THE RIVERS
RAN EAST

THE RIVERS RAN EAST

Leonard Clark

TRAVELERS'
– TALES –
CLASSICS

TRAVELERS' TALES
San Francisco

Travelers' Tales and Travelers' Tales Guides are trademarks of Travelers' Tales, Inc., 330 Townsend Street, Suite 208, San Francisco, California 94107. www.travelerstales.com

Jacket Design: Michele Wetherbee
Interior Design: Claudia Smelser
Page Layout: Cynthia Lamb, using the fonts Minion and Mrs. Eaves

Distributed by: Publishers Group West, 1700 Fourth Street, Berkeley, California 94710.

Library of Congress Cataloging-in-Publication Data

Clark, Leonard (Leonard Francis)
   The rivers ran east / Leonard Clark.
      p. cm. — (Travelers' Tales classics)
   ISBN 1-885211-66-x
   1. Amazon River Valley—Description and travel. 2. Amazon River Valley—Discovery and exploration—American. 3. Loreto (Peru : Dept.)—History—20th century. 4. Clark, Leonard (Leonard Francis)—Journeys—Amazon River Valley. I. Title. II. Series.

F2546 .C6 2001
985'.44—dc21

2001025004

First Printing
Printed in the United States of America
10 9 8 7 6 5 4 3 2 1

TO

My Mother

That patient and loving woman—who never gave up hope even months after the Foreign Chancellery of the Government of Peru had reported to Colonel Paul K. Porch, U.S. Military Attaché in Quito (Ecuador), that I had been murdered by the Huambiza Jívaro headhunters.

CONTENTS

From our perch at the beginning of the third millennium, where we can look across the vast landscape of the world and see that just about every square mile has been tramped on by one of us, has been plotted and graphed and mapped by satellites, when an "adventure" almost invariably means going boldly where hundreds if not thousands have gone before, it can be hard to imagine the enormity of Leonard Clark's endeavor that comes to life in the pages that follow.

Clark was driven by two of the oldest addictions known to man, the lust for gold and the lust for adventure. The same glittering element that drove biblical figures to distraction and damnation, that spawned the rise and fall of empires and prompted the Spanish to wipe out entire New World civilizations, obsessed Clark and sent him into the wild jungles of the Amazon. At the time this jungle was quintessential and untrammeled, a place of primal forces where every plant and animal was a predator or had developed elaborate defenses to ward off other creatures bent on killing and eating them. This was not the world of today's "rainforest," a euphemism that has stripped the tropical wilderness of its true vital nature. It was a place almost completely unexplored, inhabited by warring tribes, slave-trading godfathers, dedicated missionaries, and creatures bent on survival and nothing more.

Drawn by visions of El Dorado and a map he is certain will lead him to it, Clark heads into the unforgiving wilderness with barely the provisions to sustain him (let alone the funds to pay for them), relying on his wartime experience in Asia, his wits, and the grace of God to see him through. He finds reliable sidekicks in the redoubtable Jorge Mendoza and the fearless Inez Pokorny, and together they forge their way through a violent world where disaster lurks around every bend in the river. Man-eating jaguars, giant anacondas, headhunting Indians, and poisonous creatures of every sort are their constant companions.

But Clark, of course, is on more than just a quest for gold. He understands that wealth comes in many forms, and throughout his hair-raising mission he is constantly searching for indigenous medicines that can be extracted and exploited, collecting a potential gold mine of knowledge. Ironically, this makes him something of an ethnologist and environmentalist rather than just an adventurer, as the information he brings out of the jungle adds volumes to the understanding of tropical plant properties and their possible uses.

Again from our comfortable modern perch it is hard to imagine today's rainforest and Clark's jungle being the same place, but they are not so different. Today's tropical wilderness is more traveled, more developed, more understood, and less violent in human terms, but it is still ruled by that essential primal law of survival above all else. Today we experience it from the comfort of a lodge, or a jungle camp developed by others to take the real danger out of it. We hike with guides and marvel at the creatures and plants and their defenses against each other, but we do not face it in the raw, with bare hands, with no way out but an inexorable descent downriver on a flimsy raft into uncharted territory. Leonard Clark did it for us, and for this we can be grateful.

His journey is truly one of the greatest adventures ever recorded. And now it is back in print for all to enjoy.

LARRY HABEGGER

Executive Editor
Travelers' Tales
San Francisco, California

FOREWORD

Many explorers have traversed the great river highways of the South American Continent; few have penetrated beyond the banks to the true unknown; almost none has written an account of his exploration. I believe Colonel Clark's book, which is about the true inner vast areas of darkness, will become a classic. It is an authentic adventure of exploration and worthwhile discovery.

I am a Peruvian, a veteran resident of the jungle. I have spent a quarter of a century of my life on the main trunk rivers of the Amazonic regions. Adventure—as I personally know—is not the mark of incompetency, as many experts would have us believe. It is a barometer showing just how far into the true unknown (of the Amazon regions at any rate) the explorer has been able to go. Clark cuts into ribbons all tactical methods of advancing. He does not cover his rear against the attack of the savages. He has no consideration for bringing up supplies and protection to that point of zero where it is a calculated 99 percent risk to advance farther before turning back. He just goes!

This North American has accomplished his journey almost without funds. He was forced to live by the jungle, a nearly impossible feat even for a wild Indian. These risks, and the calculated danger, accent the extreme readability and permanent value of his book.

Colonel Clark has been unique in his method of acquiring sixty heretofore secret medicines. (Many of these, our Peruvian scientists feel, may be more important than the discovery of the cure for cancer malignancy, and may lead up to it.) Living closely with the Indians, he has uncovered their psychology and related it to their religion. He has located, and actually mapped, ancient El Dorado and its sources of gold. His discovery of oil in the Amazon will affect the lives of millions of people. In my opinion Clark's discoveries comprise the most valuable contribution possible for the reconnaissance explorer.

As Director of Colonization for the Oriente, I have learned much from this book that will help in my work of colonizing this vast jungle area. With the exception of the extremely difficult Campa territory, our Army has now occupied many key bases on the outer perimeter surrounding the areas Clark describes. This includes the oil-bearing basin which our Peruvian sovereignty established by right of formal discovery and occupation. This has been accomplished although the Cordillera del Condor Jívaros are the most difficult confederation of tribes to deal with. Like others flanking them, they are headhunters of the most malignant type. The Peruvian Government is taking strong steps to correct the shameful and inhuman slave practices which Clark found existed in and around the entire area, especially on the Gran Pajonal.

The appendices at the end of the book are the most complete, valuable, and original of any contained in the texts of South American exploration.

The author himself has answered all the questions, drawn all the threads tight. We are not left dangling. Although this journal describes a treasure hunt, it is also the finest piece of exploration so far accomplished anywhere in the Amazon Valley.

BARON WALTER FRASS VON WOLFENEGG

Jefe Ministerio de Agricultura
Dirección de Asuntos Orientales
Colonización y Terrenos de Oriente
Centro de Colonización de Alto Marañón
Puerto Patria, Loreto, Peruana

To write a few opening words to Leonard Clark's record of exploration is a privilege not often granted to an American official on the ground. Here is a book to get one's teeth into; extremely exciting and informative. Clark has actually traversed at least two of the worst regions off the main Western Amazon rivers—regions inaccessible even to the armed forces of the countries claiming this vast jungle area.

I notice he has written only on the exploring phase of his great trip, and sincerely hope a second book follows encompassing the long-occupied regions also known to him, and now an important part of the interlocking economy and social life of the greater world without. Clark is a former intelligence officer and thoroughly competent in methods of collection. His knowledge is detailed and indeed profound.

If you put your hand on this narrative you cannot shake it off. Clark has told his story as it was actually lived in the jungle. Clark's book is filled with fascinating new information—and with him we learn; but with him also we itch from the hellish bites of strange bugs; we sweat and are blinded under a glaring equatorial sun; we taste the feeling of despair from starvation; we hear the anaconda's ghost-hiss of night-tracking headhunters, under the influence of strange drugs such as the Soul Vine. We are overwhelmed by the same sickening smells when a witchman lets a poisonous snake bite him deliberately; we know the terrible sense of the explorer's uncertainty—the question of going forward into the eerie, living, creeping silence of the great bush, or retreating to safety—when the maps prove to be all wrong....

This of course is a new kind of Amazon expedition; for Clark has contrived in an informal and fascinating manner to combine information with adventure, something very rare in the literature of the past. And knowing him in the Amazon country personally, I can say he had no help, no official sanctions, few material assets. It was all completely without fanfare, though now that the expedition is accomplished Clark is in danger of becoming a legend in these parts. For capital, he had only courage; labor there was—of a grim and terrible kind. Clark above all others has proved that even in our workaday world, great rewards, moral as well as those measurable in gold, still are possible to him who dares the unknown.

I am a hunter myself, and am grateful that he has included tales of hunting in the jungles. So little of this—due to almost insurmountable difficulties in heavy jungle—is included in exploration accounts (excepting a few hunts in President Theodore Roosevelt's *River of Doubt,* in the more open terrain of the Brazilian Mato Grosso).

In his *Appendices of the Western Amazon,* I must say that the information is 95 percent new. Certainly the wildlife providing hides, feathers and meat, the trees, fishes, medicines and other useful products such as petroleum and gold, will provide priceless material for a study on the possibility of a hundred new exports to the United States and Europe.

I see he has used foreign italicized words only when an English rendition is not quite applicable. For instance, a *quebrada* in the Andes is certainly not a gulch, but a sort of Grand Canyon wrinkle in the earth's crust; a *playa* is certainly not a beach as we visualize a beach, but a particular kind of riverine sand bank or even an isolated bar, etc.

I respectfully differ with Clark on the length of the anaconda snake. The one he measured on the Morona River was 26 feet 8 1/2 inches. That is much too conservative. The Peruvian skin traders who bring thousands a year to Iquitos tell me anacondas quite often measure up to 40 feet. The Englishman, Colonel P. H. Fawcett, (who was lost while searching for a ruined city which he believed to be Atlantis) once killed an anaconda measured at 65 feet. In the Beni Swamps of Madre de Dios, Fawcett saw snake tracks which led him to estimate their length up to 80 feet. In the Beni also, the Colonel saw an animal he believed might be *Diplodocus,* the 80-foot reptile of twenty-five tons. This animal he thought might still be in existence as it was an eater of aquatic plants, which grow profusely in this region. The *Diplodocus* story is confirmed by many of the tribes east of the Ucayali, a region covered by Clark.

A note of warning must be sounded to prospectors who might attempt to reach the new gold- and oil-bearing regions. It is very dangerous even when fully equipped, the many diseases are often fatal, transportation is non-existent, many of the tribes off the main rivers are savage. Because Clark got through alive is no reason to suppose that many others could do the same. The jungle-wise soldiers themselves have been thrust back time and again, often with heavy losses.

Clark has not mentioned his own personal background and qualifications, and I think it important as an explanation of why he was able to succeed where others have failed. He has been exploring the waste places of the earth, on all its five continents, for twenty years. No other such explorer is active today. He is not of the same class as other modern-day explorers—that is, geologists, botanists, ethnological collectors, etc.—but that rare Victorian type, the trail-breaker: the true explorer whom all others must follow.

Clark's background, enabling him to obtain the secret information on the slave practices, is fantastic. He has not mentioned it, but he was actually the original pioneer of the United States armed services behind the Red Army and the Japanese Army lines, in charge of our underground organizations, guerrilla activities and our espionage systems in China, Mongolia and other countries in World War II. He has also been private advisor to the Arab League in Egypt, and to various princes and lamas in Mongolia and Tibet and to at least five warlords in China. He personally took the unofficial surrender of Formosa from General Enriki Ando three months prior to its occupation by Chiang Kai-shek and the American Forces.

Clark is the only true Tibetan explorer ever produced by the United States, excepting W. W. Rockhill, over a century ago. Clark reached the headwaters of the Yellow River. He mapped this area, together with the western ranges of the Amnyi Machen. As leader of the official Chinese Nationalist Expedition, his equipment and retinue were vast; a large staff of scientists, hundreds of troops and carrier animals, sent out by Governor Ma Pu-fang. No doubt this was the greatest field expedition of modern times.

And what a contrast, due to lack of material assets, what an incredible contrast, to Leonard Clark's Amazon venture!

LOUIS GALLARDY
Consular Agent

Iquitos

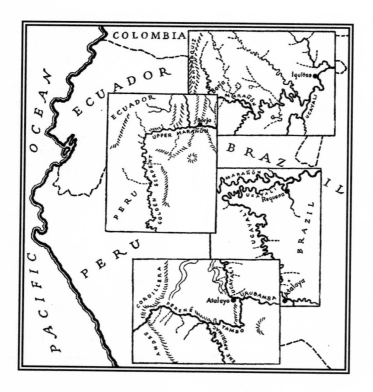

This chart shows the relation of exploration areas to each other and also the location of the maps in the text. It will be noted that the mapped areas do not relate to any geographical scale of the several countries. Each map in the text bears its own mileage scale, its latitude and longitude, and its continental location.

"El Dorado (Land of the Golden Man!) is a fabulous country of immeasurable treasure...." Thus wrote home the Imperial Spaniards of Castile and Leon. This El Dorado was richer "in tears from the sun," than all the other kingdoms of the New World. Now "tears from the sun," the Conquistadores knew, was gold, the yellowish malleable metal used as building material in the cyclopean Incan Temples of the Sun God. In Cuzco, in the Sun Temple, was the Sun God in solid gold, the rays consisting of 1,000 priceless gems; the scintillation, according to the Spaniards, was almost insupportable.

In the Temple of the Moon, the Moon Goddess was of pure silver, and at her feet were ringed the gold-covered mummies of the Inca Queens of past dynasties. In the Rainbow Temple of the god Cuycha, a seven-hued arc of gold was picked out in colors of jewels. In the "Temple of Venus" were twelve huge silver and gold jars filled with holy grain offerings carved from gold and jewels. Even the plumbing of all these temples and palaces was of solid silver. Further, in this Incan capital of Cuzco, "Hub of the Universe," whose inner and outer defensive walls were also faced with sheets of pure gold—the fascinated Spaniards saw with their own eyes in Coricancha (Holy City of Gold) the emperor Inca had an entire forest-garden of trees and flowers fashioned in pure gold and silver. The great blossoms were of clustered pearls, emeralds and other gems.

This city was watered by the river Huatenay, while all about stretched the Intipampa (Field of the Sun). The sacred Coricancha, both forest and fields, were peopled with life-sized golden mannequins of Quechuas, Arymayas and Incas at work on pottery and the various other cultural tasks of the Empire's teeming millions of people. The hoes, spades and other tools were of gold. *Huacas*, sacred statues, besides being of gold and gems, were also of an amalgam of gold and mercury; bronze; and copper.

In the metal trees were golden birds—macaws and parrots, umbrella-birds and cock-o'-the-rocks—roosting, birds of every hue with ruby eyes. There was an entire herd of llamas—pure gold, with turquoise eyes; reptiles, bugs and animals of jade and gold—pairs of each kind known to exist in the land. And not only these, but massive idol-gods of the Sun and Moon, nine former Inca Emperors, museums, monasteries, shrines and entire public buildings and walkways were of gold and silver, or covered solidly with sheets of it.

And yet, all this, the Indians wonderingly said, was as nothing compared to the source of all this gold and treasure—El Dorado! Even under too eager torture by the greedy Spaniards, the Indians (those grave and taciturn elders who knew the secret source) told no more.

The gold of Peru was hidden. A massive chain which extended around the great plaza of Cuzco disappeared, though five thousand strong Indians must have carried it. Ten thousand llama loads of gold were gathered throughout the four subkingdoms into a treasure train which reached a point only a day's journey from the capital and then was driven off the Imperial highway by the enraged Indians. To this day it has never been found. The bullion weighed 1 million pounds avoirdupois, its worth today on the Tangier world market estimated at 1 billion dollars. But for all that, it was as nothing, for it has been recorded in Viceregal, Crown, and Church archives that 20 billion dollars in gold and silver alone was sacked in the New World and melted down to plate and ingots to be taken in galleons to Spain. Bobadilla's gem-encrusted golden table, lost in eighty feet of water off the coral reefs of Haiti, was valued by the Crown at millions of dollars.

In spite of such treasures, it was something else that obsessed the Spaniards—Find El Dorado!—that was the spirit of the time. Astrologers and geographers advised that the gold must lie in the Western Hemisphere, most likely in the Amazon or Orinoco jungles. For two centuries El Dorado called soldiers-of-fortune out of every port of a gold-hungry Europe. Sir Walter Raleigh, dreaming of golden "Manoa," sailed in 1595 from London and voyaged across the Sea of Darkness to the Orinoco River, but was driven out with great losses by "ye wilde men" who shot at his armored knights with poisoned blowgun darts.

Others sailed bravely into the Golden West, putting in motion a chain of explorations that has never been equaled. El Dorado! From the Meta River on the north to the Caqueta on the south; from the Andes' Cordilleras on the west to the Rio Negro and the Orinoco on the east they searched, and few of them ever straggled back to their galleons. Von Huten combed the wilderness between the Guaviare River, a tributary of the Orinoco, and the Uaupés of the upper Rio Negro. And before him, Ordaz, emissary of Cortés (based in Mexico), in 1531 explored the Orinoco as far as Astures, the region of the cataracts; went up the Meta to be driven out by savages. Orellana in 1544 floated down the Napo and the Amazon (where he was attacked by "Amazons"—women warriors), thereby being first to cross the southern continent.

What a race of men they were!

Quesada hunted south and west, his men dying like flies of fever in the Gran Chaco and falling in bloody battles with the wild Indians, finally struggling with a few survivors up to Peru—and of the Inca being looted and destroyed piecemeal by Pizarro and his captains. Coronado was fired by Cortés's "magnificent" rape of sacred Tollan and the Mexican Anahuac Empire of the Aztecs, and the looting of the Sun and Moon Temples in the old Toltec holy city of Teotihuacan; also by the bloody wars and looting of Montejo, Grijalva and Cordova in Yucatan and the other Mayan kingdoms of Central America. Thus Coronado headed north after El Dorado (or Golden Quiviera)—greater, richer, than all these other fabulous prizes, and its seven cities of Cíbola. He reached the Arkansas River and the Grand Canyon of the Colorado, finding only seven Indian pueblos in New Mexico. Cabeza de Vaca, lone survivor of his own command, was first to cross North America from the Gulf of Mexico to that of Lower California—but no golden walls of El Dorado ever glittered on the desert's horizon, only Apaches who sometimes fed him out of pity, and other fierce tribes from whom he hid, abandoning his clanking armor, but trudge on foot he did, on and on, but still no golden towers. And so, no one of these mighty Conquistadores, fired and driven by dreams of might and glory and untold wealth, though they ripped the gold, the silver, the emeralds, diamonds, pearls and jade from the necks of these semi-civilized people, plundered their temples, pyramids, palaces and gold—none ever found El Dorado.

El Dorado, with all its heartbreak, blood and treasure, was the greatest dream ever dreamed by man for—unlike Africa today—it brought about the colonization of the Western Hemisphere centuries before it might otherwise have come. And it still lives as a dream, because no man in this twentieth century ever looks for it. But was El Dorado altogether a dream? Perhaps, somewhere, its cities and its gold still lie unknown, undiscovered.

The Indians had said it belonged to the Golden Man; now this could be no other than Atauhuallpa himself, not any *cacique* (chief) of Colombia as some scholars believe, for the Son of the Sun was the incarnation of the Sun itself! I believe that the riddle of El Dorado, the greatest mystery of the ages, still lies unsolved, and that the Chibcha tribe's Gautavita Lake legend has no bearing on it.

The vast jungle deserts of the southern continent, traversed in only a few places by even those fierce-eyed men in steel corselets, are mainly marked today TIERRA INCÓGNITA—UNEXPLORED.... There, I too, must and will search.

From the *Iquitos Diary of Leonard Clark*
August 15, 1946

~ I. ~

We Enter at Hazard

VERY explorer has two faces, the secret one and the one he shows to the world. Both my faces hid the fact that I had $1,000 in my shirt pocket, secured by a safety pin, everything I owned in this world converted to ten $100 currency bills. It wasn't much, but I was after treasure, and every treasure hunter is optimistic. If he weren't optimistic he would be something else, but never a treasure hunter. True, at the moment I didn't know where the gold was buried, but I did have a clue—one single, solitary, threadbare clue.

This clue I had obtained in the United States on May 1st, and it was June 10th, 1946, when I crossed south of the Equator and landed by Panagra plane at Lima Airport in Peru. I was dusty, disheveled, hatless and relieved, for the long flight had been repeatedly delayed since leaving San Francisco, California, on June 1st. In addition to my small cash stake, I had a brief note from an old-time American resident of Peru, to one Miguel Maldonaldo—a Peruvian who might possibly know the location of legendary El Dorado, somewhere in the unexplored upper Amazon basin.

I already knew that Peru was an ancient and highly civilized country, and that the people were said to be among the world's most cultivated, still, I never suspected that this culture would extend to the airport officials. But by all the officials, including even the Customs, I was smilingly passed into Peru, a free man and without a worry to his name. To reap the benefits of face, so important in South America (and perhaps in North America as well), I put up at the city's finest, the magnificent Hotel Bolívar, suite 216, facing the Plaza San Martín.

From this base I began hunting down my Peruvian and also trying to find an experienced jungle partner. After five days of threading the lovely old Spanish city with its flower-embowered patio walls and brown-wood balconies, searching out any number of itinerant Señor Maldonaldos, I learned that the Peruvian had left on a trip into the *monte*, but would return to Lima in a few weeks.

As to that second man, the partner whom I hoped would act as guide, I was assisted by the American Consulate people and by Colonel J. H. O'Malley, our Military Attaché, but no one could be found who would go under-financed into such a desolate region. Three weeks passed.

Maldonaldo finally returned to Lima, and after swearing on his mother's grave as to its authenticity, gave me a yellowed, badly cracked and very old Spanish parchment map of El Dorado, in exchange for a $100 bill. Of course, there was no way possible of cross-checking such a document; I simply had to take his word for it, and the hunch of my old friend back home, and go. Like the priesthood, treasure hunters burn with a faith and trust incomprehensible to the man in the street. Once he sees a treasure map, he will believe even his worst enemy, let alone a friend. I was here because of that belief, and here was a real map to substantiate that faith and hope. I simply had to find that lost land of treasure, El Dorado, no matter what it had cost others in disappointment and tragedy. Except for that $1,000 I was broke, for I had lost a considerable fortune through bad investments in China and the United States. Although I can look back now with a calm detachment, still at the moment, in Lima, I simply had to have that gold, and with the same unreasoning desperation that grips a man who loves a woman—he has got to have that one woman, though a billion others exist in the world. I knew too, that anyone rumored to be searching for El Dorado would be placed under surveillance—for there are strict treasure-trove laws regarding this sort of thing—and so great would be the rewards of its discovery that even his life would be in jeopardy.

My going into the high bush was secret, and my "cover" was that of looking for medical secrets of the Indian *brujos* (witchmen).

I was now reduced to a desperately small $700 working capital.

I decided I must leave Lima within the next few days, if not sooner. While in search of vital information on the regions ahead, I talked to Professor Cesar Garcia Rosell, head of the oldest scientific institution on the hemisphere, the Sociedad de Geografía. He was charming, enthusiastic and surprisingly cooperative; a very young man in spite of his sixty-five years. I did not dare to rouse the savant's skepticism by mentioning my true purpose in going into the interior, but as for my decision to go there in "search of medicine," I was frank.

Together Rosell and I studied his mouldy old Jesuit maps of the tierra incognita, the unbroken jungle lying east of the Andean Cordilleras. The whole strip—believed to be mostly flat-lands—called Loreto and Madre de Dios, was disputed between Peru on the one hand, and Brazil, Bolivia, Colombia and Ecuador on the other. From Madre de Dios in the southeastern quarter near Bolivia and the headwaters of the Purus and Juruá in Brazil, all the way north to the Ecuadorian and Colombian frontiers on the Napo and Putumayo, the strip averaged 1,100 miles long by 400 to 500 wide. Its eastern edge was backed up somewhere against the westernmost regions of wildest Brazil, inhabited by the cannibal Cunibos, the headhunting Mashcos on the Rio Manú, and such killers. Rosell explained that fully 90 percent of this largely disputed region was recognized by the government (which obtained its statistics from him) as completely unexplored territory on which no white man had ever left his footprint.

"Then, what are all these names on the maps?" I asked.

"Señor—please! They are only names! Sometimes an abandoned thatched hut on a main river bank.... Only *names,* to fill the great white spaces. The governments of the five claiming powers must have colonies there, must they not?—to substantiate...."

The professor continued, saying that soldiers and rubber tappers, *barbasco* gatherers had covered but 8 to 10 percent off the main rivers, and few records had been left concerning *La Selva* (The Forest), as the Peruvians poetically called this worst jungle region in the whole Amazon basin. Nearly all the original parchment reports of the long-banished Jesuits, who had been recalled to Spain in 1767, plus the later reports of the few explorers and Indian-fighting Army officers, had been lost in a recent fire at the Society's offices. He then warned me that twenty bona-fide expeditions, fully armed and equipped, many having soldiers, had come to grief on the basin's 50,000 miles of navigable waterways in recent years. Everywhere the *bravos* were rising against further intrusion. And as for the vast, desolate desert-jungle lying unbroken between the greatest rivers, very little, almost none—if the truth were known—had actually been traversed. My track must lie across these areas and I must realize they were perilous and incalculable.

In effect, for he used both Spanish and English, his very words were:

"Señor Clark, you enter at hazard; there is a grave chance you will not get out alive from Madre de Dios and Loreto, should you be so unfortunate as to penetrate even a little way after crossing the Andes. Your head could be cut off and reduced to 2 $^1/_2$ inches. You should know that in the last ten years, we have lost approximately 700 Peruvian explorers, soldiers, officials, *patrónes* and bushrangers, who have tried to get off the rivers and 'pacify' the Indians. The explorer Robuchon is only one famous case of an investigator being eaten by cannibals, but I could name scores of unknown explorers who have fallen into the hands of the corpse-eating tribes, and those of the headhunting enclave. For every Colonel Fawcett known to the world, there are a hundred such who have disappeared and remain entirely unheard of."

Had I taken into account the many white-water rapids, unknown waterfalls which blocked the Andean watershed rivers? Also the forests would be denuded of all game and other foods. He believed man-eating jaguars were common. He spoke also of death from snake-bite, black crocodiles, *paña* (two varieties, cousins of the Brazilian meat-eating piranha). He mentioned the danger of the ten-foot cannibal *zúngaro*—tiger-fish, giant electric rays capable of electrocuting a man; even freshwater sharks 3,000 miles (by twisting river beds and channels) from the salty ocean. There were scores of diseases; and ants whose single bite will cause blindness. In short, a hundred lethal possibilities existed.

"Usually our men just disappear. We never hear from them again. Others often go insane. If they get out alive they are incompetent for any sort of work. We have just received a report from the mouth of the Morona River north of the Marañón. Juan Vargas is our mapper there. He has been found in the belly of a snake, the *yacu maman*, in his own screened launch. Our government launches have a heavy wire mesh carefully covering sides and roof so that the poison darts of the Indians will be caught in them. Vargas was sleeping on the boat. The crew were camped on a safe *playa* (river beach). The anaconda, apparently hunting food, came out of the river and entered the boat through a hole torn that day in one corner. After killing and swallowing Vargas, it could not return through the hole, and was found in the engine room next morning."

"Is it possible to swallow a man whole?" I asked. "How about a man's shoulders passing the jaws? Most experts have doubted Indian claims that certain varieties of those snakes can swallow a deer weighing a hundred pounds."

Rosell laughed indulgently, though quietly, as befitting his position. "These snakes are capable of swallowing not only a 150-pound man, but a 500-pound animal such as a tapir. You see, they crush the larger bones, lather the head and unjoint their jaws. After swallowing its food, the snake's digestive juices are so strong that even large bones are dissolved. When hungry the snake will take any kind of living food—marine, crocodiles, land mammals and even man himself."

"Señor Clark," Professor Rosell concluded, rather coldly clinical and with that manner of infinite patience assumed by Peruvians when talking with the skeptical, inexperienced gringo, "it is imperative, life and death to you, that you correct your mistaken ideas that the jungle is not dangerous. These ideas no doubt you obtained from the works of so-called explorers who have not themselves lived in the true, unexplored inner jungles but have spent only a short time on some main river, or operated a few leagues from a base on the edge of the forest."

As he talked, I took notes in my cryptic brand of shorthand:

"Herpetology: scores of poisonous snakes, not much known. Rosell has glass tubes (thirty poisonous snakes from the Ucayali River alone). Divided into two general families: colubrids and vipers. Says African and Asian cobras are colubrids. Here represented in the ring snakes—corals, genus *Elaps*, short-fanged (which, like cobras, hang on and chew after striking). Pit vipers much worse. Have two subfamilies or genera; first, the many tropical *cascabels* (rattlers—*Crotalus horridus*); second, genus *Lachesis*, like bushmasters in Guianas, aggressive, vicious, no rattles (to warn you with), exceedingly poisonous, very large. West Indies' fer-de-lance here called *jararaca* sometimes *shushupe* (long-fanged snake), night-rover, 94 percent fatal. Have one of this family only three inches long—most deadly of all. Rosell says snakes have killed more people in single year than have all the elephants, lions and buffaloes of Africa since beginning of historical times."

At this point Professor Rosell stopped to mop his brow with a linen handkerchief.

"Now! The colubrid victim suffers more than any other; because of the shock to his nerve centers, his blood is incapable of coagulation and becomes watery, often breaking out through the eyeballs. Some of these venomous reptiles, especially the vipers, will attack man without provocation. We do not know why; we only know they are irritable and vindictive, and account for the deaths of hundreds of our rubber gatherers, soldiers, *patróne* Indians (workers) and others who live on the edges of the great forest, or clearings on the main rivers within it. Our rattler types are often enormous, thick as a man's thigh; their surprisingly plentiful white, creamy-thick venom does not paralyze the nerve centers but coagulates the blood, destroying the corpuscles. Of course...you have anti-venom!"

Now South Americans believe all *norteamericanos* to be rich; and though purposely I had arrived in Peru by a subsidiary of Pan American Airways, I had not dared tell Professor Rosell I had no funds to purchase anti-venom. I knew from previous experience in Latin America he would consider me a hopeless visionary, a crank, and so cease his briefing—which to me could well mean success or failure on the road to El Dorado.

I thanked Señor Cesar Garcia Rosell, and took my leave. I have no wish to appear melodramatic when I say that I was apprehensive of what the future might hold.

On the following morning my friend, Raymond Russell of the Rubber Development Corporation, had me meet him at the University of Lima. Here he introduced me to Jorge Mendoza, a tall and very handsome twenty-four-year-old Peruvian. Mendoza said he was willing to accompany me if I paid the expenses. He did not pry into my motives for undertaking such a journey, and I wrongly assumed that like most men during some period in their life, Jorge was anxious to escape the humdrum existence of working for an honest living. Jorge was not only a friend of Russell, but he possessed other excellent qualifications: He was a graduate of Lima University; and he spoke perfect English. Above all, he had once been a *montero* (meat hunter) for the *caucheros* bleeding rubber beyond La Merced (The Merciful). This was an outpost on the open eastern slopes of the ochre-tinted mesas, those icy 20,000-foot volcanoes and peaks which rose like the ramparts of the world between me and my objective.

Nothing in South America ever properly begins "today"—it's always "*mañana!*" And so we were to start over the Andes on the classical "tomorrow." At the last minute, 4 A.M., Jorge telephoned me at the hotel to say he had several things to attend to, but for me to go by train, and he would join me in Oroya. Before I could voice my displeasure over this new arrangement, he hung up. Oroya was the first leg of my journey, and it was somewhere high up in the mists of the Andes.

It was now July 2nd. I packed my suitcase, and then in something of a fever, I counted my money. I had less than $600. The city was still dark at five o'clock, when I checked out of the Bolívar. I took a taxi to the railway station. It was a dusty and cold place, with a crowd of sour-smelling Quechua Indians and *cholo* breeds dressed in bright ponchos of orange, red, and chocolate, standing about swathed to their eyeballs. The toy-sized train came in from the yards, and after the crowd and I had boarded it, jerked its way out of the Lima station.

Coal dust and cinders settled over passengers like a pall, for the windows were all open. Picking up steam, the train began demurely nuzzling a mouselike way eastward across a dawn-lit flat desert, the coastal littoral. It was appallingly wide, wide and dry and brown as a wind-unearthed cemetery of Inca mummy dust.

After several sand-and-wind-blown hours, the clanking narrow-gage locomotive left the desert to puff and labor with asthmatic wheezings up over the wide barren ochre and red bones of the gaunt Andes.

Ever mounting the *barrancas* to the first snowy domes, those of the Cordillera Huayhuash, our train strained at her gussets and jerked and clattered her ironmonger's way upward, upward, over the lip of the sierra.

A Lima business man joined me and pointed out peons in varicolored ponchos and little round felt hats, staring out of curiously yellow-red moon faces. Over the high pampas benches atop the cliffs, herds of multicolored llamas—black, soft brown, chalky white, and slate gray—scurried out of our way and stood watching among patches of rocks and cacti, or among dazzling carpets of yellow flowers. At the various stations, elegant *haciendados* flicked quirts against their polished boots.

Chaclacavo, Sisicaya, Matucana, Casapalca, Morococha and Pachacacha, round-shouldered adobe towns. By straining and huffing and clanking, we crawled into the hinterland, higher than 14,000 feet. We were in the very tropopause. The last outridge of the Cordillera Huayhuash lay couchant, like a black and yellow *tigre*, with fleas of men and women in gaudy ponchos and llama woolly pants crawling through the hair of its grass and cactus.

In the last rays of the sun we at last rolled into the sooty mining town of Oroya.

When the train stopped, I got out. Across the railroad tracks I found a hotel, a little brick shanty, whose name I have forgotten, and was given a room with a brass bed and a chamber pot. Here I awaited Jorge. All night my window rattled, and a freezing wind hammered a hard wedge of air and dust through the sill crack just above my head.

One day followed another and still no Jorge. I sometimes went fishing for rainbow trout with Jock McCrae and some of his Indians. McCrae was a Scot, hired by the Cerro de Pasco mines to raise sheep. When I tried to make arrangements to go east over the last peaks by llama train, a very interesting bit of ethnological information turned up, which made my plan impossible.

It has been established that prior to the discovery of America and the ancient Incas, syphilis was unknown in Europe. Nearby pre-Colombian Incan graves were at the moment producing—under the spades of a Lima scientist—the bones of syphilitics, due, he believed, to the Andean Indians' working with llamas and the ancient instinct for sodomy. Very likely humanity owes this curse to Pizarro and the Andean llama. There was a national law which forbade any male Indian from traveling with a herd of llamas on a trip exceeding twenty-four hours, unless a woman went along. And since all available women were working shifts in the mines, the llama trains were stalled indefinitely.

On July 7th, Jorge showed up. Among his effects was a waterproof money belt, which I immediately purchased for my own use, transferring my shrinking capital to its safekeeping. This money belt was immensely important. It was large and roomy and had button-down flap covers over each pocket. The outside material was leather, while the inside lining was of yellow oiled silk, from which had been sewn the very large pockets. Later I was to carry in these the various trail necessities such as compass, notebook and pencil, maps, papers, 35 mm films and the like.

At dawn next morning, in a freezing wind, we left Oroya for Tarma, in the station wagon of another fishing friend, Colonel R. H. Wright, with McCrae and Wright taking turns at the driving. We began climbing up out of the Oroya canyon. Up, up, we twisted and curved in dusty soaring sweeps on a powder-white, rutty road, up and over the bleak Cordillera de Huachon. At 18,000 feet above sea level, we were breathing laboriously from the tremendous altitude to which we were unaccustomed. Our heads and hearts were near to bursting, and we had to fight for breath. Under such conditions, dilation of the heart is possible. Overhead the great brown condors circled low.

Green valleys, lying between long ridges of bare granite, undulated for scores of miles to the south. Ahead of us snow peaks and glaciers towered yet other thousands of feet above our wind-whipped automobile. All about at closer range could be seen the smoke-blackened caves of the Indian herders. Wright, a cattleman brought here by the Cerro de Pasco from Texas, had bred herds of special high-altitude cattle. At one point he stopped and pointed out a herd of these cross-bred old Spanish cattle, grazing contentedly at sub-Arctic levels, waxing fat on the tough wiry *paramos* grass. In the summer he always burned off this grass, for if allowed to become too big it wore down the teeth of the cattle, and they would starve to death. As a result of the Texan's know-how, the entire cattle-breeding industry of the Andes was being entirely revolutionized after 400 years of trial and error. Such unsung men as Wright, of course, eventually exert more influence on humanity and its way of life than even the great conquerors. What Wright was doing for cattle, McCrae, the Scot, was doing for the whole sheep industry of the Andean regions. It was their job to raise food for the mines' 20,000 laborers. Here were probably the highest grazing grounds on earth, surpassed, if anywhere, only in Tibet. On the tops of ridges were any number of rock corrals, used at night for harboring the cattle from the wolves.

On the Andean crest, knifing through racing clouds and the stratospheric winds, we were at last on top, and almost immediately began bouncing down the dirt road traversing the long east slope of the Cordillera, headed east toward the haze-filled Amazon regions now in plain sight.

We entered the mouth of a narrow and dusty gulch. The way was lined with eucalyptus groves and nodding alfalfa fields, both of which were importations. Cactus hedges led us into Tarma. This proved to be a colonial frontier town of adobe and plaster built around a plaza dominated by a small cathedral, and reflecting every color in an Andean rainbow.

Here Wright and McCrae said goodbye as they wanted to return home before darkness set in. By midafternoon, Jorge and I obtained tickets on the La Merced *cameon*, and hours later, just before nightfall, we rattled into La Merced, the end of the line in every sense.

We put up at the inn called El Chalaco—and though we had no candle, not even a washbasin, and the dirt floor crawled with *buscacojones* (a small fire-ant), it did have two old hammocks which by the judicious lifting of our eyebrows we managed to borrow from the proprietress. Also available was the standard grub of the upper Amazon: *plátanos*, a cooking banana; rice, beans, red peppers ground down and mixed with oil, and *xarque* (jerked beef). We were hungry, and so had no difficulty getting the *xarque* down, though we had watched the cook whale a slab of it against a doorpost in order to dislodge the two-inch white maggots.

Being now on the edge of the Amazon jungle, the mosquitoes bothered us during the night. At dawn we got up and took a stroll through the town. La Merced probably had some fifty inhabitants, mostly traders and *caucheros*, who lived in houses of adobe and plaster which were roofed with either palm thatching or corrugated-iron sheeting. Black buzzards perched on the gables. All about stood flowering porcelain-blue jacaranda trees, and the walls of the old church were loaded with vines of purple and ruby-red bougainvillea. The poorest *cholo* (working man) had orchids growing on limbs placed in his window sills, and hanging from trees in his patio.

The church was the center of the town, and here after two hundred years, it still stood hopeful of spiritual conquest (curiously called "reducing the Indian"). A few soldiers were about, mostly Quechuas, armed with rifles having fixed bayonets. Many times in the past, the *bravos* just east had put on the *sua* (war paint) and burned out the town and massacred its inhabitants.

Jorge found several old friends, a crew of hard-eyed, lean *caucheros*. From them he bought our outfit (second hand), some supplies, and even a few sturdy bush clothes—an outlay of 160 soles-de-oro (suns-of-gold, worth about $24). I had left behind in Lima all non-essential clothes and other items. What we now had, including the new purchases, I listed on the back of my best map:

1. Two mosquito nets (with cords sewn into the corners).
2. A 12-gage shotgun.
3. Boxes of shells (one No. 5, one 0-0 buckshot).
4. Compass, aneroid barometer (calibrated for elevations), 3 pencils, small ruler & protractor (celluloid 180° gadget used in map work), 2 small diary notebooks, paper-backed Almanac.
5. Camera (Leica, with 10 rolls 35 mm film, tropical packing).
6. Two oiled silk ponchos.
7. One plug smoking tobacco (each had his pipe), 20 small boxes of matches in oiled paper.
8. One machete (and scabbard).
9. Packet of fish hooks, 100-ft. fish line.
10. Two sheath knives.
11. Food (2 lbs. rice, 2 lbs. beans, 2 lbs. *xarque*).
12. One money poke with soles-de-oro coins.
13. Two deerskin shirts, 2 homespun pants, 2 pairs heavy shoes, 2 leather shirts, socks & linen under trunks, pair old slacks & 1 shirt.
14. One pot.
15. One tanned puma skin (Jorge's).
16. One .45 caliber Colt automatic pistol (20 rounds).
17. One wristwatch.
18. One large money belt (waterproof).
19. One bottle iodine (small).
20. One flashlight (small pencil type).

All this time since leaving Oroya, Jorge had not pressed me as to our route into the bush, or our purpose for going there. That night he said:

"What is your plan, señor?"

I told him that early next morning we would start down the trail leading into the east, which the padre at the church had told me would take us to the Perené River. Jorge nodded thoughtfully, but agreed, and next morning (July l0th) we started out through the bush, following the trail through the high jungle. The way was not particularly difficult in spite of some machete work, for the season was dry, it being well past the ending of the torrential rainy season. Nevertheless by late afternoon we had only covered three Spanish leagues—nine miles. We now pitched camp well inside the edge of that mangy tangle of vegetable oddities comprising the Peruvian Gran Pajonal itself. I had been told in Lima that this was the very heartbeat of unqualified savagery in all that most extensive, unexplored region on earth, the valleys of the Amazon and Orinoco, 6 million square miles of solid jungle, the bulk of South America.

We ate boiled *xarque* and rice from the small supply which we had carried along, and turned in. We were tired and the striker mosquitoes were out early.

My route was purposely roundabout. This was for three tactical reasons. First, the Peruvian army was guarding the regions of approach where I was going in search of El Dorado because of an irregular (and undeclared) war with Ecuador over that vast no-man's tract of jungle called the Oriente—home of the Jívaro headhunters. Secondly, by really collecting medicines I would establish a bona-fide reason for being in the Amazon country, and when I reached Iquitos, I would find myself in a position to approach the mystery area from a direction not wholly covered by the Peruvians. I must hasten to correct any impression that the Oriente—an area of unexplored jungle as large as Texas—was swarming with soldiers. There were only a few hundred of them, but their little bamboo forts were on the main river highways, and exceedingly difficult to get around. And third, I was on the cheapest route from the Pacific coast into the Amazon.

I presently realized it was past midnight; yet I rolled and tossed and sweated. I simply could not sleep, though I was beginning to stiffen from the day's work and ached in every bone and muscle. There were several reasons for my restlessness. This was our first night in the big jungle. The map was burning a hole in my chest through the money belt worn bandolier-wise. There was the incredible clicking cacophony—like a million Spanish castanets—of the cicadas; the drum-booming of the huge-throated phosphorescent-skinned tree frogs; the chattering

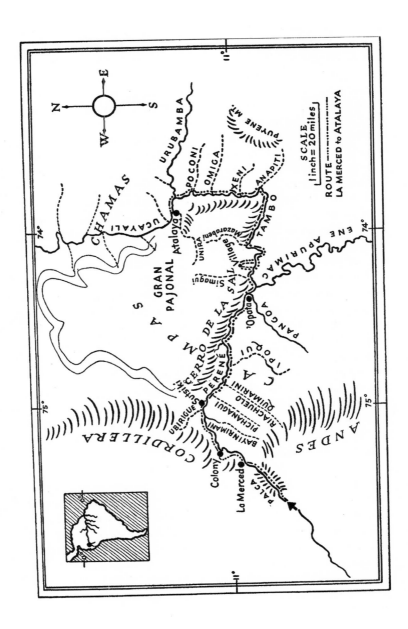

complaints hurled down from a herd of stumpy *chorro* monkeys. My head was bursting with that strange, absolutely unlooked for, musty-putrid sickening-sweet texture of an air filled with night-blooming perfumes and stinks exuding from nearby gassy swamps and banks of ceres, moon-flowers, and orchids. But to top it all, I was brooding inwardly over the problems sure to come in six months' or a year's trekking through the regions which now lay before us.

I wanted to smoke (but couldn't find a dry match) and puzzle it out, and especially to reexamine my objective—which had looked so logical and attainable in Lima, but was now, at short range, beginning to appear absolutely impossible.

I cautiously raised the dampish mosquito netting and rose to my knees on my waterproof poncho, spread on the soggy ground. Though this was the dry season, the ground never appeared to be really dry. No telling what thing was lying near, or even on top of the net. I still retained a vivid picture of what we had seen on the edge of camp, while gathering firewood just before nightfall. It had been a mottled, slowly and peculiarly sideways-moving puddle of thick coils, with a low-held, flat ace-of-spades head wide as a man's hand, cocked back, having two glinting black eyes—a column of horny buttons standing erect and whirring a high, dry, angry death-rattle. Danger could not have been better dramatized.

I got to my feet after tossing aside the net, walked four yards toward the center of our little clearing—eight apprehensive steps in an inky darkness. At the campfire, now reduced to a heap of ashes and a few pink embers, I knelt in relief and lit my pipe from a glowing hardwood coal. I put a few limbs of the smokeless *remo caspi* on the white ashes— for Indians were near—the while beating off a cloud of singing mosquitoes. I watched the ground in the spreading light for the all-too-common night-hunting rattleless *jararaca*—Rosell's orange-colored diamond-headed fer-de-lance, that aggressive and vicious type of *Bothrops* as big around as a man's thigh, whose yellow venom is a passport to a nasty and painful death. Now, a single night of this sort of thing was endurable, but could I take a year of it? Something was bound to crack, at least so Rosell and the other experts hanging around Lima had said, and I was ready to believe them.

The sky overhead through the thick limbs was an electric blue, studded with globs of stars. An itchy, hot summer mist shimmered through the mixed jumble of trees and palms, gathering wetly in prismatic clusters under the few firelit jade-green leaves. Apparently this moisture out of a clear sky precipitated from the higher leaves when the cooler breezes stirred against them, thus condensing and producing this startling bush rain. Warm spatters dripped on the backs of my hands and upturned face. Poison is quite often contained in such falling dew, for I knew that many of these trees (especially the *Sachacurarine* palm, from whose seeds, bark and leaves the Indians extracted juices used to cure snake poisoning) carried a sap that burned the skin like acid. I hurriedly wiped my face on the dirty sleeve of my deerskin shirt. The thick moisture-saturated air alleviated a flight of bobbing greenish-yellow fireflies, whose lights flashed on and off. Two varieties are so strong in intensity that the headhunters—as we later were to learn—carry them in small *chonta* (black palm heart) splinter cages, to light their way at night.

Jorge stirred in his own sagging net. I could see him in the soft dancing glow of the replenished fire outlined against a mighty white-skinned tree, an *aguano* mahogany over sixty feet in circumference. From that direction came the metallic snick of the shotgun's hammer being cocked.

"Jorge!" I said quickly—and in time. Jorge was not one to linger long when in doubt. Henceforth there would always be something to guard your life against—even the hasty action of a friend. But it was another thing that really concerned me; here there was something latent as a hangman's noose resting on your shoulders, something ghostly pervading all these massive jungles—a hangover from the Mesozoic age. The wild Indians, highly developed in psychic reception, call this *Curupuri*—the Forest Ghost. Whatever *Curupuri* is, it is very real, like a force of nature, an insidious passivity which drives men mad. It makes one pitch one's voice very low, sometimes even in broad daylight. It is exactly as if a thousand eyes are watching every instant and a thousand ears are eternally listening.

There was another strange and fearful quality too, perhaps one rooted in acoustics and ventriloquism. We had passed an Indian this morning, standing in his canoe—and using it as a sounding diaphragm—talking as by telephone to another Indian half a mile away. The strange thing was that he pitched his voice no louder than when he turned to speak with us only a few feet behind him. Even now I knew the secrets of the jungle that had never been told, I sensed that the reason lay in the fact that explorers were invariably external to the jungle, never becoming part of it as Jorge and I must from sheer necessity. Sitting in a thatched dugout canoe on a river, a net tent surrounding your living quarters amidships, is not the best way to learn of this most wonderful of all forests. To know the jungle you must live by it, overcome its host of pests, become one with it, not live a separate life, surrounding yourself with all the objects of civilization. If you do, you can collect a few rocks, insects, bird pelts, perhaps acquire a few native customs and measure a few craniums, but you will never know and feel, taste and hear and smell that which lies hidden to all but its very own. And so, if 90 percent of the contents of this journal is new and entirely unrelated, even contradictory, to anything that has been written of Amazon exploration, it is solely the fortunate result of the peculiar termite's view that Jorge and I were forced to take.

But to return to Jorge: "My friend," he answered quietly in his hoarse, patient hunter's voice, "you must be more careful. You are not in New York, you know. There are dangers here. Above all, man-eater jaguars in this region. Yes, yes, I know—you have told me that the jaguar is not normally a man-eater. But, if this is so, how come they buried Morelos' bones in La Merced only last week? And what of the thirty-two crosses in the cemetery, each placed over a man who has been killed by these cats? That Morelos cat I killed weighed 315 pounds. If wounded by an Indian's spear or arrow, these beasts get desperate and angry when the ants attack them, and after the third day they are starving and will take you from behind—hunting in singles or pairs—and crush your skull between their jaws, or bite out your spine, as one did to Carlos Garcia last season, just above the shoulder blades. A half hour ago I smelled a *tigre* only fifty feet in back of your net, when the breeze stirred for a moment. Maybe he was stalking—who knows the mind of a *tigre*? You move too quietly. I did not hear you."

This was the longest speech I had ever heard the hunter make. My ear picked up a click which told me that he was lowering the stiff-springed flat hammer, easing it down with his strong, peculiarly crooked, calloused thumb. Since the big carnivores stalk upwind, they will be found only on the leeward side of a camp, and a charge will come from that direction only. I had purposely kept my face pointed downwind at the fire, but of course Jorge could not have known that.

"Jorge, how many eyes do you think I have in my head? You warn me to watch eternally for snakes, for Indians whose tracks you picked up a mile back, for a possible jaguar some fool Indian may have wounded. I am not exactly a Brownie Scout camping out in her mother's back yard, you know."

"Look out!" he said it so softly, or rather hissed it, I could scarcely hear: "Now you've sat down in that bush, and you are probably infested with *garapatos*." He bounded out from under his net with a squirming side motion, and, grabbing up a faggot, fanned it around his head to a flaming torch, and held it close, pointing out hundreds of tiny reddish-white ticks, the size of pepper, crawling all over my legs, feet and pants.

"You see, I can't leave you alone five minutes. The *pantaloones* must come off, quick." By that time the bites were setting me on fire, for these ticks burrow through cloth and bury themselves whole in one's skin. The *pantaloones* came off in jig time. Jorge beat the pants against the mahogany tree, held them over the flames of the fire, and finally tossed them back smoking and well scorched, and it was high time as the mosquitoes were having a field day.

Half eaten alive, we returned to our ponchos and blessed nets.

Quiet settled down except for the constant ringing racket from the black jungle around us, and after fifteen minutes Jorge spoke in his quiet, husky way:

"I, too, cannot sleep."

"How did you know I was not asleep?"

"I just saw a red dot in the middle of your net. I assume you are smoking your pipe. The aroma of bush tobacco also confirms this suspicion. It is my belief that a wild Indian can smell it at least a mile off."

Five minutes later, he said: "My friend, I am concerned for us. We are down on our luck; yet, what can two men accomplish in these regions? Consider…we have practically no equipment—a dented pot, a rusty machete, a single old gun, two leaky ponchos, a pair of rotten nets. No hammocks to keep us off the ground. You have not even a covering, while I have only my puma skin."

His voice rose a little, was pitched on a higher key, but still retained its huskiness and still had the rumbling force behind it: "Why must we go into this place? What is the incentive of this expedition?"

"You are not alone in your fears, my friend," I answered in the polite Spanish phraseology, for sometimes we spoke Spanish as well as English, or even a mixture of the two, "Only the great prize keeps me resolute."

Jorge then assumed the rather didactic attitude of the university-educated Peruvian instructing the ignorant North American.

"Ah, that prize...Gold? But, I assure you, there is no lost mine out here—nothing. Nothing but death. Even the conquistadores never came back, once they went in." He stopped abruptly. Was he listening; sniffing the air; or was he, too, thinking of the other dangers awaiting us?

In a moment, lying on my back comfortably under my netting and smoking, I continued talking across the ten-foot interval.

"The purpose of our expedition, which I did not want known in Lima, is to find the wildest witchdoctors who have never seen a white man, and to talk to them."

"My poor friend. So that is it? I assure you they know nothing of treasure—only of killing, red-magic; specialists in stalking and death—both the slow and the quick. And some are cannibals. Two weeks ago the Chuncho Campas killed eighty-four soldiers a few miles from this very camp. You and I sat at the radio in the Hotel Bolívar in Lima, listening to the government broadcast of the last moments of the few survivors crying out on their radio transmitter for God and for us to help them; and then, soon after, must have come the final attack of those Campa devils with their skull-crushers. Wiped out to the last man." As a matter of fact, this massacre had almost decided me in Lima to abandon the whole idea of El Dorado. At the time the newspapers were full of the ambushing and entrapment by Indians of this military party. A very detailed account had been possible due to the commander of the column still having intact his two-way radio transmitter-receiver, a short-wave combat unit issued to soldiers in dangerous areas, and tied into the many radio-equipped Peruvian Air Force fields not only in the Andes but in the jungle landing strips at Pucalpa and Iquitos as well. The powerful transmitters here had relayed the distress messages direct to Lima.

When he had finished, I continued on the same casual pitch: "I know that many medical secrets have come from the witchmen."

"How could you possibly know this!" It was not a question, but a demand, charged with the very special Peruvian irony—an acid brand all its own—and aimed at destroying my plan, which God knows was shaky enough.

To impress Jorge, and perhaps myself, I became a bit didactic and technical myself: "Listen, hombre...here is something more portable than heavy gold bars, even if we knew where to get them; the witch-doctors have already given to civilization quinine—a white amorphous alkaloid compound contained in the bark of *Cinchona calisaya* and others of your trees. And the deadly nightshade, *Atropa belladonna*. And the local anesthesia, cocaine, contained in coca leaves. Even curare, the resinous extract of *Strychnos* type vegetation—the poison for their blowpipe darts—is used now in abdominal surgery, also to treat spastic paralysis and heart diseases…and many other medicines besides."

"But, amigo—"

"No 'buts,' Jorge; the Spaniards got the malaria cure from the Jívaros, who live in the edge of the bush east of Quito."

"This is fantastic."

"Wait, Jorge. I believe that it is true. The Indian can cure all the old diseases known to him; and he can even cure some of the new ones introduced by the foreigner. Last year in unexplored central Quintana Roo Territory south of Yucatán, I found Maya Indians using the modern wonder drug, penicillin—they call it *pozole*. The stuff was analyzed in Mexico City, and it is the same mold composition. They probably at one time had many more important medical cures, but the ancient Maya books were all burned by Landa in his auto-da-fé of July 1562 at Mani. What would you say if I told you that approximately 75 percent of all pharmaceutical knowledge has stemmed directly or indirectly from these same Amazon savages?"

Again Jorge aired his university training: "I would say you were mad. My brother is a doctor, educated in Paris, and one of our best. He says they know nothing. Amigo, if it is as you say, why has not La Condamine or Von Humboldt or Wallace and Bates of a century ago—or Baron Sant' Anna Nery made mention of it. You must be completely mistaken."

He could probably feel me squirming.

"No, you do not answer. Amigo—listen. I am returning across the Cordillera to Lima. In the morning I start. I cannot accompany you."

I took my time before answering. If Jorge meant this, I was in trouble. "Richard Gill, who worked on the curare problem, lived near Baños in the Ecuadorian Andes, and never penetrated the Jívaro interior very far, as he tells us. The secret of curare is alone worth a fortune, for science cannot reproduce it. We can take up where Gill left off, find a way through the inner jungles, and from the many wild tribes bring evidence that will point the way to science. Chemists will one day follow our maps, and get to work on our clues."

I puffed on my pipe, noting that the tobacco twist, wrapped in *tamchi* bark strips that we had purchased in La Merced, was already damp and moldy. Several of the striker mosquitoes were circling in the pink glow inside my netting.

It would certainly take time to get the hang of things here. This was no plush expedition; we had none of the "musts." In fact we had, as Jorge said, practically nothing. So far, every person with whom I had discussed my medical idea thought it was impractical, impossible, and not even worth talking about. Of course, back of us nine miles was La Merced—sanctuary, and we could still return.

"Very well, Jorge. No one believes it. I'll grant you that. So what? Does that mean it is not the truth? Does it mean that you and I cannot find the clues to those scores of diseases for which science can learn no answer? Why, the wealth to be derived from the medicines could only be matched by the treasures of El Dorado itself." I knew that the only way to get Jorge to stay on with me was to keep harping on *gold*—as potent a bait today as it was four hundred years ago. "*I tell you, it is the very biggest thing in the world.*"

"It only means, my friend, that you should have had your head examined. Dream stuff.... And your people call mine '*romanticos.*'"

"How about a little shut-eye? My pipe's out."

"I will not go. That is final. *Buenos noches!*"

"Okay, go back and be a farmer on your old man's hacienda until the tapping season. I'll make out. And don't forget to curl your tail when you leave." Desertion was easy for Jorge, for he knew the *caucheros* would soon be able to collect the milk of the highland *caucho* tree, and so his actual livelihood was assured.

Jorge's net swayed wildly. "But, be reasonable. A lone American will die."

"I intend going, and if necessary I will die." That sounded very egotistical, but the Peruvians who live on the edge of the jungle are brave men, real Indian fighters and bushmen living dangerously by their machete and gun, much as our own ancestors did a century and more ago. They respond only to the dramatic thought expressed in the dramatic word.

"Why? There is no quick cash in it. Be practical. *Caramba*!...what a fellow!"

"I still will go. I am right, and I know I am right. Now good-night!"

That ended our argument. About 4:30 in the morning, when dawn crept through the tattered leaves across an apple-green sky, I expected Jorge to pick up his poncho and head back for La Merced. At this time I could not risk telling him of my true plans—El Dorado—I must test him first, live with him for weeks on end, then I would know whether to reveal the great objective. But instead of pulling up stakes, he hung around, though there was nothing to eat, glancing at me now and then when he thought I was not noticing.

Things stood like that, a little awkwardly between us, until a shadow darted across the narrow clearing, and glancing up I saw a flock of macaws streaking by, gliding steeply.

"Water nearby," remarked Jorge, rising with our shotgun, a double-barreled 12-gage I had purchased from the legal attaché at the Embassy. Jorge slipped off. Tall and catlike I could see him winding among the fat boles of the monstrous, twisted trunks all tangled together with hundred-foot-high palms—the *aguaje*, with its purple fruit; the feathery *ubim* and the great fern-like *curua*. A few minutes later, I heard a shot about a hundred yards away. Presently the hunter was back, holding a long-tailed macaw by its wing.

It was blue and gold, and a yard long. He began stripping off the feathers. He then slit the white belly with his sheath knife, and flung out the guts (stuffed with berries of the *tucuma* palm, as he pointed out), and presently had the carcass, big as a chicken, spitted on a green stick stuck at an angle over the coals which he kicked together with his *alpargatos*-clad feet.

"We have no salt, due to the extra weight," I said. "And I'll bet you the Inca's eye it is the grandfather of all parrots."

His teeth flashed an answer. "We call them *huacamayo*. Here in the uplands are two species: the blue, and the scarlet and yellow. Lower in the Amazon flatlands I hear there is a black one. Both varieties are food, my friend, tough food for the hungry belly." Jorge took a white crystal from his pocket, and tossed it to me: "Salt we have. Yesterday I found a ledge of it. You need only crush it between two flat rocks and it is ready." And then he added with a twinkling eye—"And our teeth, at least, are sound...."

While busy pulverizing the crystal, I noticed a slight movement on the ground just behind the Peruvian where he squatted, and saw that dozens of the big red ivory-headed *sauba* ants were already blanketing out the little pile of feathers. Jorge followed my glance, and the smile disappeared.

"Strange food for even a starved ant," I ventured.

"That is the obvious conclusion. Actually, they are not after food at all. Like everything else in the jungle, they are a paradox. Let me explain: this umbrella ant collects everything it can—carrion, leaves, your shirt—anything—and carries it back to cultivate his fungus plantations, which supply his only food. Remember, if you ever get sick or are wounded out here, these ants will carry you off piecemeal, to be used as fertilizer. They will cut off your flesh while you are still living and eventually even gnaw away your bones."

"Out here is nothing friendly?" I asked. "How about food for myself? Can I find food in the jungle?"

This question, mildly put as it was, meant life or death to me.

"The jungle is your enemy. It will destroy you if it can—and it never sleeps. Even a wild Indian cannot find food in it—he lives by his *chacara* (garden)."

After a while Jorge asked: "What are you going to do?"

"Study the map." I unfolded the huge square, backed with reinforcing muslin, spreading it over my poncho so as not to dirty it. Except for a few rivers with names in large Spanish print strung along the black-inked banks, it was mostly a white blank stamped between the rivers in red ink—TIERRA INCÓGNITA: UNEXPLORED. I placed my compass on a corner, and oriented the sheet by turning it carefully until the north-south longitudinal lines pointed in the same direction as the sensitive needle. North was further determined by the slant of the sun from the left.

My companion left the fire—for no Peruvian bushman can resist a map—and peered over my shoulder as I bent closer. He said: "That line, there, is the Equator, right through the middle of the map. That's north, up there to the left." He pointed with a long sunburned hand in that direction, "Headhunting Jívaros! That's east—straight ahead from this camp into the rising sun...2,700 miles of jungle all the way to the Atlantic. That's south, there to our right... *Madre de Dios!*—500 miles of hell we have named 'Mother of God!' in desperation for a better;

nothing but Macheguengos and other tribes who kill on sight. Now, amigo, where do you go from this camp?"

"I'll just head northwards for 2,500 miles across the Amazon's headwaters system." I would never have spoken my next words if I had not been more than a little irked by his tone, and at the same time wanted to test his courage:

"Your tail is dragging, Jorge; why don't you pick it up and start for La Merced?"

The hunter calmly stepped back, picked up the shotgun, cocked the hammer, aimed the piece at a point just below my chin and said in a very offhand voice: "I believe I shall save the Jívaros the trouble of cutting off your gringo head."

"Why don't you?" I returned, as his long finger curled around the trigger, "then the courts will have the pleasure of standing you in front of a wall and shooting you."

"There is never a trial known yet in Peru, when it comes to shooting a gringo—we call it 'self-defense.'"

Jorge raised his eyes to mine just over the sights; I kept as still as I could, not blinking. Finally he said, "I do not like even a little the reference to the curling of the tail." Then in a very husky whisper: "Remember!"

He laid aside the gun and knelt alongside. "So! You'll just head north—but why? You are an American, not a Peruvian bushman—even we can't do this! Do you want to die! God does not love the foolish, here. Go west with me across the mountains to Lima, to security, maybe even a bit of love and romance, eh?, and...to life! Up north, on the west coast, are the Colorado tribe, plenty tame; all the explorers photograph them for your periodicals—no danger!"

"Jorge, I would rather take that shotgun and find my way through the truly unknown regions, with my idea as a prize to seek, than have all that other."

He grinned, but there was no humor in it, and though his blue eyes flashed with a puzzled expression and the corners crinkled deeply, there was no warmth in them either. "You are a madman, not an explorer."

"Listen, *hombre de monte*—" and, as he turned the meat slowly on its skewer, I briefly explained that in Lima, I had already talked to Professor Cesar Garcia Rosell. As I talked Jorge came and bent over the map spread on my poncho.

"Rosell says there is a single possible way for getting through central Madre de Dios and Loreto. If I can but descend the Cordillera's lower slopes for a hundred miles on the Perené River, I can then go east and north down the Tambo, which he believes connects here somewhere with the Ucayali." I pointed to the area on the map. "In this way I can float 900 more miles by river into the main Amazon up north. From Iquitos I can then swing west up the Amazon, here the Lower, Middle and Upper Marañón, and work my way a thousand miles through the disputed Oriente north of Peru proper and east of Ecuador. I will cover the back regions of the Jívaro rivers of the Tigre, Pastaza, Morona, Santiago. Jorge, don't look so damned glum. Sure, it's impossible to cut a way through this jungle for any distance. I must stick to the rivers; use them as flexible bases for reaching the inner regions where I will find the unspoiled tribal *brujos*."

I glanced across at Jorge; "In the meantime, you'll be safe in either Lima or La Merced."

Jorge scowled blackly but made no move toward the shotgun. It was just as well, for had he done so, I would have wrapped the stock around his head.

He finally gained his composure. "Does Rosell—who is not himself an explorer—assert that any man ever made this trip down the Perené, and went 1,200 miles through the jungle to Iquitos?" There was a quiet, waitful look to the hunter's hard, level eyes.

"No, he did not. He warned that this is the worst region in the Amazon Valley. Explorers purposely crossed the Andes on the Pichis Trail and hit the Ucayali low down in the north near its confluence with the Amazon, only a few hundred miles southwest of Iquitos. They thereby miss Madre de Dios and the Campa country through which the Perené must flow."

Jorge got off his knees and stepped back thoughtfully to the fire and turned the macaw, which was more than a little brown on one side, and certainly smelled good. I was getting hungry myself.

I continued, summing up: "And, Professor Rosell also says the Peruvians and their troops have reached Iquitos by circling around by ship through the Panama Canal to the mouth of the Amazon, then ascending it some 2,500 miles. From that base they have filtered up the Ucayali. But that the Perené, being Chuncho, or Campa tribal country, is unexplored, and that every military expedition has ended in extermination or retreat. Not so long ago the Chamas rose and wiped out every one of the 500 Ucayali colonists. This goes for the rubber-tappers on the fringes, too."

"You have the picture—that is correct," Jorge said, adding, with special emphasis, "But *you*—dare to run this Perené?..."

"There live the Campas, probably the wildest Indians in the head-waters, and therefore one of those *bravo* tribes most likely to retain the ancient culture and the sacred religious medical secrets."

"Why not work around the missions?"

"Because the Indians' language is polysynthetic and cannot be written; the witchmen pass down the secrets from mouth to ear, and whenever the wild Indians come in contact with missionaries or *patrónes*, and become quasi-civilized, *mansos*, they lose the legends, the knowledge, everything."

Jorge sighed, and wagged his exceedingly handsome head, with its small close ears, straight nose, and hard-mouthed and scarred face. "No man has ever come out alive from the Gran Pajonal. But we have heard from slaves whom the Campas sell to the *patrónes* that it is a plateau lying along the north bank of the Perené. Apparently the cliffs are of salt, and more than a thousand feet high. But, my friend, there my curiosity ends; I tire exceedingly of arguing. You are a very hardheaded fellow, even for a yanqui. Rodriquiz was hungry like you, only he was hungry for gold. He was a thin, ribby man, a lot more so than you. He didn't think the Campas would be interested in him. He disappeared, and years later a slave told us in La Merced that Rodriquiz was caught and emasculated like a steer, and kept in the smallest of corrals for four months till he got fat on palm-oil berries. Then they killed and ate him."

"Delightful little story," I cut in.

"You have heard nothing.... Now there is an Englishman, named Stone, who lives northeast of us in a clearing at the extreme headwaters of the Perené, where it is a little creek. This *inglés* has never left his clearing, except to explore downstream six miles. Men have been killed in that clearing. He calls it the 'Perené Colony' and he grows the best coffee in Peru. It is the only European commercial plantation beyond La Merced, or anywhere east of the Andes for over a thousand miles north and south in Peru. Now, what will you do if you reach this place?"

"I'll hit the Englishman for a dish of his tea—and then I'll figure out how to get farther east."

"I will escort you that far," said Jorge, his lips curling thinly as he rose from the map. "Stone is a good friend of mine, and though he grows coffee, he actually does drink tea—'an abominable drink' I usually assure him, which only seems to make him laugh. But for all his queer gringo ways, he is a brave, fine and honorable man."

We grasped each other's hand, and shook on the deal. I had not the money to circle South America. I needed a cover. By reversing the usual explorer's route of ascending the Amazon from its Atlantic mouth at Pará (or Belém), and by going instead through the shorter back door over the Pacific system of the Andes, I could start the first dogleg on my projected 2,500-mile journey along the remotest upper tributary system of the Amazon.

Jorge and I wolfed down the macaw, after he had deftly split it with his razor-edged *facao*, a curved, Bowie-like, ten-inch, ground-down knife of Brazilian origin. Our bellies quiet now—if you can call that digestive organism quiet as it thrashes around pieces of an ornithological rubber boot—we pitched in and rolled up our nets and ponchos. A flock of very large, black, hump-backed vultures, with black-skinned, bare, wrinkled heads, sailed into the limbs overhead, sensing our preparations for departure.

"*Gallinazas*," said Jorge, instructing me as was his habit, "Slim pickings for them here. They are dangerous—remember that!"

"Dangerous?"

"Yes. Indians will see them, and be here within an hour."

With the precious map folded and safely stowed away in my oil-skin tobacco pouch and deposited in the money belt, the shotgun in hand, our pack on my back containing all our goods and perhaps weighing a bit more than an *arroba* and a half (*arroba*—twenty-five pounds by local computation, which varies according to district), and with Jorge in the lead as guide handling the machete, we struck out for the Perené. About an hour and a half had passed as it was now five minutes to six.

As we turned to leave, the *gallinazas*, with horrible squeals and the clacking of beaks, dropped through the limbs into the clearing on strumming wings. Looking back to see if we had left anything, I realized I had no classical Rear Echelon Base Camp to Organize, no Reserves to Muster, no Flag to Raise, no Associates and Loyal Comrades to Shed a Tear with and say a Gallant Farewell to, no Last-Minute Press-Releases to Radio out to Civilization, no Troops to Tell

Off, no Trusty Indian Scouts to Screen the Way Ahead, no Precious Supplies and Equipage to Relay Forward by Expendable Porters and Canoes. But, I knew too, that the record of Amazon exploration showed that the size of an expedition bore little relation to the results it finally brought home in its baggage. In that thought, tempered with the realization that no explorer had ever before gone in empty-handed of supplies (and come out alive), I took what little consolation and hope I could. There is no incentive like that of searching for a lost land of gold. Raleigh and Orellana and those others had found that out; and I too had caught the same burning fever that had driven them on and on, many to…God knows what!

We had advanced northeast only about a mile, through dense jungle mainly comprised of a heavy stand of *tortuga* trees, threading our way down a *trocha* (net of trails) made by wild pigs, when it started raining. First, a pattering tattoo of drips, then a sluicing down of solid sheets of water. Instead of complaining, Jorge was pleased, as our tracks were being washed away. Indeed our march was taking us through country which could not have changed since the times when the great three-toed, camel-like, elephant-nosed *Macrauchenia* lived in it. Indian legends as well as fresh skins found in caves confirm this. Northeast, in the Javary country, the Indians report the existence of "horses," an animal they have never actually seen, and know only from descriptions by the *patrónes*.

We slithered along a narrow, muddy, water-streaming burrow under weird vegetable masses bound tightly together with the parasitic spiky, fig-leaved *mato-palo* lianas, all swaying in the wind. Bark, limbs, leaves, ants, strange insects of enormous size—such as the brown seven-inch "walking stick"—old birds' nests, and other trash, fell around and upon our heads and shoulders. Like the *caucheros*, we did not wear hats or sun helmets, our heads being protected by a red scarf cinched around our brows Apache-like. No man wearing a hat could get through that brittle tangle.

"I thought this was the dry season," I called out above the racket to Jorge. He was swinging his machete, at one point hacking a way through exceptionally heavy undergrowth and debris, alive with toucans making a clacking sound with their enormous yellow, red and green bills.

"Dry season, wet season—it is practically all the same here. Perhaps a little less water now than in April and May." He did not turn his head, nor did he stop working. That was the last time Jorge spoke for the next two hours, as the game trails were almost non-existent in places, and he required all his breath for swinging the machete. I acted as not only baggage carrier in the rear—no easy job in the clutching brush—but compass man as well, checking him to left or right whenever we were confronted by a new choice of tunnels.

Muddy water was soon standing four to six inches deep on the more level ground. Snakes, flooded out of their holes, were coiled on bushes and in the thorny yellow-blooming acacias. They were of jewel-bright solid colors or combinations of diamonds, rings and mottles. The *jergóns* being deep plum to bull-blood red; the whitish *mantona*; the turtle-headed *motelo-machacuys* being yellow, white, black and red—snakes never before reported in such high elevations. But the most common, which Jorge always carefully pointed out, was the *loro-machacuy*. This snake is of several varieties: the blues, the white and blacks, the greens, eight-foot whip-like reptiles and deadly poisonous, which climbed higher than the other snakes. Sometimes we had to crouch low when passing beneath. We were careful not to disturb the *loros*, as when this happened they slid off their perch and landed in the water. They had a nasty habit, too, of gliding down across your shoulders—warned Jorge as he pointed out one lying only two feet above my head. I could not believe my eyes, when we saw a thick six-foot-long rattler swimming along, as if it were a watersnake! Apparently these Amazon rattlers have taken to water.

The game trails had been made by a herd of perhaps five hundred boars called *huangana*, whose three-inch cloven tracks we saw on higher unflooded ground. Jorge said they were close by, whispering there were two kinds, these, and the smaller, collared, bristly, gray *sajino*. The latter, related to the Mexican peccary, are not considered dangerous. The *huanganas*, however, are big, white-lipped, black pigs, which attack in herds of as many (according to the *patrónes*) as a thousand head, and will bravely charge men and even jaguars. Even in the rain, their scent—stronger than that around a pigpen—lay heavy on the undergrowth, against which they had rubbed. This is caused (unlike the domestic pig) by secretions from a gland over the hind quarters; an oily, dark-brown substance believed to be a sex-attractor, but active also when the pigs become alarmed or angry.

By late morning we were hungry. Our first game was actually a scaly armadillo that must have weighed thirty pounds. Short-legged, it jumped through the water in little leaps, and we took out after it as the place was fairly open. I finally made a dive and grabbed its long, horny tail and tried to yank the armor-clad beast out of the hole it was desperately digging with long claws. But the armadillo, terrifically strong, actually succeeded in digging in, for I could not get a good purchase with my feet. Having no shovel to turn it out with, we lost our lunch. But Jorge climbed a slender *maraja* palm, and its black fruit proved abundant and edible if oily. "That's what the Campas will fatten you on," remarked he with a grin. We washed it down with a gourd half-filled with "milk," obtained when Jorge stuck the machete into a smooth-skinned reddish tree whose name I did not note. All about, were pairs of flitting, delicate pale blue violin birds, *sui-sui*.

In the meantime the wind had sprung up and was now whistling thinly. Due to the danger from falling trees, this was a bad place to be caught in a tropical storm. The rain slashed at us spasmodically. Thunder rumbled and clapped overhead. The larger *cedros* trees creaked mightily. Lightning crackled in their wet conductor tops—a mass of green and yellow orchids—so that the purpling jungle was lit up in blinding flashes. At such moments the charcoal-black silhouettes of strange, fiat-topped umbrella trees—*lupunas*, towering 180 feet into the air; *mirity* palms, with their huge, green, 12-foot-wide fans blown inside out. These last were enormous, bare-limbed trees with a scrofulous white bark, filled with waxy red blossoms huge as cabbages, that were being wrenched loose and sent flying through the air all over the weird landscape.

Having eaten, and sharpened the steel blade of the machete with a fragment of native sandstone picked up along the way, we again hit the trail. We were now making very good time, as I was in the swing of it. Our feet tiresomely plopped-plopped-plopped, as we pulled them out of a thick, yellowish-white clay. I found later that this was the universal hard-pan formation (covered by very little loam) of the entire western Amazon basin and one of the main reasons why the region will always remain a wild and savage land, for it cannot support large agricultural populations. Only ten miles out of camp, halfway to the Perené, my feet burned with broken blisters caused mainly by my feet being submerged in water. I was covered with insect bites from head to foot, and it was all I could do to keep from crying out with the terrible itching and the sharp pain. The worst were the tiny black *pium* flies, that settled on us in dense clouds, and drew blood on every square inch of skin, even under our tough leather shirts and homespun pants. The *tabañas*, green and brown and big as horseflies, were not so numerous as the other insects, though their stings (for they are blood feeders) raised hard welts a half-inch in diameter. None of these I must scratch, warned Jorge, especially those bites in which eggs had been blown.

All that day we marched—crawled would be a more fitting word— mostly in warm rains, hour after hour. The heat was so enervating, so burning, that at times I reeled from near heat prostration, and eventually could no longer even sweat. Later that day, Jorge shot a red wolf, the *jubatus*.

Shouldering our way through the tangle, the miles dropped away behind us. Late afternoon came, the skies suddenly cleared to a deep ozone-blue. At our backs an enormous coppery sun lay sizzling over the thin snowy crest of the Andes. We had now been traveling eleven hours since 6 A.M. Then a tiny light flashed ahead in a blue-shadowed ravine. Filled from side to side with jungle and torn fern-trees, the small clearing had a few sagging adobe huts clustered in its middle, huddling away from the jungle.

"That is our destination," said Jorge, "the house of Señor Stone."

"Good," I answered as casually as I could, sitting down in the yellow mud in spite of several green slime-trailing slugs. "Let's rest *un momento*." Except to eat, we hadn't stopped since turning out of camp over eleven hours before.

"No…we must hurry on! What is wrong, my friend? It is only a few hundred yards farther. Night is coming in fast; we have a very short twilight in this latitude. (Our position was: 10° 55' S. Lat., 75° 18' W. Long.) It is unsafe to stay here in the dark. That is a jaguar you hear roaring."

"Let him roar," I returned, "these blisters are worse than his bite. I will sit a moment."

"Your second day in *la selva*…your second *easy* day—is almost finished." Jorge looked down at me keenly, with a new interest perhaps. His sunburned mahogany-brown face, with its blue Andalusian eyes, the heavy corded muscles at the side of the firm mouth, showed almost no fatigue. This frontiersman was certainly a new type, a far, far cry, from the American and European conception of the typical indolent Latin-American.

It would certainly take me a full week to reach the same peak physical condition. After that, I felt, I could beat him at his own game—only I wouldn't get the chance to wipe that sneer off his face; he would presently be turning tail for Lima.

I got on my feet, slung our pack across my shoulder, and we rushed on through the gathering gloom; that is, strictly speaking, Jorge rushed on—slashing and shouldering a noisy but effective way through *garapatos*-laden growth. I just wallowed and limped along on my blisters in his wake.

I realized in a daze that from now on my sole problem in life would be one of survival, the overcoming of whatever obstacles must certainly lie ahead if I were somehow to find those witchmen and obtain the medicines. All the while I must edge closer to the great blank region on the map where I hoped to find El Dorado. Nor did I fool myself, or pull the poncho over my eyes, as the Peruvians say. It was a calculated roll of the dice—my neck against the Indians' secrets, and that passport to El Dorado–Cabeza de Vaca's golden cities (God willing!). I was thrilled in spite of my pitiable condition, but unlike my heavily armored predecessors, I didn't mind admitting the truth to myself. What meaning had the mysterious bellbird's fatal call? I did not know. But I was already thoroughly scared.

❧ II. ☙

"Beyond Lies the Unknown..."

*T*HE last limb sprang into place with a hard snap behind us, and we stepped cautiously into the clearing. Ahead was a high platform balanced in three palm stumps. On it a chunky bob-haired Indian lookout in black paint and a G-string jumped to his feet and began bellowing on a bull's horn, warning the plantation that strangers were approaching.

Immediately a tall, spare man stepped out from a warehouse door-way. He carried a carbine in the crook of his arm. Even in the gathering dusk, I saw that he wore his linen suit with a surprising air. A pukka-sahib. I had expected to see a moth-eaten tropical tramp with a tobacco-stained beard, like that hardy breed of Americans and Englishmen a hundred or so of whom are scattered all the way from the Rio Grande in Mexico to Tierra del Fuego. I was conscious that we ourselves were undermining the prestige of the Caucasian race, our pants torn, our faces and hands scratched and swollen, plastered from head to foot with mud.

"Señor Stone!" called out my companion, raising his hand. "Oh—it's you, Mendoza! Salutations and all that rot. It's bloody dangerous to come in here so late, you know. The Campas murdered Miller about this hour." Jorge whispered that Miller had been Stone's predecessor. "Do come along. It's all right now." He handed over the gun—a well-kept one—to a cat-whiskered, stumpy 200-pound Indian buck clad in an old pair of pants. The Indian's upper body was smeared with a shiny translucent red paint, *achiote*.

We approached and shook hands.

"Beastly weather for you chaps to be splashing about in," observed the Englishman, "Where are your bearers?"

"I'm the only bearer around here," I grinned.

Jorge explained we had none, which seemed to surprise the other. We stopped at a ramshackle cage consisting of a scrap of window screening nailed across the open face of a packing case, and the tall man peered inside.

"Pretty little chappie, isn't it?" he smiled. "I wouldn't touch that screen, if I were you."

I jerked my hand away—and none too soon. Something thudded against the screen. I peered closer and saw that a very large and bright-orange bushmaster was coiling and hissing, preparing to strike again. A trickle of venom was running down the mesh.

"I should hate to find that thing in my bed," spoke up Jorge. He lifted a lid on top, stirring up the thick ten-foot snake with a stick, at which it struck repeatedly, hard—like the blow of a hammer.

The planter chuckled mildly: "That's where it was found, you know, in Miguel's bed."

"Really," came from Jorge unsmiling, who spoke perfect English whenever he fancied, for he was, as I have said, a graduate of the university where I had met him, "and how is your *mayordomo*?"

"Doing splendidly, I fancy. Had to bury the poor chap. Slight case of snake poisoning." And a moment later, to me: "You're American, aren't you?" And when I affirmed his suspicions, he added, "What on earth are you doing in a place like this?"

"I'm headed for the big basin."

For a full minute the man said nothing, just stared, while comprehension slowly gathered in his pale blue eyes. Then he said in precise tones, "You're joking, of course. You would have to go through the Campa country. But Americanisms always leave me a trifle confused; you mean by 'the Big basin' the Amazon Valley?"

In Spanish I said: "That is the crux of the idea, the meat on the wishbone."

"That's what I jolly well don't like about you Americans. You lack experience—a sense of fitness. People just don't go into the Amazon from here."

"Perhaps you are right," I answered, "but we shall see."

"Oh, really…" he stammered; but not from the bumbling, muddle-headed stodginess all the world is so fond of snickering over. I have seen the Englishman operate in the worst pest holes of the five continents, I don't think he is at all slow on the uptake. He has a kind of deep inherent, almost atavistic shyness, which when stripped of its appalling egotism and stuffiness is all to his credit. Finally Stone ended with the typical covering remark, which again meant nothing really: "I'm quite sure, being an American, *you* will have no difficulty!"

"I'm sure of it too."

About that time Jorge either envisioned sleeping out in the brush amongst the bugs, or else saw signs of the Stars and Stripes and the Union Jack breaking out in the free non-imperialistic jungles of Peruana. It is perplexing to the South American that the Anglo-Saxons are more apt to bristle at each other, than at a Latin. And of course the South Americans, who always stick together, are puzzled; they can't dope it out, not realizing that under the veneer of acidity between foreign-residing Americans and Englishmen, there is usually (not always), an inner feeling of peace, and even of friendship. Both take great care not to show it. But when the chips are down, they are invariably drawn to each other. The fact remains, however, that Americans are at a great disadvantage. British literature, directly translated into Spanish by South American publishers, is full of the contempt held by the Englishman for the American, whereas our own translated literature poorly offsets this with that puzzling fawning of ours over the Englishman, which suggests we recognize an inferiority and are invariably currying his liking.

With a grin Jorge began pointing out the scenery, such as it was. Crowning a low hillock in the center of the clearing, "the residence" was revealed through a cluster of squatty palms. We climbed the hill, going through a grove of pink oleanders, while all about stretched a badly mutilated and burned-out clearing. There were rows of coffee bushes, hedged by steep yellowish hills to which clung a dripping lettuce-green rind of jungle, festooned with thick black vines and studded with flame-of-the-forest and fern trees of the lacy *shapaja* variety. On the south side of the ravine flowed the Perené—my key to the east and the Gran Pajonal, and later the lower Amazon regions. Whispering, innocent-enough caprice of crinkled tinfoil only a hundred feet wide, it moved thinly over gravels and sands of clean granite. We stepped up to a porch, smothered in hibiscus. When my elbow touched one of the flower-bursting bushes, the blossoms all sprang up into the air—butterflies, green and gold.

Inside, the residence proved really luxurious, and Jorge and I were shown to separate rooms, some thirty-five feet long, with seven-foot-wide beds, having tentlike nets suspended on frames. Darkness came. I lit the coal-oil lamp, stripped off my clothes and bathed in a tin tub, using the water in a pitcher. I removed as many bugs as possible, painted my scratches with iodine, and dressed in a clean white shirt and old gray flannel slacks. With night, due to our elevation, it had turned much cooler. I rested on the bed's cover, reading.

Suddenly I felt queer—as if something were watching me. Without moving a hair, for a snake could easily be lying very close, I moved the line of my vision over the top of the book and saw at the bed's foot a heavy-set Indian clad in a loin-strap. His face was fantastically painted in red and black; yellow feathers dangled from his ear lobes. He spoke no word, just turned and went silently across the floor toward the door on enormous bare feet. Opening his maw of a mouth, he pointed at his black-painted filed teeth. I guessed dinner was served.

I followed the Indian into the dining room. The walls here were of the rarest hardwoods in the world, brilliant red with a white burl grain. A hissing gasoline-pressure lamp hung from the high ceiling. Under it was a long refectory table, covered with white linen. I smiled when I saw it was set with Wedgwood plates having the blue Chinese willow-pattern design, showing a temple whose original in Shanghai had once been my hideout during the Japanese Army occupation of China. There was a service of silver. In the center a great silver bowl was filled with—of all things!—red English roses.

As I sat down I decided to pick the Englishman's brains for information on the jungle, and yet enjoy the proffered luxury of our surroundings—certainly the last I would know—and at the same time hold up my end by making polite small talk. We seated ourselves, and while being served by the painted "butler," soup, fish, and later, meat, I discussed with our most properly jacketed host the possibilities for settling colonists in east Peru. Millions in an overcrowded Europe were reaching out, rather desperately, for new lands.

"Before you settle them, old boy, you had jolly well better explore the place first," the Englishman suggested tartly.

"It can't be that bad," I returned with what I hoped was a smile aimed at drawing him out. "There are few explorers who will not claim that the region has been pretty well defined."

"What explorers, old boy?"

I cautiously mentioned the names of those few who had worked in a radius of some 2,000 miles—some three or four.

Stone looked startled and glanced across at Jorge, who was smiling vaguely, saying little. "Yes, I've read the books by the Americans and Englishmen. Two of the blighters sat on their hocks in their Andean houses west of the jungle. One lived with a missionary who told me the fool never came into dinner without wearing his .45. And the other fellow floated down a river inhabited by Peruvian *patrónes* for well over 200 years."

"Well, they weren't real explorers," I hastened to explain, "they were collectors and scientists. There are no reconnaissance explorers today."

Then he exploded: "By Jove! Then why don't they say so! At best, these so-called explorers come in here for a month or two, sit around some mission station, or float down some such river as the Napo, the Araguaia or the Madeira, and then trot home and spread the good word that all is known, *and explored*—by them, of course!"

Stone was wound up, and with a full head of steam in his boilers. He had struck a favorite subject of residents both foreign and domestic in these Amazon countries. I grinned sympathetically, and continued pumping him. If the jungled slopes of the Andes were to be opened, *after being explored*, could a program for settling such people be activated? Could determined pioneering men bring their families into this forest and live in peace and prosperity? Our host thought it about as possible as establishing them on the bally moon, but finally conceded—IF. And assuming (which was unlikely) that would-be Daniel Boones, who couldn't cut the mustard back in a tamed Europe, could make out in a jungle. For a period of two years such misguided candidates might be brought into the Perené Colony, screened, schooled, hardened—physically and morally—and of course, old boy, fed and clothed. They must be supplied with tools, medicinals and seeds, provided with advisors and protection against the Indians and other boogies—*but*, mind you (at this point a large finger was wagged under my nose), only a well selected group! Most Europeans could not survive this jungle, let alone get a living out of it. This was not Asia and Africa, you know. Many had tried here, but few had lived through the experience. Even the *caucheros* (for whom the planter seemed to have a very healthy regard) never stayed out long.

"This is the Amazon bush, my American friend," he said emphatically in measured cadence. "This is bloody hell! And you'll find your jolly neck exposed to the axe if you go a mile east of here. There are no drug stores and ice cream cones down there, you know!" This last, I thought, was a bit unnecessarily English.

I came up at the count of nine, while Jorge labored at suppressing a laugh, and turned again to Stone. After those two years of grace in his theoretical jungle kindergarten, could the colonists wrest a living? As a wild guess, could the higher-level sub-Andean slopes of 100,000 square miles, such as hereabouts, support one hundred white men and their families, or could it support a million such families?

"Mendoza, your Yankee friend is suffering from a touch of the sun?"

Jorge grinned. "We came twenty-one miles today in eleven hours. I shouldn't be at all surprised."

Stone whistled in surprise. "Well! He could never have made it alone, that's certain—even if he is an American!"

I was just about to continue with my own tomahawk work, when he continued, turning toward me: "You know, I can't figure Mendoza out. He is the heir apparent to one of the greatest landed estates in the country. And what does he do? He runs off into this beastly bush, hunting meat for a gang of *caucheros*. Fancy! A gentleman in his own right…a direct descendant of a Spanish noble who was one of the original conquistadores! What do you make of it?"

"Maybe he likes parrot meat," I suggested.

"Fiddlesticks! The Mendoza family controls holdings of the best coffee lands in Peru, herds of cattle so numerous they don't even know whether they own a hundred—or three hundred thousand heads. I know for a fact they have silver and gold concessions!"

"Well, you know, man always wants what he hasn't got." I glanced over at Jorge. He was very busy with his fish. I had wondered why his outfit was even leaner than my own. Probably it was a matter of pride to make good on his own in the *monte*, perhaps against the wishes of his family. Ever since he had aimed that gun at my throat, I had liked him immensely. And now I liked him even better, and was terribly sorry he was not going in search of El Dorado with me.

Stone fell to carving the beef, a juicy haunch, pink inside with an outer jacket of golden cracklings. It smelled like something out of Merry England. All at once a fusillade of gunshots boomed out from the east side of the clearing. Our heads jerked up and Stone squared around toward the noise: "I hope the blithers potted that cat which broke the neck of my best bull last night!"

Sure enough, when we trooped outside with a lantern, there was a huge spotted jaguar. It hung by its feet from a pole carried on the shoulders of a crowd of grinning Indians. It was vile-smelling, bleeding profusely at the head which was badly mangled from a shotgun blast. An iron hook was pounded into its hind hocks, and the beast was hauled up by a squeaking block-and-tackle.

"This is the third largest feline in the world," pedantically pointed out Stone, with an air of authority; then, to Jorge, "What will the bloody pussycat go, Mendoza?"

"Perhaps 280 pounds."

"No! No! Not that heavy, really!" returned the Englishman decisively, for it would be exceedingly rotten form to overdo it in front of this pair of foreigners. And then as he held up the lantern, "308—well! Well! Scales are probably off."

We returned to the dining room, and tackled that rare roast beef. Black Chanchamayo coffee, the world's finest and never sold outside Peru (except, it is said, to the Royal House in London), was served demitasse in the library. Here, where the walls were not banked with rows of books, they were paneled with a dark hand-polished pigeon-blood mahogany cut from the nearby "bush," as the Englishman called the jungle. Pipes lit and comfortably seated, we three continued our talk until long past midnight. Monstrous brown moths with yellow cat's eyes speckling their dusty wings, black flying beetles with green eyes, flying ants in red suits and silvery wings, three-inch apple-green praying mantis—all in a suicidal frenzy, pinged and swooshed against the lamp on the table. Some of the smaller bugs stuck fast to the gasoline leaking around the filler cap. From time to time, the planter bawled for an Indian to man the pressure gadget.

"That's what would happen to your colonists," once remarked Stone, pointing with his pipe stem at the dead bugs scattered under the light. "The bally bush gets them all. It will reach out and get me in this house. That bug," he pointed at a long brown beetle trying to dash its brains out against the lamp, "will cause blindness if it flies into your eye!" He whapped the bug with a paper-backed book. "That bush will get you. But I don't think you will go into it. Mendoza tells me he is returning to Lima, and of course you will have to go along with him."

An Indian, silent as a shadow, with an expressionless flat, Mongolian, blue-painted face, placed a bottle of Scotch on the table. In spite of all the humpetyumph, I was beginning to like Stone. He was really careful and conservative. Egotistical and earthy, the sort of man who really believes he is master of his own destiny, and that accident and fate have nothing to do with him. He had been rummaging in his attic, not really talking up to now. And Jorge, that philosophic paradox of the educated professional hunter, was a most un-Latin listener, full of knowledge, a deep wisdom for his years—and carefully husbanding an attendant and friendly silence toward both of us.

It is really astonishing how many people in the United States and Europe are interested in getting information (which is not available) on the possibilities for pioneering in the jungle. I explained this to Stone, and soon he was talking. The easterly slopes of the Cordillera, the bench ladder curving down to meet the steamy Amazonic flats, were probably, he believed, mainly free from most types of malaria. "Of course, chaps, that is a guess. We do not know."

The only partly and seasonally inundated bush close by, was certainly rich in commercial plants, fine cabinet woods, hide and skin animals and reptiles, and even minerals—gold, silver, copper. In places the soil must be deep enough and productive. Stone was exporting tea, coffee, castor oil, lemon-grass, vegetables, *maíz*, temperate-zone fruits such as oranges, limes, and all of the tropical fruits—pineapple, varieties of bananas, papaya, mango, *zapote, camote*, to mention but a few.

Except for horses, which cannot live here, Stone's livestock was doing well. Of course, due to the depredations of condors, he could not raise sheep even on the open Andean slopes included in his concession farther west. But Brahma cattle imported from Texas were ideal—bugs and heat seldom bothered them. He had, over the years, even beaten most parasites. To combat the strange diseases among the laborers, some five hundred of them, the Englishman injected live Gibraltar monkeys with the patient's blood, then shipped the live monkey out for laboratory analysis at Lima. Whatever medicine was returned by runner from La Merced was administered. Yes, sometimes the monkey cashed in his chips. But without this unique service even Stone could not operate here. Of course, many diseases were never identified, and for still others science had as yet found no cure.

"What happens then?" I asked, thinking those with unidentified disease were probably shipped over the Andes on the backs of those piano-carrying Quechua *cargadors* one hears so much about in Lima.

"My dear fellow, we usually bury them. In fact we have got quite a cemetery, don't you know."

Wrapped in a cloud of pipe smoke, our host, citing the facts so bitterly acquired on his own hacienda, stated his belief that if the more elevated regions of Peru were ever explored they might support 5 million people. The "right kind," he meant. After five years they might grow enough food for themselves, and eventually an export surplus for 10 million others. But it would not be easy. We were warned of the necessity for stout leadership, organization, reception and training of the would-be pioneers; for planning and financing on a large scale.... "An American loan would swing it nicely." The opening up of transportation and communication—preferably an English concession—prior to bringing them in. He spoke of the tragedy of 150 Poles, all hand-picked, based on Iquitos and lost for any number of reasons along the Ucayali River, from 1931 to 1933. Today, all of them were dead.

Stone stated that my objective was hare-brained; the Indians had no real knowledge of medicine, and the wild tribes—worse than even the Parecis of Mato Grosso—tribes practically unknown such as the Campas, Amahuacas, Guarayos, Cashinahuas and Purus out east, would attack a man on sight. The Bat Tribe (Morcegos), who paint themselves purple, and their hair yellow, recently staked out forty-three Bolivian *caucheros* to anthills. He warned me to go back, that beyond lay the unknown. And if I persisted, my head would surely end up on a post, or my body even conveniently hacked and set boiling in a clay fire-pot.

With that we went to bed. The next morning, before daybreak (July 12th), I awoke when a beam of light fell across my eyes. Jorge had come into my room carrying a lighted candle. I tossed aside the netting and got up.

"I'm going in with you," he said quietly.

"I can't pay you much, Jorge. Only $200 to Iquitos."

He smiled, "I thought I was a partner."

"You were a partner, till you quit. Now you're on the payroll until you prove yourself."

The smile broadened: "Money is not everything. Adventure counts too. Besides, I must help you. Peru and the United States are friends, are they not? Stone and I have talked it over. He says that for an American you really are not a bad sort"—here Jorge grinned again. "You see, you cannot even find the Campas' villages because Stone has heard these people cut the vocal cords of their roosters' throats to silence them. And without making friendly contact with the savages, you will certainly be attacked or starve out there."

"And don't forget the *brujos* and their medicines," I pointed out. "We must find these, if nothing more."

Jorge smiled and shrugged his shoulders. "Medicines I have no interest in. But gold! Something tells me we shall find a great deal of it."

It was not long before I was dressed and packed.

After breakfast, Stone, armed with a cane, took us down to the sandy bank of the Perené, where two six-foot Indians in bark aprons were preparing to launch a small twelve-foot canoe. The stinking carcass of a rather large crocodile lay alongside at the water's edge.

"The river is full of these devils, especially lower down," remarked Stone. "We caught that one after it had eaten my best dog. We bait a piece of *topa*," he pointed to a chunk of wood. "The crocodile's teeth become imbedded in the soft wood, and as the brute cannot submerge without drowning, we merely have to haul it in on a *cabuya* (a tree fiber) rope, and shoot it in the head.

"Speaking of reptiles, old boy, Colonel Fawcett reached the eastern edge of Madre de Dios, out where you are going. It is a country of swamps apparently. One day while running his dugouts through it, he saw a great reptilian head rise out of the jungle, but before he could shoot, the head was lowered. From the noise the beast made getting away, he took it to be some sort of dinosaur. His Indians revolted and it was necessary to return to Mato Grosso."

When I smiled, he presently added: "Don't be too sure they don't exist—we hear a great many stories from the Indians here! You may take my canoe. Mendoza will go by mule. You will rendezvous at a friendly Campa village ten miles below. I haven't seen it, but Miguel, before he died, used to say it was all right. After that, I really don't know what will happen to you. Valeria, a crazy prospector, is down there somewhere. And I hear a Puna Indian missionary is still alive. If you find these two, perhaps they can help you along farther."

I thanked this fine Englishman, for in spite of all the affectation and frumpery, there are no better men anywhere on earth. As the full light of dawn poured in an orange flood over the green rim of the Amazon Valley, I took my seat, a precarious one on a handful of sticks in the bottom of the dugout. It had been carved from a single log of *alfaro*, or *lagarto caspi* (crocodile wood) of a reptilian greenness. The baggage was wedged in fore and aft of me. The pair of paddlers, exceedingly hefty Indians, coppery as hand-polished *canela*, took their positions and warned me to sit steadily, as the river was full of— "Devils, señor!"

"Rapids and crocs," smilingly interpreted Stone. Then added, "These two men are safe enough, and they speak a fair brand of Spanish. If you want to know anything, just ask them."

He shoved us out into the river. One Indian knelt in the bow, the other squatted aft, steering with a round paddle-blade on a long handle. These red paddle-blades were painted with mystic designs to appease the river spirits. We swirled away.

"Cheerio! Take care, Yank! If you find that tribe of pigmies, mail me a stuffed one!" It dawned on me that Stone, like many others, gave no credence to the shrunken heads, but believed they came from a race of men only a foot high who lived somewhere in the interior.

Jorge waved, swung up on his mule. I watched him start into a tunneled trail of purple shadows, followed by an Indian on foot. He would reach the rendezvous about the same time as myself, for though I would travel faster, my route was much longer due to the river's tortuous winding, whereas he would go in a straight line only about a third as far. We were off! Power lay in this river, even here. I could hear it and feel it. The clearing swiftly fell to the rear, and we bobbed along with little gurgly sounds through a narrow jungle-walled slot like a cork in a mill-flume. The canoe proved to be tippy, as it was barely twenty inches wide. After a few blank stares from the bow Indian, I lay on my back and watched the last stars wink out, one by one. Vines crossed like cat's cradles overhead, and hanging from them by long, bushy tails and spidery arms was a jabbering band of *coata* monkeys. Their shaggy black hair coats had whitish patches, and they squealed in holy terror as they swung off into the towering jungle.

Immediately I began to smell new sharp delightful odors, and a few fecal ones not so delightful. These odors went away, and never seemed to return, for they were always being replaced by new ones. Blue parakeets flew up the river toward us. Clusters of reddish frugivorous bats hung head-down from limbs. They had neither feet nor legs, and they were held suspended by hooks set in their wing tips.

Once in a cucumber-green *yacu* (lagoon) the bow paddler dug in his paddle to brake us to a stop, and told me to place my ear against the bottom of the dugout and listen for the thrumming and purring of fishes in the shallows. (Science, of course, has only recently learned that fishes are capable of making sounds.) Most *huarapaches* (white men), he said, looked only ahead of them. I must look even closer ahead, much closer!—and above, as well; and below; and on both sides; and especially behind—never forget to look behind!—but above all, I must look *inside*, to see if the "soul" was black. If I could remember all this, my scope for observation would certainly be enlarged seven times....

The current's tempo quickened; suddenly without warning—swift, high-curling waves washed over us, dashing ten feet straight into the air—or so it seemed, though probably half that—banging and pounding against our thin shell of a bottom. We rode with a stiff wind against our face, plowing through a series of wild sprayheads, while the water swished over the low freeboard of the gunwales to slosh in the bilge. Then we hit still water, and frantically began bailing with our cupped hands and a single halved gourd.

Miles after, we shot around a wide steep curve, through more white, roaring waves, and surging past black glistening rocks miraculously missed only at each last instant. And then finally, amid a flock of white *huanchaco* storks—standing four feet high—we glided toward the right bank and landed on a bar. Several long dugouts were drawn up and tethered to poles thrust into deep gravel.

I was already farther east than Stone had been. The village must be close by, for a tom-tom was being thumped about a hundred yards inland. I half expected to find Jorge there. We scrambled up the steep twenty-foot bank. Black mosses, like hanks of mummy hair, dropped wetly from slippery roots. We got to the top, and beyond, on a tree-covered broad flat bench of sand and gravel, came to the village. There were ten houses perched on log piles. Vertical cane walls were topped with beautifully woven palm thatched roofs. We climbed up onto a porch some six feet high. It was springy as a bed mattress, and fashioned from the brown split *chonta* palm bark, unrolled like a mat. This *chonta* palm, whose inner heart is one of the hardest woods known, is seventy-five feet high, with a thorny trunk, and is undoubtedly the most valuable wood in the entire jungle.

Jorge was nowhere about—probably detained. Although a fire outside the huts was smoking, the place seemed deserted. I jumped to the ground off the porch, and stood still, wondering what I should do. The two paddlers had taken one look, and run back to their canoe. I was not exactly hankering to walk into one of those huts and get an arrow through my chest. After about ten minutes a score of crafty-eyed Indians came slowly out of the smoky interiors, and formed a half-circle around me. I moved back until the porch touched my shoulder.

Naked but for shirts, they looked plenty tough, and were—Stone had said—neither strictly wild nor strictly tame, either. They were crudely smeared with the glistening *achiote*, that same paprika paint made up with fish oil or animal fat, and from which lipstick is made. They stood around gazing at me, picking their noses, and twisting up their wide mouths into thin sneers, an indication they had seen white men, whom they could invariably beat at jungle lore, their gage of a man's worth. No one could hunt, track and kill as well as an Indian; paddle, grow food, or talk to the spirits of the jungle.

The nose of each man was pierced, and one brave had a four-inch red bone stuck through the septum parallel with his upper lip. The headman, a giant, finally approached. His greased hair was bobbed just above the eyes and long behind, made up into pigtails threaded with red and yellow feathers. He was a savage if I ever saw one. Around his bulging neck a talisman hung on a beaded string. I took a sharp look at this object, and saw with a little shock that it was a set of false teeth, through which a set of holes had been drilled.

I was wondering who could have donated these, when a woman (whom later I realized must be the chief's wife) brought out a gourd of *chicha*, which Stone had told me I must not refuse.

As the mixture of clots and slime slid down my throat I all but gagged, and wondered what they were. (Fortunately, it was not for another day till I found out.) The Indian said I could go no farther downriver, as this was Indian country. The whole band were stomping their feet on the ground, and crying out and grimacing angrily. My position was complicated further by the braves speaking only a few words of Spanish. Every few minutes one of them would crowd up close, his bloodshot eyes staring into mine only a few inches away. Finally, one terrific giant stuck his face right against mine and made a growling sound, probably imitating a tiger; and that started the others howling in laughter. I brought my fist squarely into his breadbasket, and he dropped like a shot. The silence was so thick you could have sliced it with a machete. Then suddenly one of the Indians whirled around. Jorge was coming up at a run from the bank, his wet doeskin shirt sticking to his back like red onion-peel. He waded in amongst the Indians. At a few gruff words from him the Indians fell back, and presently we walked over to the shade of the biggest hut. "Am I glad to see you!" I said. "What kept you?" As we were going in amongst the Indians at the hut, he explained he had run into some rotten ground perforated with armadillo burrows, and had to send the Indian back with the mule, after which he hurried on by foot. They were squatting on their painted hams, snatching tubers out of a fire-blackened clay pot. A second pot held chunks of meat.

"That tuber is yuca (cassava or arrowroot)," said Jorge, pointing, "and that is what we are going to live on mainly, if we are lucky. This other is rat meat."

"It's pretty big for rat meat!"

"We have several very large rodents here. This one is of a small variety called *picuro paca*. It weighs only about fifteen pounds."

Trying not to visualize a gigantic reddish rat, horny tail and all, I ate a piece of it, and found the gray meat to be sickeningly sweet.

Bluebottle flies buzzed and settled on us in a blanket—even tiny gray mosquitoes, though it was broad daylight and the sun was blazing high. One of the Indians cut a slash across a blood-blister on the end of his big toe and squeezed out a grub, laid by the borer *nigua*, a kind of jigger-flea. He then put his hands into the same meat pot from which we were eating. I asked Jorge to learn where the chief had got the false teeth.

He and the Indians began jabbering in a rudimentary patois of Quechua, Campa, and Spanish. Finally Jorge said, "Mostly, these people, as you see, wear a necklace of crocodile teeth, as medicine against snakes. The crocodile is one of the river gods. This fellow is the *curaca* (chief); he says he got the false teeth out of the head of a *huarapache* who was searching for *curi* (gold). The *curaca* it seems became frightened when the prospector took out the teeth and clacked them at him. He was afraid the man had bewitched him, and so speared the fellow in the back, and annexed the teeth. He thinks they are good medicine for snakes." Jorge chuckled softly, "That's the first medicine we find, eh?— my friend!"

"But I thought this village was tame...?"

Jorge grinned. "It is. We call these 'shirt Indians.'"

Presently he began haranguing for transportation. For an hour he argued back and forth. At times the argument seemed ready to boil over into a free-for-all fight. Later I learned the Campas make a show of becoming incredibly excited and violent whenever speaking on any subject. Finally we seemed to make a little headway. On the river bank the chief showed us two large pigeon-blood cedar canoes, and assigned six paddlers for each, to take us down to the Puna missionary's settlement which he called "Sutsiki."

This place, from their description, seemed to be about thirty miles away. Once we got there we would certainly be "bushed" as Stone had said. There would be no turning back. A trail did not exist in the jungle, and the river's current was too swift for doubling around and paddling uphill. The Indians somehow were able to filter homeward through the tangle; but a white man, never! Thus we were forced to buy the canoes outright, for 100 soles-de-oro (about $15), as the stretch below was wild, and there was no chance whatever of returning them even empty up to this high village.

The eating over, we embarked in the dugouts and were soon racing through a deep gulch whose slopes were usually hidden by a miasmic jumble, mostly of *palo mulato* and *algodon* trees, hung with parasitic aroids and streaming aerial roots sucking moisture from the damp air. Every limb and crotch was smothered with the prickly pineapple-like plant, having the yard-tall red blossom. Blue herons fished elegantly in the shallows along the stony banks. Suddenly we shot at what seemed like fifty miles an hour (but was probably nearer thirty) over a sandstone ledge barrier, and plunged down through a washboard of white waters with rocks sticking up everywhere like shark's teeth. I nearly pushed a hole through the bottom of my own dugout trying to put on the brakes. The worst rocks were those hidden under a thin film of swift water, for you couldn't see them until the last instant.

To dodge these dangerous shoals, the Indians continually shouted at each other, whooped and screamed, frantically digging in their paddles so that their tremendous muscles bunched up like hard knots as they drove the dugouts this way and that, braking, even back-paddling, but with it all, finally getting us through. We were dripping wet, half-swamped, and our baggage (such as it was) drenched.

At times when it was impossible to pass over a stone barrier, or a forty-five-degree waterfall, we had to let the dugouts down at the side of the rapids on vines cut from the trees. The landscape was wild, the river and the two walls of jungle dancing in green and brown heat waves. We worked hard under the blazing Amazon sun, dripping with sweat, for the heat was awful.

Nine times that day we had to beach the flooding canoes and empty them of water. Quite often there was no landing place alongside, and we had to drag the dugouts out of the river, and up and over immense boulders. The boats were heavy, and yet were so fragile they would not bear dropping, as this would crack them. Even so, we sometimes lost our grip on their slippery sides and they became badly damaged. All this labor required care and delayed our advance, and in addition we must caulk the canoes again and again—forcing twisted palm fibers into the cracks with the points of our knives and the Indians' machetes.

Once while pounding down through a stretch of loud-booming waters, dodging snags and rocks I couldn't see too well, I realized night was almost upon us. At our backs in the west, a flaming sun was dropping into the burgundy-red river. We reached bottom safely, and a purling current carried us swiftly into the darkening east. The whole jungle and its nocturnal wildlife awoke all at once—*huangana* pigs grunted in the thickets alongside; crocodiles wriggled out of the river to lie on the narrow bars and *playas* (the serpentine sand and gravel beaches), and when they opened their great jaws the jungle reverberated with a frog-like booming roar. The strange bedlam calls of a thousand unknown birds echoed in the canyon and insects by the clouds came dancing over the water. Last—but not least!—came the thin, high, awesome whine of countless mosquitoes, followed by little pings in my ears and an incredible itching of face, neck and hands.

And then, suddenly, we heard the sounds of men. The Indians in the dugouts stared hard into the trees. Tom-toms rattled. And the wildest, sing-songing howls came riding out of the jungle.

Jorge's canoe—a quarter filled with water—slid sluggishly alongside my port gunwale. "I have just learned those were Valeria's teeth worn by that *curaca*. The prospector is dead. And these are Christian voices, not those of *bravos*. We can thank the Virgin Mother that the Puna Indian missionary is probably still alive!"

↶ III. ↷

We Become Slave Traders

ONE too soon we turned in and beached the two cracked and badly leaking dugouts on the left bank. Securing them we hurried after our dozen Indians down a narrow trail cut through a dense, brittle belt of *caña brava*, a species of twenty-foot bamboo. At the end of this we found a grove of overwhelmingly sweet-smelling cinnamon trees, the *canela muena*, one of at least twelve varieties; and just beyond we entered a clearing carved out of a high white rubber jungle of the *mazaranduva*.

Sutsiki mission consisted of a hutch of some eight or ten cane- and palm-thatched huts perched on high stilts of a greenish ironwood. They smoked through their rotten old roofs, and little fires glowed red through the doorways. A burly Puna Indian missionary, whose Christianized Quechua subtribe lived in the south Peruvian Andes near Lake Titicaca, came running out of a hut holding a torch. He greeted us and pointed out a smaller hut that we could occupy. We climbed the ladder to it, and with a broom of limbs tied to a stick, swept the bark floor, dislodging centipedes some six inches long.

"*Estranjéros!* What are you here for? Men or women? I have eight *nankiratse* (slaves), strong machete men, and the price is cheap...500 soles-de-oro (about $9 each) for the lot!" wheezed the Puna excitedly, cracking his knuckles. He was about forty, his broad face was painted

49

red, his lips thin and purplish. From time to time he nervously clicked his cross and breviaries.

"We are not *patrónes*," spoke up Jorge, glancing at me rather shyly I thought, "we are going to contact the *brujos*."

"No, señor!" the Indian missionary said vehemently, "you must go back!"

"We are not Indians," replied Jorge, "it is not possible."

He and the wildly gesticulating Puna went up to the *casa grande*, a bush-house partly concealed among banana trees. As it dominated the clearing, and was the center of our stage in that camp, a detailed description should be made. The building was some hundred and fifty feet long, a massive two-storied structure of high bamboo walls; roofed with a peaked thatch of *pona* palm fronds, held in place on the underside by a cane-ribbed ceiling of the fine *chicosa*. The framework supporting this massive jungle mansion—perhaps the greatest in all the western Amazon—was of the hard *cocobolo* waterwood.

Later, after doctoring my face, which was swollen from bites, I joined Jorge and the Puna here. After hours of wrangling, I finally grasped the situation. First, it was absolutely impossible to go farther east. To attempt it was certain death, and not at all a quick and painless death.

"Campas!" the Puna snapped irritably when I questioned him for details, "Just devils!"

Jorge thought the Indian missionary himself was in a very dangerous position. Under him were grouped 160 Campas of both sexes, who were soon excitedly crowding around; a flock of sweating quasi-savages swathed in brownish-red woolen gowns called *cushmas*, patterned after the monk's robe. Their faces were weirdly painted with long black lines on the high cheek bones, and thick red slashes angling sharply downward at the sides of their wide mouths. A few had their jaws painted a shiny black, the upper half of the face, white. I believe no one has ever revealed what this fashion of painting means, for while it also frightens enemies and is a camouflage, it actually tells the true secret reason why the jungle Indian paints. It is a calling card telling other Indians his rank and whether the savage is ready for war, love, hunting, "spirit-talk," or perhaps only on a peaceful journey.

The missionary believed that at least ten thousand wild Campas lurked in the lower regions toward the east; but these would have very little to do with his 160 mission Indians. For us there would be no guide, no interpreter, no river men. "*No hay!*" screamed the Puna, apparently beside himself with fear and fury. None of these tame Indians, he insisted, with a wave of his sweating hand, could go with us for they were unable to exist in the wilds after their "reduction" or taming. Having lost the old forest culture and the secrets of jungle livelihood, they had become mission charges—*esclavos*—slaves.

From the Puna's missionary and other agents west of the jungle, the *patrónes* around La Merced bootlegged "converts" on a cash-and-carry basis, as the traffic was illegal. The Indian missionary's undercover turnover that year had been 480 slaves—certainly a big business! We argued and wrangled long into the night with this missionary, and finally, Jorge growled that—though it was against the law of the republic—our only chance of going farther would be to pose as slavers ourselves. The wild Campas—though no white man had ever come back alive to La Merced, once he went into the Gran Pajonal—might possibly deal with us that way and allow us to pass. In order to do this, and carry out such a scheme for going east, we would have to learn the business.

For the following days we bought from the Puna salt and cloth for trading purposes, and set ourselves at three main tasks. First, as no Spanish translation exists, we must begin to learn the Campa language. Second, we must prepare to go east down the unknown Perené. Third, we must find out something of the inside slave-trade practices, and they proved to be as complicated and secret as international espionage or dope trafficking. Without these three basic accomplishments, it would be impossible to even get near the *brujos*—and through their intercession with the tribe continue on our way toward Iquitos, and so eventually to the far regions hiding El Dorado itself. We must get through, for I had already spent so much money up to this point, that should we fail now, the whole venture would fall apart, and failure would be certain. I had left Lima with less than $600, and expenses along the way had added up to about $75, which left me exactly $521.18. This did not include a few hundred metal soles-de-oro carried separately in a canvas handbag.

This, then, in brief, is what we learned in those first days:

Pushing back the jungle and working it commercially necessitates the use of labor capable of existing in these terrible swamp forests—and only Indians can do this. First comes the capturing of the mind of the wild Indian, and this is done through symbolic religion. Money alone will not buy his services, for when the brave obtains enough for a gun or a machete, he quits and returns to the free life of the wastes. It is recognized by such missionaries as this Puna that psychology is stronger and more permanent than the use of iron chains, though these—and worse—too (as you shall see) are used. Among most such missionaries—and I repeat "most"—an alteration in Christian doctrine is made to dovetail with the Indian mystical beliefs.

In the center of the Sutsiki mission slave camp was an enormous thatched idol-house of bamboo. Here, on an altar, Christ was worshipped in the anthropomorphic form of a gigantic wooden image carved in the semblance of a Campa *brujo*. The idol's shoulders were covered with a sacred boa constrictor snakeskin cape, its loins girded with a grass skirt. A parrot feather headdress stood erect on its head, a band of cactus encased the brow, a skull necklace was strung about its neck, snake amulets encircled the ankles and arms. The fanged (for the teeth were pointed like a *brujo's*) face was painted terrifyingly with mystic symbols. The idol was crucified on its cross by giant pegs of black *chonta* from which blood dripped in partly dried clots—Christ's name being PAWA, (literally, "The Man of Gold").

This horrendous image was carved of the almost unknown ivory wood, *palo marfil* (said to be more costly than elephant ivory). It was daily washed in blood (taken from the veins of the worshippers) and likewise freshly painted with black *sua* and *achiote* dressed and scented. Every night the image was offered slabs of raw tapir or deer meat, tossed on a greasy stone dish. To it, in the light of torches, Indian maidens, stripped naked, their nipples rouged with a paste of *achiote* offered (as in ancient Greece) their "psychological bodies" (or, in this case, "ghost bodies") to the pleasure of the image. When a Campa warrior dreams in the night of a woman, and finds the semen on awakening, he takes this as proof that their two ghosts have copulated—hence the belief in the effectiveness of the "ghost dance." All this ritualistic orgy is to a drumming accompaniment on the sacred long drums, blessed by the high priests of the Dancing Anaconda Brotherhood, and to the mystic wailing of flutes consisting of two rows of hollow crocodile teeth. All about the men on the left, the women on the right, sit the entranced rows of Sun worshippers in a state of mass hypnotism, making obeisance to Pawa—Jesus, our Lord the Golden Man (Atahuallpa's old mystic title as the incarnated Sun God)!

No one has ever learned the outward customs nor the inward psychological behavior-pattern of the Campas. It was absolutely necessary for us to delve into this mysterious and horrid business of slavery and witchcraft combined with its twisted Christianity, before we could hope to move a yard out of Sutsiki.

In all fairness, neither the Church nor the Government in any way countenances the slave trade and its unholy ramifications. In every manner these two agencies officially fight the evil—priests, and soldiers often losing their lives. And it is a dark fight without glory, for no man dares to talk of it: a shot in the dark, and the priest lies dead on his floor, his throat sometimes cut for good measure. A bit of the witchman's poison in the food of the soldier who has captured slaves as evidence; a snake in the hammock of someone who might talk, or, above all, write. But we—Jorge and I—might pass muster, for we were becoming slavers ourselves, outwardly at any rate.

The Amazon's peonage phase of twentieth-century bonded slavery was a legalized form of perpetual indebtedness, and a quite different matter. The inside story of outright slavery has never been uncovered, much less revealed. The only reason I was able to learn this secret conspiracy and intrigue was by being forced to turn slaver myself.

Strangely enough, the Puna learned the missionary business from a white man (not a Peruvian) who, shortly before we arrived in Sutsiki, operated long enough, according to *patrónes* later met, to amass a fortune of $100,000; for ten long and fearful years this man never for a single waking moment sat in the bush house without a .45 Colt on his hip. It is estimated by the *patrónes* that this white missionary is responsible directly and indirectly for the deaths of 9,000 Campas alone, not counting slaves acquired from other tribes. Even allowing for exaggerations, the figures are impressive. Jorge's and my friend Russell, in Lima, said the R.D.C. believed the Campas numbered 15,000; Stone—with characteristic reluctance to exaggerate—veered too far in the other direction when he placed them at 2,000; while the Ucayali *patrónes* (in more contact and having a better intelligence system) place them at 30,000. None of these authorities has personally been into the Gran Pajonal; but from what the Campas told me, I would place them at a figure between 10,000 and 12,000.

Normally, the slaves are brought in young. The children are bartered for salt and cloth from their Indian parents. Sometimes a slave is a young widow whose husband either died of natural causes or more often was killed in the incessant fratricidal wars. Sometimes the slaves are young cast-offs escaping tribal vengeance for misdeeds real or fancied. But especially the procuring is of children from parents after the children have been declared "*bruja*" by a witchdoctor. Sentenced as bewitched, they must die, according to tribal law. Instead of killing them, however, the parents—among the most savage human beings on earth, incredibly avaricious, will almost always, if the chance presents itself, sell their children, killing another's child whose head is sometimes offered as proof that the sentence has been carried out.

After years of "reduction," or conversion, the children, called *nanki-ratse* (for Campa adults can seldom be broken), some often dying under the bullwhip (*pasamendotse*) are either sold or "legally contracted out as labor," by their savior missionary. This contracting or selling is to *patrónes* whose desperate need in the Amazon sector totals some 5,000 new machete and *caucho* workers each year. These slaves replace those who have died from natural causes, fighting, diseases, and heartbreak. The steady flow of slaves also allows for the natural economic expansion of the recent prosperous years. The Campa tribe, while it is the main source, is not the only one.

Nor is slavery confined to the jungle where it is comparatively safe from scandal beyond the Andean barrier. I already knew that prime slaves could be procured in Lima for 160 soles-de-oro (about $25 on the black market) per head. The brutal system exists even among enlightened Peruvians and foreigners, because it is *custombre*. Apparently, one gradually accepts slavery by not using the ugly name but by calling these slaves "Children-of-the-house." One even begins, as we were to learn over the following months, to overlook that which the Campas themselves call *guashankidanse* (punishment)—the breaking of slaves, the whipping of those seeking to escape bondage, and the use of the "wooden jacket," or even the barbarous tracking with dogs (and worse—by trained Campas, who unlike hounds never fail).

Thus, the days and nights passed; a hot, sweltering procession. We ate boiled yuca and the fibrous, white, starchy, tuberous farinha of Brazil, grown in the *chacaras* (jungle-cleared gardens of the Indians). Curiously—as a true gage of our knowledge—science has a single name for the yuca; actually, the Campas claim forty-eight types and have a name for each. Our beverage was usually cacao. Also we drank *chicha*, the fermented results of sugarcane or yuca masticated by the women and spit, together with saliva and the mucous of the nasal passages, into a trough. There it stood for a few days until it became mildly intoxicating. On the Indians it had a terrifying effect, turning them into mentally stupefied, bleary-eyed, fighting savages. It had a tangy-cool, clotted feel to it, and was sweetish-sour to the palate. Its taste, we found, varies with the tribes; but this description fits the *chicha* of the western enclave of the Campa confederation.

In the evenings, currents of hot fog-dripping air coiled through the slave camp. Clouds of mosquitoes and other pests came out of the woods, such as the night-flying *gehene*, whose sting is poisonous. If I wanted to read my paper-bound Almanac, I could only do so by getting under my netting, and it was suffocatingly hot. Nor would the net keep out the smaller and more deadly of the insect swarms. We itched incessantly though we bathed twice daily—morning and night. The worst insects were the powder flies, tiny borers who laid their eggs under our skin.

To learn their methods, we went fishing with the friendlier Indians, for only by fishing and hunting could we hope to keep from starving in the regions ahead. And not only outright starvation; but there was beriberi and scurvy to guard against. The best fishing place was where the river swirled around deep pools at the foot of gigantic tree roots buried in deep water among water grasses and lilies. Instead of fishhooks and lines, bows and arrows were used. Also reed lances and balsa or cane spears, both of which float and can be readily recovered. These were usually attached to a cord and so could be retrieved without entering the water, which was unsafe due to various fishes, snakes, and other dangers.

These fishing excursions were always successful. We filled large baskets with various fishes such as *gamitana* (dark yellow scales), *boquichico* (silvery with dark back), and *palometa* (plate-size, silver with orange spots)—fishes without English names. Many fish were heavily armored, resembling primitive fossil types, though whether related to the extinct arthrodires and ostracoderms it was impossible to determine.

One day we bought four slaves outright, paying out hard soles-de-oro—250 coins for them (about $35). Each coin was tested on an ironwood board to see if it rang true. These slaves were strong, sound, male Campas—as the Puna pointed out when thumping them, pulling on their brawny arms, peering into their mouths—and from twenty to twenty-two years of age. The price was stiff. But under no other circumstance—until bought—would they even unwillingly accompany us. They were terrified of the wild Indians. The Puna swore on his cross they would not desert once we started downriver.

Later Jorge and I were out in the forest fattening our larder by hunting *sajino* pigs, whose pinkish-white flesh we must smoke not only to preserve it in the heat, but to kill the worms. We killed two boars and were packing them into camp, when we jumped a deer. I dropped my boar and with a lucky snapshot killed the deer. I believe it was a new type, being neither *rufus* nor *campestris*, but a small gray deer living only on high ground and in very heavy cover.

A terrible thing had happened during our absence. The Puna—afraid we would demand our money back because of the reluctant four slaves—had his muscle men string them up by their wrists to the rafters of the *casa grande*. When we returned to camp, the whips were already singing and cracking. Three of the *esclavos* were hanging like dead men, unconscious. All of them were covered with welts and streaming with blood, their legs running with it.

Jorge dropped his pig. Rushing forward he whipped out his *facao* and cut down the nearest man, while I was soon hacking at the buckskin cords of the other three.

I then turned and knocked the Puna sprawling with a clip under his ear. Instantly I was set upon by a big Indian buck who grabbed up a short spear. He would have run me through, had not Jorge glided in behind him and jabbed his *facao* up under the man's right shoulder blade. With two inches of cold steel in his back, the brute grunted and dropped the spear, and Jorge pulled out the blade, brought its heavy butt down hard against the slaver's head.

The others, some eight men, were driven off—but it was not easy, for they cursed and spit and scratched and laid out with their clawed hands right and left. Except for that one spear, they had only their whips. Jorge was caught across the eyes by the lash-end of a whip. With a bellow of pain and rage he charged the Indian, seizing him by the throat, he slashed him across the face with the curved knife. From the top of the scalp to the throat the bone lay open. I got my hands on one of the whips and was soon cracking it in the howling faces of the furious mob, driving them back slowly. As the last wall was cleared we turned our attention to unlashing the legs and wrists of the slaves.

But our anger was a terrible mistake, for from that moment on the Puna hated the very sight of us, and the Indians were told lies which turned them against us. We were "bad men," slavers who would pay nothing for slaves, the kind who kill and steal. We knew the missionary would go to any length to have full satisfaction through revenge. We never again ate with the Puna, and fearing poison, prepared our own food. Although no more supplies came from the *chacaras*, we did not starve, for there was plenty of game to be had. By night one of us always guarded while the other slept. Such guarding had to be inside a mosquito net, and as a result the guard sometimes fell asleep.

Fortunately, one of the original Campa braves who had brought us to this strange camp still remained (the others having hurriedly returned). His Spanish name was José. He was twenty-four years old and an outlaw—which was fortunate for us. Intelligent, chunky, José spoke a good brand of Spanish. The Puna had once sold him, and he had escaped from his *patróne* who used to string him up and hold a hot iron against his buttocks when he was unable to meet the quota by caring for a hectare of yuca. One night José had beheaded the *patróne* with a machete blow, and now out of desperation—for the Puna was threatening to return him to a new owner—he sided with Jorge and me. Jingling coins in his hand, and tossing them up and down under their eyes, José recruited several rather reluctant men and began cutting *palo de balsa* trees for constructing two *shintipu* (rafts). Most Amazon woods will sink when placed in water. This, however, was an exceedingly lightweight, white, corklike wood, able to sustain abnormal weights. The river would likely be too wild below this point to float our big leaky cedar canoes safely through the rapids. On this pair of rafts we would try to descend the falls of the Perené to the Tambo, and thence drift into the Ucayali. We must wait, José said, four or five more days for the green logs to dry out sufficiently.

The Campa women were often pretty, but wild and shy. They spoke a separate language from that of the men; for to speak the men's language was taboo—the penalty being trial by the nearest witchman, his inevitable sentence—death. The older mothers had abnormally elongated breasts; sometimes when a woman was busy over her pots she tossed her breasts over her shoulder. I saw one of them nursing two boys, who must have been at least fifteen years old.

The Indian mothers carried their babies—strikingly beautiful cherubs—in a wide sling of blue and white beads, or from a wide strip of bark from which dangled carved monkey bones, either of which was slung across the shoulder bandolier fashion. Babies' and children's faces were painted, and strings of bright feathers, or parakeet skins stuffed with tree cotton, were slung as witchcraft "medicine" about their necks. *Achiote* was used to repel insects and to depict blood. The flaming orange-red is a symbolic substitute for human blood and like it believed to possess identical magic qualities. Many toys were seen: perfect miniature bows and arrows, war clubs and spears, stone axes and knives, houses, carved birds and animals. Some of the birds and animal objects were mythological, part of the Campa witchcraft. Other toys were of serpents, which among these Indians had great significance. This serpent cult is extensive, probably stemming from the ancient Maya, though independent of the Christian serpent in the Garden of Eden, and the Hindu Brahmins and Tibetan lamas with their mystic Kundalini Serpent Power Cult.

The archaic civilizations of the Maya, the Aztec, the Toltec and the Inca, worshipped the Man of the Sun, and also the tutelar deity, the Serpent. The pre-Anahuac (Mexican) priest-god, Tallac or Quetzalcoatl (Feathered Serpent)—which in a purer translation means "Bird-Snake"—was worshipped in the Maya cities as Kukulcan, the Solar God. What relation exists between these dead civilizations and the Campa cult of the Golden Man coupled with their Snake worship, is unknown. These Serpent Gods manifested on earth as the Thunder, the Lightning Bolt, and the Volcanic Smoke. Undoubtedly, this fascinating Serpent Cult had spread from the Yucatán Maya north to Alaska and south to the Amazon where today it is a living worship. The Brotherhood of the Dancing Anacondas is only a variation of Yetl (the Man of the Sun), worshipped by the Tlinget tribe of Canada, and the same as the Campa's Man of Gold. Atatarho, the Iroquois, who wore a mantle of living serpents, differs little from the Campa *brujo* of today. Among Mexicans, Hopis, Maya, Campas, and many other people, the sun is sometimes symbolized by the snake, especially when the tail is held in the mouth.

At this time, because Jorge and I were having many of the items prepared for our expedition into the central Gran Pajonal, we learned that the beautiful kitchen utensils of the Campas are made of *machingo*, a very hard wood or burl. Delicate cups from the shell of the tortoise and the rind of the fruit of the *tutumo* tree, are carved like the drawings on the walls of the European Neanderthal caves. Scrub brushes are of *pichana* fibers, resembling a sponge. They use wooden neck-racks for sleeping and basket pillows are stuffed with seeds of the *huimba* fruit, lighter than duck's down. Their ropes are never weakened by rot, and are stronger than good hemp, being woven from the choice inner strands in the heart of a tree called the *yanacaspi*. A cereal, which we stocked up on, is made from the seeds of the *cocona* bush. Jellies of many kinds are *not* made from animal hoofs but from botanical products, one of which is the fruit of the *huacrapona* tree. All these names I entered into my notebook.

In fact, the Indians' knowledge of the jungle and all it contained of use to man was far in excess of anything available to us. The more we learned of the Campas, even these spoiled *mansos*, the more certain I became that their medicine (*akendaronse*) at its virgin core, must be effective. I was more determined than ever to go ahead into the Gran Pajonal, come what may. Even Jorge—though as yet he conceded nothing—had picked up a certain interest (though he was always prospecting for gold) and was not so critical of my plan these last few days.

"You know—" he remarked once from his hammock (the beds were too short), "We might have something. There actually may be something to it! I have just heard of an arm being amputated by a witchdoctor, and no infection set in afterwards. Of course, it was luck...."

Very little is actually known of the savage Amazon Indians. In studying the Campas, it was impossible not to fix their place in the scale of man's culture. Had I realized the difficulties confronting us, I would have studied these Indians even more. To understand what was to befall us, they must be perfectly comprehended, physically as well as psychologically. First of all, came *Pithecanthropus* (Ape-man) of Java, about whom we know little. Lord Avebury named early man not by race, but by culture. Paleolithic (Old Stone Age) used chipped implements; while fossils and flints found in higher stratas of the stones, were called Neolithic (New Stone Age). The Campa savage, therefore was probably descended from the Miocene monkeys (round-skulled), to Piltdown man, to Aurignacian man, to Azilian man, to Neolithic man, to

Mongoloid (though the last is in doubt). In the over-all picture, then, he differs in line of descent from that of the lowly Australian bushman, whose skeleton more closely resembles Neanderthal while the Negro is no relation to him, having descended in that instance from Piltdown direct to Grimaldi, thence to Negro. Therefore, the Campa is Neolithic, if his culture in its basic essence is scaled against the European Neolithic man who used polished stone tools, pottery, had domestic animals (which the Campa has not) and was an agriculturist. Neolithic man fished and hunted, had no metal tools but used gold ornaments, lived in dwellings raised on piles, had dugout canoes. He broke objects such as weapons and pots at a man's burial so as to "kill them," and was a true sun worshipper in a religious sense. All this the Campa has attained (except for the domesticated animals). Therefore we were dealing with a primitive mind which would find us all but incomprehensible. However, luckily for us, the Campa had wide medical knowledge not equaled in any civilization or culture till a century ago.

Jorge and I worked hard compiling our Spanish-Campa-English dictionary, often keeping at it all day and into the night, until it finally swelled to several hundred words. Stone had said Japanese laborers working for him understood many of the Campa words and believed these words to be related to ancient Japanese. They were tongue-twisters too: "Early" was *kapstiekitartere*. And we nearly had fits over the pronunciation of "hate"—*maguisaneateri*. Jorge practically gave up in disgust when we came to "free"—*esparuankirerakiri*. But we hung on and in a surprisingly short time were speaking to the Indians almost entirely in Campa. The Puna knew little of this difficult tongue and we spoke to him, when necessary, in Spanish, with some Quechua thrown in. This gradually gave us an edge over the Indian missionary, and our relations with the *mansos* improved to the point where we began eating yuca again!

At last the great day came when we were ready to contact our first wild witchdoctor. The Puna was surprisingly cooperative, and too late we forgot the capacity of the Quechua for treachery. A recently acquired slave of his—called Otsiti, the Dog—was dispatched east to make the proper arrangements, for we dared not go in ourselves. Should he contact a witchdoctor, he was to say two strangers who were slavers wished to talk to him in person about bringing out 100 slaves. The slave was to explain that we could pay a higher price than the Puna customarily did (in trade goods already obtained from the missionary—salt and cloth) and therefore the deal must be secret, unknown to the Puna.

By night the messenger had not returned. "The Dog is dead," gloated the Puna.

Another Indian was dispatched, a one-armed youth called Shacha, the Hatchet. You always knew when the Hatchet was about, for he was invariably throwing a tomahawk-like hatchet with deadly accuracy into logs and even into hardwood hut frames. The handle of this weapon was of wood, painted red, and decorated on the butt with a tuft of human hair cut from a scalp. So deadly was the Hatchet's aim that the Puna kept him solely for raiding forays into the interior. It was said he could split a man's skull at fifty feet, and that he never missed.

For this brave we paid 150 soles-de-oro, buying him "skin, bones and all"—as the slavers' slang has it, getting a receipt for him. With the Hatchet went a gift of 100 soles-de-oro, contained in a small leather poke, to be presented to one of the High Priests in the Gran Pajonal. As money, the coins meant nothing to the Indians. The metal value was high—for from them they beat ornaments and even knife blades. Like all Campas, both the Dog and the Hatchet had received their odd names when nearing puberty. They had been sent to the Dream House. In the case of the Dog, we were told he had dreamed of a dog; and this was interpreted by the attending master of the Cult of Dreams, a *brujo* oracle, as meaning he had the power during sleep of transmigrating his soul into the body of a dog and could change bodies at will, and thus kill, hunt by scent and hide like a Campa dog—an enviable incarnation in Campa eyes.

During the past sweltering days of our preparations to descend the unknown river, canisters had been made from the *atadijo* tree, dried to serve as containers for *chicha*, with corn cobs for stoppers. No Indian will begin a journey without a good supply of *chicha* aboard his raft. Tobacco leaves were plucked from a few wild plants transplanted from the high Andes by the Puna. This was one of the wild forebears of our own domestic tobaccos, the ancestor of that precious plant brought from North America to Europe by Sir Walter Raleigh. He, of course, had found the Indians smoking it in their peace pipes. I tried the dried yellowish leaves in my pipe and found this primitive tobacco strong enough probably to burn the lining out of a crocodile's lungs, but in my desperation quite smokeable two or three times a day.

The singsonging hymns from the palm idol-house of Pawa, the Golden Man, whose spirit lived in the Sun itself, seemed never to end. Pawa was not actually the sun, but higher than the sun—not unlike the Mayan god Hunabku—the Divine Trinity, indivisible, not seen, incomprehensible. As among the Tibetans and ancient Greeks, drums were beaten and musical instruments played to establish contact with the forces of life, as vibrations are believed to be the secret of all universality. To each phenomenal object the link to the subjective idea of a central power is in the form of vibrations having various intensities and combinations of sound construction. A practical example would be the yogi of India who believes he will receive enlightenment by the mere repetition of the mystic word for God—OM. Forevermore, a gentle, strangely petulant, childlike chanting that in the first day or two was not unlovely, beat relentlessly first against my ears and then like rivets into the tissue of my brain.

The jungle, too, pulsing and ringing with insects as to a baton, had somehow crept into this demonic-Christian rhythm. Small drums of scraped lizard skin—white on top like kid, but shiny black and beady yellow at the sides—were softly patted, day and night, scarcely without cease. These sounds became narcotic, deadening.

The Campa dreams of the sun, is drawn up into it, and if he dies while he is thus meditating, he is returned to earth and the other worlds on its rays to become one with all creation—the flower, the earth, the snake, the water, the air, the trees—one with all phenomenal matter. That is why he talks to the objects all about him, for he believes that each has a soul. That is why he breaks the bow and arrows of the dead warrior, in order to "kill" them and free their imprisoned soul.

It was past midnight on the day after his leaving that Shacha, the one-armed slave, returned. In the darkness, he touched me lightly on the shoulder. I awoke and lit my palm-oil lamp, a shallow stone dish with a cotton wick. Jorge, who was supposed to be guarding, had fallen asleep. In the soft glow, the Hatchet was thin and wild-eyed. Behind him stood a tall Campa witchman in a fantastic headdress. They had reached our hut unseen by the slaves and the Puna master slaver. Jorge and I rolled off our cane shelves (for we had again exchanged our hammocks for the cooler Indian beds) and looked the newcomer over. It was the Devil himself. His face was divided into two sections, the upper half a dead-white, the lower half a shiny black. Below this mask and around his neck hung a necklace of great armadillo claws, that clicked whenever he moved. From the hips up, he was naked—showing a massive chest and arms as thick as a wrestler's. The hips and upper legs were wrapped in a short bright red *uma*, a different kind of Campa *cushma*. I definitely recognized the color as the beautiful lost "Chimu red" found by archeologists in the coastal deserts of ancient Chimu. This *brujo* exuded mystery! The witchman stared back at us from eyes painted in intricate blue snake scales.

In the cryptic language of his tribe, the Hatchet cautioned us to leave the hut separately, *now*, and go by different directions out of camp, and to meet at the *playa*. The stranger left first; then Jorge; and ten minutes after him, I followed.

At the rendezvous, I found Jorge and the witchman, but the Hatchet had disappeared. "He has gone to the Dream House to talk with the Ghosts of the Ancestors," spoke up the stranger, standing at a distance in the moonlight.

Then without sound, almost as if he were leading children against their will and better judgment, the witchman turned east and swiftly strode into the thick high jungle along the Perené's north bank, heading downstream. I knew we were aiming right for the inner regions of the forbidden Gran Pajonal....

ᴗ **IV.** ᴗ

Brother of the Snake

HILE standing on the *playa*, the river boiling alongside and the encroaching ring of jungle illuminated by the moon, I had a clammy feeling we might be getting into something we couldn't handle; and the Indian was already inside the edge of the high thicket. Jorge must have had the same idea, for he peered closely at me in a hesitating manner and started to speak. However, he abruptly changed his mind and turned, dropping swiftly in behind the witchman. I kept close at his heels.

We entered a scattered wild rubber grove of *mazaranduva*, 150-foot-high, blue-gray trees, standing in a thick matrix of palms and hardwoods, bound together with coiling lianas. The more open patches on the jungle's muddy floor were surprisingly well lit by the yellow moon. The guide seemed to be keeping to a very faint trail known to him, and along this we tunneled, holding our heads low to clear the limbs and parasitic growth. Guided mostly by the click of his claw necklace, we tried to keep clear as best we could of the blacker shadows. In these night shades lurked a sense of mystery and wonder. It was a jungle having four dimensions—heighth, breadth, depth, and that other, the immeasurable physical magnetism of the Indians' *Curupuri*. Even Jorge noticed it:

"There is something here I don't like!" he said.

The Indian was nowhere in sight; the clicks had stopped. We hurried along, and after half an hour, I experienced an unaccountable chill when Jorge suddenly halted in his tracks and I bumped up against him:

"Be prepared to go back," he said, after some hesitation, in a very quiet voice. "There is a snake here."

For some reason I breathed in relief. "Go around it," I suggested. "We don't want to lose that Campa."

"No! Stand very still. I can't see. But I know it is close—I just heard it hiss."

Not knowing whether the snake's head was suspended in the darkness somewhere around our faces, or wriggling toward us over the ground, we must have stood there a full five minutes, not daring to move a toe or bat an eye. The mosquitoes were awful. I began sweating, while my lower leg muscles crawled and my face twitched every time a bug touched it. Suddenly, a yard away on our right side—of all things—came the faint quack of a duck. It sounded pathetic and distressful, as if it were lost.

Jorge sprang instantly ahead, crying "Hurry!"

I lost no time getting out of there. We pushed on through the massive white-barked trees that turned all these sub-Andean foothills into a ghostly chaotic wilderness, going slightly downhill, moving through the gently creaking, sweating forest. There was something awesome in the knowledge that the jungle stretched unbroken to Cape Paraíba 2,700 miles away to the Atlantic Ocean, unbroken except for the monstrous muddy rivers twisting under the Equator.

We had to move faster now to catch up. The unerring Campa, whom we found waiting in a shadow, turned on his heel and waded through deep pools of warm water clotted with frog algae. His sacred white plume rose out of a halo-shaped basket headpiece formed exactly like the brim of a straw hat, and guided us like a beacon.

Several times the Indian had to wait, which seemed to surprise him. His manner was one of extreme wariness, combined with curious wig-wagging hand and arm motions coupled with a sort of flitting movement among the trees. Later I learned he was taking cocaine—one of the Campa drugs, which would account for his wild actions.

Very tired after an hour of rough going, we rested on a fallen log, and the guide back-tracked, standing like a shadow twenty feet away. All about now was a thunderous ear-splitting orchestration of frogs, insects, animals, and night birds. From the roaring the *cochas* on all sides must have been crawling with crocodiles. I remarked to Jorge that he usually didn't sweat so much even on a burning hot night. His leather shirt was wringing wet.

"That snake back there—" he answered, "was a *shushupe*."

"When I failed to register, the Peruvian explained that this was a maroon-colored twelve-foot reptile of intense cunning, who lured unwary victims to him. It would attack man, and in five to eight minutes, the paralyzing venom would cause death by shock. "We lose three or four *caucheros* every year out of La Merced.

"I guess the snake was after that duck," I suggested, adding, "lucky for us."

"No, it makes the sound itself—a decoy. To strike effectively, the *shushupe* must be coiled as a spring is coiled. Therefore, the *shushupe* calls his victim up close to him. Then strikes."

"There couldn't possibly be anything more diabolical out here than that," I ventured. Jorge made no answer.

With an impatient gesture the savage turned to go, and afraid of losing him, we got to our feet and hurried on, our toes awkwardly feeling a way through the mesh of roots criss-crossing the ground. Once I pitched headlong through a slippery tangle, covering myself with mud and fire-ants. I couldn't help wondering if it were true, as they insisted in Lima, that the Campas were "absolutely hopeless," even more impossible than the Jívaros, Witotos, Boros, and Cashibos—and if they really did stake out their prisoners to be tormented and consumed alive by these insects.

Worried and confused from the bites, for a single nip on the arm will cause it to become numb at first, and later to throb with a terrific ache, I floundered straight into a spiked palm, cutting my face and hands. The Campas know these spikes as "elfin darts," and they fear any person who is pricked by them, believing an evil spirit has caused him to be led there, and that if he appeases the evil spirit it becomes his ally and can be directed against an enemy. The jungle—it was fast becoming obvious—dealt from a cold pack: standing in that hot, suffocating hothouse, dripping with sweat and mud, a prey to swarms of pestilent, buzzing, night-flying sweat-drinkers, full of a creeping apprehension and despair, I came very near to quitting. After all, no one but Jorge would ever know I had fizzled out in this impossible venture. What could a corpse do with the gold of El Dorado?

The Campa was presently standing near, and I realized he was striking sparks with flint and steel into a bundled fagot of oilwood bound
about a ball of wild kapok tree cotton tied to a long stick. All the rest of
that night we moved by torchlight through the desert of jungle, an eerie
hell that could not have changed much since the beginning of the creation of the world's equatorial forests.

Only once did the Indian engage us in conversation. That was to
warn us in violent gestures and words against the *sucuruju*, a serpent
which he paced off as being eighty feet long, that lay coiled in wait for
prey, camouflaged by small trees growing out of its spine. All tribes of
the upper Amazon believe in the existence of such a monster.[1]

The Campas' memory is so accurate and vivid as to be incomprehensible to us. Their minds are trained to visualize, in pictures, every
object and every plan. In other words, sustained reasoning (as we know
it) is impossible to the wild Campa. The *sucuruju*, then, may be mystical, or it may actually be a giant reptile—but for the Campa *it exists*, and
it is real, *seeable*.[2]

With daylight in the jungle, Jorge and I breathed easier, but there
was no resting. The tireless Campa kept right on, faster than before, at
times breaking into a swift dog-lope. Twice he quickly hid us when
Campa war parties passed, tossing over us some unknown witchman's
powder—probably to kill scent. Apparently the witchman had scented

---

1. The great Peruvian missionary explorer, Father P. Avencio Villarejo, of
the Sociedad de Geografía de Lima, claims in one of his papers that a specimen
of the *Yuca mama* (Mother of the Waters) or *boa de agua* (*Eunectes murinus*),
was photographed in the Putumayo region and that its dimensions were "25
metros de largo—por 9.10 de diametro, 15 centimetros de longitude."

2. Further, I do not believe necessarily that the extinct giants of the Age of
Reptiles died out because of a change in weather causing the disappearance of
vegetation from which they got their food. A change in weather, causing high
humidity in the earth's atmospheric envelope, could, however, have blocked out
the cosmic rays sufficiently to cause the great reptiles to die out from rickets.
However, many reptilian forms have come down to us, and it is possible that in
these vast jungles yet exist forms of the great reptiles, and it could be one of
these spoken of by the Indians. Only a person who has not seen the vast depths
of the Amazon's inner regions lying off the river banks, could possibly make a
flat statement that it would be impossible. As a fascinating example of what the
witchman's warning may lead to:—

the war party, as we were in very thick jungle and he could not have seen them, for they were trotting in single file, incredibly swift, utterly silent. They were naked, painted dark green from head to foot. They carried spears and war-clubs. The strange thing about them was that they were hissing like snakes. Later we learned that the warriors believed that by so calling on the Anacondas they became invisible!

All that following day we marched, only once stopping at a deserted hut to eat wild papayas, which we knocked off the trunk of a tall, thin tree, leafed somewhat like a fig.

By evening we found ourselves in a clearing. Several feathery seventy-five-foot *pupunha* palms, with clusters of yellow fruit, rustled faintly as if complaining of the awful heat and the lack of air. There were three very large *paugotse*, the heavily timbered Campa house, perched

---

2. *continued*

Of the edentates (giant sloths, armadillos, anteaters); one was the Giant Armadillo—*Glyptodon*, known to be fifteen feet long, having bony plates set in its skin—fresh parts of whose body have already been found. While a relative, *Neomylodon* (New mill-toothed), whose skin was protected by horny plates, has actually been found together with dung and flesh, in a north Patagonian cave—the bones were broken by man! Now if we accept the prevailing scientific theory that the Amazon tribes were descended from Mongoloids who could not have migrated to the South American continent further back than five to ten thousand years ago, then it is quite possible that, today, *Neomylodon* still lives in the vast uninhabited jungles of the Amazon country.

Therefore, the extermination of the giant edentates is not yet established because the Indian legends must first receive serious investigation in the unexplored tracts, for they state that such monsters still exist. It is altogether possible, however, that with the establishment of a land-bridge (the Isthmus of Panama) between North and South America, all the great edentates were exterminated; this from a combined attack of the jaguar (introduced from North America) seeking prey, as well as the great herdsof primitive horses, the *Onohippidium*, infringing on their feeding grounds; and of course, the hunting Indians. Lest I be accused of taking Doyle's *Lost World* too seriously, it must be noted that the kouprey (Grey Ox) was discovered in heavily populated and long-explored Indo-China by Defosse only fifteen years ago—its name being *Novibos*. While I found existing on Hainan Island a type of ancient elk, the *Thamin*, which I located by following native legends confirming its existence.

on log stilts, roofed over with woven palm fans. These had no cane side-walls. Around them in the clearing were perhaps a hundred savages—men and women.

The sun was already down. There was a fire built on a mud and stone dais in the middle of one of the platformed houses. Ten male Indians squatted on their hams about it. The fire was made of nuts from the *shapaja* tree-fern. Oily smoke came from these nuts and was used as an insect repellent.

The Indians were clan chiefs—*katsimare pingatsare*, naked but for leather G-strings, and a layer of bright paint of different hues and patterns. They were sharp-eyed warriors, very burly, many of them six feet. All were crowned with the curious circular reed basket with a rim some three inches wide. A pair of feathers rose from the back of the corona, in contrast to our guide's single white egret plume. These two feathers were gracefully bowed out at their ends, and were of various colors, symbolic of caste.

Wide amulets (on arms and below the knees) of blue beads worked in intricate white geometrical patterns, caught the firelight. Disks hung from their aquiline noses, while silver and gold labrets swung pendant-ly from both upper and lower lips. From each earlobe was suspended a circular spray of feathers, the ornament being three inches in diameter. These feathers were from the red breast and yellow belly feathers of the toucan.

Jorge and I, cursing our particular brand of insanity—for we were badly bitten and itching from head to foot—followed the *brujo's* agile and muddy heels up the ladder and squatted in the circle. The ten Indians were sitting on animal- and bird-legged stools with curved tops of rare hardwoods. Not one of the Indians spoke a word for several minutes—their thin lips tight and non-committal. They were truly terrible men. Their devilish faces were carefully painted, and there was a gleam about them, due no doubt to the fluorescent qualities in the pigments. One brave's head was painted a pure yellow, his arms being green. Another was flame-red from the eyes up, the limbs and body slashed in horizontal three-inch bars of blue and black. None of the weird markings on the faces was alike: there were circles, wriggles, slashes, spots, and a strange blocklike interlocking of squares and rectangles like a Chinese puzzle. These were the insignia of mystics.

Our own *brujo* suddenly broke out with Romanesque gestures, employing the strangely violent, clickatat, singsonging, gutteral language of the Campas. The circle lolled like wolves, while listening attentively behind alert and rigid faces. They were like no other savage faces on earth, and I had been amongst the headhunting Taiyles of Formosa, the Toradjas of Celebes, the Ba Sa Dungs of central Hainan Island, the Was of north Burma, the Igorotes of Luzon, the Dyaks and Punans of Borneo—but these Campas outshone them all, and were savages in every vibrant meaning of the word.

While the witchman talked on, I took in our surroundings, with an eye to possible escape in case of emergency. The roof was thirty feet high. Directly overhead, suspended out of the shadows on long dark stringers, dangled any number of human skulls. Some were painted in different colors, and a few skulls had grass or feather crowns and eyes of polished stones. Three entire human skins were thrown across a rafter, apparently drying. I took all these objects to be medicine-cult props and not war trophies. Such heads must be kept and spoken to, fed and given offerings. It is believed the spirit of man resides in his severed head, and that it sometimes leaves the head to wander. Always, however, it returns, for the spirit yearns for the body it has lost. At such a time the *brujo* periodically makes contact with the spirit and directs it, genie-like, to do his bidding. Unlike the Mayas' Ix-ch'el (Goddess of Medicine), the nature of the Campa *brujo* is not only temporal but divine.

Bundles of five- to six-foot arrows, notched and brightly feathered, were thrust into the edge of the palm roof. They had detachable points of black *chonta* that fitted into hollow shafts. Some were flaring, some blunt or barbed. They were variously designed to slash through the tough bone and muscle of a jaguar, bring down the pig-like capybara, or even to pierce the armor plate of a killer crocodile. Those with blunt toplike points were "singing arrows" and used for stunning certain birds such as the orange cock-o'-the-rock (a rare bird which is captured and plucked of certain feathers, then released, being sacred). But the most fascinating of the array were the wide, flat, poisonous arrowheads with row on row of long serrated barbs up the shaft. These the Campas used in war, as it was impossible to pull them out of a man before the poison took effect.

Racks of black *satamendotse*, war spears, with wide *chonta* blades, stood about. Many of the eight-foot heavy shafts were banded in red and blue and decorated with clusters of feathers or patches of animal skin. Log drums, leather tom-toms, and aromatic baskets of herbs were slung from the rafters.

Our guide suddenly pointed to a *brujo*, demanding that we state our business to him. This devil was squatting in a flayed human skin, which smelled horribly. He was about forty years of age and weighed over 200 pounds. His granite face was an enameled mask of paint. Large brown anaconda scales were painted on the eyelids and around the eyes.[3]

In the Campa dialect, I told this new *brujo* we would buy slaves.

"What kind of slaves?"

"How many kinds are there?"

It seemed there were women slaves for working, others for making love. There were slaves for every purpose—*chacara* making, hunting and fishing, war, machete slaves, man-hunting slaves....

I stated I wasn't particular; I, too, was a witchdoctor who wanted to test my medicines on women, men, children. It made no difference. This announcement caused a stir among the Indians, for they broke their silence and began a terrific jabbering, showing black teeth filed to a sharp point. The sturdy platform actually quivered under their gyrations and pounding heels.

The witchdoctor's name was Iye Marangui, we were told. That was the name presented to strangers, for the Campas have many names, including secret religious ones. Translated, Iye Marangui means Brother of the Snake.

"I am Brother of the Snake!" he bellowed in my face, pounding his massive chest with a club of a fist, "I am High Priest in the Brotherhood of the Dancing Anacondas!"

Suddenly, as if at a signal, the row stopped; every brave squatted again, staring about him. For five minutes the silence was so deep it was impossible to even hear an Indian breathe. Then Iye Marangui spoke again, ending with a hiss so terrible it could only have been copied from

3. Did some link exist between the modern-day Campa tribe and the antique Aztec god, Xipe (The Flayed), who is depicted in the Mexican *pinturas* as being attired in a flayed human skin taken from a sacrifice on the temple pyramids, the *teocallis*?

that of an anaconda itself. When he stopped and stared at me, I got up. I stood in the circle and, also using the descriptive sign-language, bellowed back in Campa:—

We had traveled four times the length of the Father of Waters (the Amazon), four times the distance between the Antami (Andes) and Mama-cocha (Mother Sea—Atlantic Ocean). I spoke in this fashion because, although many explorers believe the Indians to be confined to their own tribal areas, and to be ignorant of the full extent of the Amazon's jungle, I knew this is not invariably so. Many are mighty travelers, and their system of secret code communication by drum, bull horn or voice, and by marking rocks and vegetation, is quite often intertribal in scope. The witch apparently was not impressed, though many of the Indians stared at each other.

The Campas believe that before a rock crystal can be formed, it must be backed by a Will. Apparently, the great geologist, Professor J. W. Gregory of the University of Glasgow, agrees with them for he says, "If there be any absolute difference between living and non-living matter, it should be capable of definition. But all the explanations of life and of vitality apply to the more complex forms of crystal growth...."

Iye Marangui held up a seven-inch crystal, which I recognized as a crystallization of quartz.

"This..." cried the witch, "is God!"

I got to my feet.

The purpose of my experimenting with the slaves, I told them, was to learn wisdom; it was twofold: to cure the "bewitched" and to forecast the future.

The spirit Brother of the Snakes stirred mildly beside the coals. I wondered if he would grasp this chance to show his stuff. Apparently he was communing with some guardian spirit, for every few minutes he would hiss. At last I knew he was interested, for he condescended to extend the formal gracious courtesies, up till now withheld. He directed an Indian to feed us. We were handed a bowl filled with cold chunks of fish which, being starved, we ate with great relish. Next, he spat at both our feet, each in turn. He did *huinioshirenkar*, life sacrifice, for our honor, directing one of the chiefs to kill a big, brown, scaly-tailed rodent called a *punchana*. He crawled around the circle, and with his finger marked each man with the flowing blood. The designs were entirely mystic, and were in the form of two large circles, one painted on each half of the face, and then bisected by a wavy line (the sign of the Snake) drawn through the middle.

Then he sat down in a beautiful high-backed chair carved from the precious stone-like *guayacan* with the flaring tail of one of the black *paujils*, one of the many turkeys. I rose and continued, explaining that the witchdoctors of my own tribe were wise, but that many things were unknown to them. The sorcerer jumped to his feet.

"True! Pawa's medicine is not so 'strong' as that of the *abendaningare!*"

Bellowing like a bull at me, and using sign language, he immediately made it plain that the chiefs could sell no slaves for this holy purpose, so said the ancient law. No one spoke for a full minute, as this Campa Hammurabi (lawgiver) stared at us with a terrifying snake expression. Jorge's face did not change, but his breathing seemed suspended. Now what will happen! I thought, as I sat down.

Suddenly the *brujo* reached over and took a small steaming earthen pot from the coals. With a flat stick he ladled out a thick golden manna, blew on it, put it on his tongue and began chewing. Then he took a flexible curved tube, stuck its end in the pot, and inserting the other end in one of his nostrils, inhaled. He sneezed, moaned, and carried on at a great rate, and I don't wonder with that mess in his nasal passages.

"The stuff is tobacco paste," Jorge remarked in a low voice, "I can smell it."

Two of the chiefs bounded off the platform and down the ladder. They returned carrying a man. This *manseare* (patient) was laid out on the palm-bark floor beside the fire dais. His head rolled and fell with jerks from side to side, his lips uttering moans of great pain. Iye Marangui began a series of howling incantations. This was to arouse the patient by degrees, for obviously his spirit was wandering out of his body and should he awaken and be unable to reach his body in time, he would die. Campa death was that state, then, when the soul was separated from the body, and in the Dream World.

A wooden needle was dipped into a second pot and a deep insertion was made into this man's jugular vein, the doctor's fingers working a way through the thick neck muscles. I got out my notebook and pencil from the money belt. Prayers were called aloud to a god named Gaubane. Leaning over, the *brujo* began sucking loudly on the man's arm, swollen as a result of the strike of a *nacanaca*, a deadly black-and-red snake six feet long. This same snake was tied around the *manseare's* left arm. Twenty minutes later the swelling began subsiding. The patient scrambled to his feet and walked unaided out of the circle. The devil had been exorcised! The practical Jorge dipped his finger into the pot and said its contents were seeds, bark and leaves of the *sachacurarine* palm. He added, surprisingly, that this could be worth a fortune if the compound stood up under laboratory tests.

A second man was brought up from the clearing. The *brujo*, assuming now a violently truculent mood, explained to the circle that a devil lived in the patient's stomach, and was causing him to die of *kepiare* (poison). He gave him something to swallow and then knelt and began sucking loudly as before, this time on a blue-tattooed stomach. After a minute the witch leaned back and spat out a mouthful of bones, pieces of wood and other rubbish. The sick man sat up, and presently walked down the ladder, his great splayed toes seizing the rungs as a hand would.

Jorge bent close: "I saw him put the trash into his mouth. Obviously the medicine works, and he does this other to impress both patient and audience."

Victims of malaria (*karkametstase*), and leprosy (*patarangare*), were given quinine obtained from cinchona bark for the first; and an unknown compound for the second; both would be cured, according to the *brujo*.

For a warrior, who bounded up from those waiting below, the *brujo* prepared a *matse* (charm), a pair of narrow bracelets from an iguana skin of the black-and-white variety. Savage superstition? Pure rot, as Stone would say? I'm afraid not. The charms work, regardless of what scientists and theologians believe. There are two reasons why these mystical snake charms are effective. The charm emits a faint odor, which unknown to the wearer, keeps him constantly conscious of the presence of a snake, and he subconsciously watches for it.

If, however, a snake's head rises close by to strike, the man freezes—stops all motion—for he is not afraid; he thinks the charm will protect him. And when the snake lowers its head to crawl away, he brings his knife down and kills it. The second reason is that as a field explorer I know that a frightened man emits an odor, an odor of fear, and snakes are sensitive to it. Their tongues play in and out, trying to pick up whether you are fearful and might hurt them; and when fear exists in the man, it is transferred to the snake itself—*then it strikes*! But when the man believes he is protected by the magic inherent in the charm, he is not afraid—and thus no odor is thrown off by him. Close observation will show that among savages there is invariably a good sound, if indirect, reason behind all the mumbo jumbo, if the investigator will but look for it. In other words, the charm works, but he does not know why it works, for the Indian has not the power of analytical reasoning. He ascribes its success to mystic circumstances and magic. Actually, if the wearer of the charm knew why it works, it would no longer protect him from snake bite.

All these various names I was entering in my notebook.

Couvade, we next saw, is practiced here. Not all tribes do so, however, for when I was later among the Jívaros and other savages, I saw no sign of it. A husband, "suffering" from the pains of his wife in childbirth, was given a drug to put him to sleep that night. Couvade has never been understood and has always been treated as a joke among civilized observers. The true reason the Campa husband takes to his bed in pain is because he believes that he is lessening his wife's suffering in so doing. He believes he is bearing her pain for her. And she believes it too, believes it with all the vivid and sometimes terrible conviction of the Campa mind. As a result, the wife works at hard labor up to the hour of birth, and then gives birth with little pain. She is back at work again within a few hours after having her baby. *All observers know this, but they do not know why.* Actually, this is deeply psychological, and is connected not only with the Indian's intensive belief but the presiding *brujo's* aid in autosuggestion through his knowledge of telepathy. This is often intensified by cataleptic trance, during which opium-like mystic visions are produced and seen on the retina of the eye. Therefore, the husband is not necessarily stealing the wife's thunder, in order to receive attention from his condoling friends and to get their gifts, as is generally believed.

For still another client, a *takotause* (lover) was prepared a drink called *posan-ka*, a love potion. Love is termed technically *nitasutane*. Modern psychologists, particularly French ones, have claimed that love (like the power of analogical reasoning) is the mental product of recent environment and possible only to modern "enlightened" man; that savages do not experience it. No one has ever refuted this. I found that love's psychic and physical ramifications were thoroughly known to the *brujo*. And again, we have been wrong: for the love potion is effective—it works.

The practical mechanics, aside from the psychic ones, are this: the *posan-ka* contains a powerful drug which produces a dream state, during which the lover has a "spirit connection" with the girl of his desire. He believes wholeheartedly that his spirit and hers have had a union. This has a greater significance than appears on the surface—for it may cast doubt on the Freudian theory which asserts in principle that human action stems from the sex impulse; whereas the Campa reverses the process and causes sexuality itself to stem from the dream—for, having possessed the girl in "spirit" form (according to his and her belief), he now marries her as an act of religion and consummates his love by bodily contact. On personally testing this drug later (for before leaving we obtained samples of all these compounds, which were later sent by messenger back to Stone), I found it to be so potent that it was necessary to follow up with a counter-depressant. It may be the only aphrodisiac known. It is the reason why very old Campas are—so they claim—sexually potent, and always retain young wives.

For still another, a compound of herbs was prepared in a small pot, to be transmitted by a gourd douche to a wife who was injured and so could not safely bear any more children. The *brujo* brought out a calabash, which was round with a long neck. Into it the medicament was poured. In the back of the globe section was a hole, through which the witchman now blew the medicine into the vagina. After three months of treatment, it was explained that this particular compound would make it impossible for the woman to conceive for a period of two years. It would in no way change her normal womanhood. Its use prevents the necessity for either sexual abstinence or abortion among Campa women, who are said to be capable of childbirth from thirteen to sixty years of age.

Other medicine compounds (*akendaronse*) were prepared by the two *brujos* for still other ailments. The bark of the *chuchuhuasha* tree, pulverized and placed in alcohol distilled from the *aguaja* palm, and taken orally, is claimed as a cure for certain types of skin cancer, brought on by intensive exposure to the tropic sun. Under the circumstances we could not judge its effectiveness. We then saw that when the rough-barked tree, *sangre de drago*, was bled and boiled, a brilliant red liquid was recovered, which, when taken through the mouth by women in childbirth, eliminates hemorrhages. *Huaman samana* was apparently in great demand also. The leaves are crushed in alcohol, and applied to the skin, killing internal boring insects and their egg sacs.

Jorge, hoping to capture the Indians' friendship, reiterated to the senior *brujo* that our interest was also in forecasting the future. I suspected that this, more than therapy, was the chief occupation of these medico-mediums and necromancers. The witchman at once became ponderous, and would not be hurried by the whim of an ignorant pair of white men. Hadn't he himself heard from escaped slaves that they could cure but few of the jungle's diseases?

What followed was not bargained for, and I had no other choice now or at any other time that night, but to be an unwilling witness. After all, we could not escape, nor could we do anything about it. Under the thatched roof with its dangling heads, we were sweating not only from the temperature but from our excitement as well. That flayed skin worn by the witchman was stinking, for Iye Marangui was sweating from his exertions. The floor shook under us from time to time as he or one of the others moved about.

A mortal injection of strychnine applied on a *chonta* needle was given a malformed baby. This realistic infanticide is the reason why no idiots or malformed Indians were ever seen by us in the wilds. Another child was baptized—baptized in fire and not in water. As the Fire God has power, it would be used henceforth in certain ailments, by applying a firebrand to the place of hurt so as to drive out the evil spirit causing the illness. We saw too that *brujos*, as necromancers, are concerned with calendric matters (moon calendars); incredibly complicated ritualistic practices; astrological data used in casting horoscopes, planting, etc.

A man who wished to plant a *chacara* in a new place in the jungle, brought forth soil, and this was eaten by the *brujo* and declared good, for the Earth God gave him a sign in its taste.

While all of this was ordinary routine to the witchdoctor, I, for one, was tiring. Yet I dared not relax my attention, for I knew I would probably never again have the chance for getting the medicines. Jorge's reaction was one of silence and watchfulness, and obviously he did not like the brutal phases of this practice, though he never once lost interest.

As part of his regular duties that night, Iye Marangui (after first having his patient swallow an anesthetic), amputated with considerable skill the infected and bloated hand of a brave who had been wounded while fighting. This anesthetic was later identified as belladonna. Questioned, the witchman said that formerly wooden knives whose edges were set with the triangular razor-sharp teeth of the *paña* fish, were used. Campa steel is now obtained from any kind of iron; though mainly machetes and nails. These are obtained from Campas living on the fringe of the Gran Pajonal who sometimes work for *patrónes* or have access to traders and missionaries.

During the surgery a tom-tom was patted—a device which brought the Campa mind to an indescribable pitch of receptivity—making possible perhaps that "divine healing" of the ancients. I wondered if it was magic or miracle that cured these people, or if it was mind and will over matter itself. The *brujo* fixed a red plaster-wad made of a mash from the bulb-like *sangre pidipidi* which had been boiled in water. This he put on the stump of the amputated arm—before the skin flaps were pinioned with wooden spikes. When the patient came out of his "twilight sleep," he grinned, picked up his severed hand from the floor, rose and walked out of the stoic paint-masked circle. When I asked the *brujo* why he did not sew the wound, instead of using the spikes, he answered that should the devils return (infection), the wound could be opened and treated with certain ingredients, then closed again.

Only once in all the hours did Jorge speak to me on a matter not directly related to Iye Marangui's doings. "How are we going to get out of here?" he said. "You don't seem to realize the danger."

Still another, a warrior, had dreamed that while working in his *chacara* a snake had raised its head, but before it could strike he had awakened. He now wanted an interpretation. The *brujo* went into a trance and explained that an enemy was rising against his client. Then the witch tossed sticks in the air, studied them carefully, and found the enemy to be the spirit of the man's father-in-law transmigrating by night to the body of the snake. The wicked man must therefore be killed, and not the snake.

The chief squatting next to me took out a handful of roasted grasshoppers from a monkey skin bag and popped them into his mouth. I grinned, and with a dead-pan expression, he handed me a few. I found them to be of a smoky, nutty flavor, and very oily.

A twelve-year-old girl was condemned—the *brujo* being apparently not only priest and medicine man, but also judge. Her three husbands had all died within the year. During the morning she had been declared *bruja.* She was taken under the platform, and to my horror, the only sound that came back to us was that of a club cracking her skull. I jumped to my feet, but Jorge's hand darted out and caught my arm, hauled me down hard beside him and held me there.

It was long past midnight, and still there was no sign of a let-up. A woman was found guilty of lechery. I saw what was coming and grabbed the sides of my seat. She was condemned in the presence of her accusing husband who threw her to the floor, sat on her and cut off her left breast as punishment. No anesthesia was given. She would henceforth be a slave, for he would take to wife a concubine. The woman was forced to drink a clear liquid extracted from the *sangre de drago* tree. The devils would not come to the wound now, someone explained, indicating the wound was not septic! The breast was tossed on the fire, and half an hour later, the second-string witch fished it out with a stick, peeled it and ate it.

I was so tired I could hardly keep my eyes open. By 3 A.M., the last of the patients had been brought forward. The ten shiny *katsimare pingatsare* got up, grunted and spoke in the wild manner customary with them, then abruptly cut it off, politely spitting toward Jorge and me, and left suddenly—the whole house shivering when they leapt off the platform. The two witchdoctors, Jorge and I, were now all who remained. The two Indians immediately went to sleep sitting upright in their chairs. Jorge and I lay on the bark floor and were instantly asleep. The oily smoke curling off the fire kept off most of the mosquitoes, and in any event, we were so exhausted that nothing could have kept us awake.

↜ V. ↝

"We Can't Go Back!"

I AWOKE all at once with a start, and though my eyes were still closed, a strong feeling of apprehension was creeping over me; very carefully, I cracked an eye apart and saw that daylight had arrived The first object I spied was a pair of enormous red-painted legs; and glancing up their length I saw that it was Iye Marangui standing over me, minus his suit of human skin. His thin lips were curled away from filed teeth, and in any other human being it would have been a smile. Apparently it was not the kind of smile an Indian wears when he is cutting off your head, for the witch grunted and began a terrific speech. Jorge and I sat up and listened gravely.

We gathered we had to get out—*now*. It was very dangerous here. This was a great disappointment to me as I was most anxious to learn more. However, the Iquitos officials should be impressed with the medicines already obtained. But we had no choice in the matter and must go. And go we did.

We ate more of the boiled fish while the original guide donned his red *uma*, put on his claw necklace, and gruffly bade us follow him to Sutsiki, the House of Pawa.

"*Paugotse Pawa!*" he kept screaming, "*Paugotse Pawa!*" carefully peering into our faces as if we were dumb beasts.

Then he ran down the ladder and swiftly walked into the jungle.

Saying goodbye is unknown to these Indians, and so, after one last look at Iye Marangui, we followed. To keep up with our guide we often had to break into a trot. With violent arm motions the Indian kept hurrying us along. The hours went by in a flood of sweat, but there was no stopping for rest. Several times the witch hid us, tossing his red powder around, and then squatting alongside and hissing softly while a party of Campas silently flitted by.

Thirsty, we stopped once to drink stagnant water from a rock pool, after first skimming the dead bugs off. The day was steaming hot and we were given nothing to eat. Nevertheless, we made fast time, covering as much ground in a full day as we had formerly in a day and half a night. Finally we arrived at Sutsiki, alone, for the witchman would not enter the clearing. As he turned to go, I asked his name, and he answered "Tiger Ghost."

Flocks of large green parrots swished by overhead, feeding in a grove of *zapote* trees laden with a sweet-tasting brownish-red fruit. And to the haunting pagan chant of the "Christian" hymns, and the soft *thump-thump-thump* pulsating from that monstrous church, we responded with grateful thanks; for it seemed we had indeed arrived safely home to cat and carpet after a perilous journey.

That night we slept fitfully. Once I thought I heard a sound in the room and switched on my small flashlight, but found nothing. This flashlight was carried normally in the money belt and taken out at night only to be used if necessary, as we had no extra batteries. Restless, our minds dwelt on the momentous events just past. And our ears rang with the endless songs and eerie thumpings down in the big thatch.

At last dawn came and I found José. We had a long talk, and I gave him the small packet of medicines, mostly dried herbs and powder, together with a note, and told him to find a trustworthy man who would bring them to Stone. Later, from Iquitos I would contact Stone and he could send the packet on by the Lima mail-carrying Air Force plane landing weekly in Iquitos. And since José was willing to go downriver with us, I paid him fifty soles-de-oro. My money was shrinking as I had paid out: \$35 (four slaves), \$9 (Otsiti), \$20 (Shacha), 100 soles-de-oro (Campa gift), \$15 (salt, cloth), \$10 (supplies), 50 soles-de-oro (José). That left a balance of \$521.18 − \$89 = \$432.18.

Jorge and I walked with José through the *pindu* canes with their single fan tops, and then along the crunchy gravel banks of the river until we came to our pair of balsa rafts. José pointed out one that was finished. It was a beautiful object of six white peeled logs each nearly a foot in diameter—five feet wide, twenty-two feet long. Its bow was shapely, tapered to a point, and upturned like that of a toboggan. Down the length of the sleek craft was a sturdy pole rack, its dimensions being a foot high and a foot wide, on which he indicated we could sit, and our gear and food could be lashed by vines and so kept dry. The raft had been pegged together with black *chonta* splinters, called by the Campas *kiri*. As a result, it was wonderfully flexible, yet exceedingly strong; but could it stand up to the terrific beating it would likely get? Five Indians were pounding long-bows of the same tough palm through the half-dozen logs of the second raft.

We would leave on the morrow. Tonight there would be a celebration. That afternoon the Puna exhibited twelve slave children. These *nankiretse* had apparently not yet been purchased from their parents after being condemned to die. A *brujo* had proclaimed them *cregotaranskaro*, guilty of being bewitched. The Puna tapped a long and dirty fingernail on his account book. Taking the hint, I decided to donate a substantial sum, ill though we could afford it, especially when I heard that he could not easily endure the cries of the unpurchased children should their mothers have to beat them to death. Thick sticks are used, he explained, a method of execution deemed necessary, since before dying the children must be exorcised of the malignant spirits inhabiting their bodies. While bargaining, the Puna became very angry, and he called over a woman, who began beating two of the children with a splintered bamboo stave. Absolutely silent, the naked children lay on the ground, the splinters cutting into them like a fine blade. I dared not touch the female fiend. We had divided our coin supply into three smaller leather bags. I lost no time tossing one of these bags of coins (perhaps sixty soles-de-oro) toward the grinning Puna, who then blessed me and called the savage off.

There was one thing we simply had to learn before leaving, and so from the *mansos* I cautiously enquired whether the *patrónes* on the Ucayali were in conspiracy with the Campa *brujos*. If enough children were condemned annually, such a system would, of course, supply them with a steady source of slaves. They answered, "Of course!" This eventually was to surprise me, for the *patrónes* whom I later saw were not generally such subtle men, but rather those who preferred direct action and whose methods ran to wholesale murder and capture. Later, in Atalaya, I was to find that many *patrónes* openly hire Campas for raiding not only the Campas but several other tribes as well. The Campas are superior fighters, utterly relentless, and are invariably the ones sent out. No hiding from the law is even attempted.

I made arrangements for the two children to be taken to Stone, and I wrote a note asking him to feed and care for them. I knew what the Englishman thought of the slave practices and I knew I could count on him.

Our preparations for the voyage went on all day. Duffel bags were fashioned by the women, who painted white rubber latex milk on flour sacks (brought in by the missionary as barter goods), which turned them yellow. This was necessary, for all our meager gear would otherwise be ruined by wet and mold. Also, should the balsa rafts overturn, the loosely packed air-filled bags—acting as preservers—might be saved when the sausages bobbed surfaceward. Such items should never be (though they often were) lashed to a raft.

At this time we patched our clothes. We were dressed in the tough homespun pants obtained at La Merced, and wore the deerskin shirts. These were hot though they afforded good protection in the jungle. On our feet were our old walking shoes. And our heads, as usual, were either bare or else a rag in the style of the *caucheros* was bound around the brow. This was sometimes used as a sweat-rag.

Finally, though it was late, 7:30 P.M., the *mansos* were still bringing in our last supplies from a luscious and generative earth. The music of clicking coins was proving irresistible to the Puna, who had given orders to sell. Supplies were cheap, a few brass coins buying a bushel of vegetables or fish. He not only enriched himself but was getting rid of us, and in addition would in all likelihood have his revenge too. For a few coins we bought drippy *caña dulce*, a sweet cane; heavy strings of fish speared in the warm waters of the river; baskets of yuca; two crocks of *chicha*; a basket of melons; the citrus *sandia*; and a rare fruit, the *sacha papa*. There were several stems of that golden fruit referred to by Charles Darwin's English assistant, as "bananers."

Afraid the Puna and his *mansos* might send out signals warning the tribe against us, we made inquiries and learned that signal drums are rarely used. Yet Campa news maintains an incredibly swift tempo. Bull horns are the secret in signaling between clan houses and villages, which, according to the Sutsiki Indians, cover an area of 15,000 square miles. Thousands of *ishingare*, wild savages, in the Gran Pajonal, who had never before seen a white man, already knew of our arrival at the slave camp. Polished bull horns had apparently already announced to the savages that Jorge and I were to be served a feast that night of roasted yuca and venison liver. It was also known to this amazing tribe that we two strangers put our legs into garments "hollow like bamboos."

We learned that other messages had long ago been sent out telling that we bewitched people by staring at them through an "evil eye," which was exceedingly bad since we were capturing *shiakanse*, or spirit pictures. This apparently had been explained by the Puna. In fact, if we but threw the *shiakanse* (photographs) into the river, that person would drown or be taken by an electric ray or some other dangerous fish; or, if we burned the *shiakanse*, that person would surely burn; or, if perhaps we cut off the "captured heads" with a knife, the victim of our witchcraft would suffer a like fate in a raid. And so, strangely enough, on the rim of this savage and unknown world, we two had no more privacy than a pair of goldfish in a glass bowl. I announced to the buglers that I had ridden in the night on the back of the white "king of the vultures" (the Campas believe that the condors have a king and that he is white), over the Gran Pajonal, and captured with my "evil eye" (camera) the entire tribe, and that if they harmed us, disaster would befall them all. This "black propaganda" was blasted out on the bull horns in code, caught up in the far distance, and relayed eastward in a fan shape for hundreds of miles.

It was pitch dark when José came and said our two balsas were ready. Our long journey of over a thousand miles to Iquitos would at last begin. Again the bull horns sounded and out of the jungle several Campas charged in for the celebration. We had sent out word that "magnificent gifts" would be issued to any guests. Since we could not leave in secret, we wanted good words to be blown downriver. These new people came from scattered camps, for there are very few villages amongst the Campas. The *bravos* are not socially inclined, nor communal by instinct, but are individualists—so much so that there is no head chief of the Campa tribe. Our magnificent gifts were handed out, these being in the form of several shoe buttons. They had been clipped from a pair of button shoes contained in the wardrobe of the Puna. The buttons were immediately inserted in the lip-split and used as ornaments.

Tom-toms and hollow animal teeth flutes tapped and twiddled all that hot, limpid night. All of us dripped with sweat. The large-footed and oddly pigeon-toed warriors and women, wild as well as *manso*, all flashing in brilliant paints, danced and stomped, decked out in all their radiantly savage finery. Four warriors dueled with wooden war-axes, inflicting what to me seemed terrible bruises and wounds before we could stop them. Life among these Indians is cheap, and especially when they are drunk.

The creamy bronze, straight-backed handsome women, all wore chokers of feathers, clanking shell dance-belts, arm bracelets of beads and shells and teeth, thick ropes of the irradiant wings of a chameleon-like greenish-red beetle; pulverized flowers and perfume spices such as vanilla, contained in tiny gourds the sizes of grapes and hanging in clusters between their breasts. Across the women's shoulders, bandolier fashion, were wide hand-woven cloth belts from which dangled hundreds of carved monkey bones, etched in hieroglyphics resembling the early Azilian pictures of Europe.

As the moon rose over the palm-laced horizon, the Indians gathered around the *machingo* troughs to drink *chicha*, the women's fermented saliva. Faster and faster whirled the *shingirotse* (harvest dance), swaying under the scarlet hibiscus bushes and the feathery *caña-brava* with its purple blossoms. Of the hundred Indians there, two warriors were swathed in feather coats of dazzling gold and blue, similar to those of the olden kings of Hawaii, and others in gorgeous *cushmas* of reds and oranges; plumed with feathers and ornate crowns of flowers, banded with hand-drilled seeds. Once they sang of the harvesting of the *paiche* fish, ten-foot man-killers, taken by harpoon.

As Jorge pointed out at midnight, the Indians were dangerously drunk. Above the sounds of the grunting moans of two jaguars on a ridge nearby, the flutes and tom-toms played on, a mad revelry that set the blood pounding. One blue-painted warrior dressed in a tailed puma loincloth, reeled up, grinned and spat in front of me—showing fine manners—and handed me a tube of polished bamboo.

Having received no warning, I pulled its wooden plug, and into my lap fell a small orange-colored snake. The brave explained with howls of laughter—for I must have jumped a foot—that if I had an enemy, all I need do was to put the business end of this bamboo inside his hammock and pull the cork. The snake, an *aguaje machacuy*, would do the rest, especially if you shook it up a bit. I shuddered, grateful the snake had not been shaken, and wondering who was going to get it in his bed that night.

No longer coy, the women wailed their mystic songs.

Warriors sang odes telling of many enemies they had slain, or describing new foes yet to fall under their war-clubs. Headhunting and scalp-taking in the Amazon is very often a part of the ceremonies for the harvest (or again, the planting) season. The idea is that flowing blood represents the sap of new life, that death itself is necessary for the continuous flow in all its manifestations of life in matter. Thus, a human is a human today, but tomorrow might be a yuca stalk, or a beast—no matter!—for the undying spirit is God Itself, and cannot be wetted, cannot be hurt, cannot have beginning or end.

One *bravo* had a knot of long hair hanging from his girdle, a war trophy. These men, unlike the Oriente headhunters in the north, do not usually take heads. The knotted trophies are taken in honor and glory, a by-product incidental to capturing the women and children of the slain. Campa warfare, called *manitingare*, is profitable, as the adult slaves or *manipirisi* are bartered for muskets to the *patrónes* hundreds of miles east on the Ucayali. "Victory!" exclaimed one warrior, holding up a greasy black trophy by its hair, "is sweet! Like salt on the Chuncho tongue!"

At the first faint glimmering of light announcing dawn, we brought to a close those busy days and left the clearing, grabbing up our stuff and carrying it down to the river, where it was lashed to the rafts. In a few minutes we stepped aboard our new white balsas, which lay bobbing in a quiet lagoon. We pushed them off the shore and slipped smoothly into the tumbling, swishing caldron of the river's current. As the bows swung downstream, phosphorus-sheathed fish leapt high above them. Insects moved in droning clouds. A dark-gray fifty-pound *taricaya*, one of the many turtles, splashed into the water. Flocks of ibis rose screaming off the river. We were really off!

We had learned that the man from whom the Puna had taken over Sutsiki had been successful in reaching the Perené Colony overland after forcing a hundred slaves to cut a way for him. In this manner he also got out his chests and bales of ill-gotten treasure. Had we had a vision—when we started so lightheartedly that day—of what lay in store for us, we, too, would have given every last penny to have a road cut through the jungle, back to Stone.

Shortly after shoving off (July 17), rain began pelting us. The sound of cataracts ahead crystallized inside my ribs into something between terror and exaltation. No missionary or *patróne* had ever penetrated below Sutsiki anywhere on the Perené. It was considered by the *patrónes* that should an explorer ever break through on it, he would find it to be the wildest river of the upper Amazon. We were entering the true unknown, the Gran Pajonal itself. Far away from our starting point, at its junction with the Ene, a third river was formed from the two— Professor Rosell's Tambo. Somewhere on it was thought to be a bush mission ('Opata) under Padre Antony. This man had descended the Pangoa, which heads near Cuzco. He was said to have successfully held out through several raids and massacres recurring over the bloody years. 'Opata, we hoped, would constitute the first comparatively short leg of our long journey.

Now José was a *manso*, and on hearing the roaring waters ahead, he stood up and worshipped the sun and then, to be on the safe side, prayed Christian style, with bared head, after which he marked a cross in the sky with his paddle and drew a circle with it around the balsas, exorcising them of devils.

We had purchased a fifth slave in the night, and so counting José there were six Indians, three assigned to the long paddles of each raft which Jorge and I captained. These *balseros* (wearing monkey-skin hunting bags slung around their shoulders) always stood upright for exercising better control over the rafts. Jorge and I usually sat on the rack at the stern. As we entered the head of the first rapid, the men paddled furiously, steering right for the middle of the deafening torrent where the deepest water would be found. We had scarcely rounded the first turn of them when my own balsa nearly capsized. The crew cried out in surprise; you could see their mouths open and their neck muscles strain, but not a sound came forth above the crashing waters.

High six-foot waves flooded over the long and narrow craft, washing off all of our food baskets and most of our bags of gear, together with one of the slaves, the bow paddler. This man's head bobbed up alongside farther downstream; he was saved from drowning only because he had clung to his balsa paddle. After being whirled by a cross-current out of the vortex of a whirlpool at the foot of the chute, he was at last wedged against a boulder, at which he clutched in desperation. Knowing the Indians cannot swim (except José, who was learning), I dived overboard and grabbed him by the hair, and together we floated down the current, while the others worked the raft around to a small gravel beach, where we joined it.

Due to the fact that our equipment was properly packed in the airtight latex-covered bags, these two bobbed to the surface and we got them by swimming. All of the food, however, had been lost. The shotgun had luckily been slung on a buckskin cord around José's shoulder. And the trade machetes we had purchased from the Puna at the last minute being carried in leather scabbards fastened about the waist with leather cording, were also intact. We put our waterproof luggage bags on the rack, and this time (though we knew of the danger should the rafts capsize) tied them down with bark lashings. About one basket full of miscellaneous vegetables, mostly yuca, was recovered from the shallows.

On the beach we added another balsa log to the raft, making seven in all. It took an hour to cut and fix the wooden spikes, and though still green, the extra log added a certain stability to the raft. The rain slacked off and an ultramarine sky flashed above the narrow walled slot of the jungle, a carboniferous swamp with amphibian trees footed in the river.

So frightened was I at the thought of the possibility of losing everything in the rapids ahead, that henceforth I determined to carry in the ample pouches of my Peruvian waterproof money belt the following items listed in La Merced: films (in their tropical packing), money, miniature Leica camera, passport, matches, two notebooks, two pencils, map (in the oiled-silk tobacco pouch), compass, flashlight and other essential things. My .45 was in the future never to leave my person. Only a Hollywood explorer would ever carry a gun in a holster. I took it out of my bag and stuck it into the top of my pants and under my shirt. Fortunately, McCrae had agreed to forward my clothes and other nonessentials to Quito, in Ecuador, where I hoped to terminate my journey.

Once more we shoved off into the torrent to be washed along at a terrific rate; boulders gurgled by in a roar of drenching spray, and tumbling waters full of logs and fallen branches swept by. We were blinded from the spray, but even so we could never for an instant relax our vigilance and furious parrying. Desperately we paddled away from suddenly revealed rocks; should we strike them squarely at this great speed, they would wrench the rafts asunder. Sometimes we were not quick enough, and rolled over them sideways, bumping and thumping, with terror rising in our hearts. Worse, the rain water began to swell the flood as it drained out of the jungle and poured off the yard-high banks.

"*Paña!*" called out José, pointing with his paddle at a wide patch of dark water alongside. These were the ferocious cannibal fish. Some of them actually leapt clear of the water, to bounce hard on the deck of the rafts, and the barefooted men jumped about in a lively manner.

An hour, then two hours, crept by. We were eating up the miles and 'Opata could not be many days away. Some Indians appeared just ahead, spearing fish along a bank; they had not noticed us as we swept unannounced around a bend. They let out a howl and fled into the forest, but not before two spears had been hurriedly launched at Jorge's raft a half length in the lead. The first spear whizzed over our heads; the second, however, thumped into the very center of Jorge's bag, puncturing it in two places.

José said the Indians were angry at being surprised, but that if we had a chance we would land among the next band of them in order to get more food.

A sandbar appeared and on it was an encampment of *bravos* who did not run. This *playa*, a long curved sandspit, had several small palm-leaf huts grouped around a few smudge fires. Fish were being cured in the smoke, suspended on willow racks. While women and children attended them, a score of naked men stood in dugouts tossing spears into a milky *cocha* (lagoon) just beyond the bank. We turned left and landed. A woman said the *cocha* had been poisoned with *barbasco* root, a narcotic believed to possess a male soul. (Used in airplane crop-dusting, *barbasco* provides a high percentage of rotenone.) The roots were smashed with clubs in the bottom of the canoes, which were then overturned, releasing the milkish soup. The poison soon stunned the fish, causing them to swim lazily to the surface. Strangely, the poisoned fish, eels, watersnakes and other marine life were not injured; the Indians told us they could safely be eaten. By the hundreds fish were being speared or shot with bows and arrows.

We lost no time joining in, thus securing several fine fish. Besides those seen at Sutsiki, the *liza* was here, a spiny, platter-shaped skate, but sweet fleshed. There were also several specimens of the yellow-scaled twenty-pound *gamitana*. A number of the savages stopped fishing, gathered around us with scowling faces. They were smeared red from head to foot. As we brought our own fish into camp, I noted a sick brave, stretched out under one of the palm lean-tos. Apparently something had bitten him when he was wading in the lagoon.

An old *brujo*, wearing a magnificent red-veined brown jasper necklace, was attending him. We were horrified when the *brujo* told José that the sick man was bewitched and must die. As he lay there helpless, covered tautly by a cloth, two men, quite matter of factly, drew their bows and shot broad-headed war arrows into his chest. This didn't seem to kill him, for he squirmed this way and that, and the witch finally sat on his belly, put a vine rope around his neck, and thrusting a stick into the loop, twisted it, thus garroting the stricken man before our eyes. I learned to my horror that it is impossible to garrote a man unless a helper jumps on his chest to expel the air from the lungs; the brutal job took them twenty minutes before he was dead.

Jorge came quickly over to me as I stood shocked speechless. "You must believe me when I tell you the Campas are the cruelest beasts in this whole jungle. You must prepare yourself for terrible things. The Mother of God help us if we ever fall into their hands!"

The six *balseros* were very much frightened by this sudden turn of events, and all of us extremely anxious to be off that sandbar and out of this camp.

I told Jorge to bring his raft out of the *cocha* and to meet mine at the far end of the *playa*. Here again we had a very bad scare when the old *brujo* came stomping down to our balsas in a rage. The tyrant was waving his hands and characteristically shouting at the top of his lungs. He was followed by a widely deployed pack of *bravos* carrying fish spears, and bows already strung with multibarbed arrows.

My .45 Colt automatic was carried inside my shirt under my belt, out of sight, whereas the shotgun was now foolishly lashed by a vine on top of Jorge's yellow bag on the rack of his own balsa. If this was an attack I knew we would undoubtedly be wiped out. I decided to shoot the *brujo* first and then as many others as I possibly could, should it come to that, and I slipped my hand inside my shirt and left it there. Instead of pressing an attack, the haughty old *brujo*, who appeared to be enjoying our predicament, folded his arms across his chest, shook his great mane of red-dyed hair and contented himself with hurling abuses at one of our *balseros*. This slave's father, a *manso*, had threatened to feed the *brujo* to the vultures for practicing his witchcraft on the Puna's

"Christian" Indians, several valuable slaves having died. (I could well believe that last!) The *brujo* had heard of this threat and was not going to be satisfied until "pay-blood" had been collected. Among the Campas revenge takes a curious twist: the "pay-blood" can be collected from any member of a man's family.

Now we had heard that the Campas almost always honor slave ownership. I therefore cried out, "Stand back! This man is my property!"

The *brujo* grunted in surprise, but halted abruptly at the edge of the water. The others around him also stopped, transferring their attention to me, as I sat on the rack of my raft.

Jorge, I could see, was trying not to make any sudden moves, as he carelessly undid the lashings on the shotgun. The slaves began talking fast in Campa. I pointed to the fish on our rafts and smiled. It was a strained situation; there were no smiles in return. With an unhurried movement I put my foot against the *playa* and shoved the raft off into the torrent. And Jorge immediately did the same. The stretch below should rightly have been reconnoitered, but the threat of the high waves in the *mal-paso* were as nothing compared to these angry savages. The waves came up before us like windows of white marble, and we hit squarely into them, smashing hard, but held on and came up safe and sopping wet a minute later. Behind, the surprised Indians were shaking their weapons, but made no effort to follow us into that wild chasm. For once we were glad to be caught in the grip of the river—come what may.

That night we found a deserted pole and thatch longhouse some 300 yards inland at the end of a faint trail threading back from the right south bank. We made camp, thankful to be comparatively safe. We broiled the *barbasco*-killed fish, especially favoring a silver-scaled one called *yahuarachi* and roasted a few pieces of yuca roots we found lying among some dusty old gourds and abandoned arrow shafts. It was a dusty camp of ghosts, charred sticks, old bones, skin and hair; an evil smell led us to a bundle of human bones and withered flesh suspended from the rafters, wrapped in bark cloth and corded with fibers. The bark cloth was covered with wonderful drawings in a soft red and jet black, not unlike the drawings of extinct bulls in the caves of Altamira in north Spain.

Next morning, awakened by dew dripping through the rotted thatch roof, we went into the *chacara* and dug up a few edible roots. The slaves killed a blue *guan*, a kind of turkey, and so fared very well indeed. The

Hatchet had slept in the tall sword grass close to the beached balsas in order to guard them and their cargoes from marauding Indians, or to rescue them from the river should it rise suddenly. Storms will cause the river to rise twenty feet in a matter of half an hour. Debris caught in limbs high up in the jungle indicated that rises of thirty to forty feet were possible.

On a sudden impulse José led me a few feet away from the river. Here he pointed out an Indian's body lying on its back in the tall grass. From the wound in the chest, I was sure it could only have been caused by a spear with a very wide blade. But I was wrong. During the night José and the Hatchet, while squatting in the grass alongside the balsas had smelled an Indian stalking them, and the Hatchet had in turn stalked the hunter, killing him with a throw of his tomahawk.

No surprise was shown among the others, and we coiled the lianas serving as mooring lines and started drifting into the east. Before us stretched the fluid yellow currents of our uncertain highway. Rafts of pink waterlilies drifted by, galleons for fat yellow-vested, green-coated frogs, who blinked but once, for the slaves speared them and ate the white flesh raw. The sky became waterlogged and suddenly it rained.

Big scarlet macaws rocketed by overhead through the rain. I had thought they flew in pairs, but here in the foothills they banded in flocks of from ten to a hundred. When the rain stopped and the sun came out, green lovebirds burst out of palmetto palms like steel shell fragments. Swarms of hovering *piums* formed in clouds, or bags, around our heads. Ignoring their bites, our six stumpy brown men stood upright on the balsas, praying to Pawa, with heads pulled down so tautly and devotedly that their hard wet necks bulged.

For hours we swept along the heavily jungled banks. I realized that by river we could cover as much distance in one hour as a fast-moving land party could do in an entire day. After that the risks did not seem so important, for while rafting it was possible to keep at the job from twelve to fourteen hours per day. Suddenly there was a roaring sound ahead, and spray shot hundreds of yards skyward; we had to beach. After carefully reconnoitering by cutting our way along the banks, we returned to the rafts and rode them submerged through a bad run of white curled waves. We clung frantically to the racks, with muddy water flooding up to our chests. We had just rounded a bend when three rifle shots rang out. A bullet, already spent, ricocheted off the surface of the river just ahead of my bow. From the sound I knew it had been fired from the standard rifle of the Amazon, a .44 Winchester. We dug in and paddled to the right bank, where our two balsas were whirled into a backlash—a peculiarity of the Perené—and swept upstream.

While drifting back in the direction we had just come, we finally stuck fast in a rust-colored, fetid, bubbling vegetable muck of gas and chemicals expelled from the bowels of the jungle.

We lay there, while swarms of big yellow and gray, but apparently quite harmless, water spiders, fell out of the brush overhead. We soon got our bearings and peered over the rotting timber. Some two hundred yards lower down on the opposite bank, we spotted four *bravos* moving about with that peculiar Campa flitting movement. Their bellies, shoulders, and faces were smeared with black paint. They carried muskets and rifles and were shoving along four children toward the lower end of the *playa*. José pointed out three adult bodies sprawled along the shore, and we realized that we had not been the target at all.

"*Manatingare!*" (warrior party) José whispered. Our slaves thought these were a band of slavers probably raiding for their *patróne* some hundreds of miles east of us on the Ucayali. The mission boys were badly scared, and would have waded back into the swamp behind, had we not stopped them. Jorge and I sat down on his raft and tried to figure out our next move.

"Well—one thing is certain," he finally said, with a grin, "We can't go back!"

ॐ **VI.** ॐ

"What Shall We Do Now, Amigo?"

HE slave party across the way trotted into the blue shadows at the edge of the jungle's wall. It was fortunate we did not come out of hiding, as they soon reappeared lower down pushing a solitary balsa which had been concealed by tall reeds at the lower end of the spit. They climbed aboard, and amid a flurry of paddles and much splashing, as if fearing pursuit, the Indians and their captives disappeared around the first bend in the river.

We shoved our balsas out of the muck and paddled hard through the strong current, heading across the river to the *playa*. Three corpses were sprawled in the sand, two women and a man. Apparently not realizing the presence of the lurking slavers, this family had been digging for turtle eggs. There were several holes scattered over the *playa* dug by the little ten-pound *nambu* turtles, who lay ten or fifteen eggs to a nest. The *balseros* looked around for the eggs, but these had disappeared with the renegades.

The dead Indians lay in pools of coagulating blood, and were already attracting ants and sand crabs. Vultures were flopping and squealing overhead, their naked black necks snaking in and out, their beady eyes fixed on us. Swinging two of our paddles we tried to drive them off, but they merely settled down again in a watchful circle.

José scooped out a shallow trench with his paddle. The others joined in and fifteen minutes later we buried the Indians. At Jorge's insistence we stood around the pit, our bared heads frying in the sun, while José—our self-appointed preacher—and the others mumbled the prayers learned at Sutsiki. We then rolled the stiffening bodies into the grave and leveled off the sand. Except for more vultures fighting around us and in the marginal trees, there was no movement along the river.

We cast off the lines, hopped aboard our balsas, and pushed into the current. Calls of strange birds came out to us as we drifted by. They sounded like no other birds on earth; rusty gates, shrill traffic whistles, foghorns, animal howls, clicks, beeps, bellows, roars—and there was even the persistent clanging of a bell. This last was the mysterious bell-bird, which we had been told decoys men to their death in the depths of the wilderness. Sometimes it appeared on our left, and then almost immediately again on the right. Anyone trying to locate the bellbird would certainly wander in circles. Its tolling was the most haunting and beautiful sound I have ever heard. And strangely, it was not rare, for we heard it for hours on end, day after day, month after month. The Indians said the clear tones were more dangerous than the roar of a hunting tiger, for the tiger was something tangible, something you could kill—if it didn't kill you first—but the bellbird....

In the quiet stretches we rested on our paddles, wiped the rolling sweat out of our aching eyes and squinted against the glare reflected off the café-au-lait water. We swept past the trunks of straight-shanked trees called the *incira*. This tree has beautiful burl wood of canary yellow, so hard that only the finest steel-cutting tools can dent it. Lining the banks were the tall white trunks of the *puna* tree. Tumbling out of these were fantastic ten-foot blossoms of alternate red and yellow, trailing in the water like the tails of war bonnets. Giant cedars stood by the thousands, towering into the sky, and there were the yellow *remo caspi* and the great *huacapurana*. We learned their Indian names, for not many had Spanish ones, let alone English.

Scores of the giant *arapato* palms rose sheer from the river-torn banks, these being only one of the hundred palms we eventually identified. Extensive thickets of the curious single-stemmed fan palm were common (sometimes miles long), as were fifteen-foot ferns and hedges of gaudy red lilies and leopard plants. Orchids were everywhere. We stopped under one and I counted 1,892 orchids on the single plant! Hundreds of varieties are very common in these uplands (after the wet season); but there was one blue orchid with golden eyes, more beautiful than all the others, and it was called by the Campas "Eyes of the Earth Goddess."

Rafts of floating hyacinth were among the fantastic flora of the region, floating by with insipid clouds of perfume hovering around them. These rafts of vegetation were the lurking places of not only snakes, but crocodiles. We never ventured near them except when absolutely necessary.

Although I was never fortunate enough to see one, the Indians say these vegetation rafts are sometimes inhabited by a thirty-foot poisonous snake they call "Red Lightning" which attacks unprovoked. The nearest approach to it I saw was a twelve-foot bright-yellow bushmaster that we killed on a bank—after a tough fight, for it was very reluctant to die and had an evil temper. I believe it and the king cobra, which I found in Hainan and have seen in India, are the largest poisonous snakes definitely identified.

Occasionally an Indian fishtrap swept into view; these had cane walls thrust into the river bottom, and were called by the Campas *keperotse*. We speared two carplike fish out of one of them, for we had lost most of our food in the rapids and were hungry. Every mile or so now we passed dugouts; usually they were drawn up on the white beaches, and tethered to poles stuck into the sand. Hardwood canoes will sink when overturned, and for that reason I knew we would not see any of that type until we reached the great sluggish rivers of the Amazon flatland. Apparently some order had gone out to the Campas that we were not to be wiped out in a massacre. José wasn't sure, but he thought Iye Marangui might have something to do with it. Our worst danger he felt was from isolated bands of Indians, whom we might surprise and so anger.

Apparently, in spite of what we had seen at Sutsiki, this was no slave-bled river, even here in the west. Indians were everywhere in groups on the tribal "squatting grounds" under crude shelters of palm leaves. These people were tall and barrel-chested—not at all spindly-legged like some tribes—heavy-jawed and beetle-browed, resembling the Eskimo race; absolutely silent and unresponding to our hand-wagging. Unless the *bravos* among them were armed, they would usually run and hide. The hair of most was cut all the way around in a long Dutch boy bob to the shoulders, and their dead-pan faces were usually painted or smeared hideously in black and red, and sometimes indigo-blue. One of the braves was having his hair cut with scissors, but looking closer I saw the scissors were the jaws of a *paña*.

Our watery highway was full of sudden dangers, boulders bubbling up from under us from cascading white torrents of rushing waters and flying spray. Logs smashed against us, twice knocking the baggage awry, which meant that we must stop and repinion them with wooden spikes. Hundred-yard-wide whirlpools had to be carefully circumvented. These swirling funnels were capable of not only engulfing trees, as we saw, but our rafts as well. The thunderous roar of cataracts ahead, or around us, never ceased for a moment. We were wet to the skin and it was necessary at times to sit straddle-legged on the racks, and hang on to bark straps, like pulling leather on a bucking horse, to keep from being thrown into the river.

Once we saw several savages standing in the river. They scrambled ashore on our approach, but returned with animal grunts in a few minutes. They warned us away, apparently afraid we would steal whatever was there. As we drifted closer, we saw that a large eight-foot-long bloated animal, a *sacha vaca*, or *danta*, was caught under the limbs, and it was this carrion they were after. When Indians are hungry and about to eat, they never think of anything else. Jorge and I figured there was no danger from them and paddled over. One of them began talking sulkily, saying that four days before, this beast had been speared while swimming across the river. It had sunk, but they knew that its body would come to the surface, as *pañas* had not found it. They had searched the river banks for miles, and had just located it. Though rotten with gas, the tapir was being cut up. This putrid meat was divided among the band of Indians, who began eating huge mouthfuls on the spot.

So greedy were they over the raw chunks being salvaged out of the bloody water, for the chocolate-colored animal must have weighed over 500 pounds and was too heavy to haul out on the bank, that they took too long, and a shoal of thousands of *paña* began to swarm in the water, tearing the carcass to a pulp, and driving the angry Indians into the trees above. Suddenly a limb gave way and in plunged one of the Indians! Immediately the *pañas* attacked, and but for a single scream when his intestines floated surfaceward, the man was quiet. The water ran red a second time, for the rapacious fish were ripping the flesh off the bones—a business of perhaps ten minutes.

The water all about was boiling with the frantic cannibal fish and the place became exceedingly dangerous, so we left.

Beyond the banks and through breaks in the high jungle we began to glimpse steep hills, every foot of them covered with a dense vegetation of trees, palms and all kinds of weird growth. These unapproachable hills were piled four or five deep, stairlike against the horizon on both sides of us. Living in this mass of tangled vegetation were familiar flocks of green parrots, white cranes, black kites, white king vultures, fishing eagles and hawks, partridges, kingfishers no larger than a humming-bird, flycatchers, waders—birds of all feathers, shapes and dispositions. And there were a hundred others, unknown ones, whose names I was anxious to learn. Once I shot a variation of the *inhambu*—locally a red chicken—but as it dropped into the water, a swirl showed where something grabbed it from below, and our dinner was lost. Whatever we got during the following days, fish, birds, or some small animal, was chopped up and cooked all together in a single pot; sometimes even frogs were added and certain insects—an unsavory tasting but exceedingly strengthening mess.

Around one turn the balsas swept close against a *playa* and nearly crashed into a tremendous eighteen- or twenty-foot black crocodile lying in the gravel. Frightened at our sudden appearance, it roared and hissed, and ran forward on stumpy legs with a wriggling reptilian swift-ness to torpedo straight into Jorge's balsa. The beast came so suddenly that Jorge raised his bare legs and yelled out in alarm. One of his bow paddlers was instantly knocked overboard, and that was the last we ever saw of him, though we stayed in the backwaters of the place probing and watching for an hour. The others explained that the crocodile would thrust him into the mud, and when the body disintegrated conveniently it would be uncovered and torn apart to be devoured.

Our reaction to the loss of this man was one of deep surprise as well as discouragement. All along we had expected trouble from the Campas, and hadn't thought much of either *paña* or crocodiles. From this point on we were to take every precaution possible against such a recurrence. Jorge had seen many men die in his life, and I likewise. We felt no great personal loss, for this Indian had been a silent and surly fellow. Oddly enough the Indian crew shrugged the tragedy off, and never again made mention of it.

I should explain that other explorers, and particularly European ones, have almost invariably called the South American reptilian order of Crocodylia "alligators," instead of "crocodiles," as I have done. This has long been a bone of contention, and lest I be alone in my insistence on "crocodile," an explanation is certainly due the reader. First, there are no alligators in the Amazon country. There are only two known alligators; one genus (*Alligator mississippiensis*) exists in the southern United States; another (*A. sinensis*), which is smaller, is found in central and south China. I have hunted both these alligators. There is also a North American crocodile (*Crocodylus acutus*) found in the United States, the West Indies and the north rim of South America. In the Orinoco is a crocodile called *C. intermedius*, and in the Amazon one called the cayman, of which there are three species. The alligator differs from the true crocodile in having a shorter head and broader, more obtuse snout. Also, the alligator has a fourth, enlarged tooth of the underjaw which fits not in a notch at the side of the upper jaw as in the crocodiles but into a pit in the upper jaw. South America has many sub-species of caymans, which differ from the alligator by the absence of a bony septum between the nostrils. They also have differences in the bony scales of the ventral armor. Therefore, "cayman" or "crocodile"—and not "alligator"—is the proper classification.

On the second evening just before nightfall when we landed on a *playa*, the slaves stumbled across what looked somewhat like human imprints in the damp sand. These measured fourteen inches in length and were three times as wide as my foot. They seemed to have been made by the people whose gigantic bones have been found in Andean caves. The superstitious Indians were frightened by this sight and would not take it as a joke, for there are legends about giants here, and José insisted we continue down the river even in the darkness. From the river's sound below I knew it was a crazy plan. Also the malaria-carrying *zancudos* (*Anopheles*) were coming out in whining biting hordes. Therefore we camped on the strange tracks, all of us standing one-hour watches throughout an uneventful night. At dawn of the third day, we cast off into the flood, which was not very deep.

We had not gone far when one of the sharp-eyed Indians saw a movement in the wall of trees near us on the left bank, and the mystery of the "human" tracks was cleared up. To our amazement, a tremendous black bear was standing, clawing apart a rotten tree stump from which cascaded ants. This type of bear has not been seen or yet fallen to the gun of any explorer. It is called by the Campas *milne*. It might be related to a rare bear inhabiting the lower eastern Andean ranges, said by the Campas to be red in color.

It was a magnificent sight—something one might expect to find in Alaska, but scarcely in the tangled jungles of the Amazon. Our swift and silent approach, which swept us helplessly toward the big animal, was breathtaking. I made no effort—in spite of Jorge and the others' yells—to use my pistol. It would be a poor weapon from a wobbly raft against a wounded and charging bear. Before I could stop him, José slapped his paddle sharply against the surface of the river, imitating the crack of an Indian flintlock. The bear lost all curiosity in the ants and their larvae, and with a grunt leapt into the water and began swimming across the river just in front of us. Seeing our two rafts drifting nearby, perhaps thinking them convenient to crawl upon, or else being angry, the beast let out a bellow and started straight toward my raft. The bear was only three feet away when the crew leaped overboard on the off-side. The craft steadied down a bit and I drew a bead with the Colt on the bear's nearest eye, and squeezed off. It was killed instantly, but while I was trying to drag it aboard, a swarm of the black variety of *paña* appeared, and at sight of the three-pound, oval-shaped devils leaping out of the water, for their numbers were incredible, I let go its paw. Picking up my paddle, I drove the raft shoreward. The three Indians who had waded ashore stood dripping. I was angry with the deserters and disappointed at losing the skin and skull of the new bear. This find could have been quite as startling as the Megatherium (giant ground sloth), whose skin has recently been found in an upland cave. In so huge a jungle there must be hundreds of creatures, great and small, as yet unknown. Even in the fairly open terrain of Szechwan, west China, my friend Floyd Tangier Smith was the first to capture the giant panda in 1936. While Dr. Geoffrey B. Orbell, as late as 1948, discovered in small, long-civilized New Zealand, the "extinct" bird, *takahe*.

On this *playa* we camped, where José dug into a *taricaya* turtle nest and obtained some 200 small eggs which were roasted in the fire. Before dawn we were off again, putting the miles behind us. On the fourth day after leaving Sutsiki, in the midafternoon, the head of a great cataract was suddenly announced by a dull thundering roar. We paddled swiftly to the nearest flat beach on the left side; a cliff rose on the right. Only by leaping into the river and hauling on the lines was a safe landing made just in time.

Securing the rafts to trailing *tamshi* vines, we left a slave on guard, and undertaking a reconnaissance, crawled for the distance of half a mile.

Here we turned right, and with our machetes slashed a way to the river's bank, to be confronted by a breath-arresting sight. The entire Perené crashed down a rocky staircase, its surface consisting of churned waves whose crests rose ten to fifteen feet in long curls and whiplashes of foam and white water. The Indians agreed it would be madness to attempt a passage.

In spite of this verdict I knew we had to get the rafts down somehow, or face the prospect of perishing in this place. I waded out for a better look. Fragmented boulders were thrust up everywhere, great sandstones of the Lower Paleozoic, the size of houses. Were these abutments of the English botanists' ancient continent of Gondwanaland, which existed before the rise of our continents, and on which the first life appeared?

Directly before me, across the river, rose a cliff of several hundred feet. Wreaths of fog and spray shot skyward off the chocolate surface of the river. It seemed impossible that anything but a log could emerge intact at the lower end of the two-mile cataract, for we were not halfway down. So furious was the current that José judged it impossible to lower the balsas by even the strongest *cabuya* tree fiber ropes.

"God be with us, *patróne*..." he shouted above the thunder of the falls, "*Madre de Dios*! We must certainly return to Sutsiki, or we are lost."

"But how return? No trails. Besides, we are in Campa country, it is death to move slowly."

"*Si, si, mi patróne*! We all owe God a life. When we die we will be drawn up to the God in the Sun, and he will send us out again into the worlds. All is the will of God."

Such a sun-worshipping philosophic attitude was not at all pleasing to Jorge or to me. But we were certainly faced with the chilling prospect of abandoning our balsas and striking overland for the Rio Ene some 200 miles east, as the birds go, through trackless jungle.

Everyone wanted to try and get the balsas back upriver, by using snags, limbs and *caña brava* to pull us along the banks against the current. I knew this could not be done. To climb back up the staircase of the Andean foothills was not humanly possible. I knew we could never in a lifetime return to La Merced alive, for not only was there the swift current, but not a few of the Indians behind were now aroused. And so I held out for continuing by river. In four days we had saved at least two weeks of hard jungle work. Risk or no risk, we must somehow portage our gear through the tangle, together with the half-basket of yuca and the few dried fish we still had left—the very last of all our supplies. We must skirt the cataract by slashing a way through the trees and brush on this north side and so reach the comparatively quiet waters that must lie below the falls.

The Indians turned sullen, speaking out of the corners of their mouths. Jorge was carrying the shotgun, and under my shirt I still had the Colt. He smiled and said in English, "If they get nasty, just start shooting. I'll get the Hatchet first."

"Okay," I agreed, "now let's get back."

Retracing our steps up to the rafts—mostly by crawling under the tangle—the Indians gradually cooled off and seemed convinced that there was indeed no returning by river to Sutsiki. They would try to go downstream if I would promise to make a substantial offering to the Holy Mother in Atalaya (on the upper Ucayali), should we reach that metropolis alive. To this I agreed, after Jorge made discreet inquiries and learned that it would entail a candle for each of us, to be lighted before the altar of Pawa, about which the Puna had told them.

At the balsas we began the terrific labor of the portage. Laden with saddles and bags and such other gear and supplies as we possessed, we fearfully moved out once more downhill under the vermin-ridden trees. Hoping to find a better way, we turned further inland. Between the trunks, even enveloping whole trees, hung huge silvery spider nets. Enormous hairy yellow spiders ran in and out. Countless insects were trapped in these vast webs. I saw a rare type of *Morpho* butterfly, with wings measuring eight inches across; there were even small birds and lizards. While underfoot in this vile place was the *mygale*, a poisonous bird-catching spider some seven inches across.

All this horrible mess of stiff and wiry spider webs covered us as we took turns cutting a narrow trail. Our clothes dripped with perspiration. All of us became caked with the whitish pepper-sized *isango*, a minute blood-feeding insect.

In the very midst of the spider webs we came upon a human skeleton, well gnawed by ants. The Indians fearfully examined it, and then explained what had happened—sounding a grim warning. The sinister place afforded a natural ambush, and we must watch for Indian signs. The usual method of these snake-like Campas is to lie in wait at such a portage. Usually the Indian is painted green with black, white or yellow streaks for camouflage, as this tricks and diffuses light and line. If a man passes, the scalp hunter steps from behind a tree. Silent as a shadow, the tigerish fellow shoves a short heavy spear up under his victim's lower rib, spinning and twisting the shaft so that when he withdraws it, according to our Indians, pieces of intestine, heart, lung and stomach come out on the ground. This kind of spear is never thrown; and a surprise attack thus made is not apt to miscarry, as death is usually instantaneous.

Our gear, poor as it was, would seem a treasure to these savages. Thus ever watchful, as we crept along close together, the alert José killed a *jergon*, a five-foot lead-colored snake with a delicate pink forked tongue.

As we rested, sweat-feeding stingless hornets swarmed around our dripping heads. They seemed to enjoy a peculiar fascination when hovering close to our faces, no doubt seeing their yellow bodies mirrored in our eyes, for they would suddenly dart forward into them. Beyond the region of the spiders, we came upon slippery roots, red, yellow and licorice-black, all sizes, from violin strings to ship's hawsers a foot thick. They were a special province of snakes. Three of the vicious *yguana machacuy* were pointed out by the Indians; these snakes have an iguana-type head, are very thick, and being sluggish in movement and patch-colored, are extremely hard to see. Had I been alone I would have passed them by unnoticed. The great hardwood logs lying on the ground had splintered and were all twisted about with vines and leaves, and covered by an unearthly fungus; cardinal red toadstools; yard-wide mushrooms with rippling lace of poisonous blues and creams; sporous plants spotted with browns and greens; and leprous puffballs having the glistening iridescent skin of toads. José warned me against touching any of these.

In the midst of a *caña* thicket we jumped a *tigrillo*, a small yellowish leopard-cat with black spots, feeding on a fish it had dragged inland from the river. The Mexican name for this cat is ocelot. I was nearest but dared not risk drawing stray Indians by firing, and it vanished with a snarl into the thicket, leaving the fish behind. When feeding, these cats—so said one of the Indians—will sometimes attack. Since only the fish's head had been eaten, José kept it for our larder. Here we turned right and, guided by a great thundering just south, slashed our way through the last of the tangle, and finally reached the foot of the cataract.

At the base of the two-mile drop of flumes and falls, we found a landslide of broken boulders which allowed us to reach a bench just above the water's edge. Here we stacked our precious bags of gear and the food. The choppy race beyond was full of floating timbers, branches, banana trees, clotted islands of cane and aquatic grasses, palms, and other floatable forest refuse. Swarming over the pebble beaches were carpets of yellow butterflies, including a few of the rare and priceless *Esmeralda* with its purple wings. Approaching closer to marvel, we saw that the butterflies were hovering and settling on dead things which had been disgorged by the river. On the rocks below were the carcasses of a liver-red deer and a monkey, rotting in the heat and emitting a stench.

The Indians complained bitterly. What was the use of it all? Now we had our bags and food below the cataract, but no balsas for going forward. Surely we knew there was not a stick of balsa in this whole hardwood *catahua* forest. We sat in the shade of a palm and ate, for one of the slaves had the entrails of small birds wrapped in leaves, which he had baked at the last camp and kept in his monkey skin hag. We built a fire (a terrible mistake!) and after cooking the ocelot's fish, ate that too. And then swinging our arms to keep off the hornets, retraced our steps up the trail. Two men remained to guard the supplies. It was late afternoon when we regained the balsas.

The Indians had expected to cast loose the rafts, hoping that enough wreckage could be recovered below the falls to construct one large raft capable of carrying all of us. But the river was too swift—perhaps forty miles an hour in some of the stretches—and we were without any means for collecting the precious logs at the foot and so would lose them. I said we must ride the balsas through. The most dangerous point, I hurriedly explained when they cried out in protest, was at the very head of the falls. This point might be safely passed and the bows of the balsas could be pointed forward, and kept there so as not to allow the rafts to swing broadside in the trough and capsize.

They wanted to know why we couldn't build new rafts below the cataracts. I countered with two good reasons: first, they had said there were no *palo de balsa* trees, and also the delay in cutting and drying floatable logs even if any could be found; and second, that our only security from Indians lay in our policy of a steady movement along the river. Should we take root for even a day the bull horns might well blast us out of the jungle. Surely the Indians ahead had been warned of us, and might gather for a fight. Further, our gear and food were now located two miles east. Should we lose it, we could not hope to survive in the wilds. Night was also fast approaching, and I, for one, was hungry. At the mention of food, they grumblingly threw all caution to the winds. There is no bait like food to hungry men. Four of us, including José and myself, would attempt to run the balsas through. Jorge would help us to maneuver the rafts into midstream by guy vines. After we were loosed, he would retrace his way down the portage trail and join the pair of guards at the bottom. One of us definitely had to stay with both groups. I handed Jorge my .45 Colt and the precious money belt and all it contained.

We now cut four new paddles. The first balsa, which was to go ahead of José and me, was worked precariously by paddles and vines into the middle of the river. It was necessary to cross over to the opposite bank with my own balsa. Thus suspended on a vine from either shore, this first balsa safely reached the head of the cataracts. At this point the river was only a hundred yards wide. Lying in midstream with a curl of white water over its stern, its bow only a few yards from the first wave, the balsa seemed like a whitish chip on a heaving sea. The two Indians' faces shone with vigilance and excitement, and they seemed strangely happy. Yet they knew that the two miles ahead were stone steps jammed with boulders, death-trap falls, and all the impending dangers we had viewed and calculated from positions below. A rainbow arched through the single walled slot of the river bed, but it was the only beautiful thing about that hell hole.

Before we could change our minds through fear and indecision, I brought my machete down on my vine, and Jorge, across the way, let loose his vine. The freed raft and its crew of two Indians slipped up on an oily wave and then shot into a broad trough. The crest toppled over them. Then the balsa emerged only to dash through a fearsome wall of falling white waters, which enveloped it completely. And that was the last view we had of them....

Now it was my turn. Frankly, I was more than shaky. I was downright scared. By securing a long vine to a tree and then paying it out as we crossed over to pick up Jorge's line, José and I finally worked our own raft carefully back into midstream and then we cast it adrift. Jorge stood on the shore against the palms and flame trees. His silence was moving, and his face showed that this might be the last he would ever see of any of us. But he too knew we had to try or perish in the Gran Pajonal.

Helplessly we slipped into a long toboggan slide of gliding water, swift and sure as that in a millrace. Suddenly at the bottom of the dip rose a ten-foot wave. It toppled over us, and would have torn us from the balsa had we not braced frantically against the rack with our feet and clutched the straps with our hands. We emerged through a solid wall of water. Instantly we struck a black basalt boulder with such violence that the skin was torn from the palm of one of José's hands, and my right shoulder was all but dislocated. We were blinded by water and choking.

We hurtled forward in a turbulent fall of deafening waters; a log rammed against my left leg and it felt broken. The raft smashed on, careening against a row of boulders, then sliding headlong into successive walls of water, rolling and pitching the while with such violence that I could barely make out a blur of the canyon wall on our right side. I tasted blood on my teeth.

As we tore along, I saw the first raft for a split second. Its white shiny bottom lay gleaming in the setting sun like the belly of a wounded shark. It lay toppled over on its back across a flat rock. The crew was nowhere in sight. Were they smashed beneath it?

When not clinging to the straps on the rack, we wielded the paddles trying to keep the bow straight. A constant roar filled our ears and the smashing and splitting of logs and other debris jammed, thumped and bumped around us in the declivity. For a moment I tried to calculate our speed and judged it to be over forty miles per hour.

Then suddenly I knew the first mile was passed and we were halfway down, for as we flashed under a high abutment of the right-hand cliff, I saw the red clusters of the *jupati* palm fruit. This grove we had marked down from the midway point reached during the reconnaissance. After that we plowed through such a thunderous and violent washboard of waves that I felt all was lost and yelled to the insanely grinning José to save himself. But this warning was not necessary, for that man of all gods was hanging on like grim death and bellowing: "Oh Sun! Oh Mother of God! Open your arms, here I, José, come!"

A fifteen-foot-high wave heaved us upward almost to its crest and then fell from under us. We were suddenly struck by another, like a boxer's straight left followed by a hard right-cross. The raft began to disintegrate under us and when the crest of that second wave broke, we found ourselves struggling in the turgid waters, floundering amidst the smashing logs of the raft and other wreckage carried along by the river.

The white logs rolled over and over, grinding together, and there was no grasping them. I was smashed between two spinning logs and felt as if my ribs had caved in. All this time we were being carried forward in a turmoil of white and yellow water, at an unrelenting velocity. I fought the river with every trick of mind and muscle; rolling over boulders, as a fighter rolls with a hard punch, swimming steadily when it appeared to my advantage, treading water to keep from being sucked to the bottom in the down currents and so ground to bits amongst the rounded boulders which rolled like balls along the bed of the river.

Quite suddenly, and almost together, José and I were finally swept out of the flood and carried on the foamy surface of a curving eddy. We had reached the bottom of the canyon! We bumped softly against a rock and gravel beach, which we recognized from the deer and monkey carcasses; just above should lie our equipment and our food. Miraculously, my wristwatch was unbroken, and it had taken only ten minutes to make the entire run. Somehow we caught hold of a stone. José was badly shaken and I felt as if I had received a terrific beating in a long fist fight. After a few minutes we found the strength to crawl out of the deep water and lay on a partly submerged flat boulder and a few pieces of driftwood. We had hardly caught our breath and begun an examination of our bruises when part of the first raft, which we had passed near the head of the slot, surprisingly swept alongside. It must be rescued.

Seizing pieces of driftwood, we swam out to two of the logs and finally crawled upon them. Each man astraddle a log and using the driftwood as paddles, we started after the scattered raft. The balsa logs of both rafts were now milling around in a clockwise circle at the foot of the falls. One by one they were gathered, though a few escaped in the current. With our legs clasped under the log each of us was riding, we were taking a frightful risk, for there were crocodiles in the deep pool—

we could see their snouts under the banks. We were annoyed because the two guards on the north bank above had not yet put in an appearance to help us. We became encouraged when the other two Indians, the crew of the first balsa whom we had given up for lost, pushed out of the jungle, wet and bruised. They still wore their monkey skin bags. They explained they had been washed against the shore about two hundred yards higher up.

But our joy was short-lived. One of the Indians called out in alarm from above. Our stuff had disappeared! And the two guards were lying among the rocks—dead! José and I climbed up, and there were both men sprawled on the rocks. They had been shot with arrows—green feathers were protruding out of the Hatchet's back, while two yellow-feathered shafts, one in the throat and the other in the thigh—stuck out of the other fellow. And, worse, if possible, all our gear *and food* was gone! Vanished!

Jorge showed up with machete at his side and gun across his arm, took one quick look around; taking in the wreckage on the river bank, the dead men, the absence of the food basket—and then unexpectedly groaned:

"What shall we do now, amigo?…"

ᖇ VII. ᖇ

Kill! Kill!

a THIN slice of an orange moon rose with equatorial swiftness over the tall hedge of jungle standing ragged along the opposite bank and fixed its straight shafts of light into the yellow river. Scattered bellbird calls, of varying tolls and intensities, began ringing out on our north side. I counted their locations—five, or possibly six Indians were signaling each other, slowly converging on us....

There was no time to bury the two Indian slaves. I took the shotgun from Jorge, together with my .45 Colt and money belt, and stood guard just inside the first inky shadows of the high bush. By the moon's light the others—now thoroughly frightened—pitched in with Jorge's machete and hurriedly lashed the balsa logs together with vines torn from the nearest trees. Out of the wreckage of our two old rafts they had only enough material for constructing a single raft of eight logs. When Jorge whistled softly I joined them, and we finally cast off into the strong currents not knowing what lay ahead. We had not yet rounded the first bend about two hundred feet away, when we heard angry cries and yells from the very spot we had just left.

Thankful for getting clear of that place, but apprehensive for what lay ahead, we drifted down the middle of the river through the moon's beams and the dark shadows cast by the taller trees. At times we ran into trouble, but each time we extricated ourselves with the paddles we had portaged down to the foot of the falls. Now the river was never impersonal, but very close to us, for we knew its every quirk of character.

The balsa floated dangerously low in the water under our weight, its deck awash. With guns in hand, Jorge and I scanned the left bank, for a Campa brave can move almost as fast through jungle as a white man can over open ground. The three slaves meanwhile stood upright with their hands clasped over their lank bellies, as José quietly spoke the evening prayers, impervious to the stinging of mosquitoes or the great insectivorous bats wheeling past their faces. When the prayers were finished the Indians turned their attention to the moon, very softly singing songs startlingly like those wild singsong ones of the savage Ngoloks in Tibet (who sing into their wide sleeve). Afterwards the three slaves squatted silently on their heels, peering stoically into the thick vegetation. The banks now averaged only a hundred feet on either flank. The river was very deep and sluggish in many of the stretches lying between cataracts.

Some miles beyond, the brown thatch of a hut stood out in a clearing on the left. In spite of the risk we must stop at this clearing. We were exhausted and in need of food. As we dug in our oars to make for it, hoping to find something to eat, several Indians appeared on the bank overhead. A shower of arrows whizzed past, two of them thudding into the spongy balsa logs. The bow slave, a tall and very thin fellow called Red Snake, let out a yell and crumpled onto the raft. An arrow had gone completely through him.

I drew my .45, for I had long since stuck it into my pants' top, and economically began firing into the legs of the mob; Jorge's shotgun crashed out and an Indian—caught in the act of drawing his longbow—gave a long yell and pitched off the steep bank, disappearing into the dark waters below. The Indians above suddenly broke and ran back across the clearing and into the bush at the far side. At their heels yipped a pack of hunting dogs. And following these were a silent string of trotting *bravos*, probably a rear guard, armed with flintlocks, spears and bows. We landed too far down, and had to jump overboard and tow the raft back to the open bank.

We secured the balsa to a flanking *caña* brake. Here we rolled Red Snake over on his side, and I broke off the arrowhead. In withdrawing the shaft the same way it had gone in, Red Snake grunted, his head flopped. I knew he was dead. Without a word, José put a coil of liana vine around Red Snake's neck and then rolled the body off the raft and into the water.

We hurriedly climbed the bank and deployed so that we were spaced apart and would not present an easy target. Thus we walked slowly into the clearing. Snapping on my pencil flashlight, which I had taken from the bandolier money belt, I entered the hut. It was empty. Suspended on strings from the rafters was a broken old flintlock musket manufactured in Great Britain by "P. Dumoulin & Co.," who have distributed tens of thousands of the standard muzzleloaders throughout the Amazon Valley. At close range these smoothbores will kill even a jaguar. The Campas call them *tungaventodse*. The barrels, made of coiled wire soldered over and filed smooth begin unwinding after some fifty to a hundred rounds have been fired.

Abandoned bows and arrows were both a good five feet long, the shafts tipped with *chonta* arrowheads having wicked barbs, and feathered with two split quills of toucan wing tips tied in a screw pattern. The toucan flies straight ahead without deviation, and because of the magic attached to this ability, these feathers are in great demand among the arrow makers.

Scattered over the bark floor were several wooden neck-racks and sleeping mats, a few baskets, and some crude unpainted pottery, and heavy coils of necklaces consisting of thousands of tiny black seeds of the *chakiri* plant. This was wampum money and the Indians wear them over the shoulder bandolier fashion. Some gold dust and nuggets, called *kishongare*, were in a calabash. A yard-wide round frame with a monkey hide laced to it at the edges was the gold pan, a clue of how the ancient Incas recovered their gold. A leather pouch was filled with crocodile fat, used for rheumatism, so said José. Hunting trophies were evident in the jawbones of different animals thrust in rows under the woven palm-leaf roof. Many had yuca and other food—offerings to the wandering animal ghosts—stuck between their teeth. We were hopeful at this sight, but after a diligent search found no food clean enough or free of worms, for ourselves—and yet we were starving, for excepting the ocelot's fish and the bird entrails, we had not eaten since before dawn.

Those of us who had run the rapids were all but done in, but even so, we had to join Jorge in the scouting. In the edge of the clearing, while reconnoitering for lurking Indians, we got entangled in the disgusting nets of enormous night spiders, hairy black things with red spots, busily spinning ladies' veils across the lips of pale orchids. At the bank while scouting the reeds we heard the slapping of fishes' tails rising to a hatch of flies, and lost no time getting out bows and arrows. Soon we had eight *shuyo*, a small fish with dark reddish scales. We scraped out a hole in the middle of the Indians' abandoned campfire, and after tossing the fish into the hole, covered them over with a heap of coals. The two slaves gleefully brought in a few papayas, which they had knocked out of a tree with a pole. They dared not wander farther afield in search of a *chacara*, for signals were being detected from among the real bird and animal calls out in the bush. In spite of the danger we must eat.

While the fish were cooking, I looked carefully about. Bird colonies were suspended overhead in two barren lightning-blasted trees—the *huacapu*, a practically indestructible wood used mainly for structural poles in the Campa houses. These long sack-shaped baskets, a yard in length, swung gently as cradles from the limbs, and black and yellow birds, large as crows, darted in and out of a hole in the bottom.

We couldn't sit or lie on the ground, tired as we were, for it was crawling with long lines of umbrella ants, holding leaves upright by their lower edges and looking exactly like Lilliputian boats with hoisted green sails. The fire's soft glow showed a pair of tall blood-smeared posts weirdly painted with "human ghost pictures" in white and red. Seeing them, the slaves became greatly alarmed saying these were "evil" and had to do with death, and with *kamari*—devil spirits. I wanted to douse the fire, but Jorge pointed out the food would not cook, and that since the Indians knew we were here anyway, it would make no difference. If they were going to return and attack, the fire or lack of it would not prevent their doing so. The slaves kept turning in a circle and facing the jungle, and they held their new bows and arrows ready in their hands.

Quite suddenly I realized that this campfire had not been kindled with hardwood, which often glows like coal, but by chunks of a substance which smelled like asphalt! It appeared to be crude petroleum in solidified form, and we recalled a story told by Stone.

Years before, some Campa braves had appeared at the plantation carrying several small pieces of solid petroleum. The Campas used the petroleum for making offerings to the gods and devils, mixing it with the sweet-smelling copal, a kind of amber.[1] They agreed to take the excited Englishman downriver to the place where it was mined.

Heavily armed, Stone followed the Indians in his own dugout manned by his own trusted paddlers. They had not gone more than six miles, when the wild Indians changed their minds and fled ahead, deserting him. Disappointed, and fearful lest they set an ambush, he and his frightened men turned back. Stone never dared to return, even though convinced that petroleum existed somewhere on the Perené and knowing that its existence in the eastern Andes would have great significance and value. The market was ready at hand, especially along the Amazon in Brazil.

In the meantime the signals out in the darkness were coming in closer and closer. One very excited and noisome brave, no doubt out to make a name for himself, sounded like a *soldado*, the soldier bird. There was no danger to himself, because even if we detected the counterfeit, it was pitch dark in the bush and we would certainly not go looking for him. I lay stretched out on a log and waited for the fish to bake. This job would take some time, for Amazon fish, many of them, are infested with worms. José whispered that he felt in his bones we were being watched by what he termed *antamikire* (savages). He preferred once again to board the raft and cast adrift in the darkness rather than stay here another second after we had satisfied our hunger.

By the excellent light of the petroleum-fed fire, I got out my notebook from its pocket in the money belt, and on a page made several drawings of some fifteen types of stone and wood artifacts and arrowheads, including the fascinating hieroglyphics and picture writing carved on monkey-bone tablets, and the patterns of some interestingly shaped canoe paddles found inside the house. I had finished and was completing my notes for the day, for in spite of the effort this had become by now a habit, when suddenly an arrow, red and banded with green rings, hissed into the center of the fire, scattering embers in a shower over us!

In spite of the tension we had been experiencing ever since our arrival, we were shocked into inactivity and were speechless.

When I finally let out a yell of warning, the others seized the

---

1. Copal was used by the ancient Incas and Mayas on the altars of the Sun God and Quetzacoatl.

machete and the bows and arrows, and Jorge grabbed the shotgun off a log, and in a body we ran for the house. Clattering up the steep ladder we pulled it up behind, and found ourselves in the main room. I went at once to the back wall and fired my pistol twice through the upright bamboos comprising that wall. I wanted to leave no doubt in the savage's minds that we were now inside the house.

"No, no, señor," exclaimed José, quite beside himself, "We must not fight from the house!"

"Just take it easy, José," I said. In the dark we both began quietly tearing up the palm-bark floors, while the others stood guard at the doorway.

We were not an instant too soon. From the open doorway we could see flaming fire-arrows already arching out of the jungle and knew they would crash into the dry thatched roof overhead. José relayed my instructions to his friend to take up positions at the edge of the jungle wherever shade and other cover could conceal them. We leapt through the hole down to the dark ground below. We dispersed, crawling on our bellies through shadows to such hiding places as we could find. I selected a small lean-to on which a tame macaw was roosting. Jorge knelt close by, grasping his *facao* between his teeth, the shotgun held at the ready. I wondered how the Peruvian would make out in a fight. In Lima they were always talking about how brave they were, and very proud of their bull fighters.

There was no sound from the Indians. From the ends of the clearing came the crackling of the burning roof; a sheet of flame began to light up the whole area. A ring of *puna* palm trunks stood out in sharp white relief at the clearing's edge like a neat picket fence. We couldn't hide much longer.

I picked up one of the heavier paddles I had been sketching earlier. Using the pistol at close quarters would be risky, as my own three men were scattered about the clearing. Also, I had only a few shells in my pocket and four in the magazine. However, I snapped the magazine out of the pistol's handle and crowded in two more shells—six in all. Signals began breaking out, and they told us that our attackers had drawn in closer and were waiting mutely in the sepulchral forest, watching like hawks for us to run out of the house and commit *tongashare*, literally "raid suicide." It was the Campa technique to fire a house from a distance, then to close the range, and as their trapped victims rushed out of the burning hut, to shoot arrows and bullets into them by the light from the roof.

The house was now completely in flames. The roof began to fall in, shooting up columns of sparks. The embers were dropping into the clearing where they threatened to burn my own shelter as well as Jorge's *techa*. Believing we had chosen to burn rather than die by arrows and gunshot, our attackers began signaling each other with bird calls. Suddenly, the *bravos* broke cover and dashed into the clearing, about thirty of them!—uttering war cries of triumph and firing their muskets and arrows into the burning house, a few even launching their big *wairi satamedotse*—war spears.

They were scattered all around us; wild, naked devils banded with red paint, their excited faces masks of solid rouge. They wore no *cushmas*, however, since these might obstruct their movements. It is a custom among the warring Campas never to wear clothing on a raid, for if wounded, the likelihood of a nasty infection is thus greatly lessened. The braves were incredibly evil-looking, howling, leaping up and down, and brandishing war clubs—stone skull-crushers fitted with long wooden handles—and wicked daggers set with bony edges.

"*Moyeri! Moyeri!*" ("Kill! Kill!") they cried over and over again.

They presented perfect targets against the background of the burning house. I decided to use the .45 after all, and fired twice over their heads. Complete pandemonium broke out. I think the savages would have fled, so great was their surprise, and I was dumbfounded when Jorge leapt into their midst, slashing right and left with his long knife, his gun wisely discarded in the melee. I seized the paddle in both hands, and running forward, laid out to left and right, swinging it against all available skulls and shoulders, backs and chests. I also used it in the manner of a bayonet. The Indians were thrown into confusion, due to the sudden surprise element of our counterattack.

Our knife and paddle proved more effective at close range than the bows and muskets turned against us. One savage had his hands on my throat, when I saw an arrow sink with a smack into the side of his neck— an arrow shot at me, but striking him! When he dropped, I grabbed him, trying to hold his body up as a shield with my left arm while swinging the paddle as hard with my right hand as I could.

The two slaves now charged in with swinging machete and club, howling in rage. So unexpected was their concerted attack against the rear and flank that the *bravos* were thrown into even greater confusion. These warriors would be far more effective as lone manhunters in the jungle. Though the Indians fought fairly well, once they settled down and resorted to their axes and flintlocks as clubs, they had lost the battle (having done more damage to themselves than to us), and soon began withdrawing by running off into the jungle. I once saw a Chinese guerrilla behind the Japanese Yellow River lines get into a Jap infantry machine-gun bunker and kill five men with a shovel. Nine of my men were bayoneted, including that Chinese, but he could fight. And that Jorge was the same kind of fighter.

Five warriors lay on the ground. Black Hawk, the last of the Sutsiki slaves, had a broken left arm, and José's right shoulder was laid open for a foot, while Jorge and I were cut and badly battered about head and body.

José bent over one of the savages, and after a close examination, informed us it was a famous *antamikire andandingare,* or fighting *bravo* who had been directing the reorganization and fight. His fingers still clutched the barrel of one of the trade muskets. He was further recognized by Black Hawk as a renegade *curaca,* a labor chief named Saki, in the service of a powerful *patróne* based on the Alto Ucayali. This same notorious Saki once boasted at Sutsiki that he had captured 600 Campa women and children and sold them for one musket each, or for 100 soles-de-oro per head. José said that he and his renegade band had probably slain hundreds of adult Indians in their terrible raids for slaves and plunder. We could not tell whether these same Indians had shot the two women and the man we had found higher up the river.

Though Saki's riddance was a blessing to the Campa tribe, this knowledge caused José and Black Hawk great uneasiness, for they pointed out that should word of this battle reach the *patróne,* our lives would be in great danger. It was possible that the band's *secundo* under the dead Saki would now attempt to hunt us down, fearing we had gotten evidence of his slave raiding, which was illegal. Although the law was helpless in prosecuting the slavers, still such a blunder on the raider's part might bring down the wrath of his *patróne* on his head. I tried to reassure my companions and told them I doubted we would be pursued further.

It was after midnight; following the dexterous José, we dug our fish out of the fire and quickly fled through the *caña* brake to the river. The balsa was still safely moored to its liana, and we lost no time getting aboard, for signals were once more all about. The moon, though westering, was still bright, but fortunately we were in the shadow of a great *cumala* tree, which partly obscured the raft. Hurrying, we cast off, and began our second blind drift that night.

Our way was along the bottom of a knife-gash canyon of tall trees all sparkling with blue and red phosphorescent fungus, set under a long rectangular mat of dark blue in which the glinting stars were stuck like glass thumbtacks. The river seemed to be flattening out and to deepen as the sub-Andean slopes were left ever farther behind. Glimpsed over the waving heads of *caña* thickets, we saw jungled spurs, mesas, plateaus and foothills, comprising the western rim of the mighty Amazon forest. A startled loon cried out alongside, and we cocked our two guns, for we were still nervous, suspicious of every bird call. Once a feather floating by seemed an unforgettable monument in marble to some bird's flight, indicative of the transitory nature of all life. It made me pause and wonder if anyone would ever know what had happened, should something befall the four of us that night on this wild river.

Black Hawk lay flat on the raft with his broken arm. José busied himself with his feet and left hand (for his shoulder was bothering him) at the stern of the raft, and presently fished up the dead Indian, now a skeleton, stripped clean by the *pañas*. The bones were a shiny yellow-white in the starlight—a grim object. Placing the skeleton in the middle of the raft, alongside Black Hawk, José voiced the unwritten law of all Amazon expeditions:

"None of us must be abandoned, *patróne*. When we come to a safe place, we must give this man a Christian burial."

"But—what difference does it make where a man is buried out here. It's all water and jungle...."

Jorge grinned in the moonlight—grinned in spite of the fact that he was beaten and done in. I was satisfied I had no ordinary man with me, but a tough jungle man who was not only a *montero* and a fighter, but a man who had guts to boot. There was a great deal of satisfaction in that, and I almost mentioned El Dorado—but not quite.

⤳ VIII. ⤵

A Bible and a Tiger

OR two hours we drifted through the jungle of semidarkness, putting up only a gaggle of wild muscovy duck which rose with a terrific clatter. We had put perhaps fifteen miles behind us when we were caught up in an eddy and swept shorewards against a low sand and gravel *playa* some two hundred yards long and fifty feet wide. Here we decided to hole up due to a thundering crash of waters, which announced the presence ahead of a cataract barrier. The *playa* was crawling with crocodiles, some two thousand of them, whose eyes gleamed like rubies in the beam of my flashlight; a few wriggled slowly into the river, but most stayed. In spite of this we must remain here, for we dared not risk the *mal-paso*.

Ashore on the left hand, and with our bare feet braced in the cool sand, we grabbed hold of the vine and hauled the precious raft high up on the beach and secured it to a fallen tree trunk. Jorge and I did all the work, as the two Indians were in no condition to help. Though aching in every bone and muscle, and so tired we could hardly manage, we lost little time scooping out a shallow grave and burying poor Red Snake's skeleton, consigning him to the gods with appropriate prayers to Pawa and the moon.

The hornet-like *tabañas* were frightful for we could not hear them and we felt blood on our faces and hands before we were aware of them. Our arms flaying the air, we hurriedly occupied a pair of old palm lean-tos left by nomadic fishing Indians—stinking fish heads and skeletons lay about the place. Here Black Hawk, holding his broken arm, and José with his slashed shoulder, sat as stoic as the proverbial Indian. Having lost our nets we dug a hole and built a smudge fire in its bottom to hide the flames. We took stock of the things saved in my money belt and Jorge's hunting bag, all we now had with us. Except for the films and camera, an aneroid barometer, a few matches, two notebooks, pencil, money, one machete, my map of El Dorado, hunting knives, the paddles and the two guns (with only five rounds for the pistol and nine shells for the shotgun), the compass and a few other items such as a bottle of iodine, we faced the jungle almost emptyhanded. The two Indians still had their bows and a few arrows, also two fishing spears, which they had annexed at the battle camp. Above all, we had nothing to eat.

Exhausted, I finally fell asleep and hours later, just before dawn, I awakened. A deafening wave of sound was coming out of the jungle to roll over the river; amphibian tonks and bellows, bird calls, animal grunts and chatterings, the click of cicadas and the incredible swarms of other insects. All but a few of the crocodiles had moved off into the river on their daily search for food. A few of the small vampire bats were darting about, and I knew that from now on, we must sleep Indian style, whenever possible, with our feet pointed to the fire. When no fire was possible, we must keep on our shoes and wrap our heads in cloth or even large leaves as José and Black Hawk did.

I rolled a cigarette, shaving a bit of the precious tobacco from our twist, which fortunately Jorge had been carrying in his pocket at the portage, into a piece of notepaper, and was soon blowing smoke rings into the top of the crude thatch. Jorge awakened and sat alongside, presently smoking an enormous cigarette rolled in a certain kind of palm-leaf used by the Indians for that purpose.

"Sometimes it is a great feeling to be alive, my friend," he grinned. "If that band of Indians follow by river we are in danger of being overtaken, but if they come by land, we are safe here till dawn."

In times of danger men often talk about queer and impractical things. That terrific din outside camp, I told him, was not unlike the same ringing roar of the 34th Guerrilla Army, when it was surrounded by eight Japanese infantry columns south of the terrible Fen River in

North China. With eighteen thousand Chinese Yen Shih-son cavalry under my command sent out to destroy railroads, we were caught behind the enemy's main lines and faced annihilation. We rode hard to escape, sometimes hiding in the dark and resting in rice paddies or millet fields or in the bottom of ditches, talking about—of all subjects—how we could get our socks washed if we reached the Jap-held Fen by the next night. The Japanese invasion of the American B-29 bases in northwest China was stopped cold. But out of eighteen thousand men, only eighty-three of us ever washed our socks....

Camping on the Perené that night, in a situation no less dangerous (for I can assure you there is little choice between an Indian scalping knife and a Jap bullet or bayonet), Jorge and I talked in low voices, stopping every few minutes to listen intently for the possible movements or signals of Indians scouting in the jungle. Oddly enough, we talked of more profound matters than dirty socks. And this perhaps was strange, for Jorge was a very earthy, hard and practical young man, whose mind measured the worth of all things against its peso value; while I have never been accused of being a hallowed saint myself. A contributing factor might have been that the air was muggy, motionless, cohesive; and somehow a strange feeling crept over us, and flowed over into our conversation.

All the animate and inanimate kingdoms of matter were bound together by a single dominating force which alone kept the ninety kinds of atoms in perfectly integrating ever-changing motion. It was this force (known to the Campas in a mystical sense) which created, sustained and also destroyed life by an incessant agitating of the electronic atoms comprising worlds and germs alike, and that this force was none other than God.

At this point José joined in the conversation. God, then, it presently seemed to the three of us buried in that cosmos of jungle, was manifested in man's innermost consciousness. Yet that force (God) was separate from mind and brain, which, like the five senses, were only animal tools. These were not the real essence of man—for that could only be the spirit of God, which prevailed as a base everywhere in man and even in stones.

"Well," said Jorge quietly, puffing on his stogie, "I'll probably be disowned by my family, and excommunicated by the Church. But I think somehow, seeing how it is in this jungle, that 'God' is consciousness, separate from matter—which itself can only be electricity (electrons, protons and neutrons) in various combinations—and that His will is what gives the atom its motion and even its conception…that there is no beginning and no ending, but only eternal change…Therefore there can be no real death, but only little unreal deaths…."

Yes, that strange night the Peruvian, the Campa and I agreed that our individual body of atoms and its guiding mind was separated from the Will, the God, within us. And that this separate subtle universal "I" (God) was linked through ever-changing but never-lost cycles of chemistry into yet other atoms and molecules, even those contained in fertilizer. And that that binder, the inner consciousness, could only be released to freedom with the ultimate reality, when our individual outer minds were enlightened and saw the truth. We somehow understood that night that man had lost God, not because man had sinned, for what does God care about the sins and good deeds of man, but because man had turned for salvation outwards, to worship before his own alter-ego (the ideal of humanity). This because he foolishly put all his hopes for life eternal into creating a Greek Utopia on earth, instead of discarding his own personal ego and humanity en masse, and turning inward toward God Himself. For some reason, I was pleased when José said quietly: "Señor—you would make a good Campa *brujo!*"

When dawn (our fifth) came, we cut off our philosophizing and began wondering about food. José and Black Hawk complained that with the excitement gone they now felt awful from the fight, and that *niguas* had crawled under their toenails and laid eggs. This must have happened days earlier, as the blister sacs were painful to the touch. José obtained splinters in the forest and we set Black Hawk's left upper arm, binding the splints with wide bark wrappings. With a handful of *chonta* needles, Jorge and I pinioned José's cut together, and he smeared a concoction on his right shoulder obtained from the *retama* tree. With daylight, Jorge and I covered the smudge with sand and built a smokeless fire in the shape of a star, the butts of five dry logs of *quinilla* forming the crux and furnishing coals. We had no intention of letting the smoke rise above the trees and betray our presence to hostile Indians.

While Black Hawk and José slept, Jorge and I speared five fish, for at Saki's camp we had obtained not only spears but bows and arrows. Our appetites soon sharpened at the smell of the fish sizzling in the bed of coals. These fish were the black type of *paña* (there is also a silvery one), and amazingly the eight-inch to a foot-long disk-like fish were delicious. The *paña*, with red gills and tail and pink belly, were easy to see, and had been decoyed in close to the *playa* by Jorge, who had dangled his bare feet in the water! This was doubly unsafe, due to the presence of several crocodiles lying on the surface. To spear a fish you must judge its speed and depth from the V-shaped ripple on the water above it. In casting the spear, you aim, if the fish is down two feet and moving fast, about sixteen inches just ahead of the point of the V. It is a knack which can only come with experience.

After eating it was time to move on, but we were so beaten up from the battle, that we now decided to stay rooted for the day, come what may. Though this was only our fifth day on the river, we had covered a hell of a lot of ground, in more ways than one. Urgently needing attention was also repair work of another nature. A tropical ulcer, apparently flyblown—for a one-inch white worm was pulled out of it—was now forming over my right ankle.

While discussing where we would hide the eight-log raft, we were interrupted by a hissing: José stared quickly around our feet, thinking a snake was buried in the sand. Black Hawk suddenly pointed with his good right arm, and we saw a flock of eight white swans floating serenely down the river. Jorge saw them too, and seized the shotgun, but changed his mind when he remembered Indians might be lurking near. The birds were fully fifty yards away and moving downstream fast. We hardly dared breathe, watching all that good meat getting away. José, estimating they would drift no closer, quickly strung his bow—which he picked off the ground with his foot—and in spite of his shoulder hurting, put an arrow neatly through the lead swan....

Amazed and delighted, Jorge and I retrieved the game by using the raft, and none too soon, for a crocodile was swimming toward the bird. And then we hid the balsa among water grass growing farther upstream.

With this food in hand we felt secure against the jungle. José took on the job of plucking the feathers, holding the bird between his feet. In the meanwhile Jorge, Black Hawk and I rested on the sand, for whenever we tried to sit up or move about, we ached in every bone. I finally lay back and all but fell asleep, for the early morning was the only cool part of the whole day, and the breeze moaning in the feathery bamboos at our back was not only a lullaby but drove the insects away.

I figured we were fairly safe in our position on the edge of the *playa*, for if Indians appeared on the river we could retreat unseen into the thicket. Indians, I mused, would not be able to get through the dry bamboo brake without making a noise. I soon got up and investigated a slight sound, but found only a *capitaris*, one of the tortoises. Again I was dozing off when two ostrich-appearing birds, grayish brown in color, apparently flightless due to short wings, and tall as the average Indian, walked out of the thicket only a few yards away (which gave me quite a start!) and began feeding over the *playa*. At the water's edge, one of them tossed a frog into the air, caught it on the fly and swallowed neatly at a gulp. We idly watched the birds for several minutes. José shook his head at me indicating they were not good for eating. The real reason was that Indians believe this species to be sacred, and so will not kill it. Finally the great birds strutted back into the bamboos, and probably bedded down against the heat of the day.

Next, a strange small reddish animal came hopping out on the *playa*, and at a sign from me, José put an arrow through it. It proved to be a marsupial, complete with belly pouch. The curious thing is that these animals are found only in South America, North America (the opossum), and in Australia. Later in Ecuador, I learned of a rare type found there in the jungles and named *Caenolestes*.

The two Indians now promoted from slaves to free men (with receipts to prove it) squatted under their lean-to out of the scorching sun and began picking fleas out of each other's long black hair. Soon they were chanting contentedly from their tiny Bibles, a remarkable product of Sutsiki ingenuity, which they carried in the regular jungle waterproof, raw latex-smeared leather bag, knotted to a thong around their necks. These Bibles (four inches long, three inches wide and two inches thick) were wonderful books made from sheaves of removable Campa paper obtained from hand-trimmed leaves of the *mishquipanga* plant, and bound between two boards of the sacred *culebra caspi*, a very fine-grained wood marked with snake-like mottling.

No translation from the Campa (which has no written language) to the Spanish had been attempted; instead, strings of drawings ran in columns up and down the pages. A drawing of Pawa, the Man of Gold, walking on the surface of a *cocha* was meant to convey the story of Christ walking upon the waters. These pre-Stone-Age Bibles were the most fascinating books I had ever seen (though the Panchen Lama, spiritual ruler of Tibet, had once shown me in Kumbum some original illuminated manuscripts in Pali). They were painted in the beautiful "lost" earth colors of the Andean civilizations, and were as artistic as Egyptian figures.

After considerable thought, for at one time I was familiar with the various code systems used in espionage, ciphers and cryptographs, I got a workable idea for translating the Bible into spoken and written Spanish. I took José's wonderful Bible and added to it a system of translation comprehensive to the Campa mind which (as previously pointed out) visualizes pictures and is exceedingly swift and retentive. In front of the picture of the Inca-like Christ, I now drew before the watchful eyes of José , who at first was anything but delighted at my boldness, a picture of a crane, whose Campa name is *Chris*. Right after it on the same line I placed a turtle whose Campa name is *To*, followed by Latin letters of the Spanish equivalent *Chris-to* (Christ). This, coupled with the pictures already in his Bible, would give José an ideographic and phonetic Bible in spoken and written Spanish. Also, the end drawing would convey its true meaning. For the first time his Bible was comprehensible in both spoken and written languages.

Jorge, too, was delighted, and enthusiastic, saying that by this system the government could translate various other books for the use of the illiterate savage Indian tribes and nations, and teach them to *write* and *speak* Spanish.

"The political consequences are apparent!" he shouted on a somewhat (for me) disappointing note, with no thought to the cultural implications.

José's new Bible:

The ancient Peruvians of the Cordilleras had no system of writing or numeration. They used *quipus* to record events, knotted pieces of string or leather varying in length and colors: if the thread was black and knotted—the knots corresponded to so many nights; if white, to days; thus now, and for the first time, the Campas had (theoretically) a written language. And no people are greater than the information contained in their books. The significant fact was that not only could the Campas benefit, but also every illiterate people throughout the whole world. Publishers could open a new field here, for all illiterate peoples are fascinated with the written word when illustrated and concerning themselves, their own costumes, etc. In Turkestan, I once saw a Sart merchant pay $1,000 (silver *what* = $1 U.S.) to a Tungan for a $1 copy of the Koran printed in Arabic in England. The Campas love books, and today they have only guns, machetes and *aguardiente*. Whenever I brought out my almanac, it drew Indians like flies, for they were more fascinated with this book than even with the shotgun, compass, or watch. They are not fools, as I was learning, and understood that knowledge would help them to better lives.

We lolled under the palm-leaf shelters making needed repairs on our tattered clothing, sewing on buttons carved from the ivory *tagua* nut, and closing torn places. Our needles were Indian, the palm "elfin darts," thread was obtained by pulling strands out of a hunk of sinew which Black Hawk carried in his monkey skin bag.

At this work I nearly suffocated from the heat. Further, thousands of insects settled on us, and a strange panic, a suppressed fear of their hovering eternally with never a minute of respite from their stings, came to me then and was never entirely to leave me for the next six months on our way to El Dorado.

Jorge and I scrubbed with sand in the river, washed our clothing, spreading it out on the stove-hot boulders where it soon dried. When José asked why we didn't get rid of our hot and itchy beards, we answered that we had lost our razors. He went into the jungle and soon returned with a greenish paste, which he smeared on Jorge's face. A few minutes later he told him to wash it off. When Jorge came back from the river, he was clean-shaven as a matinee idol. The Indians use this paste to remove every hair on their bodies except that of the scalp. I was not long in following Jorge's example.

We towed our raft from its hiding place, and screened by some tall rushes, tore it apart. From the eight balsa timbers, together with four other logs cut from the jungle, we constructed two rafts of six logs each. Should we lose one raft, we would still have a second one to fall back upon. We found no *palo de balsa*, but used logs of *cetico*, a lightweight wood used by the Campas for fishing rafts. It contained a high percentage of cellulose and could be an important source of wealth. The

Indians say its seeds are sown widely throughout the jungle in the droppings of a certain bat that feeds on *cetico.*

The two Indians were too badly off to help us much, and when the job was finished, we hid the rafts on our north bank and got back under the palm coverings. I prepared "coffee" from the charred palm kernels in the battered Indian clay pot we had found on the *playa.* As I was bending over the coals, the mumbling prayers from the Indians' lean-to ceased so suddenly that I glanced up in alarm. Three horse-haired *bravos* in purple and red paint, with their scalps done up in hawk feathers, were running out of the bamboo thicket. They were armed with bows and arrows, and one of them had a musket. A couple of silent dogs bounded along at their heels, while farther behind in the shade squatted a bevy of women and children.

I got up and walked toward them with empty hands, for they were startled, not having seen us till then. I was almost up to them before they lowered their weapons. I beckoned to the savages and led them back into camp where they lost no time feeling around in the dead coals for yuca. Much to their surprise there were none, and José told them we wanted to barter for food. Huge smiles crawled over their painted faces. They too had nothing. I suggested we join forces and try for a few fish. A pair of *garcettas* were hovering and screaming over the river, indicating that a run of fish was in progress.

Since we had that morning broken all but a single reed spear, and had no floatable arrows suitable for fishing, we borrowed some from these people. Their faces being banded in purple and red, I realized now this was the mark for Indians fishing-bound. Had I been alert, I would have noticed before that their scalplock feathers were those of fish-hawks. We spent an hour in the rapids, where the Campas indicated fish by shouting "*shima!*" whenever they spotted one. Fish were moving upstream by the school, and at places where the waters ran shallow, very considerately exposed their dorsal fins as targets. Soon we had impaled and landed thirty-two large dark-scaled fish, whose Spanish name Jorge said was *punuysique.* These together with the swan were soon broiling over the rebuilt fire. Unless smoked, nothing is ever saved for a rainy day, for flesh soon spoils in such heat. That is why the Indian gorges one day and goes hungry the next. His is a hand-to-mouth existence, unless he binds himself to a *chacara.*

The Indians wouldn't talk while they were busy stuffing themselves, and they ate prodigious amounts. Afterwards we squatted around the coals and threw on certain leafy limbs whose smoke drove off the insects. These Indians were on their way to a great festival. They explained that annually, at the end of the rainy season, the Campas hold war maneuvers and dueling games all over their country. The *patrónes* estimate the war and war game casualties total at least ten percent (dead) of the entire tribe annually.

A repellent old woman waddled over, and after shaking a calabash rattle around us to scare off any devils, packed off half our campfire to make one of her own back in the thicket. About this time the three braves put their hands into their greasy monkey-skin bags and took out hunting feathers (called *chivangue*) and exchanged them for the fish-hawk feathers in their scalplocks. They shouted incantations to the hunting gods and after picking up their long-bows and some hardwood arrows, together with the flintlock, invited us to join them in a hunt. Black Hawk and José didn't like this idea at all, and while they stayed behind to watch camp and the rafts, Jorge and I went along with the Indians.

About four hundred yards downriver they showed us where they had very cleverly hidden a dugout canoe in a deep ditch covered over with dirt and planted with ferns. This they excavated and dunked in the river to clean it off. Two of the hunters were ferried across, and followed by their *garapato*-infested dogs, turned into the jungle on the south bank. The canoe then returned. Pongee, the oldest brave, with a face like a polished mahogany knot, took Jorge and me in his dugout. He worked his long paddle soundlessly and deftly, like the tail of a fish, so that we lost no way in the current. The river was a hundred yards wide at this point, and in its middle we waited for an hour under a boiling sun. Once in a while, a tiny green and white kingfisher, not much bigger than a thimble, would strike the water. He seemed to have trouble finding a fish small enough, for each time he would fly into a tree and squeal angrily.

"What are we hunting?" I asked the Indian.

"*Maniro*," he whispered, which I knew was the red deer, called *venado* by the Peruvians. Deer would be bedded down in this midday heat.

On the south bank opposite, a small tributary opened its narrow mouth into the Perené. The waters were red and the Indians said no fish lived in it; therefore it is likely to have been poisoned by a copper deposit somewhere higher up. Such rivers are known as "starvation rivers." Scores of unknown, unmapped, and unexplored feeders had already been marked on my map in dotted lines, some having vivid colors—white, yellow, black, green, red—depending no doubt on the geology and the vegetation of the regions through which they meander. At this particular point on the Perené, the usual sand and gravel had been replaced by dykes consisting of great blocks of fragmented sedimentary stones.

Suddenly farther up the small red river we could hear the dogs barking. They were on a line about five hundred yards back in the jungle, and we could easily follow their swift and erratic course as it slowly bent in toward us. From the tone of the dogs' voices, game had been jumped. In five minutes they were working very close, weaving in and out of the massive thicket.

Suddenly, *without warning of any kind,* and straight off the ten-foot-high bank, sprang a tremendous jaguar, its build very heavy and ponderous, weighing certainly not less than 350 pounds.

"*Manite!*" screamed the Indian, all his caution gone.

And it really was! The Perené jaguar is three times the size of the African leopard, and is as large as the normal African lion or the Asiatic tiger; and it can be just as dangerous as these other cats.[1]

As the massive yellowish black-rosetted beast struck the water, it sank. Its broad head soon reappeared, turning squarely toward us. I had a slight tremor inside, for I am not one to pooh-pooh a tiger! Once in Yucatán, in broad daylight, I saw an unprovoked attack by a jaguar, and a man was killed in the flash of an eye. In China on two different occasions, I had seen a total of four men die in tiger charges. A shotgun, loaded with a charge of deer-pellets (0-0 buckshot), is no weapon to face a jaguar!

Pongee was moving the dugout forward now (forward, of all directions!) and the tiger spotted us kneeling in the canoe some fifty feet away. Digging in his paddle the crazy Indian shot us forward, while I cocked the old shotgun and prayed. When we were eight feet off, the cat suddenly changed course and came straight for us. I threw the gun to my shoulder and fired.

---

1. The *tigre* (tiger) is called *otoronongo* by the *caucheros,* who greatly fear it; its Latin name is *Felis onca.*

The tiger disappeared in a mass of blood, but reappeared alongside, for our momentum had carried the dugout over the spot. Its paw, spread with claws as wide as a man's two hands, ripped a chunk out of the gunwale of the canoe as it tried to get aboard—and then the beast's tremendous weight flipped the canoe completely over!

In that split second we were splashing about in the river with a wounded tiger in our midst. Not only that—its blood would soon draw the *pañas*. I grabbed the fool Indian by his hair as he floated past (in one hand he still clutched his bow and several arrows) and started swimming for the north bank on the far opposite side, Jorge following. The jaguar turned and struck out now for the same near bank from which it had sprung. The three of us were swept downstream for three hundred yards before I felt shallow bottom with my feet. Puffing from our exertions, Jorge and I managed to crawl up a steep gravel bar.

Taking turns at pumping water out of the Indian's lungs, we soon had him sitting up and blinking, though frankly, Jorge was all for dumping him back in again. We could see the dugout caught between two rocks some four hundred yards downstream. We waded down to it. In spite of the tearing water around our shoulders, we finally succeeded in getting the dugout righted and emptied, and after dragging it back to the spit, climbed in and headed upstream. Driftwood poles picked up along the bar supplied the motive power. We located the spot where we had foundered, which I had noted was between a rock and a certain palm, each located on opposite banks. Here Jorge and I began diving desperately. On the fifth try, in moving water at least fifteen feet deep, Jorge came up grinning, holding the shotgun by its barrel!

The dugout was so small it was a terrific job to get aboard. The only way was to climb over the stern, for by attempting to come over the side we nearly capsized it again. We were no sooner safely in when we heard a stick crack just above our heads on the same south bank from which the jaguar had sprung. To our amazement we now saw an antlered red deer streaking out of the jungle; it too leapt off the ten-foot bank and struck the river with a splash. Its head rose and it began swimming across to the other side. Pongee let the dugout drift, which corresponded to the rate of drift of the animal. When the quarry had reached midstream, he began poling furiously until we shot alongside.

The Indian now threw his pole down, strung his bow with a red arrow (painted for easier finding in the bush), for though the barrel of our gun was loaded, it was wet and useless. At a twenty-foot range, the Indian shot just under water, hitting the buck high up in the neck. Surprisingly, the buck still continued to swim strongly. The Indian only grinned when I made motions to shoot again, as I was afraid of losing it. We continued drifting right along with the deer. At last the *pañas* got to it, and struggling greatly the buck left the river to bound into the jungle on the same south side from which the dogs had raised it. This did not seem to disturb Pongee, though by now I was boiling with fury inside.

The Indian leaned on his pole, and with a mighty shove drove the dugout into the mud of a high spit curving off the south bank.

"*Shetaki!*" he grinned, pointing to the buck's tracks, which were already filling with water. At his heels—and in spite of a wounded tiger lying somewhere close by—we tracked out our quarry where it lay deep in a thicket of fan cane, about 300 yards inland. Pongee explained to José , who had left camp and crossed the river on hearing the shotgun's blast, that the deer had not died from the arrow striking the neck, but from the snake venom in which the family dipped their arrowheads.

"Snake poison!" I cried in disgust. "Then we can't eat the meat."

But José pointed out that the Indian was withdrawing the arrow, and with his knife cutting the flesh away, so that when he finished a hole some four inches in diameter went right through the neck. "Well, it can't poison us very much," decided Jorge.

Since the carcass was covered with ticks, we butchered the buck on the spot, and packed the meat back to the dugout. José , who had crossed the river below in the rapids, now got aboard with us. Later in camp (Pongee having returned for them), the other two braves and their panting dogs joined us, carrying the skin of the jaguar! They told how they had intercepted and speared the wounded tiger while it was still on the ground. Cornered, it had made no move to take to the trees. I traded them out of the skin but for no consideration could they be parted from the teeth. With holes drilled in them and strung on a neck-lace, the jaguar's teeth would be powerful hunting medicine.

Oddly enough, the Indians gave us every scrap of the strong-smelling venison. The reason was obvious. The Indians do not know how to remove the musk glands. Actually, however, no Campa eats veni-son, as it might be a *brujo* in a favorite animal disguise. This taboo is called *kandakandedro* (law).

Jorge sighed, "What a life we lead! First you write a Bible, then we are nearly killed by a tiger."

After Pongee and his friends departed that evening, on their way to the war games, we ate the liver and smoked the venison by impaling pieces on stakes around a smudge fire. Hardwood smoke is the best since it gives a wonderful flavor. In such hot weather there was no other way to preserve the meat, and so we had to risk the smoke being seen or smelled out. We set guard, each standing two-hour watches till dawn. Nothing appeared but the crocodiles.

Then we loaded up and with two men on each of the new rafts, we paddled out to the swiftest part of the current. José and Black Hawk took firm seats in the middle, while (at the bows) Jorge and I wielded the paddles. Soon we were smashing side by side down through the cataract—a vicious and blustery place. Fortunately, the two balsas proved to be strongly pinioned and lashed; they pitched, rising and falling on the yellow flood, slamming hard but always rising to the surface intact. The jungled hills seemed filled with spray and flying water. Again we were eating up the miles. At the very bottom of the reverberating gorge, we skidded along the high right side of a broad whirlpool, and only by the hardest kind of paddling did we manage to get clear of it, and over its bulging lip and out into the flowing current once more....

ᕙ IX. ᕗ

Our Lord Be Praised

ECAUSE of hardship, exposure and lack of sufficient food, we were becoming surprisingly weak. Yet three times that afternoon we slashed our way through a very dense jungle of purple-flowering *puva* trees, crawling on hands and knees around short but cataclysmic falls of from half a mile to a mile in length. Three times the rafts were turned loose by the two Indians and run through the torrents empty, while Jorge and I recovered the wreckage at the bottom. The swimming was dangerous in such fast rough water. We lost four logs of the twelve by this method, and even those eight recovered were now so waterlogged that they barely held our weight. Still, we dared not risk making up a single raft again, though its stability, as against the four log rafts, would certainly have been greater in rough waters.

At another wild place, we let the rafts down slowly on vines. For a mile we climbed around massive marginal rocks, wading in the shallower places up to our chins. This was necessary, in spite of danger from possible lurking *paña*, for we feared to let them go empty, or to ride them through, as there was no gathering pool at the bottom of this fall. Had we done so, they would certainly have broken up and been swept away, leaving us stranded. All that day the mists were spinning off that stretch of the river, and *puma garzas*, small brown herons, shrilly cried

132

their fishing tally. But in most places the banks were not nearly so high, and we knew we were almost at the bottom of the Andean slope.

At the last of the falls, during a half-mile portage, the one-armed Black Hawk, while hopelessly pursuing a band of friar monkeys with a stone in his right hand, spied a *lagarto*, or cayman. The crocodile slept about six feet down in the bottom of a clear pool. We had eaten the last of the deer *xarque*, most of which had been washed overboard, and were wondering if this particular reptile meat would help stave off hunger that night.

The Campas eat a certain green crocodile called *jacaré tinga*. These are carnivorous reptiles and yet eat any rotten refuse. Some were said to be poisonous owing to certain worms in their flesh. The Peruvians will not eat the two species which they recognize as the dangerous *lagarto negro* (black), and the smaller *lagarto blanco* (white).

Finished with the job of collecting the rafts' logs and pounding in the wooden spikes with rocks once more, we wearily crawled back through the flowering jungle to the pool containing the *lagarto*. Reaching the shore of Black Hawk's pool, some hundred feet long by fifty wide, I saw that the crocodile was a smallish green-brown one, not more than twelve feet in length, and weighing perhaps 300 pounds. But even so—after it was recognized as a "black"—José and Black Hawk would not wade in and pull it out on the beach, where I could crush its head with a boulder. Even if we should be able to chase it out in the open, I dared not fire the shotgun, for Indian smokes were all around, rising above the tree tops.

"Señor—*patróne*...be reasonable. It's murder. It's murder!" José cried out above the noise of the cataract to the north. Nevertheless, Jorge waved the *mansos* (no longer slaves) aside and cut a long flexible liana, while I, also innocent of dallying with *lagarto negro*, cut down a sapling. Soon we had contrived a lasso on the end of my forked pole—some seven feet long. Now for snaking out our dinner, worms or no worms. I could already smell its tail baking in a bed of coals.

Thinking to stir the croc up a bit so that I could slip the noose over its head, I approached waist-deep in the pool. When I was within some eight feet, and it still hadn't moved, I poked the thing in the ribs wondering if perhaps it were dead. Jorge following just behind had been quite sure that the thing had died at the bottom of the pool, for it did not appear to be breathing. Suddenly the whole pool blew up in my face, with an expenditure of energy comparable to that in a five-pound charge of TNT. A column of water shot into the air, and the crocodile leapt clean out of the pool. I fell backwards from sheer shock at seeing at least a million three-inch teeth gleaming in the sunlight. Jorge dragged me clear of the water.

'The bastard's alive,' I was finally able to remark, and probably unnecessarily. "*Madre de Dios!*" exclaimed Jorge, "That bull *lagarto's* alive all right."

"Well—it's your turn," I suggested, handing him the pole.

In the meanwhile the crocodile had squirmed back into the pool, and now was lifting his flat and altogether ugly head out of the water for a survey of the situation. What he saw was that Jorge and I now blocked his way to the main river, a very foolish notion on our part. "*Muy peligroso*—dangerous?" I enquired of José, just to be sure.

"*Si, si! Muy peligroso!*" The fool Indian was laughing so hard I thought he would fall off the boulder on which he had perched himself.

Since Jorge hadn't availed himself of the opportunity for taking over the pole and its vine lasso, I waded in a bit more cautiously this time, holding the pole out as a fender, just in case. I still hoped, somewhat vaguely it is true, to drop the noose over the jaws and snake it out bodily.

Just in front was the head, its jaws wide open, the mouth a great reptilian maw of a cotton whiteness, all lined with long curved teeth. Slowly I approached.

"Now! Now! Drop the noose over him," yelled Jorge from the shore "Don't wait. Oh!—*Sacramento!*"

"Shut up before you scare him," I yelped back, "Who in hell is catching this *lagarto*?"

José and Black Hawk started a broken record of: "*Muerte! Muerte! Muerte!*"

Now *muerte* means "death," and I feared they were right; further, it was my death they were referring to, and not the crocodile's, but there was no retreating before their horrified gaze. I thought of that tail broiling in the coals, and took hold of myself. Suddenly the beast lunged forward with a horrible hiss. I retreated backwards as fast as I could make it through the deep water. At the last instant it ducked its head under the surface, and lashing the pond into foam, came like a torpedo straight for me. The jaws surfaced where I had been, and the reptile tossed its great head into the air with a roar.

That gave me my chance, and I dropped the noose down over the beastly head. The crocodile spun on its tail and churned its way across the pool, while I hung on to the other end of the pole. The lashing tail all but jarred my head loose from its moorings. Instead of tugging like a small crocodile it felt more like the lunging of a wild horse, and I was dragged clear across the pool and out the other side, where I finally regained my footing. And now it began running on its stumpy legs, this time over land, and heading around the end of the pool for the river itself. I lost my footing and the thing was presently dragging me over boulders and old drift logs.

"Head him off!" I finally managed to shout at Jorge, who seemed convulsed. "Hurry up!"

At this, Jorge was thrown into an even greater spasm. José, however, stirred himself and ran toward me, and forgetting his shoulder heaved at the *lagarto's* head a rock, which, due to the armor plate, didn't faze it a bit. Bellowing, the reptile swept around in a backlash—and all those misguided authors over the centuries who have been calling these saurians "sluggish" should have been there on the end of that rope! It fouled the line on a boulder, and squirmed back for the pond while I still tried to bring it to a halt. By this time the mud in the bottom had riled up, and the bull slid into deep water, hiding among the larger stones. The noose was still around the bloated neck, still fastened to the pole, which I released to save myself from drowning.

Jorge at this time seemed to recover from whatever ailed him, and jumping in, laid hold of the pole which was describing a circle in the air. With shouts to José for help, he began pulling the crocodile out of the pond. Its green slimy head finally appeared at the water's edge. Here it opened its jaws a yard wide, revealing rows of yellow-white teeth, and made a loud hissing noise, simultaneously rushing forward on its claw-armed feet. Jorge dropped the pole and let out a grunt. Once again the beast headed for the river, but this time I was ready. As the bull opened its jaws to snap off a leg, I was able to ram a pole down its gullet. At this parry the beast changed its mind and headed back for the pool. Seizing the end of the pole, I somehow lifted the crocodile half off the ground in my desperation, and dragged it twenty feet back from the water.

"Get the shotgun!" I croaked, forgetting all about the Indians.

At this point the noose broke, and as Jorge was standing in the way of escape back to the pool, the saurian contented itself with making short charges at us, which we eluded only by some exceptionally fast foot work. José came sneaking up with the shotgun, which he handed to me. But it was no use now; after that wonderful fight and all that pluck, only one little crocodile against two men, I just didn't have the heart. I aimed three times right between its eyes, as the bull danced back and forth sideways, hissing and bellowing, puffing itself up to a third more than its normal size, but each time I had to lower the gun.

"Oh, to hell with it!" I finally said.

I took the little Leica from its pouch in the money belt, snapped a few photographs, then carefully backed away and we waded down the river to join our rafts below; the black *lagarto* believing he had won the fray, was last seen still thrashing around the rocky promontory, now stubbornly refusing to take either to the pool or to the river. That night we went hungry.

And hungry though we certainly were on that stinking mud bar hidden by palms, I was not sorry; for to me the crocodile—with the possible exception of man—is the most fascinating of all living creatures. His family tree goes back to the origin of reptiles more than 300,000,000 years ago. Man is an offshoot from the same tree. Therefore, as I explained to Jorge who was both shocked and amused, eating that crocodile would not be a question of cannibalism, but only a matter of degree as to what constitutes cannibalism. Jorge thought I was suffering a heat stroke, and so I explained.[1]

---

1. Plato stated in effect that man was a chicken-like biped without feathers. The ancient Greek philosopher was closer to the truth than perhaps even he suspected and certainly all mankind after him till recent years. Jorge Mendoza, the hunter, and Leonard Clark, the explorer (and our two Campa friends), were the end products of modern man who descended from Cro-Magnon whose ancestors were primates evolved from primitive mammals. Both the crocodile and these mammals probably (the paleontologists are not in exact agreement) descended through different groups from earlier reptiles The possible blood link between crocodile and man follows in logical order from the Age of Reptiles downward. From *Rhynchocephalia* descended those living crocodilians I had seen in the Ganges of India chewing on human corpses from Holy Benares. These are the gavials, and their ancestors (closer to the family tree of man) were fifty feet long; their bones are seen in Pliocene strata. From the ancestors of this rather bloodthirsty branch, *Rhynchocephalia*, or an even earlier forebearer,

Next morning at daybreak we floated serenely down the river—and nearly starved. Hours later, I was only able to lure two buzzards close enough to shoot. But they smelled so bad we could not eat them. By midday, we came upon a flock of *pava*, the great black turkey known as *Penelope superciliaris*. I shot one but it fell into the water and a crocodile got it. We continued down the river. We must have logged a hundred and fifty miles since Sutsiki. Gradually we became aware of a distant roaring of tumbling waters, and wondered what it might be—a high fall in the Perené, or a new river...?

Then it dawned on me; we were already half-way down the Gran Pajonal—after seven dangerous labor-packed days we had actually reached the mouth of the Rio Ene!

Somewhere, close by, must be Padre Antony.

Soon we heard a drum beating to the south on the right bank about a quarter of a mile ahead. José cocked his ears, and deciphering the code, spoke: "The drum says 'A feast for the Serpent. A feast for the Serpent.'"

A clearing, covered over with bamboos, appeared through the trees. According to my map, as indicated in gigantic print, this was CUPIROPATA.

---

came the toothed lizard-bird, *Archaeopteryx*, the ancestor of all birds, who laid eggs like reptiles. *Theromorph*, the Mesozoic ancestor of the mammals was followed by *Dicynodons*—beaked but with a primitive shoulder blade—an egg-laying reptile mammal, was followed by *Tritylodon* (Three-knobbed Teeth), who gave birth to small mammals (teeth with tubercles) who suckled their young and never laid eggs; and thence evolved *Cynodonts* during Lower Jurassic times, who dropped reptilian scales and took on a plastic-like skin with hair. *Cynodonts'* blood warmed a bit, since being carnivorous it required great activity for catching food. With all this activity, *Cynodonts* evolved out of its reptilian three-chambered heart the four-chambered one of the mammal. And so eventually from a common ancestor with the crocodiles, the mammals produced the primates...and those two men who wished heartily that night they had the old scales back (the bugs were bad)—those two reptiles with a new soul and hearts so soft they could not even kill a dear old cousin for food and so were starving. Jorge thought, that in that case, it was a downward spiral of devolution (for man) rather than an upward spiral of evolution which must end in God or nothing... Curious idea, that.

It took us a long time to beach the rafts, for we were weak from semi-starvation. We walked two hundred yards inland down a narrow sandy trail. I realized then what the Perené's conquest had cost us: the lives of four men; Black Hawk's broken arm and José's wound; we were ragged beyond belief, practically emptyhanded, and as wild-eyed and lean as scavengers.

Suddenly in the trail we were intercepted by a tall thin priest in a brown homespun cowled robe bound at the waist by a knotted white rope. This could only be Padre Antony, a Peruvian, the most famous missionary of all the upper Amazon tributaries, the twentieth-century Doctor Livingstone of the whole wild region.

"I have been expecting you," casually remarked the smiling priest. His expression changed as he took us in. "Follow me to my humble house, and rest where it is cool. I must feed you immediately."

"Padre Antony, how could you expect us? How did you know of us?" asked Jorge.

"My sons, the Campas' signal horns have been telling a strange story for many days. But I expected slave buyers. And you have come down from the heights of the Cordillera. My congratulations, señores! All of you are safe for the night. Our Lord be praised...."

℃ **X.** ℃

The Bellbird

E limped along at the Padre's sandal-clad heels. Long pointed shadows cast from the Andean peaks, lying unseen at our right, began sliding swiftly across the Amazon Valley. Once while resting Padre Antony told us that his own route to 'Opata had been from the Cordillera down the Pangoa River, which comes in from the south. We passed an unfinished brick church, a very small one, which the priest told us he had been trying to raise for two decades. Part of it was charred and blackened by smoke, the result of Indian raids. A couple of hundred feet in front of this ruin, standing like gigantic birdhouses on high mahogany stilts, were two immense cane and thatch longhouses. On one of these was a wooden cross.

A group of Indian girls stood in the compound. They had been rescued by Antony and were now in training as nurses. Pressing through a crowd of whooping brown-skinned *bravos*, we climbed a ladder and entered the larger of the two houses. Here a surprise awaited us. We were presented to five whitely starched Peruvian nuns. The women recently had descended the Pangoa, which lies west of the Ene. There was Madre Carmel, very ancient, wrinkled and jovial; Sister Manuela, who sat like a Buddha behind thick glasses; Sister Angelito, who was young and wonderfully beautiful; Sister Ignacia, businesslike and brusque; Sister Teresa, a shy calm little woman who only the week before had seized a stick and driven off a jaguar after it had killed the only milk cow in east Peru! The nuns greeted us with joy and immediately made us feel welcome.

We were invited to sit in wonderfully comfortable cane chairs on a wide bamboo veranda overlooking the endless Amazon country stretching eastward. The house was on the edge of a low bench, and our elevation, determined by my watch-sized aneroid barometer, was now only 1,200 feet above sea level; eastward lay a plain of solid jungle, broken only by gigantic black, yellow, and white coiling rivers and sun-glazed yellow swamps, stretching out over the horizon 2,600 miles to the Atlantic Ocean. Only a thin blue mist rose out of that continental basin of bush, and wisps of its fog sucked up by the sun danced in a dazzling sky of reddish copper. A hundred yards from the porch flowed the Rio Pangoa, some 300 feet wide and very yellow. Under the fat indigo clouds of evening, this river clutched at the silken pendant of the thundering Perené, some 400 yards to the north.

The Ene, I saw to my surprise, was marked wrongly on the maps. It lay still some miles farther east. We gazed with something like awe for a hundred miles out over a vast primeval expanse of undulating jungled hills and flats woven into the long green skirt of the Andean Cordillera, and into the foggy-blue sarcophagus of the unexplored upper Amazon country. Somehow through this terrible place, we must make our way. Great efforts and great dangers lay ahead and for these we must rest at least for a night or two and gather our strength. Reprovisioned, we must hurry on, for if delayed, the fall rainy season would prevent our ascent of the Marañón after we had reached Iquitos. Except for the River Pangoa, which Padre Antony had explored, the country about lay unknown. Even this priest, the savant of the western Amazon, who had labored to erect this little mission for twenty-five long and brutal years, had never entered any of the region off the main rivers.

I would not have been surprised that evening to see pterodactyls winging up out of those swampy desert-jungles. It was a breathtaking sight. Behind us crouched a row of volcanoes, flaming red roses against a steely sky, with the diamond-bright Southern Cross standing overhead. Actually, these "volcanoes" were probably fires started by the Indians to make garden clearings.

An Indian woman in a Mother Hubbard brought a kerosene lamp which she placed on the rough-hewn table. Mother Carmel, playing hostess, industriously wound up an ancient and very rusty Victrola. A rare little monkey called by the Quechua name of *pichioco* crawled up my leg and perched in my lap. The racket of green and yellow parrots roosting in the small orange grove below came up to us. And there was the clinking of cockroaches against the lamp; the splash of cormorants striking the river; and then the measured haunting evening song of the bellbird. Against this screen of woven sounds, there suddenly wheezed forth a Vienna waltz, strangely jarring in that wild setting where nature moved dominant, and always perfect.

Jorge fed the cuckoo bird, and got it to fight with the *pichioco*, and then jovially settled down to Chinese checkers with the sisters. Padre Antony's tonsured head shone in the lamplight; he was thin and hard, lithe at sixty. He smiled mildly when I observed, "Father, you have a second California and Florida, right here!"

In the clearing extending before us to the river's bank the orange trees were perpetually in bloom, exuding an aroma of almost overwhelming sweetness. Gardens containing rows of tobacco plants, alligator pears, limes, mangos, bananas, papayas, sugarcane, hedges of wild pineapple, and a score of other exotic fruits. There were also wavy plantings of lettuce, zigzagging lines of tomatoes, little hillocks of corn—the first we had seen—and groves of yuca.

"Yes, it is gratifying," Father Antony said somewhat grimly. "It represents a quarter of a century of work. But do you in the United States have savages, snakes, diseases, insects, tigers, and all the rest to contend with?"

Time after time 'Opata, which was the abbreviated name used here, had been burned to the ground by the Campas, its priests murdered, their hearts torn out of their chests and offered to the mysterious Snake Gods. Rebuilding his mission again and again, Padre Antony had become famous even beyond the Andean barrier. A prince of the Church had told me he bore a charmed life. Each time after being burned out, the priest had raised the great palm houses with his own hands. The last instance was only a few years before. Both houses were a hundred feet long, fifty wide. They were roofed with small white balsa poles lashed neatly with split *nucño pichana* fibers and attached to golden *huasai* fronds some fifty feet from bamboo floor to central ridgepole. They were, indeed, jungle palaces. In a small wing of the church was an organ. This the Padre had brought down the dangerous Pangoa in a dugout. And before that, the organ had been carried over mountain trails in places 18,000 feet above sea level!

He was now trying to cut a trail by machete overland from 'Opata to Atalaya on the Alto Ucayali, the head of Iquitos navigation which lay a bit over a hundred miles east of us. If successful, he would automatically open up 300,000 square miles of these rich foothills to colonists from Pucalpa and Iquitos. But—here he sighed—as fast as the *patrónes* came in on the upper Ucayali and enslaved the Campas, just so fast were they murdered and their houses burned out.

To the strains of Hoffmann's "Vienna Waltz," Sister Manuela announced dinner. After grace had been spoken by me, and I had to skip lively, we were apologetically served beef consommé, fricasseed chicken heaped on a mountain of rice, a salad of lettuce and tomatoes with a tart vinegar-wine dressing, yuca light as *tinamou* (a local quail) feathers, and mashed potatoes souffléd with wild pigeon eggs; then came baked fish, treated with wild limes, roast venison, tiny red bananas, powdered milk, orange juice, followed by a richly satisfying and elegant-smelling black coffee demitasse.

All this bounty, except for the powdered milk, had been produced at the mission and was in sharp contrast to the food eaten by other settlers in the jungle. The whole Amazon Valley of over 4,000,000 square miles is a starvation region. 'Opata lives better because its missionaries work and experiment, while the *patrónes* dream only of making a quick fortune so that they can scramble back to Lima. With the exception of perhaps a score of families, the Amazonic region east of the Cordillera is considered a grab bag, and not fit for a permanent home. I often soberly wondered what our own pioneering ancestors could have made of this wild land: perhaps little more than these hardy descendants of the old Spaniards. Nor is there a single American pioneering in that entire three thousand miles of jungle!

By midnight Jorge and I were dozing in our chairs, and smoking new corncob pipes (for the Padre grew excellent tobacco). Finally we were given tallow candles and led off to bed. Our beds had white mosquito nets. They were real wooden bunks made by Padre Antony, and there were wonderful mattresses of flour sacks sewn together like bags and stuffed with clean grass.

The last sounds we heard were the kindly voices of Padre Antony and eighty-year-old Madre Carmel, wishing us good night. But that night was not such a one of quiet bliss and relaxation from our eternal vigilance as I had anticipated. Habits acquired on the Perené were not easily given up. A *shingirotse* was going on out in the jungle. The air was full of pounding drums and wild yelling, and I could visualize the painted, drunken savages dancing. I got up and walked to the veranda. Already, long before dawn, *huangana* boars were rooting noisily in the yuca patch nearby. Overhead the blue-black sky was split by bolts of Cordillera lightning and the horizon flashed white with tropical electric displays.

Hours later in a flaming orange dawn I still sat entranced on that veranda, feeling a cool breeze from the unseen peaks some two hundred miles away at my back. I gazed out over the sparkling cliffs of the Cerro de la Sal—a sheer wall of salt facing the high plateau of the Gran Pajonal. It is the belief of the jungle-wise *patrónes* of the Ucayali, that this is the most savage region on earth today. And having come down through much of it, I could well believe them.

Already in the early daylight, *mansos* dressed in straw hats and with pants rolled above the knee, gathered purple grapes for the sacramental wine. Padre Antony approached with long strides, flaying his brown robe with the knotted rope in order to remove the dust, for obviously he had already been digging.

Though sixty, the missionary looked like a man of forty. The priest explained he had just dug a grave. A woman had been killed in the night, her body dragged off into the brush, where it had been partly eaten. The villain was the same tiger which had killed the cow. This tiger no longer hunted wild game because it was suffering from an old spear wound and so would always be a man-eater.

"How terrible!"

"Yes," he agreed mildly, "but it is all part of this jungle life. Last week a *zúngaro tigre* (tiger fish) dragged a boy from his canoe. His fishline had been wrapped around his wrist. The day after, a *yuca maman* (boa) swallowed our only sow. Such little things. Always we must watch. Recently three men have been killed by savages. And in the last months five others of our mission men have been killed and eaten by a single tiger roaming this region."

"Perhaps the same tiger as the one last night?"

"No, another—a three-legged one. It makes a circuit here every, seven or eight days."

Two months before, a man had died in this very clearing from loss of blood due to a night attack by vampire bats. Three children had also been lost to these bats.

I brought the Padre inside the sleeping room, where Jorge was stirring, and got out my map. The maps of Peru were obviously all wrong for this region, and so Antony and I spent an hour sketching in the relative positions of the mouths of the Pangoa, the Tambo, the Ene (which is the lower extension of the Apurímac rising south of Cuzco), the Perené, and several tributaries which I had noted entering the Perené on both banks. The larger of these Perené tributaries come in on the right, or south bank, and from west to east are the Riachuelo, Quimarini and Ipoqui. The Padre was very anxious to know about these rivers, having never been farther than five miles up the Perené.

"Many times," he confided, "I have tried to go up the Perené. But each time I have been driven back by the Campas. In all, perhaps I have lost twenty men!"

I suddenly turned to the priest, looking him squarely in the eyes, and asked: "Padre Antony, are there slaves on all these rivers?"

"No..." he answered evasively, "none of these wild rivers is inhabited permanently by *patrónes*, only the Ucayali." Nor would he say anything more.

While having breakfast at the house, we met a young Spanish priest whom we had not seen the night before. Later, when he was alone with me, he unveiled such a moving story of human misery as has rarely been told. The wild remote Indians of the Gran Pajonal, the *bravos*, are evidently in a favored position of defensible isolation. Few raiders can ever penetrate that far and live. But the marginal clans of Campas, who live on all sides of the highlands of the Gran Pajonal itself, are being raided every day of every week in the year and taken as slaves. Most of the slaves are women and children. The situation here was the same as at Sutsiki, except that the missionaries did not deal in slavery. This was confined to Campa raiders hired by the Ucayali *patrónes*.

The *patrónes*, some of them immensely rich, fear an uprising among the tribes such as that which wiped out Atalaya. An extensive and elaborate system is in operation for the dispersal of new slaves to the planting and *seringal* areas along the Ucayali, from which escape is all but impossible.

"You see, my friend, slavery cannot be abolished. Our economy is built on it. As long as each tree will produce thirty kilos (about seventy-five pounds) of rubber, there is no hope of relief. Slavery must always be deplored, but must never be abolished. At best we compromise, and make the life of the slaves a little less brutal."

"If this were known in the United States—surely something could be done."

"My poor friend!—The United States buys all our rubber!"

The slave *curacas* sell or barter their human cargo to the *patrónes* at the current rate of one human being for one musket, or if guns are not available, for 100 soles-de-oro, or again, for three machetes.

Often the *curacas* do not deliver the slaves to their *patrónes*, but sell them to the launch operators on the Alto Ucayali, who in their own turn, transport them to still other remote districts in the jungle and sell them to *patrónes* who are desperate for labor. Some *patrónes* estimate that 5 percent of the entire Campa tribe is sold into slavery annually. Basing their figures on an assumption of 30,000, this would mean that 1,500 new slaves come from this one tribe alone.

The present feud with the *patrónes* dates from the first rubber boom during World War I, when the priests tried to stop the uprisings and mass murders. At that time the only Amazon river brought to the notice of the outside world was the Putumayo. Sir Roger Casement reported to the British government that on the Putumayo and its tributaries thousands of Indians had died, due mainly to the brutal driving of the Peruvian *patrónes*, the cruelest of all the Amazon *caucheros*.

After the appearance of British gunboats on the Amazon, it was assumed that slave conditions had changed, and that the men responsible for the atrocities had reformed. They did not reform; and the slave conditions have not changed. Nor was any attempt made to enforce the laws that were passed prohibiting the slave trade. Newspapers in Peru are well aware that the situation in the Amazon area has deteriorated. They have been told that from one tribe alone, 1,500 are sold into slavery. They know the plight of the Indian, but they are afraid to print the story.

It is to be hoped that the free press of the United States will show more courage, for it is our country that buys this slave rubber. Is it any wonder, therefore, that we are so thoroughly hated in the interior regions of South America?

Patrónes claim that the reason the padres and other missionaries are burned out and killed is because they not only deliberately tame the

Indians for subletting to labor recruiters, but also molest the females They quote, as example, 'Opata, Piches and Tapiche, all missions bordering the Gran Pajonal, and all burned out and the inhabitants killed.

A few days before our arrival, two Campa women made their way through the jungle to 'Opata where they took refuge under Padre Antony (a priest admittedly above morals attack). When their Campa pursuers, hired by a *patróne*, demanded them back at the point of rifles, the brave priest entered the church on some pretext or other, and reappeared with a cross in one hand and a carbine in the other. At this they left, very angry, for his reputation is such that few men dare face him in open fight. Also, it is believed that no bullet will kill him, so charmed has been his life in this wildest of all lands. There are forty girls at the mission being trained as nurses. These girls either escaped to this refuge after being condemned by witchmen, or fled from slavers, or from their *patrónes*.

I was to realize later that the result of this grim situation was to make Padre Antony the prime object and the symbol of "evil." The *patrónes* were bringing the full weight of their great power, cunning and wealth against him. From Lima he had already been ordered by government and Church to restrict his activities. No newspapers could print his accounts of the slave conditions. The *patrónes* were launching a fierce and effective psychological attack against the Church as personified by padres such as Antony. All the other priests were knuckling under—all, but the obstinate Antony!

The *patrónes* accused the missionaries of dealing in women for the brothels of Lima and the coastal cities. Again, according to these men, the priests had become the breeding instruments of the new socialistic Aprista party, Moscow-trained and fostered, and were populating the rivers with half-breed *cholos*. There is some flame to be detected in this smoke, as one priest alone (according to information obtained in Iquitos) is the father of fifty-three children. Both reasons, say the *patrónes*, are the real cause of their missions being currently burned out. However, my own investigations lead me to believe that the majority of malpractices against the Indians are started at the bottom by the *patrónes* themselves.

It became more complicated to hear the gossiping priest accuse other missionaries (whose names and denominations we will not list) of supplying labor to the *patrónes* for personal profit. It is a very lucrative, cash-on-the-barrelhead, undercover sort of business, and the temptations must be great to all kinds of adventurous men. So desperate are the *patrónes* for new sources of labor, due to prevailing high commodity prices in the Americas and Europe, that they are bringing in thousands of Aramayas and Quechuas. These highland Indians usually die of lung diseases not long after entering the jungle. (They are systematically dispersed and shuffled so that escape to the mountains is impossible.) Only in the high, rare, cold altitudes of the Andes mountains, where they were born, can these civilized Indians exist. They have no resistance against jungle heat and humidity, diseases and pests; many often die of a broken heart.

Later, Padre Antony explained that it was the witchmen who condemned the children to a horrible death for possessing the evil eye. These *brujos* are part of the organization. They are maintained and used by the *patrónes* who live along the rich banks of the Ucayali.

All this information on the slave practices was absolutely essential, if I was to get through to Iquitos. For without such knowledge I would be unable to deal with the *patrónes*.

Having finished our coffee, little jovial Madre Carmel escorted me around the gardens while Antony went about his chores. We fed the eight hens and the red rooster—so precious that by night they were suspended in cages from the rafters of the house. Sometimes snakes found them even there. Then she showed me the unfinished red-brick church on which Antony had been laboring for so long.

It was a building which he fervently hoped neither the *patrónes'* *curacas* nor the *bravos* could burn down. He had fired the bricks in the earthen kiln. Building a church, Madre Carmel pointed out with a smile, was a sizable job for one man saddled with a hundred duties. I realized without saying so, that the Padre's ambition of completing the structure in his own lifetime would not be accomplished. Still, such men often live to a round century, which would give him yet another forty years of labor.

At the longhouse we were rejoined by Padre Antony who, arm in arm, took me to the nearby Indian encampment. Here, the *shingirotse* was still going on at a great rate. Tom-toms throbbed and Indian yells rent the hot and humid air. Cocaine-drugged women lying nude except for the *manendotse* beads, and *chicha*-drunk befeathered *bravos* reeled around us, devilish *achiote*-painted faces leering stupidly into ours, already in imagination transported to the mystic realm of the Great Snake. I must have revealed my shock, for Antony explained tolerantly that his work was not so simple among these Campas.

"Yes, you are surprised by this sight, señor, but if I put a stop to it, they will decamp within the hour. Our poets notwithstanding, the noble savage is not always noble, any more than the civilized man is always good. Once more 'Opata would be burned to the ground. These people you see are not the wild *bravos* of *la selva*. Strangely, such people do not know moral evil, for they have no knowledge of sin. The ones you see, however, are Indians who have been polluted by *patróne* contact. Perhaps I can save one out of the twenty, and this will be the patient and thankless labor of many years...."

"Is it worth it, Padre?" I asked, "Why not let the Lord Himself work his own inscrutable destinies with them? Surely, when the circle of destiny closes full, all will be known and illuminated, and even the Campa will be saved."

Padre Antony smiled, for he was a man having few flies on him. "Ah, my friend. You are a Campa philosopher; but I am a Christian and cannot wait for God to save them."

He sighed and continued: "I am practical. From these semi-wild natives I am attempting to combat the slave system. Also I teach them it is evil to kill, and to burn, and to enslave; that it is more evil and sinful to practice fratricide, or to sell their women and children to the *patrónes*. Above all, I am attempting to destroy the awful rule of the Snake."

With José, who joined us (he had just finished adding extra logs to the rafts), I stepped aside and then and there bartered for a ten-year-old boy in exchange for my machete, worth thirty soles-de-oro. The parents were fully satisfied. Then turning to the Padre, I said: "You don't seem to be getting very far with your teaching, Padre." Antony smiled wryly and answered patiently: "It takes time, señor *yanqui*, this work isn't accomplished overnight."

I presented the slave to the Church and asked if these, and the girls, were the only Indians 'Opata had. Antony replied that they were all of his *real converts*, as the tamed ones invariably drift on down the Tambo and into the Ucayali where the *patrónes* cleverly promise much *aguardiente* (white rum) and little work. The Church was poor and had no money for clothes or machetes.

It was, I realized, a one-way road for the Indian, any way you looked at it. The State wanted his lands and wanted him for labor. The Indians preferred the status quo, but so had the American bison, no doubt. Once de-savaged for laboring, he could never again return to his wild free *bravo* brethren. For he had forgotten the fierce ways and the strict survival culture of the wilds, had lost the primitive tigerish vitality (which has to be seen to be understood), and so could no longer support or even defend himself. Wild Indians kill tame Indians for the mere fun of it, or else send out children, boys eight or ten years of age, to hunt them down for the experience.

Before us in the encampment the Indians were amusing themselves by putting a white *mantona* (snake) in a cage with a *churro* monkey, reveling in the monkey's terrible screams of fright and its final death agonies some minutes later. Three drunken couples ran off, and José explained after much probing on my part, that the women had become excited over the *bravos* because of it. Antony said it was so—"They are a strange people, señor!" I could well believe it.

Back at the house, José continued to instruct me: "In Lima," he said, "you can buy a fairly good slave for 100 soles ($15)." This compared favorably with the Sutsiki Puna's asking price of $10 each.

When I showed surprise that he should know about slaves so far afield, he answered in a worldly manner, "The price, señor, is high because *gasolina* is so expensive and the *launcha* costs are terrible on the Ucayali, due to the system of the slaves being passed from *patróne* to *patróne* through the river *capitáns*. Even so, it is profitable, for some *capitáns* sell as many as a thousand slaves a year."

Slavery indeed, as I was eventually to document, reaches into high places. There are senators in Lima who will laugh at the drop of a martini cocktail at the crazy idea of slavery existing in this enlightened world, while yet maintaining Campa slaves in their own homes as servants. These Indians are by natural instinct cleaner in their physical habits than any other tribe. Unknown to the management, there are two in the Hotel Bolívar in Lima. Powerful are the vested interests supporting this slavery practice today. And there is no doubt that more pressure than mere warnings will be brought to bear on Antony for his unwanted humanitarian work,

"Some day, señor," continued José, "this good man will disappear and no one will say what happened. He has been here a long time.

Partly because of him, the Alto Ucayali is being opened again to agricultural colonization by the Iquitos *patrónes*, who need slave labor. But soon these people will not need him...then!" He drew his finger across his throat.

When Antony returned to the house we decided to leave Black Hawk with him, as the broken arm would make it impossible for our friend to survive in the rapids of the wild rivers below. "Not only is the Tambo very precipitous and full of rapids," warned Antony, "but there are many savages along its banks. You must prepare for trouble."

It was then arranged that three of the mission's *mansos* be given us on loan as far as the headwaters of the Ucayali. Also we obtained two spare mosquito nets and two ponchos, and a few other essentials such as a pot to cook in, and a few clothes to replace our ragged ones. For all this bounty the priest would take only $15 (about a hundred soles-de-oro in currency rates) which fortunately I still had in my money belt. Since I had lost a full bag of coins on the river at the foot of the great falls, where the two Indians had been killed (and had paid for extra slaves, machetes, provisions at Sutsiki), I was now reduced to ($432.18 − $57.20 = $374.98) to cover all my expenses to El Dorado.

By midmorning, solid heat rolled up out of the valley, as we loaded our six-log rafts. They had been dragged out on the sand to dry, and with two extra logs added to each, now floated a bit higher. They were still waterlogged, badly beaten and even splintered.

Much as we wished to remain, we could not stay longer. It was now July 24. And an early fall rainy season was predicted by Antony on the Marañón. We must hurry.

We cast adrift into the swift current of the Pangoa. Standing on the ten-foot bank with the charred church as a backdrop, Padre Antony and the five nuns waved and smiled a gracious goodbye. They were sworn to stay until their death. And then a bend suddenly swung behind us and the jungle obliterated them from sight.

"What a noble man," I thought, as I struggled at my paddle through the boiling rapids. "Surely Antony loves the thorn and not the rose!" He himself could not understand the chain-reaction of his nobility and love for mankind, nor comprehend that he too, though by different methods, was the foe of the wild Indian.

Yes, the wild, mysterious tolling of the bellbird for centuries has lured men into the great jungle in search usually of some intangible prize. But for whatever prize such hopeful wanderers follow its beckoning songs—planters, scientists, adventurers, men who have escaped prison, diamond- and gold-seekers—of all these, few ever return again to their homelands. It lures Padre Antony, that good man, to his own destruction, its tolling to him—I believe—a hymn of freedom for the last red slaves....

ꙮ **XI.** ꙮ

Signal Smokes!

*I*N the bright late-morning sun, we shot through the dangerously shallow rapids of the Pangoa junction, to be instantly caught up in the grip of the Perené and swept eastward some four miles on the crests of its current, both our decks awash. How splendid to be free again!—to dash through the boiling waters, our rafts' bows pounding up great sheets of foam and water, the four alarmed Indians and Jorge and I doused from head to toes.

The river was no longer tinged a café au lait, but was now an oily chocolate brown. We swirled up to the broad mouth of the Ene which disgorged through a gap in the right bank of the Perené. Above its shallow cataract mouth, the Ene lay like a wide mirror under low parrot-green clouds. On the water's surface was floating a great flock of pure white *garcas*—egrets and ospreys, their plumed heads turned upriver. All about was a veritable monkey jungle, herds of the brown-blackish *ebus* swinging through the closely grouped trees. A pair of serious *saturninas*, tiny apes, squatted on a limb calling plaintively. It was unusual to hear them, for they are a rare nocturnal breed.

From this point on, the Perené and the Ene combined to form the deep, broad channel of the mighty Tambo, which snatched up the rafts and carried them along on its turbulent bosom. Soon the current bowed swiftly against the base of white cliffs edging the tableland of the high Gran Pajonal.

Towering above us on the opposite bank rose a vermin-ridden, flower-studded tangle of palms and trees, interspersed with groves of wild banana—an herb and not a tree—and spiky monkey-trees and various ginkgo-like growths. There were living fossils whose ancestors were arrayed above our heads in laminated Miocene strata. All this strange dawn-age vegetation capped undulating hills leading ever upwards to purple, stone-crested mountains.

Beyond them, to the south and east, lay also the forbidden Rio Urubamba. In Lima I had been warned that on the Rio Purus, also lying in that region, blood was flowing. Many *caucho patrónes* had been killed off by the Indians. In 1943 the Alto Ucayali *patrónes* obtained permission from the government to hire Campa mercenaries to attempt a cleanup of the Machiguengas. At the same time Carrena, a powerful *patróne*, operating with Campa mercenaries, offered to put in *esclavos* for the Rubber Development Corporation to tap *caucho* on the Yura. The fierce Machiguengas wiped them all out.

Troops, in carrying out the rubber program in Madre de Dios, contacted the savage Amahuacas and fired their villages slaughtering all Indians they could find on the Alto Purus. This had fearful consequences, for the surviving savages cut off the soldiers, isolated them and then slaughtered them.

As a consequence of this slaughter, no Atalaya *patróne* now dared to go up the rubber-rich Rio San Alejandro. Cashibos were shooting all Indian mercenaries and whites on sight. Such, in brief, was the reputation of the rivers spread before us, while on the Tambo itself, still a part of the forbidden Gran Pajonal, no *patróne* dare operate from the south Ucayali bases.

Anything could happen in such a country, and Jorge and I looked to our guns. The whole vast territory for hundreds of square miles had never been traversed anywhere off its main rivers. Scores of large tributaries feeding both the Urubamba and the Ene rivers originated from this area. This was very likely the wildest and most difficult jungle yet to be explored.

Two miles after leaving the Ene's mouth, the Tambo abruptly turned left (north), roaring along in the bottom of a deep canyon walled with more white salt cliffs. Much of the formation was lime, derived from the bodies of ancient sea life, precipitated through water and laid down in massive bands. The floor of the canyon was narrow and choked with giant flowering trees of many unknown kinds, some having enormous blue blossoms, some red or white—these being the colors of ancient primitive flora. After a few miles the Tambo changed course again into the east. We were now flanked on the north by the main perpendicular escarpment of the Cerro de la Sal.

Painted savages began peering out of this thick jungle at us, but we were always gone before an effective attack could be prepared. Even so, a flight of poison-arrows flew around us three different times. Four shafts—some five to six feet long—whistled into the rafts where they stood at a high angle, quivering. Yet there was no hurrying the rafts faster, or no landing possible to fight it out.

The *cerros* continued thrusting skyward, in places sheer-walled for over a thousand feet. The rim of the Gran Pajonal was capped by strange cycads (such as are found in coal beds) and languorous heat-dripping palms, one of which was identified as the edible *asshy*. Pendant lianas were strung like black cables across the face of the cliffs. Red and yellow streams trickled off the banks into the Tambo. Here in these concentrated chemicals was the secret of the various pigments in the Amazon's multicolored rivers.

Once a straight needle of smoke appeared dead ahead, perched on the very rim of the plateau overhead. Signal smoke. War drums (separate from signal horns) began rattling to left and right.

José cried, "We must not land! Keep to the middle of the river!"

The three new Indians suddenly pointed overhead, and we caught the movement of hundreds of vultures circling in the sky; others were perched in the taller trees along the banks, and neat rows of them sat on shelves in the cliffs of the mighty escarpment. All this was an indication to our Indians of death, of stinking bodies lying in the underbrush, the grim tally of the internecine wars of the Campas.

I got out the map, which (together with the two notebooks) was a sad-looking relic after so many dampings, and began marking it with my pencil. Up into this vast country reached many unexplored rivers. There were tributaries of tributaries of the Amazon, wide as the Mississippi, greater than any river of all Europe.

We could see Indian houses on the cliffs and low banks of the mighty Tambo. At places the river broadened to three or even four hundred yards. As we drifted by the Indians silently fled into the woods.

When an Indian is hunting near his house, painted so as to be almost invisible in the jungle tangle, he always moves with a peculiar reptilian slowness, the snake's awful certainty of success. He stops while still standing on one leg, freezing all motion, stares intently up into the higher branches, moves again…until the stalked bird flutters through the leaves and thumps on the ground, killed by the poisoned blowgun dart.

Unexpectedly, on a turn, almost blinded from the glare caused by heavy evaporation, we came upon a pair of Indians—fortunately only Antony's *mansos*, poling a dugout upstream with a cargo of solid macaws, blue parrots and other gaudy birds. Due to the belief that many such birds cannot be bred in captivity, the nests are robbed of their baby birds and raised in the houses of wild Indians. Many such exotic birds are sent to the markets of the Orient, and I had seen rare Amazon birds in the Calcutta bird mart, still others in Malaya and Egypt. Though tame, these two "shirt" Indians (though without shirts at the moment) snatched up their bows. We kicked our boulder anchors overboard and swung around to a stop, the tugging current foaming along our sides. The Indians cautiously closed the distance, keeping to the edge of the river, and finally came up to us.

Their faces, shoulders and arms were painted a shiny black enamel, a greasy concoction of *yotoconti* (a war paint). We realized that this is used to cut down the glare from the river's surface. Their teeth were painted black and filed to sharp points, to resemble snake fangs. In exchange for Jorge's bandanna handkerchief, they reluctantly gave us a small basket of three-inch *chonta* palm worms. Antony had given us a basket filled with vegetables, but we had lost this in one of the boiling rapids.

We upped anchor and were carried along for miles through the most beautiful jungle I had ever seen. Finally we began searching the banks for a place to make camp. With night approaching fast, and an unknown river ahead, it was imperative that we find a spot that was defensible. After many days of taking chances with the Indians and losing much of our apprehension, and our good rest at Padre Antony's, we decided to risk a fire. After all, the Indians must know of our being on the river, and though we were not starving, we were certainly hungry. Finally we headed in for a landing. We beached our rafts on a curving sandbar, shaped like a boar's tusk, some quarter of a mile in length on the right side. It was covered by a great flock of pink spoonbill flamingoes, so tame they didn't fly but merely walked off a hundred yards or so.

A small herd of *cotos*, a large reddish monkey with a long tail and a terrific gutteral roar, gamboled over the beach. I felt safe on this beach, as it looked defensible. With nothing to eat but the worms, I took a chance and stalked the *cotos*, and taking careful aim with the Colt, shot one of the four-foot-high bachelors, whose absence could best be spared by the herd. The *coto* howlers live in pairs in what are called *bancos*, usually the fork of a tree, and are seldom seen in herds on the ground.

After cleaning the monkey and singeing off its hair, we spitted the grotesquely boyish carcass over a dry smokeless fire made of the fine fuel, *capirona*. We found its haunch delicious. The four *mansos* ate the partly digested contents of the stomach, puzzled that Jorge and I should pass up this delicacy which was considered by them to be the choicest of all.

We had located our campground just in time. Indians were, as we had suspected, obviously everywhere about, as we saw from their code signs: stones placed in various ways; marks on twigs thrust into the sand; grass knotted in such and such a way. This last code was especially intriguing. The ancient Incas, unlike the Mayas, had no recognizable system of writing. But for all that they sent messages and kept records in code by knotting strings or clusters of fibers. The system has never been deciphered, but it is possible that the Campas hold the key to the lost language.

We had just finished eating when José pointed over the tree tops across the river, and cried:

"Signal smokes!"

Indian scouts must have immediately marked us down, for two fires were being lit on the top of the Gran Pajonal not five hundred yards away. The flames mounted high, belching columns of black smoke.

On that north side we were fairly well protected by the deep moat of the Tambo, a hundred and fifty yards across, and flowing swiftly at this point. Few Indians would dare attempt swimming it. At the far end of the *playa* stretched a roaring staircase of waves which would prevent any war party from coming upstream. At our back, along the edge of the *playa*, was a row of *bombonaje* palms. These palms stood some two hundred feet back from the river, with white sand all the way between.

If anyone tried to cross this open space in the night, he would be seen. In short, we had chosen wisely, for we realized now that had we continued we would have drowned.

After eating the monkey we were still hungry, and so we tackled the palm worms. But even so, since it had been a hard day, we wanted more food for the six of us. As the Indians had marked us down, there was no point in not hunting again. The *playa* was obviously a favorite stamping ground for wildlife, as indicated by the skeins of tracks left in the sand. The ones with the enormous claw tracks with a heavy line furrowing down the middle, were crocodile. Others were the cracks of *milne*, the new bear; tapir (a pachyderm belonging to the rhinoceros family); coatimundi, a raccoon-like bear; wild pigs; red deer; ocelot; *ronsoco* (capybara). Also the giant *tamandua* anteater, a toothless monstrosity measuring a yard at the shoulders and covered with long hair striped in black and white, and having a very long thin head. There were jaguar and puma tracks. On the edge of the *playa*, alongside the jungle, was a *cocha* so filled with crocodiles that not a yard of water was free of them; there must have been thousands.

While one of the *mansos* stood guard in the edge of the jungle, we rested, lying in the clean granite and quartz sand. The signal smokes had ceased. After the moon came up we prepared to hunt, for come what may, we would need food in the days to come. Animals will lie up in the cooler parts of the jungle by day, but like to come into the open under cover of night. One of the *mansos* began whistling on a crocodile tooth, producing short plaintive sounds, and presently he was answered by a herd of *ronsocos*. We knew these strange beasts were good to eat. They are pig-sized, with a red coat and webbed feet, an amphibious rodent, whose flesh was devoured by the Campas with relish. This Perené *ronsoco* is a variation of the lower Amazon's capybara, which has been variously described as "sheeplike," "piglike," "guineapig-like," "rabbitlike." I was very anxious to inspect one at close range.

I cautiously crept off into the darkness, crawling along on my belly, a few inches at a time, peering into the darkness along the edge of the sand bank as I did not want to crawl into a nest of crocodiles. I had an awful fright when a long, black snake came out of its coil only a few feet from my face and slithered off into the river.

The little sounds of whistling from the *ronsocos* came closer, answering my own decoy—for I had borrowed the Indian's crocodile tooth—and finally, not fifty feet away, I made out seven shadowy shapes. Aiming very carefully, I fired, dropping the foremost. With squeals of terror, the others plunged into the river and swam across to the other side. I retrieved the dead *ronsoco*, and found that it weighed about 125 pounds. Dragging it back to the campfire I saw that none of the other descriptions really fitted it. Actually, the animal is an overgrown member of the cavy family, to which the tiny and very valuable chinchilla belongs. We skinned it, and saved the fat for our Campa stone lamp, given us by Padre Antony.

It was now ten o'clock. A half-moon shed its greenish-yellow light over the white *playa*. Suddenly—and with no warning whatever—a feather-shafted spear, whirring oddly, came out of the darkness and, slid, like a sharp knife into butter, right through the side of one of the *mansos*. The wide, bloody blade stuck out of his back. With a grunt, he pitched forward on his face into the fire. In a flash, Jorge kicked a heap of sand over the coals, twisted around in a sitting position, the shotgun flashing to his shoulder. But out of the darkness rimming the edge of the white-trunked jungle came no horde of angry *bravos*, only the usual night racket of the insects.

Caught in the open, our Indian guard probably dead somewhere at the foot of the palms across the *playa,* we were obviously within range of the spear thrower. I couldn't believe the Indians on the Gran Pajonal had been able to cross the river and get on our flank. It seemed more likely that only a few strays were out there among the trees. I began digging a hole in the sand with my hands. There was no point in charging an unseen target, with the chances of receiving a spear through the chest. The others soon caught on, and in five minutes we lay in the bottoms of five pits. Peering over the top of mine, I carefully studied—foot by foot—the dark fringe of rustling palms But not a man-made movement or a suspicious sound came out of the shadowed jungle.

Now men react in different ways when confronted by extreme danger, and by death. I once saw a professional soldier—a colonel—who had been dropped by parachute behind the Japanese Army lines in China to inspect my command, actually wet his pants in front of all my guerrillas engaged in attacking an enemy post. Jorge, a very different sort, a hunter and jungle man who lived constantly with death, was laughing very quietly and grimly.

"What's so funny?" I asked, though I knew there was nothing humorous about that grim laugh.

"Well, my friend, I can't pin it down to any particular thing. I merely find I am laughing."

I turned to José alongside, gazing slit-eyed into the jungle. "Can you make me *shirondantse* (laugh)?" I asked. Curiously, there is no such idea as a "joke" comprehensible to the Campa mind. Life to the Campa is too terrible, too real. Nor have I ever seen a Campa laugh or smile, unless, perhaps, you do so first, then he will follow your example thinking it is polite and mannerly. José, however, was used to the queer ways of the *Huriapache* by now.

"*Si, patróne*," he answered guilelessly, not taking his eyes from the jungle.

"Do so," I suggested.

"*Si, patróne*. But it is difficult. Perhaps this will do—who knows? A Campa *bravo* near Sutsiki once constructed a bamboo monkey cage." José glanced from the jungle across to see if I were listening. Satisfied that I was, he moved his eyes back to the wall of trees. "*Patróne*—this man used to sit inside the cage so that the monkeys could come and laugh…."

All this time we were waiting for death to come out of that tangle of jungle across the way, hearing only the ringing of the insects, seeing nothing….

Finally I answered: "Why? And what would a Campa know about a cage for a monkey?"

"But, *patróne*! He wished to call the spirit of the monkey to him, and capture it in the cage."

"What's so funny about that?"

About this time Jorge was chuckling. "The two of you are very amusing," he pointed out. "I will explain what José means…."

For a moment he hesitated, for the air was full of crocodile roars—though whether Indian signals or from the disturbed reptiles in the *cocha*, we had no way of knowing. Then Jorge began speaking. He was engaged rather unsuccessfully in this business of explanation, when for no reason at all I burst out laughing.

"What's so funny?" enquired Jorge, a trifle hurt.

But there was no time to explain. All I could do was hiss—"Sssst!"

and point toward the bush. For out of its shadows and between the palm trunks, were coming an army of cat-footed savages...walking in a strange crouch and well spaced apart, not charging, but walking—advancing slowly and silent as death itself, straight toward us.

For a moment I was too stunned to act. Then Jorge threw the shotgun to his shoulder, drew a quick bead on a six-foot warrior in an enormous headdress, and pulled the trigger. The shotgun blasted the stillness, kicked back, and the headdress flew through the air. But not a single warrior of all those skulking behind wavered. There was not a sound out of any of them—no war whoops—nothing. They didn't miss a step, but kept coming in that odd tense crouch, silent as shadows, skulking across the *playa* in full sight under the moon, skulking with inhuman certainty of their prey and straight at us.

"*Sangre de Cristo!*" spat out the Peruvian, reloading.

☙ XII. ❧

The Killing of the Catsiburere

I KNEW my original estimate of the *playa*'s defensibility had been wrong. The Indians had somehow crossed the river. We were in a jam. Jorge—with narrowed eye, the shotgun's stock seated hard against his jaw—was grimly swinging its barrel along the front rank of the advancing *bravos*. He seemed undecided on a target. Finally, when the gun's front sight stopped midway through the arc, I knew he had singled out for his last remaining charge of buckshot an enormous, predatory-looking Campa brave. The Indian was well out in front, wearing a basket crown with a white feather rising from the back of its narrow corona. This time the gun was not aimed at feathers, but at a man's belly.

"Hold your fire!" I ordered him. I struck down the gun, which roared out, plowing a furrow across the *playa* up to the Indian's feet. "It will do no good."

"These devils will burn us at the stake!" he cried out angrily.

With no other choice but to lie in the ooze of those deathtrap holes until the unwavering Indians came up and stuck their spears into our backs, I got up in full sight and started toward them as casually as I could. They were only fifty feet away and plainly visible in the moonlight, over a hundred warriors fanned out over the *playa* with others still slinking out of the somber shadows behind.

They were hard-faced, naked except for purplish-red loincloths and claw-and-tooth necklaces, hideously painted. Fully armed with battle-axes, blowguns, spears, bows and arrows, two of them actually carried nets. They came to an abrupt halt. The closest savages drew back their right arms, but did not throw their saw-edged spears, apparently await-ing a signal from the white-feathered chief.

"Ho! *Indios!*" I called out, holding my hands palm upward to show they were empty of weapons. I walked slowly forward, came to a stop in front of the tall Indian who was standing well out in front of the others. I recognized him instantly...

"Iye Marangui!" I exclaimed with involuntary surprise. This was the witchdoctor we had watched that night in his house near Sutsiki.

The grim face remained absolutely wooden, a complete deadpan, but he opened his maw of a mouth and grunted:

"*Taimroki Matse!*" (White Witch!)

I checked an impulse to extend my hand and shake his own, for this practice is abhorred by Campas who, like certain Moslems, do not wish to contaminate themselves. Instead, I spat at his feet, and pointing at the moon bellowed that its light was good for hunting, that the spirits were subservient to him on such a night, and that we, like all men, must pre-pare to join Pawa soon.

The customary formalities of greeting over, I turned on my heel and walked back to the pits. Jorge and the two Indians were uncovering the fire and building it into a huge bonfire of flames. The horde of silent Indians followed me across the *playa,* gathered in a tight ring around the blaze. Jorge and I, together with José and the 'Opata man, were caught in the center. Iye Marangui stepped in with us and squatting on his heels began a thunderous oration, which from time to time José had to piece out and interpret for me. Apparently the *manso* they had speared at the fire was a "bad" Indian, an evil-eye who had been con-demned to die but who had escaped to 'Opata.

When the witchman had broken off his tirade, I asked him a question:

"Where is my guard?"

The witchdoctor pressed a great thumb against the side of his throat and grunted significantly. I knew they had killed him.

I continued: "It is a great distance from your house to this *playa.* How long did it take you?"

"Suns!" he grunted, holding up three fingers, meaning three days.

We then knew that there were secret war trails through what was believed to be a pathless tangle of jungle, trails on which a Campa brave can run fifty miles in a single day. That they had come in three days seemed incredible, but there they were.

I knew that a powerful sorcerer of Iye Marangui's stature had not run a hundred and fifty miles merely to see that a sentence of death was carried out on an Indian he had declared *bruja*. I sensed that our fate was in his hands, but I knew better than to question him directly as to why he had intercepted us, for the Campas are intensely indirect during any form of conversation.

With a wild singsong series of sounds interspersed with grunts, he gave a command to an Indian standing just behind. This Indian instantly leapt forward and held out a very large and cumbersome bag—a cased *coto* monkey skin, with the shaggy brown hair still clinging to it.

Iye Marangui untied a buckskin cord at its neck, and began drawing out various objects: little packets in bark cloth, small skin bags, carved green jadeite stones in the form of frogs (symbol of the Rain God), bundles of feathers and other items. He started painting his heavy-jowled, flat face. He used *achiote*, the bright orange-red paint mixed (in his case) with snake oil, rubbing it all over his head, shoulders and arms. From a tiny sack he took a cobalt black paint and smeared it carefully on his forehead, finishing with a single glaring Brahmin-like white spot between the eyes. He removed his white feather *paquitsa* (headdress), and put on instead, over his own long thick hair a grim anaconda's head, rigidly mounted so that its mouth was hinged open as if striking. Poorly tanned, it emitted an incredibly vile stink, unusual for even an anaconda skin. The snake skin, a mottled black and brown, which was attached at the back to the headpiece, was about twenty-four feet long and a yard wide, and this Iye Marangui carefully coiled around his great body.

A spotted jaguar skin was spread on the sand for him, and on this the sorcerer sat crosslegged. The mounting flames of the fire played over him and the ghastly greenish glare from the moon picked out highlights in the paint. Jorge pointed out that the snake's eyes were probably diamonds. The stage for jungle sorcery, red magic, was set....

Iye Marangui began swaying back and forth, his eyes closed. Sweat broke out in beads on his devilish face, for the night was sweltering. All at once he cried out in a discordant chant, which must have continued for several minutes, for suddenly I realized clouds had blotted out the moon and a smashing deluge of rain was falling on us. But not an Indian stirred, though like cats they hate rain. The downpour soon passed, the moon returned, and only a monotonous drip came from the dank jungle beyond, and the drone of the returning insect hordes.

Suddenly the sorcerer's flint-edged eyes flew open, and the chanting stopped. "I, the Brother of the Serpent, will dream!" he bellowed in a deep voice.

He then set about a self-imposed hypnosis. Certainly in the *playa*'s shadows moved the shade of an old Frenchman named Dr. Franz Mesmer. After a few minutes the *brujo* seemed to have become a disembodied automaton swaying before the fire, into which he stared unblinkingly. The trance was induced quickly, partly through the eardrums, by the intricate sound pattern of a tom-tom beaten by one of the Indians. This was aided by the conventional system of a reflection from some bright object on the retina of the eye, in this case a large quartz crystal held in his fingers. Thus began his savage séance with the jungle gods.

All at once, without warning, the Brother of the Dancing Anacondas began screaming in a tiny voice—the opposite of his usual bellowing tones. José started whispering hurriedly in my ear, sometimes lapsing into Campa: "He is talking to the *catsiburere*, an *itasolenga* (spirit), a malignant man-dwarf, which in adulthood stands only three feet high. It has the hands of a man, also a man's head with white hair. One of its feet is clubbed, and short. Its skin is white. From its shoulders grow red hair and the wings of the white king vulture. It is the worst monster of the jungle. When a man is confronted by the *catsiburere* he becomes paralyzed with fright, and the dwarf falls upon him, and breaks all his bones. It has the strength of a thousand devils, it is *antanukire* (fierce, fiendish), and it eats of the flesh of its victims until the belly touches the ground and the wings and body are dripping with blood."

José was obviously becoming frightened. All about us were the straining faces of the savages, their hard, narrow eyes staring in fascination at the face of the witchman.

The *brujo*'s thin, feeble voice picked up a note of whining, and I nudged José. He turned toward me and began speaking in a very frightened voice: "The *brujo* says—'Man (*champari*) has come from the stars (*enpoguiro*)...and to the silent (*pimagerette*) stars, he will return at death....'"

The *brujo*, that two-hundred-pound hunk of bone and muscle, who had not flinched at the prospect of death from a shotgun, began sobbing and crying out plaintively as if the coils of the anaconda skin were crushing him. Presently his voice rose to a terrific pitch—shrill childish tones of anguish, and he began scratching at his painted chest with talon fingernails, drawing blood. Tears dripped from his eyes. Then Iye Marangui pitched forward on his face. He was shaking violently from head to foot. He raised his head with a jerk, got unsteadily to his feet. He was still wrapped in the snakeskin and he tossed his demon's head this way and that, as if to clear his brain of sleep, hissing all the while. His eyes flew open. His face became ravenous, contorted with a cataleptic insanity, alternately twisting from grotesque expressions of fierceness to those of fawning. One instant he was a snake striking out at us; the next he was a feeding tiger roaring on all fours; then a vampire darting here and there, swooping about the fire, sucking at his own arm.

Here was unbridled art, or sheer madness. He seemed suddenly symbolic of the Campas' *andakangare* (a difficult word—perhaps a mixture of terror and danger), something supernatural. Then in a peak of fury he began running around the circle of Indians, who seemed to be frozen with fright, smelling at each in turn. Abruptly he broke off and leapt toward Jorge and me as we sat near the fire with José and our 'Opata Indian; all the while stomping in a thumping dance around us, smelling at each in turn. Abruptly he broke off and stopped in front of Padre Antony's man, pointing at him with the large crystal still clutched in one hand, hissing, and screaming crazily "*Notqui! Notqui!*"

Now *notqui* merely means "eye," but he was not referring to any ordinary kind of eye, for two warriors sprang forth and dragged the poor *manso* out of our midst, and throwing him hard to the ground with a terrific slam, held him struggling on his back near the fire. There was something malignant, merciless, urgent in their manner. The witchman grabbed up a firebrand, and after the others had brutally forced their victim's mouth open with the butt of a heavy spear, he plunged the burning limb with its flames into the *manso's* mouth, and by screwing it around, forced it straight down into the throat.

The back of Jorge's hard fist appeared from nowhere and knocked me solidly in the chest as I tried to rise, my hand already under my shirt and closed over the .45's grip. "Sit still, you fool! Do you want us all stretched out and killed like that? *Las bestias!*"

José said, "This is the killing of the *catsiburere.*"

The most terrible cries of anguish came from our poor friend undergoing that awful torture. His legs flew about, twisting this way and that, in what must have been an incredible agony of pain. The smell of burning flesh filled the air. Finally, after a time, a long time, he was still and quiet—thank God the man was dead. The witch rose to his feet a bit weary from his exertions, tossing the firebrand carelessly on the fire. He was satisfied, in fact he shone with virtue—hadn't the devil been driven out of a *catsiburere* who was living in the guise of a man?

"Ah! *Está bien!*" cried Jorge. "Now what!"

ꙮ XIII. ꙮ

The Soul Vine

SOMEHOW I must extricate myself from this predicament, and the two loyal *camaradas* who still remained alive with me, and the best method for doing so was to be sympathetic toward the savages' beliefs. To be sympathetic I must first understand them. This was going to be difficult, for the Campas, swayed by Iye Marangui, were proving anything but "simple primitives," and were dominated now by ghosts and malignant spirits, not mere fancies to them, but real living phenomena.

Ancient primitive, intuitive man—who today still lives on in the vivid mind of the Campas—had learned how to produce visions; even in recent historical times the Greek Delphic oracle and the primitive Christian saints resorted to them for warnings, prophecy, advice, comfort.

And so the Campa too can produce actual visions which appear before his eyes; day and night, he sees phantoms all about him—trees bend down and speak, snakes turn into human figures before his very eye, flowers melt into crocodiles. A man at Sutsiki had one night leapt out of his bed, straight from deep sleep, and run off into the jungle. Half an hour later he returned with a wild hog slung over his shoulder, which had walked into a trap set with a bamboo spring armed with a spear. When questioned, the Indian replied that he had gotten there just in time, as the pig had nearly wriggled off the spear. When I asked how he knew the pig had been trapped just at that moment, he stared at me in amazement, finally replying: "In my dreams I saw the spear strike the pig in the shoulder!" But now Iye Marangui was demonstrating how the Campa savage differs from all other methods known to priesthood and to science, in inducing such ecstatic visions. And it was a most astonishing thing.

The Campa witchman gets through the various phases of privation, isolation, fasting, and intense contemplation, with the deliberate use of a powerful drug called *camorampi* (Spanish, *soga de muerto*), literally, in Campa, "Soul Vine." The Jívaros use it, and they call it *natema*; other tribes call it *haya huasca*; it is some sort of unidentified jungle vine which is boiled with *cowa* leaves.

If after drinking the powerful drug, a man should see (visualize) a red parrot, its skeleton visible through the feathers (as under X-rays) and obviously made from solid gold—the sibyl *brujo* will explain, while in a trance, that the man's "friend," a "spirit," has warned him that his house will be burned by enemies and his women and children sold for *kishongare* (gold). The *brujo* warns the man to prepare for war—and being of a warrior race, he knows that he should attack first. His nearest neighbor is Parare, the Wolf; that's the guilty one. Kill him!

Preparations are then made to kill the Wolf. First, the priest, using one of the several types of telepathic communication which they claim to possess, sends out a dream (the translation is "spirit") to do battle with the "protective spirits" hovering around the Wolf. The *brujo* fashions a spear of wood and poisons it, and into this mundane object he dreams a spirit; next he launches the spear into the air toward the *paugotse* (house) of the enemy of his client. Having thus destroyed the Wolf's "spirit helpers," his client can safely destroy the body of the Wolf itself. The former dreamer then lies in ambush, as only a Campa can, and easily kills his enemy. The head is taken, or a scalp of hair; its spirit is now transferred through devious magical processes to that of the taker of the head.

As for the body of the dead man, Campas will bury it in the nearest river or *cocha*, though more often they burn the bodies. A witchman, however, is buried in the earth, together with his broken witch-cult objects, for to burn him would cause the sun to go out.

The Peruvian calls the *bravo* Indian treacherous, a subhuman object fit only for destruction. It should be understood that the Indian is not treacherous, in the sense implied, but is only carrying out his convictions that he is doing right. Doing "right" seems to be a universal instinct; but what constitutes right, and what constitutes wrong, differs with society and what it considers best for the majority. The Campas, feeling no obligation to the tribe, kill each other whenever an individual's interests seem threatened, and this is called "good."

Again, when an angry Campa goes in desperation to the witchman to get an interpretation of his dream, the following may develop: The warrior explains what he has dreamed that a certain man gave him a present. But when he happily goes next morning to the man's house to claim his present, he learns to his chagrin that the scoundrel denies remembering ever making the gift. And so the Indian who had had the dream goes away angry, feeling cheated. In this case, the sorcerer advises him to kill the welcher for his obvious crime of dishonesty, and at the same time to transfer the spirit of the departed to his own train of "helpers" in payment of the debt.

Iye Marangui that night on the *playa* asked me, the White Witch, how I would have settled the affair of the last dream above stated, a case which he had disposed of that day. I suggested hanging the head in a tree and letting the vultures dispose of it. At first he was astonished, but after reflecting smiled craftily, admitting it to be an excellent suggestion. He pointed out for all to hear, that the vultures would eat the gift head, and having annexed the soul to themselves, would be friendly to the head-taker, and one day return to claim the body of the head-taker when he too eventually died. Out of gratitude they would bear his own spirit into the air toward the Sun, Source of Creation!

Still cloaked in the snakeskin, Iye Marangui—enveloped in an air of terrible sincerity—now prepared a great mystical ritual. He seated himself on the jaguar skin. An Indian brought him a flat basket with a small lid on it. The witch removed the lid and thrusting in his black claw of a hand, dragged forth a coiling grayish black snake some three feet in length. I flinched, for it was one of the *alfaningas*, as yet unclassified, and one of the most deadly of Amazon reptiles. He took the snake in one hand, while with the other the Indian held a polished disk of *curi* (Spanish gold), five inches in diameter.

At a sulky howl from the *brujo*, a wall-eyed Indian elbowed his way through the crowd and entered the inner circle around the fire, carrying a small earthen bowl painted a dull rusty red.

"It is the *camorampi*," whispered José.

The *brujo* now put down the wriggling snake and the golden disk. He grasped the bowl in both hands and drank its contents. As he did so, the lethal *alfaninga* crawled slowly over the sand toward me, and then slid across my bare hand and into my lap. I could feel my entire spine tingle as the flat, lead-gray head raised to mine, the tiny black beady eyes fixed coldly on mine, and the whitish pink forked tongue darted in and out only a few inches from my mouth, getting my vibrations. Humans, as I have mentioned, undoubtedly betray fear on coming into contact with a snake, and snakes are receptive to it, and are frightened in turn. The snake was cold, but cast off a faint musklike odor. The *brujo's* flinty eyes locked with mine, and he seemed both surprised and pleased. I would do. I was indeed a witchman.

He loudly finished gulping down the last of the draught, picked up the disk and, leaning forward, grasped the snake at its middle and placed it between his teeth. Instantly, angrily, it struck at his face—again and again—its fangs spurting twin streams of yellow venom. Then he removed the snake from his mouth. The two objects—the golden disk and the snake—he continued to hold throughout the ensuing ceremony of ritualistic magic, which was to last for two eternal, tensely torrid, mosquito-hellish hours.

The helper scampered out of our presence to join the crowd, all of whom were keyed to a high pitch of excitement and apparently frightened. The Anaconda Brother, this black-and-red painted savage, this witch savant could perform wonders equal to those of scientists—as Jorge and I knew from remembering what had happened in his own house. Now he explained that he had drunk the *camorampi*, the wonderful Soul Vine. This drug—unknown to science—was very like opium, apparently, in the De Quincy-like dreams it would presently bring on. José explained that it would compose the witch's earthly shell in a state identical to death (*kamingari*), so that his mind, encased only in its essence (*pinarotse*), or envelope of spirit, should move freely into the fateful future. Mind, explained by José as "lightning particles," would eventually return to the "dead" body on the *playa,* and so again become alive (*ayantare*). Thus the body could be used again and again, in the service of the gods as the "clay" instrument, or totem, for conveying to the Indians, the true (*kiaria*) intelligence, which the freed mind had gathered beyond time and space.

Jorge stared fascinated, for he knew we were witnessing a most remarkable event in sorcery, something that no Peruvian ethnologist had seen before. In fact, no stranger had ever learned anything of the secret Campa religion. The Puna, perhaps the most intelligent outsider in contact with them, had sneeringly told us—the ignorant newcomers—that "*Los Campas*" had none, they merely worshipped devils. But now, for some strange reason known only to himself, Iye Marangui calmly explained that before he could look into the future, his spirit must first travel to the high spirit places. Thinking me a *brujo* like himself, he wished to exchange ideas. At least that was what I wanted to believe. Had I known what was in his twisted mind, I should never have had the nerve to observe the facts, much less jot them in my notebook.

A sacred snakeskin drum began pounding—rising and falling with monotony. José bent close, saying in a low half-whispering voice that the patron Campa devil Kamari was being called by the *brujo*. Kamari was a dark shade who walked in the jungle (*antami*) or slept in the *nija*, the deep waters of rivers and lagoons, or even lived among the clouds. Like the *brujo* whose servant he was, the God Kamari could enter anything, everywhere, and at will. He could turn into a jaguar and cause it to pounce on a man. He could creep like the anaconda, hide like the tapir, or run like the deer. That is the true reason why these four animals are never eaten as food. Kamari was malignant. Normally he appeared as a manlike creature, with a large birdlike beaked nose, much like that of the Sun God Ra, whom the ancient Egyptians believed to be the ancestor of their Pharaohs.

To create an impasse and so nullify the evil efforts of Kamari, the witchman must also seek the aid of Pahua (pronounced with a Quechuan inflection as Pawa at Sutsiki), the "Man of Gold," who lived in the middle of Ureatsere, the Sun. As José whispered on, the *brujo* correlated his ceremony and symbolically began worshipping before a new small fire which an Indian had built on a hastily erected stone dais. José explained it typified Ureatsere. Yuca, the god-given Campa staff of life was then fed to this symbol of the Sun. And to the flames were added copal. The actual fire, *pumaare*, was kindled from special sacred wood called *enshato*, which had been soaked in the "hot blood of the sun" and in the "hot blood of man killed in sacrifice." Blood, the Campas believe, is that fluid substance which links all living matter; the blood of the animal is that also of man. Even the juices of plants, the saps of trees, is blood in a different form only. Strangely enough, this is the present belief of science.

The gleaming, sweat-dripping, black-and-red-painted *abendaningare* rose from his tiger skin, and symbolically glided snakelike around the "Sun," keeping time to the gently patted tom-tom, while all the Indians chanted in a high wailing chorus and incense and food sacrifice were consumed in the votive flames. Thus having appeased Pahua, and having asked the Sun God's aid against Kamari, who typifies the "Spirit of Evil," the witch proceeded to worship Pachukuma.

This third deity in the complicated Campa pantheon (which in cludes Gods and Goddesses of Earth, Water—or Rain, Air, Fire, Space), was a sort of diabolical knight-errant ghost who acted as a Hermes-like messenger, or liaison, between mankind and Pahua. Both Pahua and Pachukuma were formed in the image of man, explained José, adding, "even as Christ and Lucifer," as if to explain his belief in both religions.

Letting this sink in, he continued his explanation: All about over the *playa,* the mystical Anaconda was crawling, wending its way around and through us, sliding up through the tree tops and out into the sky. "*Patróne*—that's why everyone is crying out and pointing all about and up toward the moon. They say they see it!"

And so the way was being cleared for looking into the future, a future explained as being predestined and fatalistic, a future in which man's free will played no part. The Brother of the Dancing Anacondas squatted again on his jaguar pelt, and symbolically recognized "death," by rubbing his white-spotted forehead against a human skull clutched in the vise of his knees. In both hands he held aloft to the moon the squirming *alfaninga,* and the golden disk. After questioning the fascinated José, I took the snake to symbolize "shadow wisdom," and the disk to be "man's control of the sun and the moon, for it reflects the rays of both, symbolically linking earth to these celestial bodies."

As the sibyl *brujo* struggled against the spirit of Kamari, he cried out as in a nightmare, rocking around on his hip sockets in a circle, holding aloft the symbolic snake and the shining disk. The food sacrifice sizzled out, burnt black, even as did Moses' offering in the wilderness. It might have been a human Inca sacrifice, instead of merely a vegetable one, for sometimes captives or condemned "third-eyes" (evil-eye) are burned and children fed to an anaconda.

The drug began telling: the *brujo* was apparently falling asleep, for his head was nodding. His features kept a rigid dignity for he was *listening*, said José, to the wind god sweeping through the "worlds" (stars). He began writhing in grotesque antics, dancing violently from the hips in ecstasy now, as a *jergón* snake sways before a fright-paralyzed bird. José believed the witch to be gazing into the golden face of Pahua. After half an hour of this swaying back and forth with a sort of grinding yogi movement, his black and red arms rigidly held aloft, still clutching the snake and the disk, he began a most terrifying dirge.

The minutes flew past; suddenly Iye Marangui dropped both snake and disk on the sand, and awoke from his sleep, shaking. José said he was not outwardly conscious, but in communication with the gods. The sorcerer spoke very slowly. His voice rumbled in a deep cadaverous bellow which echoed most unnaturally in that thick sound-cushioning jungle air—perhaps reminiscent of that other Indian's ventriloquistic voice we had heard during our first day in the jungle.

It had an unaccountable quality, such as might have been caused by a human voice echoing from the far end of a long hall of stupendous height. This is what José said in as free a translation as it is possible for me to render:

"*Looo* (uttered in along drawn-out voice)...I, the *abendaningare*, a *hatingare* (traveler) have seized the sacred Anaconda, which in a thunder clap bears me instantly to a mountain top on Cachiri (the Moon)."

A long silence followed. Would he go on? Every eye in the grim-faced circle seemed to be asking that question. And then again came the great echoing voice—and again whispered José:

"*Looo*...Pahua is directing me to face Quipatse (Earth). *Looo*, the Earth is red in *tampea* (the air), like the Sun in tiger-mating time. A cloud covers Earth. Pahua sends Pachukuma off on an Anaconda, and he strikes it aside from the sky (*inquite*), that I, the *abendaningare*, may view all. *Looo*, I see *cuengare* (a fearful, or dangerous scene) of *champare* (men)! They, friends (*shanitka*) and enemies (*huairi*), burn together and strange flames of hell (*kiaratse*), rise among them all; *unila* (earthquakes) and *empoguiro* (comets), fall from the skies all black! Thunder and lightning fall amongst them, like particles from the Sun...."

This was followed by a deep silence, shattered by the Indians breaking out in a terrible wailing, each straining to watch the witch's face. Then:

"*Looo*, Pahua—that Shower of Gold, is appearing on a mountain nearby. Pahua sends me on the back of my Anaconda, to the center of creation—the Campa nation!"

The *brujo* awoke. Had he been to the earth's satellite, as José and the others believed? Or was his mind a well-ordered house of auto-suggestion? The witch was obviously bursting with hauteur and pride, though his dark eyes reflected a tense fear, and his great hands shook.

"Of course, since we don't know the answer, we may as well put it all down to indigestion," said Jorge.

That broke the spell, and we found ourselves once again back on the *playa*, and faced with the desperate problem of getting away. But the possibilities did not look bright. The Indians were engaged in a terrific pow-wow among themselves. Iye Marangui peeled out of his anaconda skin, and hustling into a red *uma*, gruffly bade us follow him. Already the others were grabbing up our mosquito nets and ponchos, and various things scattered about.

"We are *esclavos*," groaned Jorge, getting to his feet. "Remember what happened to Rodriquiz, the prospector? I warned you none has ever escaped alive from the Gran Pajonal...nor shall we."

José, who had been cocking an ear toward the babble of the crowd around the fire, turned to me and whispered tensely: "It is worse than that. They say Iye Marangui wants to eat your heart, to add your knowledge to his own."

"Then that's the explanation for their cannibalism...." I finished for him. "The Incas, Aztecs, and Mayas offered human hearts to the Man in the Sun, none other than the Campas' Man of Gold. And the astronomer-priests ate the hearts afterwards. The ancient Bird-Snake culture actually still lives in these jungles."

Jorge and José both stared in amazement, while Jorge finally sputtered: "Are all yanquis mad? But come, my friends, *vaya con Dios*—go with God."

ᘳ XIV. ᘰ

Captives of the Cannibals

*N*OT knowing where we were going—or why—or what would happen to us, we were shoved along and prodded with spears to the far end of the *playa*. Apparently the Indians were headed east, downriver. But then we were driven left into a rocky jumble, the beginning of the *mal-paso*, a roaring defile filled from side to side for 200 yards with the swift-flowing black and white waters of the Tambo. Into this deafening torrent the horde of a hundred warriors unhesitatingly plunged to their chins. A few carefully strung out behind a guide, who held aloft a firebrand snatched at the last moment from our fire.

Obviously the Campas knew of a secret ford for crossing. Though the river raged around us, tugging madly, for we three were flung in bodily and nearly drowned, we slowly waded across the slippery rocks lining the ford—a submerged dyke or reef—and emerged dripping on the opposite bank. Soon the party began stringing out and creeping along the face of a white salt cliff rising just beyond.

The moon was hanging low in the heavens now, but our way was bright enough once we climbed clear of the jungle's top. I followed close on the heels of a mule-legged *bravo*, with enormous red-painted feet and great toes splayed out for gripping the narrow, precarious path. Apparently this yard-wide shelf was caused by a steeply slanting fault, its surface was covered with loose stones and salt which had weathered away from above. Once on a bend, the fault narrowed to a foot. I was forced to place my shoulders against the wall, and trying not to look down hundreds of feet upon the jungle below, worked my way slowly around to safety.

Sweating and puffing for lack of breath, we struggled for a thousand feet up to the top of the plateau. Earlier we had seen signal fires from the same plateau, and now saw, bending away before us to the north, an endless tangle of palms and trees—the heart of the central tableland of the forbidden Gran Pajonal! The Indians began trotting down a narrow trail into the tangle. We were driven on after them, but after an hour, Jorge and I could no longer keep up, and the column slowed to a swift walk. From time to time I was tripped up by vines in the darker places, but was instantly prodded on with a spear in the hands of a grinning fiend following close.

We had gone all of ten miles from the edge of the rim, when daylight came, and some time after, Jorge, José and I were marched swiftly into a village of five houses, swarming with silent women and children. We were shoved into a hut on the far side. We lay on the earthen floor breathing hard, absolutely done in. I noticed that there were no windows, and the air was stifling. Overhead on heavy beams rose a V-shaped old grass-thatched roof, filled with vermin. Greenish spiders began coming down on long strands. Several red millipedes were crawling over the ground and so we finally got up and sat on a log lying near the wall opposite the doorway, and stared about us.

Logs were being brought to the open doorway and fixed upright in the ground, and bound with thick vines of *tamishi*. All around the hut the Indians were crowding and peering through the cracks between the logs, jeering and spitting at us. At midday a woman's hand pushed a small wooden trough through a gap under one of the logs. José cried out for water, but only jeers answered him.

"Captives of the cannibals…" groaned Jorge, as he got up and crossed the floor. He picked up the trough, smelled at it in disgust, and examined the contents. He held up one of the sour-smelling things in it, a cluster of rotted berries, a plum-sized fruit covered with scales. He bit into one, spitting out the scales and a yellow pulp. "Oily—tastes like acid. Probably that's what they fattened Rodriquiz on."

José remarked forlornly that they were fruit from the *mirity* palm, and added that when the pits, which looked somewhat like red golf balls, were baked and pulverized, the Indian women use them as abortives.

"Another medicine for science," said Jorge. I saw that his darkly tanned face was deeply lined and grim. He was not only tired in a physical sense, but even his mind reflected the ever-mounting tension of worry over the uncertainty of our situation. Unobserved by me before, this tiredness must have been accumulating for days, and only now showed in the spiritless eyes and the hard lines around the mouth. His hair (like my own, I realized) was long and tangled. And likewise his pants and shirt were dirty and even torn.

Hungry, we ate some of the pulp, and soon the floor was littered with the red pits. Vermin started coming in, especially a swarm of tiny pink ants that bit like fire. Jorge called them *pucacuras*, and warned against letting one bite anywhere near the eyes, for the acid in the stingers would cause painful and usually permanent blindness.

I heard some giggles from the other side of the wall just behind our log perch, which was elevated a foot on short posts. I glanced down just in time to spot a thick black snake wriggling along between my feet. I raised my shoe with a yell, which brought more giggles.

"It's all right," spoke up Jorge after a quick glance. "A *mussurama*—it won't hurt you. That one eats snakes."

A few feet away the *mussurama* coiled up in a hole filled with ashes and dust, its head raised a little, staring at us and darting out its tongue, but otherwise offering no harm.

"Why did they put it in here?" I wondered aloud.

José spoke up: "*Patróne*, it is only to see if we can be frightened. The children did it."

"The little bastards" I thought, but said: "Playful little devils, aren't they?"

Jorge said gloomily: "Perhaps it would be better for us if it was venomous."

All day we stayed in that sweltering dungeon, the dirt floor a filthy mess from old food and yuca expectorated about. With night we still remained miserable for they brought no light. Since those peering through the cracks couldn't see now, I began scouting around—while wondering where that damned snake was—trying to find a way out. The base of one of the logs proved to be pithy with rot, but when I drove a hard sliver into it, I found the core solid as a rock. The walls were of the metal-like *moena* wood. There was no use trying to break through. Mosquitoes flew in through the cracks and settled on us in clouds. It was the most awful night I had ever known. There was no sleep for Jorge or me, though José dozed off from time to time.

Next morning we heard the Indians outside in the village. But the only thing we saw of our captors was a woman's brown, scrawny hand at the crack under the wall, a hand quickly withdrawn, for Jorge slammed a rock at it. For breakfast we had more of the *mirity* oil berries. It began to look as if Jorge were right.

To relieve our tension I began questioning José about the Campas.

"Where shall I start?" he enquired.

"Start with the women," I suggested, "they can't possibly be as devilish as the men."

He started at random, and what he had to say wasn't very heartening. The women often mutilate the fallen after battle. It is due to their nagging that most of the killing is done—to obtain slaves and so lessen their own work. No woman wanted a man who could not kill another and protect her. As for the wives, he continued, on seeing me frown, they are reasonably faithful to the split-cane couch, but if one should prove otherwise, the husband whips her before his clan to "clean his face." In the case of the husband's stepping out, his spouse—or collective wives—whip the poor misunderstood miscreant along with the "other woman." Some wives will place the juices of the terrible *floripondo* plant in the husband's food; the poison attacks the brain tissues, turning him into a zombie-like slave, who comes and goes at her direction, a witless thing that she beats before all the other women.

"This," said José, "is *pashueitingare* (shame), avenged."

My interest aroused, and wishing for some single spark of human kindness, I asked about love, and learned that "love" is not necessarily a psychic state evolved by civilized man. The savage also marries for "love," which he calls *nitasutane*, because "he likes to be in 'love' throughout his life." To this blissful somnolent state, so desired by the more impractical male, his first wife apparently does not object, since all secondary wives are under her iron rule. José believed that the love impulse is very strong among these virile Campas. One morning just before Jorge and I had arrived at Stone's, a "wild" woman was found hanging by her neck from a tree limb. On inquiry, the intelligent José learned that the woman's husband had died while serving as a laborer, and "loving" him, she had committed *tongashare* (suicide), and so followed him to the Sun. Suicide is very common, and is usually committed by the taking of poison. Having exploded the modern theory of man's newly acquired capacity for "love" I felt satisfied for the moment, but not José, who was wound up.

The loving Campa *bravo* must ask the woman for permission to marry her, and not ask her father. Should she bite his nose and perhaps playfully bang him over the head with a club, it means she is interested in an offer. The wedding ceremony to the Sun God is enlivened by *chicha* and a shindig, songs and a little casual fighting with war clubs, rites to the minor gods and propitiation to the devils; and then follows the building of the new house with the aid, usually, of the happy bridegroom's brothers or clansmen. The *Matse* (Old Witches or Old Grandmothers), instruct the bride in her love life to come. Their tools, persisted José with great interest, are wooden carvings depicting the various positions available to the sex act, not unlike those—I gathered—seen in the murals of Pompeii. If possible the ingenious Campa seems to have outstripped civilization in devising a few new ones on his own, bringing the tribal total up to some forty. As he described some of these Jorge and I could not help wondering where sex leaves off and acrobatics begin.

Campa divorce is practiced with no ceremony other than the husband trading his wife off for a spear, a house, or a feather headdress he might fancy. If it is the wife who wants the separation, she is a wise woman who picks a better clubman than her ex-husband, for he is very apt to hunt her down and brain her. In any case the matter is settled between husband and wife.

"How about the men?" I asked.

José told us that each man fashions his own bows and arrows, his tools and canoe, burns the jungle for his garden patch, makes the cloth and most of the ornaments, these last being sacred.

Campa blowguns, or *tepi*, are bartered from the Chama tribe on the Ucayali. These guns are nine feet long. They have a slender, tapering tube of split *chonta* fitted with a mouthpiece of hollow bone. This mouthpiece is cemented with pitch and gum, while the tube itself is bandaged with fiber, polished black or dull brown. The bend of the bore is so finely drilled that it allows for the slightest drop due to weight. He warned us that the *tepi* can shoot with deadly accuracy at 100 feet, and hit a large target such as a man at a range of from 200 to 300 feet. The darts are ten inches long and contained in a section of bamboo. A type of curare poison, called *moca* among the Chamas, is also bartered for. It is prepared by the Chama witchmen, *cucucunas*. Other poison for darts and arrows may be the venom of snakes. While most upper Amazon tribes are familiar with some form of curare, the Campas are not. Chama *moca* is so virulent that a mere flesh wound will kill a lion, bear or tapir, though all these larger animals must be tracked down after being shot with a *tepi*.

Moca is undoubtedly a therapeutic agent similar to insulin. *Moca*, curiously, "relaxes" to the point of death, explained José, who had seen men die of it. The amazing thing is that the Campas themselves have an antidote. This is a quick application of rock salt applied to the wound after it has been slashed open with a knife, together with oral dosages of salt water. This is not too dissimilar from our own intravenous injection of salt solution for plague. If this is not done quickly, *moca* can cause nerve paralysis, limpness, nausea, asphyxiation, heart stoppage and death. Normally the Campas do not use the *tepi* in war against members of their own tribe, as a *bravo* can pluck out the ten-inch dart, make slashes parallel with the veins, and treat the wound with salt. Thus, not only *moca*, but snake-venom-tipped arrows are used solely on strangers, as Campas also have cures for the two main types of snake bite—and inject both antivenoms when in doubt.

When raiding, the Campas ferret out a village or a hunting camp or clanhouse, arriving at their target just before dawn. The psychological element aimed at is surprise. If the tactic and the carnage are successful, all the males will be killed, the skulls of the wounded bashed in. The women, babies and children are taken captive and later sold as slaves to the *patrónes*. (Few are the adult male Campas who have not killed at least once.)

If any of the Indians in the village has escaped the slaughter, they invariably rendezvous in the jungle and counterattack the raiders, attempting *asarmatandingare* (revenge), and to recover the slaves, and perhaps grab off a few of their own. Sometimes the counterattack is staged in the jungle after the raiders have split up their party and are returning to their own homes, but usually a few days are allowed to lapse as the enemy's guard is then relaxed, and also there is time to pre-pare ghost-spears and other magical rites.

These rites are conducted with musical instruments, *tamboros* (drums) and *sungares* (flutes). A dance, the *jubesherie* is held; the dancers wear belts of little jingling shells. Ornaments worn by the *bravos* are strictly defined as badges of distinction and grading, being taboo for all except those who qualify. Bracelets are of ivory, cloth, col-ored fibers, teeth, claws, animal and reptile skins, feathers, wood or beads, for the Campas believe that if metal is worn, the flesh will rot. After the dance the warriors start off for the manhunt.

José warned that should we be able to escape, we must beware of the trails. Traps and snares, *nofate*, are abundant and make both game and man trails exceedingly dangerous for strangers. The man-traps are called *samerense*. Deep holes are often placed in trails and runways, embedded with rows of sharp bamboo stakes, designed to impale strange *bravos* out raiding in the Gran Pajonal. Any explorer who should leave the Perené, the Tambo, or any of these western rivers, should be warned that moving inland without a local guide entails con-siderable risk.

José pointed out that three *caucheros* trying to get into the lower Tambo, and cruise for "weak rubber" trees, were victims of traps. Two of them fell into man-traps and were killed by poison. The third was captured after being taken out of a trap, and secured to a post driven into an anthill. The insects ate him alive. The skeleton was placed in the *caucheros'* canoe and floated downriver a few miles into Atalaya, as a warning for other Peruvians to stay off the river.

"All this is certainly fascinating," I pointed out, "but for the life of me, I can't see a ray of hope in it for us."

"*Patróne!*" José cried out in despair, "There is no hope. You see what they did to our three 'Opata friends on the *playa*. These Indians will tear our hearts out, and Iye Marangui and other witches will eat them. The people will eat our bodies. Believe me!"

"The damned cannibals!" whispered Jorge in English; then in Spanish to José, "The next thing you will be telling us they will feed us that *floripondo*."

"They will! They will!" cried José, quite beside himself. "They can amuse themselves longer with us when we are under the spell of this drug. A man does not die easily once he has drunk *floripondo*."

"We must get out of here!" The Peruvian spoke with such violence I was sure he would bring the guards down upon us.

With nightfall we were weak from hunger, for nothing since morning had been shoved through the hole, and though we cried out for water, none had been brought.

Three hours passed in total darkness on that second night, when I was suddenly aware that José was hunting around. When I idly asked him what he was up to, he didn't answer, but after a while joined us on the log. I struck one of the last precious matches. (I still had four in my oiled-silk map case which of course had been in the money belt under my shirt and not taken from me as had the .45.) José had found the *mussurama* and crushed it under his bare feet, and was biting the black hide off, and actually eating the meat along the spine. Jorge and I were sick at the sight, but José appeared not to notice. As a Campa he was not doing anything unnatural to his instincts.

We listened through the cracks and when the village had settled down, and our two guards outside the door were quiet, I boosted Jorge up to the ceiling on my shoulders. It was pitch dark, but he managed to feel his way into the rafters at the back of the hut and soon dry grass was coming down upon my head. I knew he was making a hole through the thatched roof in the corner.

"Pssst!" came from above, "Reach up your hands."

I lost no time in complying, and a moment later found myself dangling in mid-air, and presently pulled up to the rafter on which Jorge was standing. Then together we reached down and José was hauled up, though when his knee thumped against the log it made a loud noise and my heart nearly stopped. The stars were shining through a small hole just overhead. Crouching on the rafter, we waited ten minutes, then José began climbing through the gap. His legs disappeared, and from the rustling in the thatch we knew he was lying on the roof, *outside.*

All at once the blood began running cold in my veins. One of the guards at the door was getting up. We could hear him talking with the other one. Suddenly the *thump-thump-thump* of his great feet could be heard on the ground. He was coming counterclockwise around the hut. There was no way to warn José outside, and we felt that all was up.

The guard made the last turn just under our corner. The next sound we heard was a soft grunt. Jorge pushed his shoulders through the hole and I followed. Immediately we saw that José had heard the guard, and when he was passing beneath, had jumped straight down, apparently striking him on the head with his great hard feet. José already had the man's spear in his hands and was thirty feet away at the edge of the forest. We leapt down to the ground, only twelve feet below, ran across the dangerous open space, and found ourselves crouching with José in the shadow of a small tree.

José whispered something, but I didn't understand him. Jorge hissed in my ear that we must take off our shoes. We dare not make a noise. This we did, and when I stepped out of mine and put my feet down on the bare ground, I stepped into a nest of fire-ants.

My feet throbbing and half-paralyzed, Jorge and I started out after José who was moving as only a Campa can—silent as a black *coralito* (coral snake). He knew our shortcomings, however, and moved very slowly, holding limbs aside for us which we could not see, for the slightest noise would draw the remaining guard. Any second now he might find his friend at the back of the hut. At last we were far enough away so that we could risk moving faster. We had not gone two hundred feet, however, before a scream went up behind us.

I wanted to run, blindly—do anything to hurry. But José clamped his hand, which was hard as a vise, on my shoulder. "Do not move, *patróne*—" he whispered.

We waited motionless for a very long time, all the while the yelling Indians streamed apparently out of the longhouses and gathered behind the hut, only a stone's throw away.

"You go," suddenly whispered José, pointing into the depths of the jungle. "Hurry!"

Jorge and I moved out as fast as we could under cover of the Indians' racket, though actually at a very slow fumbling walk, due to our bare feet and also that we could hardly see in the jungle of air-roots and vines. Ten minutes must have passed before I realized that José was not with us. "Where is José?" I asked Jorge in a whisper of alarm.

"I don't know. Hurry. Make not the slightest noise. The Indians are quiet—*listening*."

"But, we can't go without him! Besides—we would be lost."

"For God's sake—hurry!"

And so we went on and on, until we came to a small opening in the tangle where a single ray of light shot down from the star-filled sky. All at once I smelled something that struck terror at my heart. An Indian was near, and only a yard away....

I felt around with my bare feet for a rock, and finding one I picked it up. "

"It is I, *patróne*."

"José! How did you ever find us?"

Ignoring the question (for we probably had sounded like a herd of wild boars, even with our bare feet), he said, "We were being followed. I returned and killed the man."

His hand grasped mine and guided it along the flat blade of the spear; it was wet and sticky.

"Knowing a Campa is with you, they dare not follow until daylight," he whispered with grim satisfaction. "Come!"

We kept at José's broad humped back as he forced a way through the jungle, always with unerring instinct picking the best and more open places through the mass of clutching vegetation. Once we struck a trail, but he would not let us take it, warning of traps. "Besides, scouts will already be watching all the trails."

An hour later through a gap in the trees I saw, after getting my bearings on the Southeren Cross, that the Indian was taking us on a line into the southeast, not south where our rafts were lying on the *playa*. Without those rafts we were in as bad a position as a shipwrecked sailor on a desert island. The Indian said we must abandon them, that warriors would start for the *playa* immediately on finding we had escaped. He hoped to intersect the Tambo far below the *mal-paso*, but first we had to reach the edge of the plateau.

"Hurry—*patróne*! There is no time to talk."

For five hours José took us slowly through that awful jungle thicket. Twice the Indian warned that he could smell a snake, and both times we had carefully to circle the spot. Walking with bare feet, we were anything but easy in our minds.

Finally, at dawn, and in full view, as there was no cover, we stood on the bare rim of the Cerro de la Sal. A thousand feet below roared the Tambo. Here the Indian left us hiding in a grove of palms and scouted west along the brink. Half an hour later he returned. He had been unable to find a way down. Next, he tried the eastern direction—and this time brought us along with him, for we must either find a way or be lost. The Campas would be well out on our tracks by now.

Expecting their yells behind us at any instant we limped along on torn feet, hurrying up as fast as we could, with José stopping often for us to catch up. Finally in desperation, though reluctantly, he brought forth our shoes from inside his shirt. He had picked them up though Indians had been everywhere. Gratefully we put them on and then, though we left easy-to-see tracks and made a terrific racket, we really moved out now, running behind him. At last José found a way off the plateau. It was down a steep rockslide that partly filled the head of a narrow canyon which cleaved the *cerro*. Taking care not to break our legs, we started down, sliding through rock screes and clinging to tree roots and lianas, until finally after half an hour we found ourselves at the bottom of the Cerro de la Sal.

Running as best we could through the jungle we lined out for the river, and three hundred yards beyond the cliff came upon its bank—a rocky, sandy stretch. José plunged unhesitatingly into the deep water. We dived in after him. Swimming hard, we finally succeeded in getting across after being carried downstream some four hundred yards. The Indian would not permit us to climb out on the far bank, but instead, started wading shoulder-deep along the muddy edge of the river. Once he pointed out an immense stingray, lying on the bottom. We splashed after José for a quarter of a mile until he turned right and crawled out of the water to enter a patch of bamboo.

"Rest!" he gasped, and then calming down explained that he must return to the river and make seeable tracks upriver from the point where we had reached the opposite bank. This would throw the trackers off, and above all delay them—for he swore that in addition to their dogs the Campas themselves could hunt by scent. The heat from the sun would eventually burn off the telltale scent, but in the meanwhile he must act! When the Indian left, I crawled back to the river and eliminated our tracks by tossing dry sand around.

All day Jorge and I laid low in that thicket, and had finally given up José, thinking that he must have fallen into an ambush, or been run to the ground. But with nightfall he came crawling in stark naked through the bamboo. He called out in a low voice first, for he knew we would arm ourselves with clubs and he might otherwise be brained on entering our hole.

"Braves are hunting everywhere," he warned, "be very quiet."

Animal and bird calls were all around, on both sides of the river, and these he whispered were signals. Also, during the late afternoon, tracks inside the thicket indicated that a warrior had passed within only fifty feet of us. José went on to explain that he had back-tracked through the water and crossed the river over to the cliff side, and then turned upriver along the bank making a few vague impressions where the trackers would find them, pretending we had waded toward the balsas and done it rather awkwardly. That would throw them off for a while, for they would search the trees and every foot of ground for a mile around the rafts.

All night we lay up. Though we now had water it was our second day without real food other than the worms and *ronsoco*. I was weak and nauseated, but after vomiting felt much better.

When Jorge and I awakened at dawn, José had vanished. We kept a careful watch, not speaking, and by midmorning I heard just the slightest rustling sound behind me, and on turning quickly, saw José standing in an opening between the bamboos only four feet away. It gave me a terrible start. Grinning, he whispered,

"Four warriors I have killed. I have a raft hidden just below."

He had found two paddles on the raft and he also had weapons slung about him, a bow and several arrows in a lion's-tail quiver, a spear, a blowgun and its bamboo section of darts. From his shoulder hung a skin bag with several objects in it such as feathers, a bracelet, and a bamboo tube of *achiote*. Every Indian carries such a bag (measuring eighteen inches long and a foot wide), and in it is not only his make-up kit but all sorts of odds and ends such as flint and steel, medicines, arrowheads and charms. In one hand he clutched by its tail a fair-sized monkey—the *huapo*.

"*Carne!*" hoarsely whispered Jorge.

José soon had the skin off the monkey, which together with the head and guts, he immediately buried in the ground, fearing vultures would come and reveal our hiding place. He was soon handing Jorge and me small pieces of meat cut with his newly acquired Campa knife.

"You must chew it well!" He would not let us eat too much of the raw meat, and withheld it after a few mouthfuls.

Pointing up at several crow-sized birds with black bodies and red heads darting back and forth overhead and chattering madly, José scowled: "We stay here today. And if those soldier-birds do not reveal us—tonight we move.

The Indian picked up his blowgun and fitted a thin, brownish dart together with a twist of cotton, into its mouthpiece breech. *Pffff!* went the dart, and one of the birds came tumbling down. When José crawled slowly out of the hole, his eyes narrowed and twisting up at the jabbering flock, I felt that it would not be long before all of the meat hunting soldier-birds would be lying dead about that thicket of bamboos.

Jorge was stretched out on his side, listening intently to a persistent Indian signal—the cat mew of a fishing hawk. I couldn't help grinning, for I knew what this son of the conquistadores thought of the shirt Indians.

"You know—" he said soberly in a very low voice, his ear still cocked toward the river bank, "That José is a good man…our good friend too."

ᘓ **XV.** ᘔ

Escape on the Tambo

*I*T was long past midnight before the last Indian signals echoing off the high salt cliffs on the far side of the river ceased. This final one was the persistent gobbling of a cock-turkey, a *piuri*, repeatedly summoning the hunting savages to him. It would have passed as a real turkey, except that these birds seldom gobble after sundown, at which time they go to roost in the higher limbs.

Even then we dared not move out. Crouching in the thicket we listened attentively to every sound that came from the trees and especially from the river: monkey chatters, the splash of fish—all were now judged genuine. But José seemed to be waiting for something, and when an hour had passed, I suddenly realized what it was when he glanced up into the sky: clouds were covering the heavens and the stars, a complete darkness creeping over the jungle.

Very quietly now we crawled through the bamboos, squirming along on our bellies, until we reached the river's south shore. José snaked into the water and we followed, taking great care not to raise the slightest ripple, for the surface was shiny with minute phosphorescent life. We feared the Indians more than the denizens of the deep. Twenty feet offshore we were in water up to our chins, and immediately started floating out toward the channel. From the middle of the river as we were being carried along, we could make out various objects, tall trees lining the low banks, and flotsam islands of hyacinth floating alongside. Despite the mosquitoes and the danger from snakes and crocodiles, we swam into one of these, a free island some half-acre in extent. To keep afloat, we need only spread our arms over the mass of the high bulbous stems.

We must have drifted downriver for two hours when José broke away from the hyacinth, swimming with only the barest ripple ahead of him, toward the left bank. Jorge and I were right behind, propelling ourselves along as cautiously as he. Reaching shallow water, the Indian waded silently into a *cocha* beyond the line of the trees.

Crouched in the river, Jorge and I waited for twenty long minutes, and then the Indian appeared pushing a narrow balsa raft ahead of him. By this time the rods of our eyes were so well adjusted to the darkness that we could see very plainly. We slid aboard and were once more adrift on the river. I seemed to be counting the inches linking us like a chain back to that bamboo thicket. Though rain was presently falling, and it was still dark, a flock of *yungaruru* pheasants began calling in their peculiar two-toned song, a very high note and a very low one—thus we realized that dawn was not far off.

Soon after, sand began flowing in the river, hissing under the raft, a sure indication that swift water was ahead. We dared not beach and risk an overland reconnaissance and so continued blindly on. A hot, rain-filled wind began blowing in gusts upriver, cavorting the raft this way and that. By energetically plying the two paddles we ran a 500-yard stretch of resounding white water, shooting through a winding slot of stone walls. At the bottom we extricated ourselves from a whirlpool, and once more glided silently on. I couldn't help it, I kept staring back over my shoulder.

There was more light on the river and we would certainly be visible to any Indian watching this stretch. The loyal José took the bamboo tube of *achiote* out of his skin bag—part of his swag—and handed it to me: "Take off your clothes, *patróne*."

Though fever-laden *culex* mosquitoes were swarming over the bright yellow surface of the river, I lost no time in complying. Jorge followed my example. We helped each other smear on the red paint, especially on our backs. Feathers were tied in our hair, which was long, and from the far banks we must have looked like three *bravos*. Delighted with our Indian appearance, José got out a pair of snake bracelets from the bag and slipped them on my arms. Our precious clothes and shoes and my money belt were hidden away in José's skin bag.

Several Indians swept into view, watching us intently from a high bank on the right side, but not a signal came from them as we drifted by. Birds began flying back and forth across the river, starting their day songs; but like many birds of these jungles they never finished their songs but usually stopped on some impossible and maddening note. Gaudy wild chickens such as the *gavilán* and the *trompetero*, were perched in the trees, the roosters beginning to crow. Still marching on our left, well back from the tangled bank, rose the sheer cliffs of the Gran Pajonal, soft white, streaked now with thick veins of orange.

A black thundercloud rolled up from behind and kept pace with us. The *pit-pit-pit* of the rain studded the tawny surface of the river. Sudden explosions and crackling electric fire broke the cloud asunder and after a violent tropical deluge, the sun shone copper in a pale blue sky; daylight had come. Though apprehensive, I saw that we were getting into lower country, for wide sandbars began replacing those of gravel. Stones still continued to clink musically as they bumped along the river's bed. These were well-rounded stones which would be ground down to sand and eventually, in the Lower Amazon basin, be pulverized to mud. That morning I was reminded that the earth turned through space (for the stars wheeled past overhead), that the mountains were washing into plains as in aeons past, and that we were part of the immense microstructure of this spinning ball of iron and nickel, mud and stone and water.

The skies presently shone with streaks of yellow, due to high-elevation dust, the jungle all green and shining in its rain drops. As the balsa, an old waterlogged one, drifted low in the torrent at fifteen miles an hour through gentle ripples, waves washed over our bare feet.

Hours later, while watching for Indians—we could hear signal drums—I suddenly spied a herd of large wild animals—pigs!—only 300 yards away.

We forgot our terror of the Indians and remembered only that we were starving. It would be necessary to approach at least within a hundred feet if we were to use José's bow and arrows effectively. We dug in the paddles, but could not beach the raft until swept some 200 yards below the herd. The pigs' eyesight was obviously bad, though José warned that their scent faculty was excellent, and we must be careful as the pigs were dangerous. Fearing they would run away, I grabbed the bow and two of the arrows and leapt ashore. I approached through a strip of covering *caña brava*, taking care to creep into the breeze which, due to a wide turn in the river, was coming downriver.

I could presently hear the pigs rooting into a bank close by. Slowly raising my head I saw that many of the animals were standing up to their bellies in the water of a shallow *cocha* choked with water lilies. They did not appear to be alarmed. Getting down on my belly I sneaked through the *caña* to within eighty feet of one of them. Carefully I fitted an arrow to the bow, and not daring to stand up, crouched on my knees and drew it. I judged the bow to be a sixty-pound one. The bowstring twanged, and the arrow zipped through a thin branch of leaves, striking the boar in the belly.

Instantly the herd stampeded, splitting into two bands, throwing up their ugly heads and squealing. At first they milled about, then both herds lined out taking to the river on my left, plunging in and swimming for the opposite side. At this point the Tambo was very swift and over 300 yards across. José apparently saw the pigs for he yelled as if to hurry the leaders on and I saw the raft slide out to intercept them. Jorge was frantically paddling, and José knelt in the bow, Campa spear in hand.

I glanced back to the *cocha* to see if my pig was down. About twenty squealing boars were following a big black pig with an arrow stuck in him! But the boar was far from dead…he was circling away from the river, head well up, trying to get my wind. Suddenly he had it, and charged through the water straight for me, grunting and making a frightful noise. I made a grab for the limb above me, pulled my legs clear in time to save them from the furiously clacking ivory tusks.

There are two species of pigs in the Campa country: the gray-brown, white-collared peccary named by the Campas *biratse*, which weighs up to eighty pounds, and the big, black, hundred-and-fifty-pound *huangana* such as these, whose name is *shintori*.

The tree in which I found myself was not more than six inches in diameter and very shaky, but so furious were the *huanganas*—leaping up at me, gouging their tusks into the trunk, even trying to dig out the roots!—that I risked climbing a little higher. I finally got eight feet above them, but dared not go higher for the tree was shaking and swaying wildly. The worst pig of the lot was the one with the arrow in his guts, and so violent was he that the shaft broke off. I was sick with disappointment, fearing he would now live to get away.

From my perch I could see the whole panorama on my left, and an amazing sight was revealed, for it was a rare occurrence. The entire river, from side to side, was a solid mass of black *huanganas*—perhaps a thousand of them.

Jorge and José beached the raft and began shouting and throwing stones at the pigs at the bottom of my tree. They wheeled and plunged through the thicket and at last took to the river for presently I could hear them splashing only a little way above the raft.

I jumped down and recovered the bow and the last arrow, and taking their tracks followed at a run. Incredibly, my boar was lying on its side in the mud not a yard from the river, gasping. Apparently the arrow was poisoned and it had taken the fifteen-minute time interval since being shot for the venom to work its way to the boar's brain. The poisoned tip, of course, was still inside. José gleefully tossed his spear, which I caught butt-end first, reversed, and drove the point into the pig's heart.

We decided to dress out our kill. Jorge and José had killed three pigs, spearing them with the captured spear after bringing the raft into the midst of the swimming herd. A thrust into the neck proved all that was necessary to kill. They had the three animals on the raft, and so we dragged all four onto a clean rock shelf. We worked fast at the butchering as swarms of blood-flies were beginning to gather. We knew Indians were near and we must get back on the river. All at once, I was aware that the crimson water about us was furiously alive, and we were barefooted.

"*Paña!*" yelled Jorge.

That awful word startled us into action. Only because we were standing in very shallow water, and thus able to leap out instantly, were our feet saved. These particular *paña* were the silver ones, having the same pink belly as the black variety and no more than nine inches long. The chisel-toothed little demons tore at the pigs' entrails lying in the water. Part of the school jumped into the air, tore the meat out of the carcasses themselves, for we had been washing out the lower parts and they lay in the shallows.

Grabbing the pigs by their ears, we hauled them safely out on the beach; one of the *pañas* flopped out of a carcass, and I kicked it away from the water. I was bending over to examine this fish, when suddenly it flopped up, cutting a deep gash in my right knee. I held it down with a stick, and saw that the teeth are triangular. The Indians use these teeth to sharpen their blowgun darts.

The pigs' carcasses finally gutted (and I was very careful to remove the broken arrow point before cleaning out the insides), and the hides left on so that the flies could not blow the meat, we bound them up in cool elephant-ear leaves. We knew we must risk a fire, for we were now too weak to go longer without food. After building a fire and cooking the hearts in the coals, we shoved off into the current and ate our first real meal in two days.

As we drifted along the river turned a yellow-gray. It was always changing its complexion according to the sky overhead, but now it obviously was deepening. Every few miles we slid through narrows and violent cataracts, with pale placid stretches in between. *Patos* were everywhere on these quiet places—mallards, wood ducks, and strange Amazon varieties—all hissing and quacking. We dared not risk our last three game arrows, for they were hardwood and would sink and be lost.

Scores of black crocodiles appeared now on every bank, and since they had never been hunted, could sometimes be approached as close as fifty feet. They lay with their great white mouths half open, watching us and warming their cold reptilian blood. By day, most of these saurians lay on the river bottom catching fish, but in the evening they crawled out by the thousands to enjoy the milder slanting rays of the setting sun. In the daytime, however, if clouds covered the hot sun, they would immediately crawl out of the water.

Turtles like the twenty-pound dark-gray *taricaya* splashed into the river from their sunning perches of logs and mud banks. The *taricaya* are capable of laying from 200 to 300 bantam-sized eggs in a single night, and in the upper river they had provided one of our main foods. Others seen were the seventy-five-pound *charapa*, which lay from 50 to 100 eggs; the smaller *cupiso, motelo, teparo,* and *asna charapa*—all being gray in color, with the exception of the *motelo*, which is yellow-gray. The *asna charapa* is easily identified by its knotty shell.

The ancient sedimentary fossilized sea bottom became more pronounced, for it was stripped of its overburden of shallow forest-earth. Great ribs of a black tarlike substance, harder than flint, lay exposed in thick bands across the uptilted fractured white and gray rocks. The earth's crust had been forced upward by enormous pressures from below, and as a result, the surface was broken. Even so, the chances were that at depths of four or five thousand feet, the original structure was intact, for the whole area appeared to be favorable for the geologic formation of oil basins—petroleum. Seepages were indicated by oil floating on top of the *cochas* beyond the river banks. Without a seismographic sounding, the extent of the basins could not be determined.

It was becoming obvious that we were getting into a heavier game country. And though the Amazon is not considered a game country (except for the open Brazilian Gran Chaco, sportsmen give it a wide berth), we counted some fifteen varieties of big game, including a pair of jaguars. New animals to us were the eight-foot *lobos*, whose fur is valuable; and the nutria, here a great tropical otter of the same length. Another strange animal was the shaggy bearlike *oso hormiguero*, approximately nine feet in length. There were also *puchanas*, a very large rodent. Once we beached to examine a sloth, the *pelejo*, the acme of slow motion, hanging by long hooks upside down on the underside of a limb.

We climbed the *pelejo's* tree to see what lay about us. Except for cliffs on the north side, there was nothing but jungle—as far as the eye could reach; but directly south, rising out of the flat tangle was a high mountain known to the Campas as Puyene, unmarked on any map, the last of the major Andean spurs reaching out into the basin. José said Puyene was inhabited by a tribe known as the "bat men," people who have no eyes, and, like bats, hunt only at night. Later that day we saw five naked savages standing on the right bank, wearing masks of bark across their eyes. These masks had two slits cut into them, which were no doubt the reason for the Campa name of "bat men"! Apparently they mistook us for Indians at first, for we got within twenty feet of them before they broke and ran into the trees.

José told us in Spanish and a few words of Campa that south of Puyene lay the "Golden City of the Three Sacred Huacas of Pachacamac." Now Pachacamac, I realized, was the ancient Incan god who had created the Sun God. He was the Universal Maker, All-Pervading Spirit, and his golden image had once stood in Cuzco between the massive gold and silver idols of the Sun and Moon Gods. The Inca priests had conceived a trinity: Pachacamac (Creative Agency); Pachaca Mama (Earth Mother); and Contici (Thunder God—literally, Thunder Vase). Very little is known of these gods.

When I asked José how he had learned of Pachacamac and his lost city, he answered: "The Inca, Aymara, and the Quecha *Huaris* (Great Ones)—*muy antigua!*—taught our *matse* (witches)."

"What are the Three Sacred Huacas in this city?" I asked.

"When Pachaca Mama produced all animals, plants and man from the same cloth, Pachacamac breathed a soul (*shiakanse*) into them. Then Pachacamac manifested as Manco Capac, the first Inca. He descended to earth and taught man all things. He is Pawa, the Son of the Sun! Manco Capac founded Cuzco, and on an altar placed three great eggs—one of gold, one of silver, one of copper—from which were born kings, priests, slaves. With the death of Inca Atahuallpa at the hands of the Spaniards, the Incas took the three cosmic eggs into the east. These are the Great Huacas. They are in Pachacamac's city of gold, just over there!" José pointed south, toward the mountain of Puyene. Somewhere in that direction, inside that vast region encircled by the Ene, Urubamba and Tambo rivers, might indeed lie that golden city.

We continued on, and two hours before dark we saw still other savages, naked and painted a bright blue. They were heavy-set men, very muscular, who fled with incredible agility away from the beach. They carried huge battle axes some four feet in length of a dark reddish wood. Rings dangled from their big hawk-beaked noses, and six-inch plugs were thrust horizontally through their earlobes. Their hair was bright red, long and coarse like a horse's tail, and streamed back over their massive painted shoulders. José called these furtive savages Machiguengas. The tribe numbers some 5,000. Silent, sadistic devils, they make swift forays against the Campa at night, committing bloody atrocities, burning, taking slaves. José explained that recently the *patróne*, Pereira, while working south out of Atalaya, captured twenty-five Machiguengas, and planned to set them at work growing coffee. The captives were yoked together and marched to the Pongo de Mainique, where they promptly broke out of the shackles and slit Pereira and his men's throats and escaped. Since then it has been impossible to capture any of them, and sure death for any *patróne* who would try.

With nightfall terminating that long day, we came upon an encampment of eleven warriors of an unknown tribe whose stamping ground is on the Purus, farther east. We knew we were on the edge of the Campa heartland, and that where strange Indians dared to come, we, too, were much safer than at any time since leaving 'Opata. The Indians were tall and slender, completely naked but for yellow paint streaked with black bars. A few had a strange basket covering and were peculiarly deformed. This tribe practices a strange form of phallic culture. They believe that God is a generative being, and that He manifests Himself on earth in the penis. With growing boys the organ is hung with graduated weights, and progressively stretched, so that in adulthood the male organ—as we saw—is elongated to a length of a foot to a foot and a half, and is usually carried in a basket.

When José enquired into their business on the Tambo, these *bravos* excitedly explained in a monkeylike chattering brand of Campa, a few words which all the tribes understand, that they were hunting Amajuacas. The Amajuaca tribe had been raiding on the Purus and burning huts, and this war party was counterattacking. We figured we were practically out of danger for the moment, for the Purus' scouts must have reported that no Campas were about.

We set up a bivouac of palm fronds at the far end of the *playa,* after driving off a herd of peculiar black-and-white pinto crocodiles. We washed off our paint and put on our clothes against the swarms of *borrashudo* mosquitoes. Since we must have provisions to continue on our way, and the pig carcasses were beginning to stink, we butchered them, and throughout the night smoked the meat on stakes encircling three smudge fires. José, Jorge and I gorged ourselves on meat. We bought yuca from the basketmen, in exchange for the four pig heads—great delicacies judging from their howls of delight. These they cracked open with rocks and placed on their fire for cooking.

We stood guard all night, for the savages' encampment was wild with drum-beating. They were making a human fetish doll out of clay, painting and befeathering it, offering yuca to it. Indians believe that spirits can enjoy the essence of food. Finally they speared the fetish, thus gaining the help of the *mamas* (spirits) against their enemies, the Amajuacas.

The *playa* was a nasty place to be, for there was no natural defense, and at the first sign of dawn we embarked for Atalaya. According to my map it lay below the Urubamba's and the Tambo's confluences with the Ucayali, and could not be more than sixty miles in the north. Soon the Tambo flattened out and widened to some 300 yards, and was running clear and very deep, a pale sea green in color with clean gravel and sand *playas* sandwiched at frequent intervals between mile-long banks of mud.

Under the jungle's roof the shiny red trunks of a new type of *cedro* trees, weirdly resembling Chinese iron landscape pictures covered with red rust, glistened in the morning light and dew. The white and yellow *huito* trees stood in thick groves. These trees are used by the tribes for rafts, as the wood is floatable. Giant 120-foot-high *moriche* palms danced gracefully in the hot damp dawn breeze.

Some hours after leaving the *playa,* the Tambo's course bent directly north. From time to time we saw canoes filled with Indians, and Jorge and José talked to a few of them. They did not belong to any great tribe but were clans who lived on the various feeder rivers entering the Tambo. From these Indians we obtained the names of the larger tributaries. The dotted lines on the map plainly showed that all about us must be a network of unnamed rivers and tributaries. Very often, these dotted lines ran through country devoid of actual rivers, whereas the white blanks on the map were often actually places where great rivers did pour into the Tambo. We were now eleven degrees south of the Equator—and as we were swept north, the rivers entering the right bank were the Anapiti, Xeni, Omiga....

I began the work of correction, which I had promised Professor Rosell I would do, as he had lost most of his own maps in the fire already mentioned. Real mountains were obviously ignored by the cartographers in Lima, while in vast swamps they had sketched in mystical ranges such as Almagro's Golden Mountains which the conquistadores had reported seeing out here. Towns of the *caucheros* were boldly marked where none existed, or ever had existed. Rosell, indeed, had been familiar with actualities when he had said: "Names! Names! Only names!" as he had tapped his fingers on the wall map depicting east Peru.

But for all the vagueness of our position on the map, we were otherwise in fair shape as Jorge said. "Escape on the Tambo. I just can't believe we are almost through the Gran Pajonal."

So many Indians were running away from the *playas,* that José thought we must look to them as if we were *patrónes* out on a raid and returning empty-handed to Atalaya, and that it couldn't be very far away.

Once, some girls bathing beside a wallowing pair of manatees—gentle cow-like creatures—froze at sight of us, then dashed through the shallow water to hide among the trees. These *manatí,* the great herb-eating seacows of the Amazon rivers, were mistaken by the old Spanish explorers such as Orellana, for mermaids. The *manatí* suckles its young, and from a distance the breasts are deceptively like those of Homo sapiens.

By midmorning we realized a great storm must have hit the Andean highlands days before, for the run-off into the Tambo surged to alarming proportions, overflowing the low banks. We had great difficulty keeping in the channel, and out of the jungle. During the space of half an hour, the foamy flood rose twenty-six feet under us! There was no trace of banks or *playas,* only trees lining the way, and the river's color turned from its pale sea green to an ashy gray—twisting dangerously this way and that with many currents and eddies. By paddling furiously we managed to keep out of the worst places, though we nearly went down in a very small but deep and steep-sided whirlpool. We breathed in relief when the flood reached its peak and started to ebb.

What a demonstration! The team of weather, water, and gravity was grinding the Andean Cordilleras—earth's mightiest mountain mass— to silt and mud. We also realized that the noise of the sub-Andean canyons had gone, and that there remained only the vast, silent plain of the basin itself....

Such mighty floods are the reason for the many large inland *cochas* being miles across and teeming with such fishes as *curuaras, tucunaris, sardinas, carachamas, puñunderos, turushuques* and *puñoisiquis.*

We finally found a thin sliver of a mud *playa* above the flood, and here we camped. We felt safe from all possible pursuit. By the firelight (we had found driftwood higher up among the trees), we anxiously studied the map. We had been unable to locate the oasis of Atalaya. Of course, years before it had been burned out by the Campas. But now it was supposed to have been rebuilt—the "greatest city" for a thousand miles south of Iquitos.

"Where the devil is it?" puzzled Jorge. It certainly had to be somewhere in this wild region of swirling waters and swamped trees, somewhere at the headwaters of the mighty Ucayali, that little-known river reputed to be as large as the Mississippi.

That night we were routed out; a new downpour of rain was raising the river, swiftly carving away the island on which we were so precariously perched. The current was filled with logs and whirling debris, which crashed together in a log-jam, piling up only a few yards away over the entire upper end of our tiny *playa*. Our only chance was to tie up the raft, and take to the trees. This we did, climbing into the limbs of a giant *zapallo*—which we soon found to be swarming with yellow ants. We were afraid to move around in the dark after our firebrands had burned out. The small flashlight was of no use as the batteries were practically dead. And as for the firebrands drawing possible Indians, that was the least of our worries. José had warned against parrot snakes, the tree-climbing *verde loros*.

That night, as if we had not already enough troubles, we were attacked by a flight of vampire bats. While wedged in a crotch of the tree, José fell asleep and lost a great amount of blood to these bats. Strangely they had tapped only his big toes and the veins above the ankles. The bat does not alight, as it has no legs and feet, but hovers. The wound cannot be felt as an anesthetic fluid is present. His feet were covered with blood, for the bats had drilled several deep cone-shaped holes. He was alarmingly weak from loss of blood. Such an attack on even a cow or a horse will often cause it to die during the night, and is the chief reason why there are no horses and cattle in the villages of the upper Amazon. Up till then we had escaped by pointing our feet toward our campfires, and wrapping our heads in cloth or large leaves, Indian-style. We had nothing with which to dress José's wounds.

And when dawn finally broke, I saw that this was not the end of our immediate troubles; Jorge was shaking violently, his face haggard, and he was burning with malaria.

I descended the trunk, swam over to the raft and worked it around to the tree. After much difficulty I got both Jorge and José aboard where they lay stretched out full length. Once more we were in the Tambo's flush, and though still flooded, it was slowing down. I must paddle hard in order to keep to the swiftest part of the channel, which was sometimes in the middle, sometimes on one side and then on the other, and dangerously close to the swamped trees.

A giant crocodile tried to climb over the stern, probably mistaking us for one of the rafts of debris floating along. We were half under water from its weight before I could drive it off with my paddle. Later I began counting the reptiles lying about on floating logs and on the banks whenever these appeared. I scored five hundred crocodiles in less than an hour, and then stopped.

Ours was an amazing journey through a reptilian paradise.

Crocodiles raised their long spade-flat heads from the mud or logs in a queer crook, while our raft was yet a good half mile off—and then quite often dashed wildly for the river. Others would slip in quietly, or even let us glide past within ten or fifteen feet, lying unconcerned in the mud, warming themselves through grinning jaws, while plovers picked the rows of long, sharp teeth. There were two kinds that day: a large mottled pinto with crazy-quilt white and gray patches, and a pure black one. The armor-plated black, the *yana lagarto*, or *lagarto negro*, is especially dangerous, being unpredictable, and if surprised will often attack. Skin hunters lower down on the Ucayali, sheath the bows of their canoes with steel. Harpooning them is a very hazardous business. One monster the three of us estimated as being twenty-three feet in length. However, the majority of the Tambo crocodiles did not exceed twelve or fourteen feet.

Seventeen torrid hours were spent that day on the river. But we had put many miles to our rear. As I steered with a fishtail twist to the oar, my eyes and ears ached from watching and listening. Sometimes we got caught among floating islands, literally crawling with snakes. Driven by the flood they were coiled on any floatable object. During this time I shaded Jorge and José with palm leaves where they lay on the wet deck, their faces and hands cracked dry. All of us were burned the color of mahogany. There was no camping at nightfall—both men were in too desperate a way. And so I kept on into the darkness, laboring at the paddle which I had turned into a sweep at the stern. We passed the broad mouth of the Urubamba coming in on the right bank.

An hour later: "Ah, *patróne*," groaned José, "the great city of Atalaya is close by."

"Where! Where!" I exclaimed, for I was very excited, "I can't see it."

"Close by, *patróne*—look sharp! I can smell smoke."

But no lights appeared anywhere in the twin walls of unbroken jungle. Due to our inaccurate map, setting a course by dead reckoning and compass was impossible, for there was no way of establishing an azimuth. The river had become so very wide it was like a sea in the dusky darkness, and I was wondering if we hadn't already entered the Ucayali, the greatest of the far west tributaries of the Amazon! In desperation I landed on the left bank, and made a reconnaissance by climbing into a tall *zapote* tree. At last I reached the crown. Over the tree tops were several little gleaming lights in the west. The "city" was on a high mud bank on the left (and not the right as shown by the map). "*La Ciudad Grande!*" I shouted for the benefit of José and Jorge below.

Climbing down and casting off in great cheer, I peered hard into the darkness for it would be easy to overshoot and impossible for me alone to work the raft back upstream against the current. Then suddenly we made out on the left bank a palm-thatched cluster of some dozen

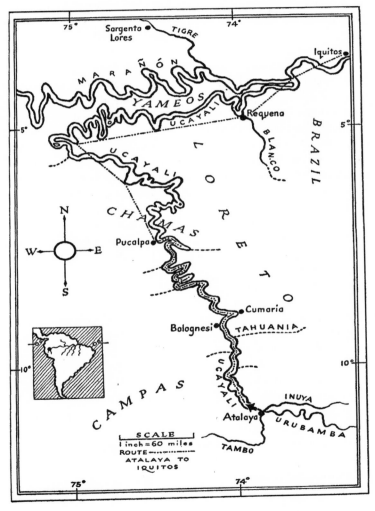

miserable shacks. I cautiously felt my way down a long staircase of rapids, and then paddled furiously. Near the bank a crocodile slid into the water, disappearing under us. We grated to a landing: it was nine o'clock.

José got up and staggered ashore, tying up the lines. I grabbed Jorge under the arms and we crawled after the Indian up the steep bank. It was about ten feet high, but we finally made the top. Before us, only a stone's throw away was an old California-type adobe perhaps 150 feet long with a low porch all along the front. I knew this to be the Franciscan mission of Atalaya when I saw its bell and wooden cross among the stars.

José pulled at my sleeve, exclaiming, "*Señor patróne! Es muy grande casa! Magnifico!*" Everything in this life is comparative, and even to me it looked like the Empire State building. We limped across the clearing (in the upper Amazon plazas there are no plantings, purposely kept absolutely bare, as this is a great relief from the surrounding jungle). I banged on the massive rough-hewn mahogany doors. Slowly, after ten persistent minutes, they creaked open on hinges of forged iron. A black-bearded, white-robed priest in a peaked cowl, holding a dripping silver candelabrum aloft, peered out with a frightened expression in his dark eyes.

"*Buenas noches, Padre,*" I said quietly, so as not to startle him further, for being ragged we must have presented anything but a reassuring sight; "I am a *norteamericano.* I desire medical aid, food and lodging for my *compañeros.*"

" Señor! *Es imposible!*" the friar held the clustered candles nearer. "From where, señor, could you possibly have come?"

"From Lima, Padre; down the Perené and the Tambo. And I have a letter of introduction from the Bishop of Lima to you."

That did it. Mumbled exclamations of amazement cackled forth from the black beard, which was draped over the entire ecclesiastical front. He introduced himself as "Padre Pascal—Alegre Al Pascal." A second cowled priest now joined us at the door—"Padre Angel Arellano, Vicar de Legado, Bishop of the Rio Ucayali, founder of Atalaya in the Year of Our Lord, 1932."

"*Exploradores!*" wailed the astonished Bishop. "Here is chickenpox. Pain. Anemia. Whooping cough. Malaria. Leprosy. Many other troubles. We are poor…even hungry, in Atalaya. But—you must be our guests!" A servant was sent to the river to fetch our things up from the balsa. The

Bishop beat off swarms of striker mosquitoes already settled on us and we strode into what seemed a medieval hall of stone and plaster, with wooden beams fixed substantially in the ceiling. The place echoed with our footfalls; the doors were slammed shut and bolted behind us. Thank God, I thought—as I stretched Jorge out on the top of a long table.

Later, when the Indian returned and Padre Alegre saw nothing but a monkey bag, a blowgun and its darts, a bow and three arrows, and two badly used paddles, he seemed worried. But not long after when he spotted the sixteen smoked hams and the eight racks of pork ribs, he jumped as if shot through the heart: "Manna from heaven!" He wagged his shiny tonsured head. "And the city is starving, señor! Twenty-eight children have died of whooping cough. And all the others are hungry. Even the soldiers. We are planning to evacuate six hundred miles north to Pucalpa!"

"Then why not issue this food to the town?" I suggested, waving at the heap.

The Bishop Arellano cut in on the bearded Alegre, smiling, "Tut! Tut! Do not worry our guests. They have troubles enough. Come, good friends, we have bread and a little wine and with your fine jungle ham...but first, the children! and then the adults in the city, and afterwards why should we five not partake of God's bounty ourselves, here, caballeros."

The food was carried away by several Indians. Soon Jorge was propped up in a chair and José and I, together with the priests, sat down at the great table now spread with a clean white cloth. We sipped red grape wine while waiting for the breech-clouted servants to bring on the ham and bread.

We toasted Señor el Presidente de Peruaua, and Señor el Presidente de Estados Unidos—and then the Bishop leaned forward, and in a confidential voice: "What political party do you favor, señor?" I assured him that I was an explorer and had no political favoritisms, but when pressed admitted to being a Republican. "A *Republicán*! That explains your presence in *La Selva*. You are a political refugee from your country!"

"But no! señor," I hastened to correct him, "We *norteamericanos* do not imprison or persecute the opposition party when it is out of power."

"Señor! Peruana is a free country. You will have sanctuary from political oppression here with us!" he exclaimed. And from then on, due to the efficient grapevine, the Peruvians of the Amazon believed me to be an American political refugee, and as long as I was on the Ucayali, I was always greeted by the priests, the fort commanders and the *patrónes*, as "*El Señor* the Republicán—the political refugee from Estados Unidos!"

At last we got to bed. I was thankful above all else to have reached Atalaya—having crossed over the Cordillera from Lima and bridged the Gran Pajonal into the Amazon country, a straight-line distance of 300 miles, twice that by our route. The great danger of this part of the trip was over. The date was July 27, twenty-five days since leaving Lima. And I was especially thankful that Jorge had proved himself, and that once he was well again I could now take him into my confidence. As explorers armed with all our information on this particular segment of the unknown sub-Andean regions, we would be welcomed in Iquitos, a hotbed of intrigue. We were now in a position to strike out for El Dorado itself.

↫ XVI. ↬

Ucayali Adventures

I WAS in bed, and it was still black night when the old cracked iron bell suspended from a rickety gallows-like frame above the thatched roof, began bong-bonging at a great rate; a wild rooster added an exclamation point to this announcement of a new day and a pattering of bare feet could be heard in the hall outside my monastic cell of a bedroom.

I was just turning over on my boards, with some vague idea of sleeping until the rainy season commenced, when Padre Alegre rushed in with a lighted candle, a huge smile in his beard, and rousted me out. "Adios, señor. Get up! We go to the garden for coffee."

"*Mañana, mañana,*" I groaned, "It's pitch dark outside. May the good Lord forgive you."

With a gleeful shout he grabbed the mosquito net from around me and tied it in a knot overhead—"Now, lazy one. Get up!—or be eaten alive by the *moscos!*" And he rushed out of the cell, the whole mission echoing with his merry laugh.

By the time I had bathed and shaved (for a razor, a bar of soap and a bucket of water had been left behind with the candle) and dressed, daylight was bursting through the narrow slit of a window set high in the thick adobe wall. The Padre had loaned me a clean pair of white duck pants and a white shirt until I could get some decent clothes of my own at the trading post. I joined the two priests and José in the garden at the rear of the building. It was surrounded by an adobe wall enclosing an acre of palms and orchids and strange flowering trees in which a flock of tiny parrots—the singing *chirricles*—were feeding.

"Welcome! Welcome!" shouted the Bishop Arellano, a tall, thin man of about fifty, "Our garden is cool so early in the day. And we have coffee in your honor."

I was handed a cup of this steaming black brew, noting that the "coffee" was made from burnt corn, as real coffee is very dear in Atalaya. Arellano said that Jorge must stay in bed, that his fever was mounting, and that we must prepare to live here for the time being. I thanked the Padres for their kindness, and they assured me they would do all they could to bring Jorge's fever down.

Padre Alegre, a younger man than the Bishop, entertained us with tales pertaining to the history of the Ucayali. Since it was down this great river of a thousand miles (450 airline miles) that we must go in order to reach Iquitos, I listened intently.

Not many years before, as time is measured here, the Chamas and the Campas rose up and massacred every *patróne* on this part of the river. When Lima ordered soldiers upriver from Iquitos on a punitive expedition, they were ambushed and, after a terrible slaughter, were driven back with losses running into the hundreds. At that time, Arellano, only recently appointed Bishop of the Ucayali, went in alone and talked the victorious tribe of 5,000 over to peace. Reoccupation of the Ucayali gradually followed, and in 1933 (less than twenty years before), Atalaya had been raised from its ashes.

War exercises, however, were still being held by the Chama nation, many deaths resulting from the massed *macana* fights. The Chamas are mainly fishermen, harpooners of the great *paiche* fish, and their main weapon in war is the heavy double-edged *macana*, or war-axe. Recently over a hundred of these Indians had been killed and maimed in a single duel. Campa *curacas* (chiefs) call in hundreds of their own warriors for these war exercises. They are paired off in two long ranks only fifteen feet apart—and armed with blunt-headed arrows, which they shoot from bows of great power, some being six feet long. At a signal the duel begins, the warrior's object being to hit his opposite number in the eye. As soon as first blood is drawn, the fight usually gets out of control and becomes a deadly melee. Sometimes serrated arrows are fitted to the bow strings.

The Campas, especially, are unbelievably skilful at dodging. Because of these war games the *patrónes* were very wary of an outbreak on the river.

The mission's water boy, a Campa, had only the week before been condemned by a class of Chama witches called *mueraya*, as being the spirit devil *yoshy*. Animals too are the abode of *yoshy*; a wife is called *yoshy aiir* (woman devil), and white men are also *yoshy*. Padre Alegre had found the Campa boy hiding in the jungle near Atalaya, almost dead from a beating administered by the *muerayas*, and had rescued him. As a result of this the witchmen were preaching war against the Church. The boy was called over to us, and when he grinned, I saw that his teeth were filed to sharp snake fangs, and that he still painted them black with the *yotoconti* plant juice. His legs and hands also were partially painted.

The boy hobbled over, for he was still badly off, and presently (to the astonishment of the Padres), I gained his confidence by speaking Campa. He said that dogs are seldom used on the upper Ucayali for recovering runaway slaves, but that men of his own tribe are set on their tracks instead. Campas are far more efficient in the swamps where the dogs lose the scent in the water.

Flogging and other punishments, including confinement in the "punishment coffin," were still being practiced, not only by the *patrónes* but also by the government officials stationed here. This torture box the Campas called *phingebitsare cajonarnise*, (literally, "insane coffin").

The box, as I saw, is not confined to *mansos* and wild Indians. That afternoon (in the center of the plaza) a soldier was put into it head down, where he remained for four hours. So violent was his screaming that the Jefe de Guarnición, at the garrison on the knoll nearby, turned the box over on its back for the remainder of the night so that Atalaya's inhabitants could sleep more comfortably in their hammocks. A Campa laborer was also immured in the box for forty-eight hours and, when released, lay unconscious on the ground for thirty more. When I approached the poor man with a gourd of water, I was run off by an angry soldier standing guard. These cruel punishments were being meted out for misdemeanors such as drunkenness, disobedience, and theft.

An Indian who got the "box treatment" because of laxness at the *patróne* Ratteri's camp returned afterwards and shot seven arrows into his owner.

While examining the Atalaya torture box I found that the victims had actually chewed holes in it trying to get out. Of course, this punishment is not allowed "officially," and there are laws on the books forbidding it.

Coffee finished that first morning, we went to the church—a tiny, white, wooden structure with a tremendous cross, facing the treeless plaza; and at José's suggestion I had a candle burned on the altar for each of our eight companions (we counted Black Hawk in) lost on the Perené and Tambo.

That day, July 28, was declared a fiesta, and as this was not only Sunday but Independence Day as well, we all trooped back to the church. In the front row of pews, regally attired in a starched white uniform, elegant with gold braid and sword, sat the grim Indian fighter, Capitán Manuel Luna Coha, Commandante of all Frontier Forces facing Brazil and Bolivia. His military district was not much less than the area contained in the United States east of the Mississippi. His international patrol line was some 1,000 miles long, and as most of the district was absolutely unexplored, it was of course never possible to patrol. With this powerful man, who was virtual king in a country larger than the greatest countries in west Europe, Jorge (who was carried in) and I—our old clothes washed and mended—sat in state.

"El Capitán—how is '*el kimono des mortes*' (the kimono of death)?" I ventured by way of small conversation.

"An Indian is in it now," he smiled pleasantly, if somewhat condescendingly, "We keep the law here. He will begin to raise a racket if the Bishop does not get on with High Mass. By the way, señor, are you a Catholic?"

"No, señor; normally I am a Methodist, though sometimes I think I am a Mohammedan or a Buddhist. But at present I lean a bit toward the Campa witchmen—sun worshippers, you know."

"Levity is not appreciated here, señor!"

I had a premonition I had better not try my luck too far. Troops with fixed bayonets stood at attention along the whitewashed walls. After the trooping of the Colors, the Bishop Arellano presided at High Mass.

In the early afternoon we reviewed a parade of a hundred troops; lean, hard, Indian-fighter type of men—thoroughly dangerous, and, I suspected, far more profitable as friends than as enemies. A small cannon was fired at intervals throughout the day; there was much patriotic singing and marching, pounding of trap drums and piping of flutes, followed by a soccer game—a national sport second only to bull fighting.

I have seen soccer played on all the continents and on any number of islands, including England. But I have never seen a game in which heads were bashed in, legs broken, and with a free-for-all at the end. The casualties were four broken legs, three broken arms, three cracked skulls—minor injuries such as sprained necks, black eyes, broken fingers, etc., being scarcely worthy of mention. The game was played between *Patróne* vs. Army. As judge of this melee, and remembering Solomon in time, I declared the game a draw, the money prize was split. In that way I escaped a mobbing.

Greatly concerned over Jorge, whose fever was not abating, and the possibility of high water on the Marañón, I was extremely anxious to start downriver, but no canoe was available. A raft was out of the question as it was too hard to handle in the current among the many shifting sand bars.

Late that afternoon José and I hunted in the jungle and came in with three boars, which we smoked that night and presented to El Jefe and to the missionaries. José created a problem, not only because his shoulder bothered him occasionally, but, as he was working willingly for white men, he would not be tolerated by the Chamas downriver. Therefore I knew I had to make plans for him to remain in Atalaya. He no longer painted, and with his long hair cut short, and dressed in clothes obtained from the Padres, he presented a good appearance.

Atalaya, I saw, was the central collecting point for all bartering and trade between Madre de Dios on the east and the state of Junín on the west, with Loreto just north. Northward, 150 air miles (300 by river) on the Ucayali was Pucalpa, the next important center, and 400 air miles northeast of that, on the Amazon lay Iquitos (*Perla del Amazonas*). At both these towns there were commercial agents, actually storekeeping traders. Atalaya's leaf and can warehouses were stuffed to overflowing with loot from the jungle: bales of sun-dried deer hides, and those of peccary, howler monkey, crocodile, boa constrictor, and other snakes including the anaconda; nutria; *lobo*; jaguar; ocelot—and in addition to hides were heaps, all helter-skelter, of tortoiseshell, beautiful Chama pottery; twists of tobacco; stacks of the seven-foot salted *paiche* fish; feathers and plumes such as egret and umbrella bird; rare bird pelts for the museums of the world; Indian weapons and culture artifacts; great black balls a foot or more thick of the smelly, sweating *caucho*; stacks of *barbasco* root; baled kapok; even beer bottles filled with gold dust; bars of silver; pokes of diamonds; baskets of medicinal herbs; logs of rare cabinet woods; boar's ivory and vegetable ivory; Brazil nuts; cacao; and many other products. One enterprising Peruvian woman fashioned copies of rare orchids from *paiche* scales, painted in wonderful Indian colors—the most beautiful and ingenious art I was to see anywhere in the jungle.

On Monday, July 29th, Padre Alegre rushed into my cell, crying, "Hurry, señor! Your Ucayali adventure begins."

It seemed the monthly mail launch had arrived only three weeks overdue from Pucalpa. We ran to the river bank. Sure enough! It was a single mahogany dugout having a forty-foot length and a five-foot beam. This *Queen Mary* of the river was powered by an ancient automobile engine. Since the launch carried a cargo of yuca, which was being avidly bartered in exchange for some of the contents of the warehouses, Atalaya's population decided to hang on—Indian troubles or no Indian troubles, Jorge was carried aboard on a litter.

We said our goodbyes, and I paid José off in hard money obtained from the mission. The priests assured me they would make José the first Indian capitalist on the Ucayali, purchase *barbasco* cuttings for him, and get him started as a small plantation owner. Other money from my money belt changed hands with the *garreta's capitán* for our passage and for a spare pistol; and then the Commandante Coha came down from his fort, and together with the two kindly friars, waved from the high bank as we sped northward downstream on the river. The Bishop Arellano called out that before reaching Pucalpa, we would come to a very fine house called Cumaria, and for us to stop there and give his respects to the Patróne Dolce. Jorge and I were somehow sandwiched between bales of deer hides and stacks of *paiche*, both crawling with flies and bugs of all kinds. The Bishop Arellano had given us a rubber poncho, and on this Jorge was lying.

In a few minutes we passed a large river on the right bank, one of the mouths of the Rio Urubamba which was in flood. The Commandante had just mentioned that a month earlier sixty soldiers had set out to explore its headwaters, but had been wiped out by Machiguengas.

With a mild breeze created by our forward movement in the five-knot current, the insects from the jungle were not nearly so bad as ashore. All day we sped down the ever-broadening Alto Ucayali. At places even here in the headwaters, the river was a half mile wide, running in broad loops through a very snaky bed. Though logging north, we were usually headed either west or east, We were paralleling the Andean Cordillera whose *cuchillas* (spurs) could be seen across the flat jungle regions on our left. Only the month before, twenty-three *patrónes* from Atalaya had been lost to Campas and jungle, trying to cross forty miles over to the hills where gold had been discovered on the "Black River."

That night, driven off the river at midnight by insect swarms of the *mosco común*, a new tiny gray mosquito, we stayed under the nets we had obtained in Atalaya, pitching them on sticks over a sand *playa*. From March to September, insects of many varieties are so bad on this river that most Indians and Peruvians stay in their houses, and for hours at a time will wrap their heads in cloths, and simply wait for the season to pass. The worst plagues are the *violenta picadura* flies and the *virote zancudo*. The death rate is very high. Such insects are so minute that no mosquito net will keep them all out. Bites often result in tropical ulcers, which appear as running sores all over the body. We were camped amongst a party of G-stringed Chamas. And very colorful these Indians were. At this place a *paiche yoshy* (fish spirit) had taken revenge on one of the fishermen who had harpooned it, for his son had fallen ill.

In the light of the Chamas' fire, we saw a *yobue* (one of the many, classes of witchmen) making "medicine." He was a short thick man, his body painted black, his face blue, his long hair dyed a bright red. He wore a cape made from the skin of the red spider monkey. The witch was drinking *oni*, the Chama brew of *aya huasca*, for producing visions. Later he sucked the spirit out of the boy's chest, displaying clear evidence to an admiring audience, in the form of a dime-sized *paiche* scale. The *yobue* then propitiated the water spirit by hanging a piece of salted *paiche* on a nearby limb.

These Indians dress in beautiful bark cloth, somewhat like South Sea Island tapa, having designs of various colors drawn in Inca-like patterns, and of a mystical meaning. Their headdress is a band of bark, at the back is a single feather—usually an egret plume or a heron crown. The braves wear a half-moon silver piece in the nose, and a disk dangling from the lower lip. Their musical instruments, played during the witch's séance, are flutes, tom-toms, strings of shells, and gourd rattles.

A marriage ceremony had taken place earlier, and the old women—according to Chama custom—were busy performing a clitoridectomy, destroying the bride's virginity with a *paca*-cane knife. These old women are *curanderias*, herbalists, and know how to pack the bride with an herb-treated mud to prevent infection as the result of the operation. All the Chama women paint the lower half of their hands and feet black, also the legs from below the knee to the ankle.

Another woman in this camp had been accused by her husband of infidelity during his absence while harpooning *paiche*. Now infidelity among many Indian tribes is punishable by death, but not so among the Chamas. The woman coyly claimed, as do all the women of this strange nation, and most ingeniously too, that a jabiru stork had attacked her while bathing at the edge of the *playa*. This satisfied the husband for a while, but after mulling it over he got another idea (after we were all fast asleep!), and accosted the warrior whom he had decided must be her lover. That night—for Indians never have my particular time for sleeping—we witnessed a most amazing sight.

The guilty lover went about receiving compliments on his prowess as a seducer, and then approaching the husband, bowed low to him, who returned the bow with great dignity; and then accommodatingly the culprit leaned over as custom demands, allowing the outraged husband gravely to cut a deep six-inch circular gash in his scalp, revealing the bone. The Indians then giggled happily, thus ending, in a very civilized fashion I thought, the whole episode. The family honor had been avenged. I noted that the partly shaved scalplocks of all the adult braves bore these curious crescent scars, the proudly worn decorations of successful lovemaking by these balcony-climbers of the jungle. The Chama scalp knife has a stubby wooden handle, but is shaped in a half-moon, the blade being only three inches long around the cutting edge. It is strange, then, that these promiscuous Indians should fight with shields and the four-foot wooden war axes for their brides.

We were away early next morning. Schools of whales, fifteen-foot dolphins, began whistling and plunging around the *garreta's* bows, causing the hollowed log to roll precariously and nearly swamp—for it was without a keel. There are two species of these *delfín* whales (freshwater whales)—*Delphinus fluviatilis*, and the *Inia geofrensis*, both of which the

Peruvians call *bufeo*. They are probably either an environmental adaptation from the days when the Amazon Valley was part of the Atlantic, or else they have followed the Amazon for four thousand miles to reach these headwaters in the Ucayali. They are a complete mystery. In any case, the great saltwater mammals today have adapted themselves to fresh water where Indians believe they actually breed. It was necessary to steer the *garreta* sharply away from them, for should we strike one we could easily founder and go down. There were twenty-three whales in this herd.

No less amazing, on this our second day, was the list I worked upon showing the major edible fishes found in the Ucayali. By nightfall it reached the fantastic number of thirty-seven varieties. This exceeds, for a single Amazon tributary alone, all the known edible fishes of any importance in all the inland North American waters combined. Obviously, starvation here has little cause for being; it is not that the soil and climate cannot produce food, for the savages (as we have seen) and even the semi-savages, though in contact with whites, live well.

It was midday, for the sun was standing directly overhead, when a small dugout overturned not far from us. There were two men in it—an old one, and another about twenty-five years old. As we changed course to rescue them, we saw that an anaconda held the young one in its mouth, while the old man (his father) was hacking away at the snake with his machete. We came alongside and saved the old fellow, but the son was crushed and drowned. We pulled the snake aboard the *garreta*, and as it was only half dead, an Indian finally managed to cut its head off with his machete. It was twenty-three feet long and a foot in diameter—the skin a golden color, with black irregular designs running over it. The Indian set to work skinning the snake, as the hide was valuable.

All that day, and in the others to follow, the wind was generally from the southeast or the east. From January to August the temperature hovers at 82–89 degrees Fahrenheit. On the Ucayali rains average sixty inches annually, with the heaviest rainfall in March. Each year the river overflows its low jungle-clad banks to cut new channels. During this time whole islands, even ten or fifteen miles in length, disappear, and new ones form.

At rare intervals—sometimes fifty or a hundred miles apart—standing high on stilts, were the big bamboo-walled, thatched houses of the *patrónes*. Hundreds of Campa, Chama and Yámeo, as well as Indians of other tribes, were kept here as "children-of-the-house" (mostly adults), working in the *barbasco* clearings. Near these houses on one or two of the exposed *playas* were heavy crops of rice. The seeds had been broadcast only a month before with no attempt at cultivation, while on the more elevated ridges scores of unfamiliar and exotic fruits and strange vegetables were flourishing with little or no care. (See Appendix.)

During our second night, coming in on the east side, we passed the rain-shadowed Rio Tahuania. Jorge was sleeping, and so I climbed up on the cargo of *paiche* and hides to watch it. An old Campa was squatting there, dressed in a ragged breechcloth. I passed him a bit of tobacco, which he rammed into the bowl of a very short Indian pipe with a two-inch stem, and soon we were smoking and taking the night breeze.

The old fellow pointed his pipe at the Tahuania and remarked that as a youth he had been to its headwaters. Knowing several *caucheros* had been killed on it recently, I pressed him for his own story. He explained that his father had been killed in the Gran Pajonal by raiding Cunibos. While he and another Campa brave pursued the Cunibas, they had turned up this river and at its source had learned that by dragging their canoe over a small ridge, they could launch it in the Rio Vacapista. This they did, and floated into the great Brazilian Yuruá, where they had found the Cunibos, killing all four of them.

Now if this be correct about the Cunibos' secret raid highway through the western jungles, it would be possible one day for an explorer to immortalize himself, by descending the Perené (or the Apurímac and Ene) into the Tambo and Ucayali, thence ascend the Tahuania to the headwaters of the Vacapista and so down the Yuruá into the middle Amazon and eventually the Atlantic. Thus he will have crossed the continent on a new west-east route—thereby matching Humboldt's north-south navigating of the Casiquiare Canal joining the Amazon system with that of the Orinoco.

I had lost count of the many unexplored rivers entering the Ucayali from both east and west: savages, cannibals and headhunters live in their headwaters. All that day Campa drums thumped from the forbidden hills on our left. Stolid Indian slavers with sinewy bulginess of muscle, enormous legs and arms, moved swiftly with flashing paddles over the river, their musket barrels sticking prominently over the gunwales of their dugouts. Prosperous *kanesare*, handsome Campa raiders, flamboyantly dressed in rich flaming-red or orange *cushmas* paddled by with live cargoes of silent children and women.

Our *capitán* steered clear of them when possible, for these slavers were very wild looking, though classed as semi-savage. On the *playas* they moved swiftly, with strangely inhuman tigerish movements combined with the Campas' *perante*, a kind of laziness seen only in dangerous wild animals; a combination that never failed to fascinate me. They were natural homicidals, with the long bobbed hair of women which they endlessly caressed in an effeminate manner. Their broad red-brown faces were painted and tattooed with tribal marks. They knew little Spanish and used sign language whenever we unavoidably drew close. Besides the muskets and .44-caliber Winchester rifles, they carried a heavy array of knives, blowguns, spears, and bows and arrows. On one *playa*, a group of them were making arrows from the flower stalk of *cañarana*, dressing the ends with a dried *paiche* tongue—the file of the jungle.

Next day at Bolognesi we saw five miserable shacks constructed of crooked sticks and withered leaves, perched on a stenching mud bank on the left side. The place was littered with discarded crocodile bellies cut from skins. We took off nine fever victims and a cargo of thirty-four slaves. We were crowded together, and the stench of the sick especially was most unpleasant, if not at times nauseating. Since leaving Atalaya the only food we had been given was a single *cutia*, a reddish, rabbit-sized, sour-smelling rodent, interesting only because its incisor teeth were used by the old Campa to scrape the bore of his blowgun.

After casting off from Bolognesi (printed in enormous type on my map), living conditions among the slaves and the fever patients became so vile that on the following day I picked up Jorge in my arms, and deserted the *garreta* for a clean *playa*. I preferred to take our chances with the wild Chamas. The last straw had come when two men had died from yellow fever. The stench in that heat was so awful I insisted on the *capitán* stopping long enough to get them underground, but he would not, owing to certain governmental red-tape which must be attended to first.

It was hot as the top of a stove in that sand, but as army ants were everywhere in the jungle alongside, we had to keep to the spit, where I built a leafy arbor to shade Jorge. Even so, after a cooling cloud crossed under the sun, the ants—in countless numbers—invaded the open *playa.* In desperation I rushed about gathering dry rushes, forming a barricade around Jorge, and then firing it in time to catch the first wave of them. In spite of this we were already badly bitten. Beyond the flames, for a hundred feet to the jungle, was a solid blanket of ants. These were the driver ants, *Eciton hamatun,* a one-inch red ant, having a white head and no eyes.

Safely within our ring of ashes and embers, for as fast as the ants came they died, I sat watching the river. In the afternoon a party of five hunters drifted along in a large *obada* (a broad, shallow dugout). These Indians were giants, naked except for G-strings of glass beadwork done in geometric patterns of red, white, black, and blue; while their entire bodies were painted red. High-standing collars of beads encircled their necks, with other bands at their wrists and legs above the knee. They were a wild-looking crew, shiny with fish oil, and I recalled Padre Alegre's story of a band of them being camped on a *playa* across from Pucalpa. A few weeks before, a general of the Peruvian Air Force had descended on the Ucayali's metropolis, and seeing these Indians conveniently across the river, thought he would taxi over and take their pictures to show his incredulous friends in Lima; this he did. The Chamas objected strenuously, thinking the General and his party of five officers (armed with .45 automatics) were capturing their *yoshy* spirits. In full sight of the infantrymen stationed across the river, they rose and cut down the entire group, killing the six officials, and fled intact.

I smiled at the Chamas and offered a little tobacco. They turned in to the beach (after looking us over very carefully), and carrying their spears, bounded ashore. Soon they were stuffing the tobacco into small pipes shaped like the butt of a cigar. They squatted around on their hams staring at us out of cruel, scarred faces. Two of the men spoke Spanish. As they didn't seem particularly hostile, I got up and packed Jorge aboard the *obada.* All at once they jumped in, and picking up their red painted paddles, began working the canoe along the tangled right bank, keeping very close to the trees.

I soon saw they were hunting egrets, two of which they killed with blowguns—the Chama *tepi.* Officially egrets are not killed. Since there is a ban against their importation into the United States, the feathers are smuggled into Europe and the Orient (especially India) where they command big prices.

As we floated downstream, one of the bucks showed me a copper axe-head he had found in one of several old jars on a "hill top." Perhaps these were the graves of Inca explorers, and it is interesting to speculate that the ancients may have penetrated deeply into the savage Amazon country. If so, their route would have been via the Apurímac, Ene, Tambo and Ucayali. Other burial urns were there, the Chama said, ascribing them to the "Old Ones." We could not examine the site, however, because of Jorge's condition (for he was far from well). I hoped to find some *patróne* who would take us in. For all that, the Indians made it clear with wild gesticulations and loud voices, that they would not be hurried.

Once, when I asked them if they had seen any large animals lately, one of the Spanish-speaking men answered that years before it was common to see very large animals on the east bank come out of the jungle to drink. Idly I asked about their size. This brave pointed to a tree about forty feet high! All these riverine tribes have legends of such beasts existing in the jungle lying out toward the Brazilian frontier. Except for a few clans living on the rivers, these jungle tracts are completely uninhabited; at least so say the Chamas. Can any man say what lies out there?

The *obada* swept gently around the broad turns, and by evening we came alongside a clearing on the right bank. There was just a chance that a house lay somewhere. The Chamas reluctantly beached the *obada*. They took out their muskets which had been concealed under a bundle of animal skins. They remained behind as they had no intention of being taken as forced labor by some *patróne's* press gang. Unable to walk far, Jorge also stayed behind to watch our things and do what he could to prevent the Indians from leaving us stranded. After examining the cartridges in the cylinder of my pistol, a rusty old .44 revolver bartered from the *garreta capitán* at Atalaya, I cautiously made my way through a patch of bamboos. On the other side I saw a very old and gnarled orange grove. It is never wise to barge into such a place, for many *patrónes* keep Indians who will make short work of a stranger. The *patrónes* often are at war with one another, and of course there are the Indians who quite frequently lay siege to such places. Friends usually enter only after giving certain signals.

Some two hundred yards inland I came upon an immense stone and plaster house, painted a pale blue with white trimming! This could only be the "fine house" which the Bishop had called out to us on our leaving Atalaya. Even so, I could not have been more shocked. By comparison with the cane and thatch houses along the Ucayali, it seemed more like some house that belonged in Lima instead of in this jungle. The tropical garden surrounding the building was incredibly clean and entirely in apple-pie order.

What manner of people could live here—?

I felt of the stubble on my sunburned chin, and glanced down at my tattered clothes, which were none too clean. I looked more like a Crimean refugee, or a hobo, than an explorer.

Striding up to the house, I rapped on the massive door. No answer. I brought my knuckles down a bit sharper. Still no answer. I tried again, hard this time.... Again no answer. I thought perhaps they couldn't hear, and so I finally banged with the long barrel of the old revolver. In a few seconds the door swung slowly back on wooden hinges, creaking like an oxcart's wheel.

A huge Chama brave in a blue loincloth stood in the doorway. He was a fearsome object, his heavy scowling face all tattooed in blue, while his massive torso was black as an inkwell. Seeing a strange *yoshy* (white devil), he turned and ran silently on bare feet into the depths of the house, leaving me at the threshold of I knew not what. Inside it was quite dark. I could make out little of the interior except that it was, by comparison with other Ucayali houses, elegantly furnished.

"Oh! *de casa!*" I called out, as custom dictates. Not to yell "Oh! *de casa!*" on approaching a house in these jungles is to invite a bullet through your head.

No answer.

I must have remained there five minutes when a woman dressed in black appeared in the doorway. She looked me over rather sharply, and addressed me in dignified Spanish, using the quiet even tones of a Peruvian grande dame. When she learned that the wild man before her was an American explorer, she spoke pure English, the first, other than Jorge's, I had heard since leaving Stone's. She bade me enter the house of "Cumaria."[1]

I followed the lady through a furnished hall, until on the far side of

---

1. Every house in the western Amazon has a name which appears on the maps as a town.

the house we stepped down to a wide veranda. The wall was decorated with jaguar skins, horns of big game, Indian feather mantels, raybursts of spears, blowguns and war axes. A radio stood on a table. The four people lounging in the chairs glanced up and looked me over coolly, taking in the tatters, the broken shoes, the whiskers, and especially the unholstered .44 thrust into a rawhide string serving as belt. Their faces were studies in arrested surprise.

Two were exceedingly chic and handsome young women, one auburn-haired, her companion a brunette. The two men were blond and exceedingly stalwart, packing holstered .45s on their hips. As their eyes narrowed on my rusty old gun, I thought—if they both draw and get the drop on me—I still have my sheath knife hanging on a buckskin cord between my shoulder blades. Also there is no known defense against a knife at short range. All were attired in white clothing.

The Doña Masenza Vd. de Dolci now presented herself and two sons, and a daughter-in-law (whose husband was away in Paris), and a daughter (the auburn one). She enquired whether I preferred a brandy to the tea which a servant was bringing in at the moment. I explained that tea was very bad for my somewhat delicate constitution, and at my murmured assent in favor of the brandy, Julio filled glasses for me and Guido, his older brother. Guido raised his glass, sniffed inaudibly, and in perfect English said:

"Colonel Clark—I give you 'Garibaldi'!"

This was somewhat startling, both the army rank and the toast, but somehow the first fitted in with the unusual circumstances... and the radio. I was too worried about Jorge to give a damn about Garibaldi. "Garibaldi?" I answered.

"Giuseppe Garibaldi," emphasized Guido. We turned the bottoms up.

The Doña now explained—before I could mention Jorge—that her deceased husband's father had founded this estate, house and family, in the last century. He had had the misfortune to kill a favorite officer of Garibaldi in a duel, and had fled first to the United States and thence to this remote spot in the wilds of the Amazon country, where he had died with his boots off at a fine ripe old age.

"You see, Colonel Clark, like yourself the elder Dolci was 'a political refugee,'" spoke up Julio.

"A political refugee—?"

"Word has reached us from the Commandante's radio in Atalaya that you are a '*Republicáno,*' and that you are being searched for by the '*Democráticos*'...."

Hearing about my companion at the river, Doña de Dolci proffered an invitation to stay the night. And so the brothers and I hustled back to the river to fetch Jorge, and to dismiss the Chamas with gifts of trade tobacco. Supporting Jorge, we returned to the house in the last glow of sunset filtering slantwise through the blossoms of the old orange grove. Doña de Dolci showed us to our rooms, telling us dinner was at nine.

The Amazon Peruvians' custom of extending hospitality to all who come, even to strangers, was indeed a fortunate one for us, particularly since one of us was ill. Here in the interior food and shelter were given the traveler and he was restocked with fresh supplies on his departure.

Soft puddles of candlelight danced on the broad base of a candlestick. I glanced around the large room and found it trimmed in rare hand-hewn *palo sangre*, blood-stick. An enormous black bedstead of ironwood stood against the wall, its white net billowing in the hot evening air which blew in through the window. The several chairs were of the *mashonaste* wood, with its twisted grains of green and red. Such woods put to shame even the rosewoods, mahoganies, and other fine woods shipped out to the civilized world. On the wall hung a gold-framed painting of a very severe looking officer in full dress uniform and decorations, perhaps the founder of this bit of paradise the midst of the *Verde Inferno.*

I stripped off my dirty clothes and bathed in a sitdown bathtub with arm rests, and I smoked a fine long cigar. Then I shaved and dressed in the white trousers and linen shirt that were laid out by a servant. I joined the others in the large salon. Jorge was there propped up in a chair and surprisingly bright. Malaria is a disease which brings melancholia, usually relieved as soon as sources of worry and hardship are removed.

I sighed in contentment and lounged in one of the long crocodile skin chairs. Without so much as a reference as to how we had reached this place, we launched into a heated discussion of Leonardo da Vinci, Emerson, and Chekhov. Jorge was in his element, and, much to my amazement, looked like a new man already. Dinner was announced by an Indian.

Seated at the table with its white cloth, on which stood a branching candelabrum filled with candles, we seemed to be a million miles from our recent starvation camps of yuca and fish on the Perené and Tambo.

The daughters, dressed in white, were beautiful in the soft lights. Serí (Sa-ray) talked with great animation. Jorge who had insisted on being propped up to the board, was fascinated; in fact he looked remarkably like a fish being harpooned; and I was a bit concerned for El Dorado.

"You are the first explorers to have stopped here," said the Doña. Then added, "We are so happy it is not true, as the radio reported, that you had perished on the Perené."

After questioning us concerning the slave practices upriver, the lady said: "We are more progressive here. We abolished slavery at Cumaria a decade ago. And it is hoped other families will follow our example."

We were served course on course of marvelous dishes reflecting the fertility and industry of Cumaria. Gone were the lean days of fish, yuca, rats, and chonta worms. We had hors d'oeuvres consisting of pale green palm hearts tasting somewhat like a mixture of artichoke and asparagus tips and decorated with small turtle eggs. Soup followed—what soup! Made from the choicest varieties of turtles found in the river. Several kinds of fish were offered on silver platters, with names as picturesque as their flesh was delicate. There were aromatic dishes of roast partridge and turkey. Meats included a saddle of roast venison in wine sauce, and a pinkish-rare roast of tapir that melted away on the tongue. Vegetables and salads were of varieties strange to our palates. Then came wooden platters heaped with bananas, sliced papayas, pineapples, *sacha* mangos, grapes, *zapotes*, oranges, *shimbillos*, and finally salted Amazon cashews, and roasted breadfruit nuts. We adjourned to the veranda where black coffee and brandy were served.

For eight days Jorge and I were guests in this house. After the first four or five days, Jorge was practically whole again, for quinine was available. Our gear, such as it was, was overhauled, our clothes mended, food packed and stored for continuing on our journey, and a large canoe purchased from the Chamas. I played soccer and hunted with Julio and Guido by day; and by night, all four of us killed *paiche* with harpoons; or dug in the *playas* for turtle eggs; or sang; or maybe played poker.

Jorge was well enough to continue our trip, so at dawn on Monday, August 9th, we said our goodbyes, really hating to leave Cumaria and these good people. The young ladies waved handkerchiefs prettily from the bank, Doña de Dolci kissed us as if we were her own sons, and her sons shook hands in a way that showed they would never see us again, but would never forget us either. Watching his face as he stared like a sick calf at the beauteous Sarí, I wasn't too sure that Jorge wouldn't one fine day come back, perhaps after his canoe had been loaded with the gold of El Dorado.

After we had pulled away from the bank, Guido called out: "Remember—no explorer or hunter ever made any money. If you are too late to ascend the Marañón, then come back, we have a million hectares of mahogany and Spanish cedar that should be thinned out!"

Four days of hard paddling brought us into Pucalpa, a third of the way down the Ucayali. The date was August 12th, two and a half months since I had left home on June 1st. Pucalpa was a metropolis of some fifty houses, cane and adobe, the fronts all neatly painted blue and white. We took a room at the small *posada* on the plaza. Stationed on the west bank of the middle of town, was Mr. Ernest J. Aish, the agent for the Blue Goose Oil Company, who kindly exchanged a $100 bill (which the bank would not honor). My expenses since 'Opata had now reduced me to $314.28.

But we were headed for a great disappointment in Pucalpa. A letter at the Commandancia awaited Jorge, telling of the death of his brother, the head of the family. Jorge must return at once to Lima. At this time I paid Jorge—much against his will—a chit for the $200 promised at Stone's. The chit would be redeemed when he sent it to my family in San Francisco.

When we reluctantly parted company, partners now, it was with the fervent hope that Jorge would rejoin me in Iquitos. His return trip to Lima would be on the old Pichis Trail, the route purposely evaded by me in order to obtain the medicines in the Gran Pajonal. He was entirely recovered from his malaria now, as the quinine at Cumaria had broken the fever. He would join a group of traders en route over the Cordillera.

A thousand troops were stationed at a camp not far away in the jungle, and their commander, a colonel, came to the *posada* and invited me to move into his own quarters. It seemed that the Commandante's excellent friend, the Bishop Arellano, had sent word by fast Indian paddlers, that I was a "Coronel" and a political refugee, and should be shown all courtesies possible. I gladly accepted, after explaining to the Colonel that we *norteamericanos* did not persecute each other when our political party was out of power; that as a matter of fact, I was in no danger from a firing squad of the *Demócráticos,* and anyway, I had only voted a couple of times...but he interrupted by saying in a great burst of heat: "Tut! Tut! señor, you do not have to explain in Peruana."

"But my dear sir!" I cried out in desperation, "I have as many friends who are Democrats, as I have who are Republicans!"

"Ah—the clever one..." he came back, "We must keep an eye on you."

Two days after arriving, a deal was made with Commandante Doig, for flying me next day by army plane to Iquitos: military aircraft may sometimes be chartered for private use in many countries of the Amazon. Due to Indian troubles downriver, no boats were running and I had to get out of there somehow, even if it was by air and expensive (though as a matter of courtesy they allowed me to pay only $50 for the gasoline). That night after dinner, two Canadian geologists, who were in Pucalpa, Donald A. Taylor and John MacGill, took us to their launch and showed us a water barrel in which was kept a dead boa constrictor that had swallowed a six-foot crocodile. MacGill was interested in the geological formations I had described on the Tambo, and was leaving next day in his own amphibian plane to reconnoiter there.

At dawn they saw me to the airport to my own plane, and shortly after taking off, the army amphibian Catalina plane roared over the Ucayali. While following its great yellow serpentine course, I saw thousands of *cochas* lying beyond the banks glittering like polished amber in the hot sunlight. The flat jungled floor of the valley was heavily creased and folded by a series of endless coils and curves, hundreds of them to the eastern horizon, showing that the Ucayali changes its channels by pattern. Tons of gold must lie in those old water courses. The right wing pontoon of the Catalina grazed the thatched roofs of Requena, an Ucayali town on the east bank as large as Pucalpa, which had been undergoing siege for over a year by the Blanco River Indians. Except for airplanes it was isolated, as no river *capitán* dared attempt a landing. Several had tried to land soldiers, but these had all been killed. After dropping supplies to the garrison of half a company (about a hundred men), we continued on. And a little later we picked up the Amazon. The pilot banked steeply to the right, and followed its broad, yellow waters for some sixty miles into the east (with considerable northing).

At 8 A.M. (August 15th), I spotted a sizable clearing in the jungle filled with a mixture of thatched and red tile roofs, and knew I had, reached Iquitos—"The Pearl of the Jungle"—that Timbuctoo of the Western Amazon.

When the Catalina landed on the bumpy cow pasture of an airdrome, I realized I had been on my way from Lima (which I left on July 2nd) for six weeks; and fourteen weeks from the time I had decided on the trip back home on May 1st—a month before I left the United States. The remote territories of Loreto and Madre de Dios were practically independent (in a political sense) of Lima. Also Loreto was under martial law due to fighting over the whereabouts of the frontier with Ecuador. As a result of the two factors, I was put through stiff customs and immigration formalities. The rusty old .44 was clapped under lock and key, as if it were a cannon. My passport (something of a blotter after its many submergings) was taken up as though I were entering a new country. Several uniformed officials put curt questions to me, and my intentions were demanded.

With it all, my family history back to and including my great-grandfather, and eight photographs of myself, were required. Now my great-grandfather, unfortunately (for me), was a considerable Indian fighter, and had been shot full of arrows and killed after a long and bloody career in California, Nevada, and Oregon territories. When I explained this, I was greeted with scowls of black suspicion: "Ah, señor. Fighting *Indios* in Estados Unidos may be legal. But—in Peruana—no! It is not permissible!"

From the airport a police officer accompanied me to Iquitos in my own taxi. The Indian driver tromped his bare foot on the accelerator, making his turns on two wheels. The tires squealed in protest. Pedestrians scattered like headless chickens. But in the midst of all this perfectly normal confusion, the policeman's pointed questions indicated I was not considered to be altogether a tourist, but an adventurer, far (too far!) off the beaten track, and as such, under official suspicion. As a matter of fact, there were rumors about that I was a political refugee—and that I might be planning to create a new country by organizing a revolt in the disputed Oriente....

If I had undergone bitter hardships so far in closing the distance to El Dorado, I knew now they had been justified—for only by establishing myself as a bona-fide, and particularly a useful, explorer, could I even hope to continue.

"Why Don't You Take Inez Along?"

FTER all that badgering and hours of delay, it was high noon before the claptrap taxi entered Iquitos' outskirts and began careening through the pinched, muddy streets.

Indians carrying balls of rubber and banana stalks on their heads threaded along the narrow sidewalks. Peruvians—mostly *patrónes* in Panama hats and white suits—strolled by; black-robed bearded priests strode along under black umbrellas. The patio walls were topped with dusty fronds of banana trees, showers of red hibiscus, and rows of black buzzards. The air was filled with a terrible stench—raw rubber and hides, these last mainly crocodile and anaconda.

We pulled up with a rattle and a bang at the baroque three-storied hotel, the Malecón Palace, tallest building in the city with a front of solid blue and yellow Delft tiles. At this famous rookery of the richest *patrónes* (Iquitos has had more millionaires per capita than any town on earth), the policeman left me, saying I must report at the police Commandancia after I had found a place to live.

What I most desired while awaiting Jorge was a clean and quiet room where I could get my bearings and plot our way to the western reaches of the unexplored Oriente.

I entered the hotel. On enquiry of the concierge, I found that no rooms were available. I returned to the street and (riding in an old horse-drawn victoria) began a search of all Iquitos—a city of some 15,000 inhabitants.

Finally, in the dark, I located a *pensión* operated by an old maid señorita, a Brazilian with a mustache. After a great deal of haggling, I arranged for a room with board. Since most of the city's foreigners were said to take their meals here, I hoped to find it a good listening post. My desire, of course, was to remain secret, but I must learn all I possibly could of the political situation and also what lay before me in the land of the head-shrinkers. I was no sooner bathed and dressed (for I had purchased about $25 worth of Peruvian clothes) than the dinner bell began clanging.

Downstairs in the large bare dining room, the señorita bustled around, shepherding her little flock of paying customers. These were adventurous-looking males of a tropic and cosmopolitan character. Two were elegantly turned out in white Palm Beach suits, and a pair were in khaki bush-clothes such as one sees in India and British East Africa. One beefy-faced Irishman of six feet four, a Mr. Leo J. McCarthy-Barry, was dressed in white pongee silk shorts with pleats. I pushed my own shirt tail in a bit farther, and tried to smell out the grub.

We must have been half-way through dinner when Inez Pokorny came into the room. She had on a white dress and she was slim. Her small head, the wary shine to her green eyes, the round neatness of her figure and the way she stood for an instant in the doorway, was cool, steady, infinitely appealing. It brought every man at our table to his feet.

She evidently had her regular place, for there was much hustling about and seating her at the far end. I asked what an American girl was doing in such wild country and was told that she had been eight months on her way up the Amazon in riverboats. This was a feat—we were given to understand by Captain Ian Rokes,—not previously performed by any lone foreign white woman.

We all sat down again, finally, and after some chitchat back and forth conversation became general. McCarthy-Barry spoke testily of the six thousand troops stationed at Iquitos who were confiscating all the food. Someone else mentioned the Peruvian Navy's latest exploit up the Amazon "disguised" as trading boats.

The Peruvian officials were jittery that the Ecuadorians might invade Loreto State, which comprised most of northeast Peru. As a result, a counter-invasion of the disputed Oriente north and west of

Iquitos was being prepared, as Peru had intentions of annexing it. Digesting all this, I realized I couldn't have arrived at a worse time.

My own end of the talk was dubiously held up by guarded answers to questions on the possibility for colonization, and the chances for finding oil on the Alto Ucayali and its tributaries, for obviously the whole town knew where I had been.

The girl, Inez, moved her dark green eyes my way, over my comment that at least one terrible obstacle must be overcome in the upper Amazon, before any chance for realizing these ambitions could even be seriously considered—and that was reducing the percentage of lepers here, surely the highest on earth. Even in Iquitos there were approximately seven hundred lepers, many of these unfortunates roaming the streets. There was no institution to care for them, only a holding camp of the crudest sort out in the jungle. Over 2,000 lepers exist on the middle and lower Ucayali alone. Contaminated *patrónes* and the tame Indian and *cholo* populations under them were fast spreading the leprosy plague among the healthy savage and semi-savage tribes—ultimately dooming these to extinction.

The following week passed in preparing for our journey. McCrae, in Oroya, had sent on (c/o U.S. Consul) a small bundle of my things. I missed Jorge, and it was that week I got his radiogram. I sat staring at it and couldn't believe what I read. He said he was now head of his family. He must direct its estates. His days of adventuring were over. *He could not come!*

Late summer terminated with a lightning storm and a very humid temperature exceeding 100 degrees Fahrenheit. A hundred degrees of dry heat is nothing; but in the tropics it is terrible—and it cost the lives of over 100 people. Above all, it meant the approach of the rainy season. And all this time I was still mopping my brow through the sweltering streets of Iquitos, undecided and alarmed, especially by the Dutchman's stories. This Henk W. van de Putte told incredible tales of murder and arson committed by the savages of the Oriente. Alone, would I be able to go up the Amazon to its extreme navigable headwaters by canoe, a trip no explorer had ever been able to accomplish? I finally decided at least to make a strong attempt; further indecision could only spell fiasco and my ultimate ruin.

To begin with, I had made a report on the situation in the districts Jorge and I had traversed. The government—in spite of the tense situation here—could not but show its gratitude. Surely they would not give me a decided "No, señor" on my plans for going upriver.

I called on the young American Consul only recently appointed, Mr. Lewis Gallardy, whose influence was great. Now I had seen hundreds of American consuls scattered over the world, and while most of them are a pretty sad lot, this Gallardy was the first who exhibited any sympathy at all for me and my problems. He had been doing all in his power to get a decision from the Peruvians. That morning he said: "Clark, old sock, I have bad news for you. Your troubles are only beginning. Officially, they will not say 'no'—but the word on the grapevine is that you won't be permitted to go; too many hush-hush army operations in the Oriente. I suggest you explore the Napo, the favorite river of your tribe." He grinned at this last, but I could see he was disappointed.

I now went to the Army Headquarters facing the Malecón, the street edging the Amazon. Coronel R. Ravines Cortés was the new Commandante for all Ground and Naval Forces in Peru east of the Andes. I safely got by the guards, and eventually found him in the inner compound of the Ministerio de Guerra, Commandancia General, Division de Selva. The Coronel, a man of the world, suavely assured me that I would have no difficulty with his forward garrisons. They would be ordered "immediately!" to assist. My explorations in the headwaters of the Amazon would "not" be blocked. The Coronel's power was absolute in a wild region greater in area than any held under the command of an American Five-Star General.

Yes, the Coronel was in direct contact with the Ministry of War in Lima. If the Minister of War radioed a favorable reply to my request, he himself would issue the necessary field orders to his subservient commanders: transportation, radio communications, sale of food, protection all would be mine. He would even pave my way to the Peruvian Army headquarters strategically occupying the entire western Oriente—that is, the rivers Morona, Santiago, and the Alto Marañón (upper Amazon). I was, of course, extremely relieved. I thanked Coronel Cortés, who had already received all the necessary documentation required of me, and the proof of my being an "*explorador*," and not a spy. Unfortunately, and unknown to myself at the time, the Peruvian Embassy in Washington had uncovered the fact that I had been a spy— and the fact that this activity had been limited to war duty made no difference in their evaluation of me.

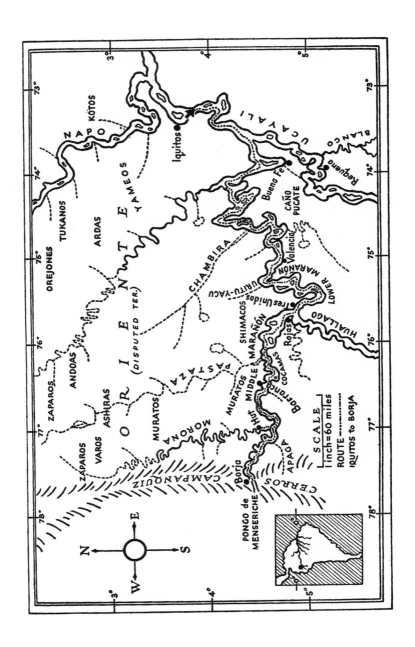

SCALE
1 inch = 60 miles
ROUTE ·········
IQUITOS to BORJA

El Dorado was mine—back in my room I got out the maps: from Borja (that same army base) I saw that I could set out for the Rio Santiago, which joined the Amazon from the north near the Andean foothills; and I could try to find a way up the main stem of the Amazon to Bella Vista, a town said to be in the high eastern Andes.[1] This would be difficult, for no explorer had yet preceded me, and it was all head-hunting country—Jívaro country. After locating El Dorado, I would take as much gold as possible to carry out; and go as far up the Amazon as was practical by dugout canoe with Jívaro paddlers; and then recross the Andes into northern Peru and eventually into Quito, Ecuador.... For the first time, things really looked practical.

Not wishing to impose on the Army too much, I went into the streets and tried to find other transportation. At the offices of the Flamingo Oil Company, the agent assured me that the company launch, carrying a geologist, was going to attempt to reach Borja, about 700 river miles west of Iquitos. This was on the Pongo de Menseriche—the ill-famed gorge through which the Amazon flows out of the Andean spurs. I would be welcome as a paying passenger. The launch would be leaving in three days. I could hardly keep from yelling "Hurray!"

Ever since arriving in Iquitos, and after hearing from Jorge, I had been trying to find an interpreter. Everyone was, of course, eager to risk his neck "exploring," but in the end some valid excuse was always forth-coming.

I needed information on the Oriente, and I turned to the Peruvians, but they were very close-mouthed; the sum of my gleanings being, that due to the *patrónes'* recent infiltrations of the main rubber-bearing rivers of the Oriente, and their attempts at "civilizing" the riverine head-hunters, the *bravos* were becoming exceedingly hostile. They were killing from ambush and burning out the *patrónes* on an unprecedented scale. True, most of the warring tribes had moved off the main rivers, but they were not exterminated (as some *patrónes* hoped); they had only disappeared into the vast flat jungles and swamps where the sol-diers dared not follow.

Haden, the Adventista missionary here, said Indian converts called

---

1. I had a letter of introduction to a man in Bella Vista from Señor Carlos Rubio, an Iquitos missionary.

the Santiago the "worst river in the entire Amazon basin." Not long before, 110 Peruvian troops were massacred after unwisely seizing two Jívaro women. The attack came before dawn, by less than twenty Huambizas armed with war axes and muskets.

And so it went: everywhere I was met with discouragement, and was given the chilling advice not to try, that even a snake could not crawl through the Oriente without the Jívaros chopping its head off.

One night after dinner, I talked to Inez. She had a way of being unexpectedly feminine, and she suddenly asked if all was well with me. I said yes—on the whole. I would surely go; the oil company's launch would be leaving soon. Charlie Simmonds asked: "What about your interpreter, did you find one?"

"Sure," I said, "me."

Rokes turned to speak: "Why don't you take Inez along—she knows the dialect. She has been planning to go up the Ucayali by launch to Pucalpa and cross on the Pichis Trail over to Lima."

"Now, just take it easy," I said, and then blurted out, "I'm not going to be saddled with any woman."

Johnny said quickly: "The fact remains that no woman has ever ascended the Amazon above Iquitos, for the same reason that no male explorer has gotten beyond the Santiago's mouth. They just disappear."

Our friend Hugo Fanelli, of the Standard Oil, a Chilean geologist of long experience on the Amazon rivers, burst out in fervent agreement to Rokes' statement. "All you people who just sit on your chairs in Iquitos think the headwaters are merely rivers to send boats up, nothing being required other than a good motor and plenty of gasoline. Last year, when I was on a feeder of the lower Ucayali, my boat overturned and I nearly lost my life. I was marooned in the jungle for over a week, and lost three men—driven crazy by insects and lack of food. Walking out, I lost my best *cholo* when a savage stuck him with a spear!"

It was getting late and the mosquitoes began wearying us. We escorted Inez back to her room in the Malecón, a habit of us foreign bachelors each night, and then departed separately for our own quarters. I counted my money. After deducting the Pucalpa expenses and the ones in Iquitos, I had $169.88.

At breakfast next morning, I came to the señorita's table half asleep, not an unusual occurrence after a long night of study—for one thing, I was trying to learn a few words of Jívaro with the aid of a missionary padre. Everyone was in his place—Inez at the head of the table. I said my good mornings around the board, drank my coffee, and finally started on my sliced papaya.

Simmonds was saying: "Hello. Wake up. It's all settled. Congratulations!"

"Congratulations for what?" I asked.

"*She* has made up her mind to go with you. She says she'll be ready to leave tomorrow morning."

I concentrated on the last of my coffee. Presently I found myself alone at the table with Inez. The last thing I wanted was a female on such an expedition, dangerous or not.

At last she said with a wide smile, "I'll probably have a lot of things to buy. Would you tell me what I'll need?"

Suddenly, with tremendous relief, I remembered we had all been discussing a picnic the day before. Surely that was it. I answered: "Oh, why not get the General and the Dutchman to pick up a few cans of sardines, some crackers, and maybe a few bottles of that excellent Oporto over at Johnny's?"

She cocked her trim head, with an air as if a trifle puzzled: "You aren't very bright this morning, are you, Mr. Clark?"

"Don't worry about me. I'll be wide awake by the time the picnic rolls around."

She looked me squarely in the eye and said, "Clark, I am going up to the Amazon headwaters with you. I know the river patois, and you do not. Perhaps it would be better if you accompanied me to the market, then I am sure to get everything I will need for the trip."

"If you were a gentleman, you'd wait to be asked."

"No woman is a gentleman," she reminded me, "and if she waited to be asked, she wouldn't travel very far. When a woman wants a thing she has to seize her opportunity."

I fell in with what I thought must surely be a joke, for no woman was so dumb as to go into Jívaro country; and so I accompanied Inez on her shopping tour. To everything on which she asked my advice, I said to humor her, "Yes, take it. Much better to have enough, wherever you are going." Of course, I wondered what in hell she would be doing with a flashlight and a dozen batteries, a machete, boy's-sized khaki pants, and a lot of camping equipment, such as a hammock, on a boat trip to Pucalpa.

By 11 o'clock, with the sun a melting white blob of heat, my arms loaded with all this gear, I was dripping. I found myself being steered unwillingly around to the oil company's office. After assuring "ourselves" that the Higgins launch would cast off next morning, we left. Much to my surprise, the girl now led me around to the office of the Army Commandante. Where I had had a difficult time getting past the officious guards, she just waltzed in—receiving full attention, snappy presentation of arms—and, of course, eyes right. The Coronel received her with gladness, and though he brushed through the formalities with me, eventually finished his pretty compliments, and turning, bruskly assured me I was solid, "*muy firmo!*" with the Army. I was not to worry; he had just received "instructions" from the Minister of War himself; I could count on him to do all that these "instructions" called for....

Inez then had a lengthy chat with the Coronel. I didn't catch much of it, as they were both rattling along in a chili-spiced brand of Spanish—but I wasn't fool enough to overlook the fact that a pair of female green eyes could top all the cold male logic in the world. Outside in the street, she looked at me sidewise under those long eyelashes, and in a teasing voice—"I'm so glad. Everything is arranged now."

"Why not?" I conveyed the idea that I usually managed to take care of myself from breakfast till evening, and without a great deal of assistance from the rest of the universe. I thought she smiled faintly at this.

"All right, lone wolf," she said, "get on with you."

I was herded like a pack mule up three flights of stairs to her room in the Malecón Palace; here I dumped the packages and gladly left.

That night, after dinner, the entire table assured me, in roaring voices, that all I would have to do now was put my John Henry on the "dotted line," and everything would be settled. I looked at the paper the grinning Charlie Simmonds was thrusting under my nose. It was a terrifyingly legal-looking document relieving me of all responsibility concerning one Inez Pokorny...while engaged in exploring the Amazon headwaters in my company.

Of course, it had to be a practical joke, and though I don't approve of them, I decided to play along rather than be a spoil-sport. I knew that most of the Oriente tribes, and notably the Muratos, will murder for a woman—any kind of two-legged woman. Currently, traders were exchanging one woman for two muskets, or a woman for a shrunken head trophy. The standard gage was: two muskets = one shrunken head trophy = one woman. The shortage was in women, not shrunken heads or muskets. My friends, of course, must know this.

And so I signed, with an exaggerated Latin flourish.

Carrying out the jest, I enumerated all of the useful things she could do. Calmly she listened, politely covering a pretended yawn. She could wash my laundry and keep my clothes mended. Keep up my notes. Clean my newly acquired .45 Colt. Straighten out melted candles. Take notes on bearings of rivers and mountains I would be discovering. Take soil samples. Oil my shoes. Nurse me when sick. Boil drinking water. Shoo flies off me. Stand watch at night in hostile country. Learn the Jívaro dialects. Scout. Catch fish and make lists. Bring hot tea while I rested from the day's heat, and just to keep her out of mischief, she could learn to harpoon *paiche* so we would have something to eat. And do the cooking. She could make a hydrographic chart on the last thousand miles of the Amazon by sounding the channel every hundred yards…I then suggested that we all meet in the morning, and they could see me off. To my absolute surprise, Inez laughed—right in my face.

The launch, Pokorny now informed me, was leaving at 8 A.M., and I was to be packed and aboard.

I was up long before dawn, packing my things in a new waterproof flour sack painted with latex. I felt like a bank robber in a hurry to go somewhere. I hustled downstairs and paid up my bill to the señorita. A *cargador* lugged my bag over to the river opposite the Malecón Palace. The Higgins launch was supposed to be tied up there. It was not yet in sight, and so I sat down on my bag. I was dozing off when Inez slowly and somewhat insolently, I thought, marched up. She was surrounded by the usual covey of male loafers who obviously didn't have much work to do in this tropic paradise.

"Hello, you're late," I greeted them, for surely they had come to see me off.

But not at all; they were just strolling in the cool of the morning with Inez. I could go jump in the river for all they cared.

"Trying to sneak off, eh?" came from Inez, "Well, for your information the launch has already left without 'us.'"

I suggested we walk over to see the agent, who happened to be standing in front of his office. To my inquiry concerning my transportation, the agent answered with a red face that he had sent the launch off because he couldn't afford to "stick his neck out" now that the girl was going too.

So she was going!

It was common gossip by night that the Army was sending a boat up to Borja. It would sail on the following day with a company of troops. When I rushed over, with Inez clicking along on high heels behind, and asked the Coronel about this, he beat successfully around the bush—for he was an uncommonly good diplomat; so much so that when we were shown outside, I was feeling splendid—but suddenly realized he had said "No." Exactly what he had said was that its sailing had been postponed "indefinitely." Now translated into Peruvian, "indefinitely" means "never." Therefore, I was not totally surprised next day, to find this boat, too, had already gone.

"I'd better handle things," says Inez.

I exhausted every possibility, even traders' bum-boats, going upriver. Then I contacted all of the mercantile companies. I could learn nothing definite about their launches, though these were obviously leaving one or two every month. I tried to figure a way out: I fished off the bank, catching a twelve-foot shark, which had probably come up from the Atlantic; but that was all I accomplished, and I couldn't even get the señorita to cook it. It was obvious that no one would carry me upriver; Gallardy had been right.

One day while fishing off his wharf, I was telling my troubles to Herr H. Fenning, a beet-faced German boat-builder and ex-soldier-of-fortune who had once come to South America to fly for some rebel army. He was a very decent sort of man, and had the reputation of being the best shipbuilder on the whole river; and finally he suggested I call on a friend of his whom he had reason to believe was getting a private *launcha* ready for an annual trading trip to Borja.

About that time Inez happened along, greeting her good friend Herr Fenning. I climbed the bank, with her panting right behind and Herr Fenning in tow. Together we were conveyed in a horse-drawn victoria to the house of Fenning's friend. Seated in a small but luxurious salon, I faced a courtly mannered Austrian gentleman of about fifty-five. Baron Walter Frass von Wolfenegg was in charge of Peru's new program for colonization bases in the Oriente.

Three hours later, Baron von Wolfenegg, late of the Austrian

Hapsburg hierarchy, whose estates had been seized by Hitler and then by the Reds, agreed to take us 700 miles west. Inez must dress as a boy; it was "impossible" otherwise. Indians would likely attack. No white woman had ever been there before, and no telling what would happen. She would certainly bring a fancy price of many muskets to the raider who took her.

"But Inez's not really going!" I exploded.

The Baron sipped his warm beer, raised a pair of very blue eyes to mine. "Herr Fenning and I are friends of Miss Pokorny, and if she can't go—then you can't. That's that!"

"Okay," I finally agreed, and not without a sinking of the heart, "I'll be burdened with her...."

"And don't you forget, Coronel—if you do not protect her, we Iquitos gentlemen have a very good strong rope that will just about fit your neck!"

ᴄᴊ XVIII. ᴄᴏ

Drums on the Marañón

S EPTEMBER 3rd was announced by the howling of big monkeys—the short-bodied, long-limbed, long-tailed bull *macke-sapas*, raiding the *chacaras* in the city's outskirts. All was ready; the day had dawned for departure. Our friends cast off the lines, yelling farewells and wishes for good luck, The blank-faced Cocama Indian pilot spun his wheel and the forty-foot cabin cruiser, *La Patria*, confidently pushed her newly painted white bows away from the bank into the river.

The turbid channel of the Marañón appeared ahead, and proved full of floating islands and tangled masses of trees. It lay a full mile off Iquitos, which is merely perched on a high bank of an arm of that mighty stream.

Down in the snug cabin, his face the color of hawkmeat from the torrid heat, and smiling beatifically, von Wolfenegg—free from his duties as president of the Iquitos Chamber of Commerce, happily ruled his logbook. Inez, dressed coolly in blue shorts and a silk handkerchief of the same shade, energetically banged enormous hand-forged nails into the walls for hanging up clothes, binoculars, guns, and cameras. I peered into the jungle as it moved sternwise, studied the wild currents lashing over the river's two-mile-wide surface, and the storm clouds in the sky—and none of it looked good.

Powered by an old automobile engine, the launch kicked up its own breeze. A second breeze was coming from the direction of the Andean Cordilleras, some four hundred air miles in the west (about 700 miles by river). Both breezes, however, were neutralized each time we veered into a deeply looping bend, thus going along with the tail breeze coming downriver. Our compass was swinging as much as 180 degrees, or half a circle. Hour after hour, the endless vine- and flower-trailing circle of jungle standing sheer along the low mud and clay banks, streamed past without a single break. Many of the trees were 200 feet high. The only difference here, from the Perené and the other rivers I had passed, was that the Amazon was many, many times larger. Little gaudy chickens called *manacaracos* screeched among the leaves. Dense clouds of the fishing birds—*tuqui tuquis*—were overhead, diving over the boat with gull-like screams and the clacking of beaks.

As I trolled for the black-armored *carachama mama*, flashing in schools at the bows, I had plenty of time to observe details in the jungle. The sheer-cut banks, some ten to fifteen feet high, revealed plainly the shallowness of the loam lying on the hardpan clay formations, so unlike what I had expected to find on the floor of the greatest of all tropical forests. This poverty of soil was the result of constant leaching by floods and rains. Blasted forever, I saw, were the high hopes of those dreamers visualizing great migrations coming from an overpopulated Europe; thousands—perhaps millions—no.

With night came clouds of mosquitoes—vicious, whining gray clouds. The stings of these new ones were strangely like little pin-pricks. Mosquitoes vary: were I blindfolded, I could have named the very river (had I ever been on it previously), by the difference in their bites. As *La Patria* was screened, we dove down into the cabin. Even so, the smaller insects and bugs got in, and it was so hot the sweat oozed out of us like water squeezed from a sponge.

Wolfenegg, pink-faced and puffed from bites, sweltered in the moving puddle of light under the swinging tin lantern hooked into a ring-bolt in the low ceiling. Fanning himself, he told a strange story: Years before, his head bookkeeper, Cesar Hernandez Ludeña, had reported, on coming to work one morning, that he had contracted leprosy. Itching sores were appearing on his tongue and the underside of his arms. Examination by the Iquitos doctors, Ponce de Leon and Eliseo Reategui-Page, Ludeña's fears were verified, for the tests (made in Lima) proved positive. The poor man was committed to a riverboat heading downriver for Manaus, and he was put under guard. Orders were to drop the "patient" off at the leper camp below Iquitos. Here he could conveniently die.

Nearly crazed from the mental shock of his awful fate, the poor bookkeeper leaped overboard to end it all. But instead of drowning, he began to revive. He started swimming and eventually escaped his keepers and fled into the jungle. Having no family or friends to protect him in Iquitos, he had no choice but death—and death lurks in a thousand disguises in the jungle. But unequipped as Ludeña was, without food or weapons, he did not die.

For an entire year, apparently, this bookkeeper—who had never been in the wilds before—wandered half-mad on the unexplored Brazilian border, somewhere south of the Amazon, and up and down the Rio Blanco and the Javari. He lived with various savage clans and tribes, taking whatever medicines the *brujos* gave him. Though living among headhunters and even cannibals, he was not killed, because the Indians believe that a crazy man is the "friend" of the Snake Spirits. On Ludeña's return to Iquitos at the end of that strange year, he was again examined by the same two doctors. They now found that all trace of the leprosy had disappeared. Their old patient was miraculously cured! For the next five years Ludeña was re-employed by Wolfenegg, and the dread disease did not reappear. He eventually married, fathered healthy children, and was living a very useful and happy life.

Now before the Baron Walter Frass von Wolfenegg had become a Peruvian, he studied medicine in Vienna and served as a combat infantry doctor in the German Army (he was probably the first parachute-doctor ever used in war). Therefore, he thoroughly acquainted himself with his friend's case, and studied hundreds of case histories of lepers in Iquitos. He finally decided that certain of the *brujos* know of a cure for leprosy. He discovered that the beneficial results of the standard chaulmoogra-oil injections, used in Iquitos, were as nothing to those produced by the Indians. As a result of all this, von Wolfenegg and I became fast friends when he learned of my own discoveries among the Campas and Chamas, for he had been unsuccessful in interesting European or American scientists to investigate the matter.

We were presently tied up at a *playa*. It was raining. While sitting inside the cabin, and more or less secure from the great hard-shelled

Amazon insects drumming against the screens, we gazed through the square windows out on the moonlit jungle. Tomás, the cook, came quietly and pointed: a jaguar was lumbering out of a strip of *caña*. It suddenly saw the boat, hesitated a moment, then continued heavily and indifferently over to a fallen palm where it lay in the sand, reaching up with its claws and sharpening them on the trunk. Later the tiger got up, stretched and yawned, and walked across to a turtle—a *charapa* weighing some seventy pounds, which was laying its eggs. With its paws the tiger flipped the *charapa* out of its hole, pounced upon the big reptile, and set about digging the meat out of the shell. First the cat bit off the armored head, and then with its claws scooped out the shell much as a bird cleans out a snail.

His dinner finished, the *tigre* walked back into the *caña*, and even in the rain I could smell it. We began playing cards. Over a hand of bridge, Inez asked Walter whether he had ever personally seen a jaguar kill a man whom it had attacked. Yes, he had: absentmindedly he came forth with a small slam, and then sitting back with his pipe, gave the following eyewitness account:

Von Wolfenegg was gathering *marfil vegetal,* the valuable ivory nuts, on the Rio Huiririma, an affluent of the Napo which enters the Amazon on the north bank below Iquitos. One early morning he and his Koto Indians, while crossing an open patch in the jungle, came upon an enormous *tigre* feeding on a deer's carcass, obviously just killed. The range was a hundred yards. One of the men, Juan José Tamani Huavara, threw his .44 Winchester to his shoulder and fired. The shot was not fatal, only creasing the thick, bull-like neck. The *tigre* instantly became crazed, not only from its painful wound, but also because it had been interrupted at feeding: the beast tore up a swathe of jungle, roaring all the while, and suddenly charged the five men who were standing in a group.

Though unarmed, they stood their ground, and finally killed the *tigre* with their machetes, but not before the great cat had clawed them, and with its fangs torn off the top of Huavara's shoulder, leaving the arm all but dismembered. Now here—to von Wolfenegg's mind—was the interesting part of the affair: a village of Orejone Indians lay close by. To this place they packed the Koto Indian who was moaning in pain, though the white man had already administered morphine from his belt kit and bandaged the shoulder. As the ivory hunters were eight days and nights by canoe from Iquitos, there seemed no chance for the mauled man.

The village *brujo* ran into the jungle for certain herbs. While these were steaming in a pot on a fire, he hurriedly removed the bandages from Huavara's shoulder. Chanting, the *brujo* began ladling on the hot brew. This appeared to be very painful to Huavara who screamed and had to be held down by his friends. The *brujo* then sprinkled on a powder and wrapped the shoulder in leaves and fibers. Two days later the bleeding had stopped, and the opened veins were closed.

The witchdoctor told Wolfenegg to return for his man in thirty days. The Austrian's estimate was that no possible chance existed of saving either the arm or the man. The arm bones were even broken and disjointed. There were only a few shreds of flesh and ligaments holding the member to the body. The ivory hunters left, gathered their ivory, and in thirty days returned. Wolfenegg had to show his men that he did not abandon followers. They found Huavara not only alive, but well, and able now to use the lower part of his arm, and even his hand.

The Orejone *brujo* would not barter his trade secret to Wolfenegg, though eight muskets were offered. Indians for hundreds of miles around the Rio Huiririma were constantly brought to this *brujo*, and his power—because of the secret—was great.

Morning came; at this point, even 2,670 miles west of Cape Garneeleira on the Atlantic (by straight-line air measurement), the Amazon was enormous, being from a mile to three miles wide. It turned and squirmed like some living anaconda having its head chopped off, whipping through the flat endless marshes and the eternal jungle. I began checking the accuracy of the United States Air Force maps, and, though these showed the Father of Waters flowing from the west, that was about the extent of their accuracy. Islands, even a mile to ten miles long, were generally ignored, rivers the size of the Missouri misplaced. God help any airman who came down in this part of the world, granting one ever had reason to be here in the first place. On the left (south side) we passed the mouth of the Ucayali.

Next day, opposite Pucate Island, we turned into the narrow mouth of the Caño Pucate, which wanders away from the south bank and was believed by the Iquitos *patrónes* to flow cross-country to the Ucayali. Its ramblings are unknown, though they are assumed to be through a dismal swamp of trees. It is the route used by the so-called "White

Indians," Yámeos, when raiding out of the Rio Mazin down into the Chama country. Such tribes as the Shimacos also use it, coming down from their Rio Chambira.

"Buena Fe" is here prominently marked on the maps, but characteristically this town proved to be a solitary one-roomed cane hut on sticks. While Walter talked with its *patróne*, a *cholo* with five tame Yámeos, Inez and I photographed several grayish-white and pink porpoises. These were very large, and rocked our canoe precariously as they dived around it. They were at least fifteen feet long.

Once more headed up the Amazon, on a northwest tangent, we passed a *bota*, a large balsa, floating downstream to Iquitos. It was loaded with balls of rubber and stacks of crocodile skins. The river flowed majestically, but now narrowed to a mile in width, always one bank being cut away like soft cheese by the sharp edge of the current; the opposite side built up in the form of flat, crescent-shaped *playas* of sand and mud. Two days beyond the Yámeos' raid-canal we came to the Tigre River, flowing south out of the Oriente (which lay along the north bank of the Amazon). The Tigre River was inhabited by Jívaros of the Zaparo tribe and by Ardas, a little-known forest tribe—whose drums could be heard rattling.

Our Cocama pilot warned that the drums were sending out warnings of our going upriver; we must tie up to the south bank that night. Instead, we three fished until midnight after anchoring well offshore, catching both varieties of a tiny eel-like three-inch fish called *canero*. Its pinkish-gray blotched skin is smooth, like flesh, the head large, with barbs set in the side on hinges; a demon more feared than the *paña*, crocodile, poisonous water snakes and electric eel. The *canero* darts into the human body, through the anus, the vaginal passage, the penis, even the mouth, and instantly expands its poisonous barbs so that it cannot be withdrawn. The only known remedy from a painful death is the Indians' *huito* fruit, which kills and expels the *canero*.

Beyond the Tigre, occasional breaks in the wall of jungle revealed that the Marañón sometimes shifts its channels, for old ones were seen. These were fast silting up with sand and mud. I realized that the Inca gold must have been in higher ground, as shown by my map to El Dorado. The whole country was of the wildest aspect—a mangy jungle through which the great chocolate-colored river flowed. Over it brooded the hushed ghost voices of the wilderness, broken only by the quick scurrying of wild things. *Cuenpaccha,* or "spirit fountain birds," flashed bright as peacocks strumming by overhead. Great flights of wild canaries were everywhere.

We were overcome by a sense of claustrophobia, of being hemmed in; for always the rim of multicolored trees coiled around us, limiting our vision. It seemed we were afloat not on a river, but in the middle of a lake or tropical lagoon, for, due to the wide turns in the river, not much of it could be seen at one time; it was like a greenish-brown mottled boa constrictor coiling slowly around your head.

In order to avoid the swifter currents against which we could make no headway, the pilot occasionally bumped the boat across a bar searching for a way to right or left, shuffling like a cautious old man through a maze of foamy shallows and ever-shifting sandbars. The river's course was so looping, that our course was sometimes north, sometimes south, and it even bent back into the east!

As the days went by, new tribes began appearing: Urarinas and Zámeos, hunting the *playa* chickens called *tibi.* These red-and-black-painted Indians kept away from us and offered no trouble. Always at least one loaded rifle was kept on deck.

One day Inez ingeniously snipped a button off the tail of my threadbare shirt and sewed it on at the collar. Walter winked and dove into his own duffle bag, plotting similar repairs on his wardrobe. Inez was now wearing khaki boy's pants and shirt. She was proving a good companion, intelligent and an asset. She helped out in the preparation of food and even kept the living quarters clean, and made up our beds in the bunks. Due to the heat and the unaccustomed routine of boat travel, none of this was easy for her. She kept a log notebook on sounding the depth of the Amazon and was at work for hours at a time correcting the maps. I taught her how to strip my newly acquired .45 automatic Colt, and how to clean and assemble it. I felt that should anything happen to me, the knowledge would come in handy. In short, she managed admirably.

Vegetable-ivory palms began appearing along the banks. Several Zámeos, however, instead of collecting the useful nuts, were darting their canoes into the jungle's edges hunting crocodiles and snakes. Only $28 a ton was being paid in Iquitos for ivory. And as only 300 to 500 ivory nuts are gathered from each tree twice a year, and the trees are well scattered through the jungle, it was no inducement. Some of the Zámeo canoes were re-enforced with slabs of ironwood, for the harpooned crocodiles often attack, thrashing about wildly and biting at the gunwales. While watching them, Walter explained he had once doubled the egg production of colonists near Iquitos by feeding crocodile meat to the hens. This crocodile country was mainly palm-*caña* thickets, the long, single stems carrying four to five hundred blossoms of a brown feathery stuff like pampas grass. With every hour we were getting into the deeper regions of the true unknown.

A canoe-load of braves of the Pinchis (or Taushiros) tribe floated out of a river on the right bank—wild men—but they only looked us over quietly, then disappeared back in the tangle. Had I not been staring at that exact place we would never have known Indians were there watching us.

One day a hot sandstorm blew howling across the wide sandbars, swirling wildly through nubbins of palm-jungled effluvial islands cut by the current from the main jungle body. This blinding sandstorm raged across the Marañón, smashing with a squeal into the damp jungle—which swayed wildly—and sticking to it like dust to flypaper. Birds overhead, crying in alarm, were caught up in the wind: strange birds like the plumed *montete*, exotic birds like the brilliant *paucar* and *ruiseñor*—species that have yet to find their way into the world's museums. The sky flushed a burning yellow. The air was clogged thick—hot and sticky, but dirty. Inez grabbed her laundry off the roof, for the winds swooshed like demons across the darkening, purplish river. The Indian crew slammed the shutters over the windows. Everything on deck, including the chicken coop on the roof, was lashed down. And then in the midst of this wild storm, came a deluge of rain! The wind and water together ripped into us....

The boat began spinning on its keel, round and round like a top. We held on grimly, afraid of being swept overboard, for we were caught up in the currents and waves were pouring over us. The leather-faced Indian at the wheel looked alarmed. The boat was crashing into logs and carried along with them, flung about like a straw. After a desperate hour the storm ended as abruptly as it had begun and the last sand sifted to earth. We straightened out, chugged away from the current and continued along the edge of the wrinkled coppery river, our decks ankle-deep in mud.

It could have been worse. Earlier in June, all this flat region had been inundated by floods, as we could see from the debris high up in the trees. Years before, in 1938, nearly the whole of Loreto lay under a sheet of water. People desperately gathered food by pulling on limbs through the drowned forest and forcing their canoes into the tops of the trees where they found bird nests and eggs. Millions of wild animals died. The tribal *brujos* announced that the end of the world had come. Whole jungle tribes took to the trees—Omuranos, Secoyas, Vacacochas, Yaguas, Omaguas, Cahuaranos. A million souls—Indians and the few mestizos and whites—prepared to die. And then the waters suddenly receded, leaving the dead everywhere on the jungle floor and along the banks of the rivers.

The bordering jungles of the Marañón are flooded annually, from January to June. Forty-foot rises come overnight. Huts vanish; *chacaras* are wiped out; food becomes scarce; beriberi breaks out. Only a few houses on high, hardwood stilts are not swept away. At such times the milk in the bark of the *seringal* groves may keep one alive. Few fish are caught in the muddy waters. But sedge islands carrying wild animals, birds and reptiles, sometimes float by. Canoes are sent to these islands and the animals are slaughtered. Sometimes a meat bonanza is hit: the season just past was a rich one for the Secoyas, who found some four hundred deer stranded on an island. The Indians *ran them down by foot*—killing three hundred of the animals.

Food plant seeds, I realized, are benevolently scattered over the river *playas* by the same hot winds we cursed, by the treacherous currents we fought, and by the very birds we killed and ate. Most parasites growing on the trees are seeded by parrots, who carry seeds in their beaks. Seeds are even distributed by man—in the droppings of the Indians.

We pushed into a *mantablanca* belt; clouds of fiendish, microscopic mosquitoes, that covered our skin, biting smartly and laying their eggs in sacs which soon were itching like fire. We stuffed our pants' bottoms into the tops of our socks. But it was useless—*mantablancas* can penetrate the ordinary cloth used in the jungle. I must have had thousands of bites on my body. A Ticunas brave we had picked up, who was being hunted by Marubos savages, crushed the leaves of the *huaman samana* tree, rubbed the juice on our skins and killed the pests. We blessed him, for our own salves and exterminators fazed them not at all.

Night came, swiftly gliding on shadow feet, and we tied up to the left bank. We retired early to doctor ourselves. Suddenly the boat heaved under us, rolling and pitching! A roaring of sliding earth deafened us. We were thrown violently out of our bunks to the floor. I crawled up the ladder, and once on deck saw that an enormous wave was rushing against us, the decks awash. The whole bank for a mile had caved in! There was no sleeping the balance of that night, for we had to stand guard and fend off drifting logs as best we could. The boat's planking was badly buckled, and we began taking so much water that the pumps could barely keep us afloat. The bilges flooded and two feet of water stood in the cabin. All seemed lost, and I began bailing with a pail, Inez pitching in alongside. Somehow we kept afloat till daybreak.

In the dawn's light we disengaged ourselves from the debris which had fallen or floated all around, trees, limbs, islands of sedge. All this time the engine was going at top speed, throwing water over the sides. I had once owned a forty-foot yawl and so knew something about caulking. Tomás and I got underwater alongside, and began working twisted fibers into the cracks, smearing a pitch along the seams. At last we had the bottom plugged, and the boat pumped dry. It was a mess, but we were floating.

By late morning we were under way once more. I began to wonder if we were ever to reach Borja, yet hundreds of miles away. At one place Walter pointed out an enormous swamp tree. He had once sent some of its wood, a branch, to Europe. It was so hard, that only the Germans' finest steel-cutting tools could penetrate it. This wood was of a jade color, and like that stone, it would not rot. Finally, in Iquitos, a table top was cut and polished, which when exhibited in Lima won the coveted international prize from among scores of rare tropical hardwoods.

We slid past the mouth of Chambira, coming in from the north, inhabited by wild tribes of Shimacos, Urarinas, Cocamillas and Aguanos—headhunters who fight the Jívaros to the west and north. As we plowed deeper into the Indian country, we passed camps of savage Zavas, painted warriors wearing cloaks of bird feathers. The Baron puffed with the burning heat, and played cards with Inez. The ex-headhunting Semigaye mechanic avidly (too avidly! as we were to see) read the Spanish edition of the *Reader's Digest*, an old number included among Walter's books. The political articles were a little over his head, but he was fascinated by the drawings. The cook, a Mayoruna (savages of the back forests), contentedly chanted strange Indian lullabies, the while scraping fish scales, or plucking *mariquiña* feathers. The *mariquiña* is a bird with the flavor of a seagull; but we were reduced to eating its flesh, for fresh meat was hard to come by. Cannibal fish, the *peje doncella*, usually struck at my food-fish after I had hooked one, taking it behind the head or by the spine and cutting the body away as with a razor.

What we wanted was red meat, and we finally found some. It was tapir flesh in the possession of some of the wild Rio Tigre Quechuas, whose camp we came upon; but they refused to be traded out of it. I watched hourly, uselessly, for the white scut of swamp deer. Though the air was filled with the wings of four-winged thrips, Inez and I fished with flies which I tied from various hairs and feathers. The cook grinned in amusement, for fly fishing is unknown here. He explained that Indians will tie a fly to a string, then tow it under water and when a fish strikes, they spear it. He was incredulous when we brought several fish in to him. Walter, shotgun in hand, watched overhead for *paujils* and *pavos* (turkeys) roosting in the trees, but usually without luck.

One afternoon we came to a shack in an acre-sized clearing on the left bank opposite from the Oriente side, and turned in to it; this "plantation" according to our maps was none other than Valencia. It was not a savory place—the ground being littered with stinking old turtle shells and yellow crocodile bellies. We were greeted by the owner, an old man, who introduced himself as Don Garcia. There was nothing to eat here, he said, so I prepared for a fishing trip. For the benefit of the millions of American licensed fishermen, I will tell of that fishing trip—for none (so far as I know) has ever been included in past exploration books, though the Amazon is the world's largest and finniest river.

Two hours before darkness set in, the "*Patróncita*"—the crew's name for Inez—and I, took *La Patria*'s dugout and started out to try our luck. The hollow log was paddled by the stony-faced mechanic, one Monte Negro, Chief "Black Mountain," whom Inez insisted for some unknown reason on calling "Jefe Mono Negro," a point which considerably irritated the proud Semigaye, since *mono* means "monkey." Black Mountain worked the canoe along our south side of the river, which was being attacked by the lash of the current, moving us cautiously among the wreckage of fallen palms and other trees.

I knelt in the prow and cast my hollow cane spear ahead into ripples, or thrust it into any of the fast-moving submerged fishes. Thus, after an hour, the canoe's bottom was covered with many flopping fish.

We crossed over to the right side of the Marañón, at this point some half-mile wide, swinging in a parabola course with the seven-knot current. We reached the Oriente forest on the north bank, and again I began tossing the spear into the moving points of the V-shaped schools. Nearly always the barbed steel struck meat, for many fish were here. The varieties were numerous, and often armed with poisonous spines. They ran from a foot in length up to five feet. Inez got over her squeamishness when I began casting aspersions at female explorers, for the fish were flopping about in the canoe, splashing water over my backside and throwing off my aim. And so with an unladylike growl in her throat, she whacked them with a machete, or speared them again. She moved around in a lively fashion so as not to be bitten and raked, especially by the spiny if scaleless *mota* and other dart-armed devils. You never knew what you had on the end of the spear thrashing around in the water, and when boated, often turned out to be energetic and dangerous *sabalo, turushuqui* or the red and yellow spotted *peje torre.*

Actually, Inez was appearing in a new light, for she had weathered better than most men could under the circumstances; was particularly patient under the swarms of insects, the heat, the monotony of our diet, the sandstorm and dangers of the river. Also she worked hard, and she was clever at handling the Indians along the way, far better than either Walter or I. So far, I did not regret having taken her along, but something in my bones warned me that great dangers and hardships lay ahead—and I hated to see her risk her life, perhaps lose it, just to gratify a mere whim that she wished to be the first explorer to cross the continent via the Amazon. At that time I assumed, mistakenly, that a woman just traveled to be traveling and didn't need a motive. Like most outdoors men, I have little use for the type of explorer who must rely on a stunt to put his expedition across, because he is lazy or basically incompetent and unable to obtain new and interesting information.

A warm evening rain caught us in the midst of solid schools of the silvery-scaled *mañana me voy*, a fish I had to kill at all costs, and eat, if only for their charming name. While the rain pelted us, the phenomenal run of *mañana me voy* flashed mockingly around the dugout by the thousands. With Black Mountain frantically steadying the little craft's bow upstream, I began casting three cane spears, automatically retrieving them as they boomeranged back on the current. Crocodiles slid in, and began striking the schools from below, causing the *mañana me voy* to burst out of the river in silvery cascades.

Garza comúns and pelicans and eagles and even dolphins—all greatly excited—moved in and attacked. Hundreds of birds dove down into the depths, splashing the mica-flashing water over us. We were soaked, but as the birds surfaced with a fish in their beaks, we yelled with joy. A great flight of red fishers, the *garza rosada*, flapped about our heads trying to get at our fish in the dugout, their sharp beaks snapping; but we drove them off with the spears, though with considerable loss to our cargo.

The dugout was riding low in the water, seemingly a third filled with fish, and so we raced back to *La Patria*, now some two miles downstream. Our heads held low, we shot under the dripping overhang of the jungle.

"Well, Inez, how do you like jungle fishing?" I asked while making a place for myself among the slippery cargo.

"I like worms," says she.

"There aren't any worms in this jungle," I said. "And another thing—you nearly tipped us over when those crocodiles were feeding back there."

Now I didn't realize there was anything in these words to cause anger in the human breast. But the next thing I knew, I was smacked across the teeth with a sizable specimen of *mañana me voy*.

"What's that for?" I asked. I could see that Black Mountain was steadying the canoe so that I could pitch her to the crocs, because that's what an Indian would have done.

"Don't you ever speak to me again!" wailed this other one, eyes flashing.

She was a temperamental woman and at times I did not understand her, but she needn't have worried, for as far as I was concerned, she could start swimming over the Andes. Presently we were alongside *La Patria*. Tomás, the cook, was delighted; and though we had been eating fish until it was coming out of our ears, our food problem was settled for the next few days. In counting the catch, both large and small fish, he studiously worked up to ten on his fingers, then began on his toes—and so, miraculously arrived at "twenty!" Now that is as far as most Indians can count, and I was curious to see what would happen. But this Tomás was a man of parts. He stopped, grinned enormously at me, and made a big mark on the wall with a grimy finger—and then started all over again. When he had finished, there were four marks, but three fingers were left over. Now what? He was really stumped. Finally he took three of the smallest fish and heaved them overboard. His smile of satisfaction was so touching, I couldn't help but stifle an oath already forming in my throat.

Chief Black Mountain reported that his engine was frozen tight and broken down. Not only were the bilges flooding, and now impossible to keep dry, but we couldn't go any farther on our journey. He had forgotten to put oil into the crankcase during all that time we had used the pump at the slide downstream. And Borja by map seemed very far away.

We stared at each other in dismay. There was no chance of walking overland through the jungle. If we abandoned ship, could we continue by dugout against the ever-increasing flush of the seven-knot current? Plainly it was either that or turn back!

"You go down to Iquitos—" cried Inez, pointing the first finger of both hands at me, "So that I can continue by Indian canoe!"

Walter suavely remarked that we had come only half-way, and it was still three or four hundred miles, as the river coiled, to the foothills of the Andes—the Cordillera Orientale, which she must climb to 18,000 feet elevation in order to get across to the coast. Unknown jungles blocked the way, jungles filled with headhunting Jívaros. No explorer in all history had ever broken through. She would forfeit her life. The last explorer anywhere in the region had been the Britisher, Commander George Dyott, who some twenty-five years earlier had been captured hundreds of miles south of the Amazon near Moyabamba—on the edge of the wild Jívaro country—and barely escaped with his neck. The two American explorers associated with the Oriente, he went on, had lived near Baños, a town near Quito—and never got very far east into the jungle; perhaps (according to Iquitos experts) twenty miles at most.

"You see what you are up against," I added. "The only real explorer who ever had any success here was the heavily armed Up de Graff, an American adventurer and *cauchero* who traveled on some of the rivers sixty years ago."

"I'm not going just twenty-five miles into the jungle from Baños; and even if I'm no *cauchero* armed to the teeth, I intend continuing. I have reasons of my own for not stopping here. I may seem just a poor, weak woman, but I'm going through the Oriente."

"The exploring fraternity isn't going to bless you," I put in, wondering what "reasons" she could have that would make her so determined.

"I'm not afraid of Indians. Headhunters—pooh! Bugs bother you worse than they do me. Any real woman can get through this jungle. I've made up my mind to go up the Amazon, and nothing and *nobody* can stop me."

I couldn't help grinning at von Wolfenegg. He was standing as if stunned with a pole axe.

"Ah, mademoiselle—I begin to understand what our General Staff has not understood...no wonder we have lost two wars. But the answer is—No!"

"Come on, Mrs. Stanley," I coaxed diplomatically, "Just prepare to float backwards for a while; I'm going to try and break through somehow, but you're not."

"Ah! Ah! mademoiselle! Please do not throw my crockery at him." And Walter lunged forward to save his best and only plate without a crack.

Stranded as we certainly were, a Robinson Crusoe existence began for us. Black Mountain was "promoted" (no one is ever "demoted" in South American jungles) from mechanic to man-about-camp. He built a rack of limbs, and after splitting our fish, placed them on it for drying. *La Patria* became a house anchored to the shore where she couldn't sink. The chicken coop was hoisted on land and a bamboo corral held the last two egg-laying hens. Steps were hacked in the mud to the top of the ten-foot bank.

Hoping I suppose for a miracle, we waited, with Walter stewing in his juices, fanning irritably and reading from La Fontaine as he taught wrinkled old Don Garcia, the *patróne* ashore, to speak French. The damp heat was oppressive and the *mantablancas* fiendish. Ashore, every bush was covered with tiny red and white *insangui*, skin borers, and to collect a thousand of them all you had to do was just brush against whatever they were on. Silent Uritú Indians from the jungles behind the river, glided in dugouts along the shore, spearing fish. A whole river of fins now churned upstream past us, millions of flashing fins and scaly backs. I could hardly wrench my eyes away. One day our friend was dismayed. Inez had been stretching Walter's precious sounding line under the weight of our combined laundry, which though not prodigious was phenomenal for the poverty-stricken Amazon. We were all of us wearing khaki pants and cotton shirts.

"Good *Gott*! Inez—with the line stretched out I would be in deep water when I wouldn't be. Mademoiselle, I luff you like a brother. But...ah, well, you keep it." His heart simply melted at sight of that close-cropped, curly head, with its golden Pan face, supported on a slender, lean stem of incredible grace. He was a hardy veteran of the wilds, this man who had left a soft life in Europe to become a man-of-the-jungle, but he also loved beauty, especially in all its womanly forms. "Why don't you love her? Everybody loves Inez. You, her kontryman. She loves everybody but you."

"Well, if you really want to know...I think women—" I started explaining, and a bit too loudly as I afterwards learned to my sorrow, "—belong in their father's house, or in their husband's house, or at least in somebody's house." I could see Pokorny edging in a bit closer. "Anyway, they don't belong gallivanting around this neck of the woods, full of head choppers worse than the old Apaches."

It was finally agreed that one Inez Pokorny had to go back, that if anything happened to her we would have it on our conscience. I made preparations to continue alone. Tobacco was sliced off a bark-wrapped twist Jorge had handed me on our departure in Pucalpa, and then I rolled the crumbs between my palms and stored them in a holeless sock. The tobacco pouch was used exclusively now for my maps. Other things included: a change of khaki pants and shirts, socks and a hat purchased in Iquitos, poncho, machete, flashlight and six extra batteries, pencils (three), small diary, Leica camera, eight rolls of 35 mm films (tropical packing), compass, aneroid barometer, fishline for sounding, .45 Colt, twenty rounds of shells, a few medicines including mosquito dope; mosquito net, trade tobacco, rock salt, pot, sheath knife, wristwatch, small can of corn "coffee." Exposed films and the two old notebooks had been mailed home. I still had the old money belt, and it held the same invaluable items carried on the southern rivers. From an Indian I purchased a sack of *chimbilla* pods. No self-respecting pig back home would eat the black, oily *chimbilla*; but then, there is a considerable difference in the standard of living between a wanderer in the Amazon jungles and a pig in the United States.

That night the moon was fairly full, and in search of other food for my supplies, Tomás and I boarded the dugout, he squatting in the bow, and I in the stern. At the last minute Walter suggested that Inez go along too. Wedged in the bow in the manner peculiar to Amazon Indians, who prefer that end of a canoe for paddling, Tomás dug his broad paddle into the water, shooting us forward into the night, surging upstream against the current and close under the snarled jungly shore. Like a zoo lion that sleeps and yawns all day, our usually inert cook had become with night a jungle rover—a true Mayoruna.

His alertness to fish flashing along the gunwales was electric and instinctive. Also he would instantly point with his chin to any rustling sound on our left side. I mentioned the danger from *culebras*, snakes, possibly coiled on the banks, which we could touch at times, but he apparently relished skimming close and revelling in the thrill, for he paid no attention to my warning. Once a canoeful of befeathered Indians silently drifted by within twenty feet, after Tomás had dug in his paddle and backed us into a lagoon, waiting, grinning like a demon. His paddle was incredibly powerful, swift and silent.

We had been gone about half an hour when he speared an iguana off a bank, calling it "river chicken." Far off, in the south, toward the unexplored Rio Samiria, came the off-key eerie cry of the *chuchuberi*—which was explained as a headhunter's ghost.

The jungle spread around us, high as a fifteen-storied building; to describe its varieties of leaves, their sizes from thirty feet in length to microscopic pinpoints; their various shapes, colors (red, gold, green), perfumes and stenches would involve a task not unlike describing the individual grains of sand on a beach.

Schools of the nocturnal *sapochunchi*, a scaleless dark-skinned fish, sounded like the sandstorm we had endured. The fish slashed in flame-like phosphorescent colors around us. The moonlight gleamed an oily gold and green in the jungle and on the water.

After an hour the Indian swung us across the river. In the middle of the channel we struck a shoal-run of *dorados*—a giant goldfish. The impact with those fish was so sudden, I thought at first we had struck a submerged *playa* and would founder in the fast current. Actually, the river was some eighty feet deep here. Tomás yelled in alarm, then with a desperate laugh began pounding his paddle madly on the water, trying to clear out a space for the dugout to float. The moonlit air was full of golden fish bursting out of the river, leaping, cascading.

I saw that the canoe was fast filling with fish. I began scooping the *dorados* out; kicking at them. And then, just as suddenly, the Indian broke clear and we floated off the island of fish, free once more.

The dugout shot forward under the paddle, and the swimming eyes of stars peered over the gunwales, moving in the murky depths below like lost worlds. Lying still in deep holes below, I knew, would be such fish as the giant *arapaima*, some four hundred pounds in weight, and fifteen feet long. Thick, shoulder-high blobs of foam, through which we cut at heart-gripping speed, indicated storms higher in the Andes, reminding me of my ultimate destination. All this time Inez was perfectly still, balancing the canoe nicely, saying nothing, a perfect companion on the river at night. I realized then how badly she wanted to go west.

After threading *cochas* jammed tight with great *ishpingo* trees, for hours on end, and spearing a load of the white, black-banded *shirapiras*, it was suddenly 3 A.M. Tomás swept in a long gull's arc back across the enchanted river. Walter was waiting on deck like an old brood hen, lantern swinging in hand, scolding us: "*Mein* children! Oh, you worry me so! Don Garcia's men say that Jívaro Achuares are wearing black warpaint…three men have been killed and decapitated very close—just in back of the house!"

We hauled the fish aboard, and had barely gotten into the cabin when suddenly Tomás hissed for us to be quiet. We stood in the dark, listening. A very faint rattling sound was coming through the jungle out of the north.

"War drums—"

There was no sleeping that night, for the drums were finally all about us. At dawn, old Don Garcia was in a great dither: "War drums on the Marañón. That is bad!"

Walter announced that he had made a decision. He must float with the current the 300 miles back to Iquitos: he would cradle "that damned poat," (no longer his "*La Belle Patria*") between two balsa rafts that had appeared in the night. Their owners, hearing the drums, were expecting the worst. Glad for the additional re-enforcement the *balseros* now agreed, for they were bringing a rich cargo of skins and rubber into Iquitos.

At daybreak, Walter took me aside and talked seriously. Inez, he said, had made up her mind and was going to continue on west. With the

Indian outbreak, it was no longer safe for her to proceed to Borja even in his launch; but now that he had to turn back, the risks were much greater. Since she was determined to go on, it was up to me to see her through. As a result of this conversation, I decided to take Inez along. The decision was undoubtedly helped along by the sober fact that she was damned useful in a practical sense, particularly in dealing with the Indians. There was no doubt but that I had changed my mind since leaving Iquitos, and after talking to Walter, there seemed no good reason for leaving her stranded in Valencia. Furthermore, I was in a sense obligated to von Wolfenegg for having transported me thus far. And though I felt deep concern for the risk to herself, this concern in the final analysis was no greater than I should have felt for any woman (or man either) who was perfectly willing to take her (or his) chances on the same basis as I was doing. And finally, like battle, exploration is not the place for indecision and squeamishness, and since Walter insisted she knew her own dangers and accepted them, that decision to take her was made final and irrevocable.

All that day we worked in the water cradling the boat between the balsas, and in the night maps were studied and marked with notes and corrections. Food was discussed. Money was counted. Letters were written to Gallardy, Johnny Rokes, Van de Putte and our other friends. Ashore, at the "casa grande" of Valencia, we signed a contract with the ancient patróne, Don Garcia. Everyone swore on his mother's head or his grandfather's grave. To honor the great business, this ingenious man wore his shoes; they had been made by dipping his bare feet into rubber latex, and then allowing it to dry while still on.

He had contracted to send us in a dugout with Indian paddlers, who spoke considerable Spanish, to Tres Unidos, five days west at the Boca Huallaga—mouth of the Huallaga. Tres Unidos was the only town (six houses) in the 600-mile stretch by river channel between Iquitos and Borja. Walter looked puzzled, as did we: our best maps indicated no such metropolis in the middle of the headhunting country. But Don Garcia swore on his wife's cross that it was there.

Our business settled, we went to sleep on the boat, awakening at 4 A.M. Outside, rain sluiced down as if an ocean were being dumped on us. Our scant belongings were transferred to Garcia's hut. The badly scarred La Patria, most of her paint long ago rubbed off, was lashed tight, secured between the pair of balsas. With the rafts' great sweeps moving slowly back and forth like the flippers of turtles lying on their backs, *La Patria*—disabled and helpless, with Walter stalking her deck like Napoleon heading for St. Helena—moved decrepitly toward the middle of the river. Here the current caught her up and moved her eastward. Walter had looted himself and forced upon us a whole gunnysack jammed with food—two pounds of beans, one of rice, a pound of black sugar, a little of his own rock salt, some hardtack, and ten small cans of vegetables, two bottles of red wine and a cup of native coffee, a dozen *plátanos*. Five empty beer bottles were included, for holding boiled water, as we had no canteen.

These empty bottles were a useless luxury. So far, since leaving Stone's, I had not boiled my drinking water. I had purposely taken it out of the rivers to see if it were contaminated. Surprisingly (and counter to the belief of other explorers), I had found that the Amazon waters (in the west) are uncontaminated, and if one does not take water out of them below a human habitation (a few hundred yards below), it is quite safe. On a laboratory test later made in Quito, it was found I had not picked up a single parasite or germ.

We were provisioned for the last few hundred miles to Borja fort, perhaps months away. We could have eaten it all in three days. And any week now the rainy season would start, and the rate of the river's current would bring my trip to a halt.

"*Adios, mis amigos! Hasta luego!*" floated back a forlorn voice. Walter bowed deeply, daubed his eyes with red bandanna, and tossed Inez her last bit of continental *beau geste*. Mingling with the bullfrogs' *tok-unk-tok-unk*, the clamor of parrots, came Walter's fading voice—"Oh—la, la, mademoiselle...the Iquitos Chamber of Commerce luffs you!"

She was shivering in the rain like an orphan in a city alley. We plodded back to the hut through deep puddles. On Don Garcia's veranda, we sat forlornly in creaking chairs; but after awhile she began playing with a *leoncito* monkey. The Don asked me to doctor his eyes. The *pucaruru* ant had fed at the corneas, which I saw had become opaque. It was a very common ailment on the river. Van de Putte had said milk applied quickly was the only cure.

Dinner at Don Garcia's was excellent; dried salt-cured *paiche*, and *fritos*—fried bananas sliced thin and baked crisp as potato chips. The *paiche* here supplies most of the meat eaten on the Marañón; it is a tremendous fish of twelve feet and more in length, weighing some seven hundred pounds.

On the cane wall I saw a calendar: today was *Friday the 13th.*

Even so, tomorrow we must prepare our dugout.

"Now what's wrong?" Inez glanced at the calendar: "Oh—so now you're worrying about having a woman along." She was completely disgusted. "I won't jinx you."

After a long quiet period, she said, "What do you call yourself?"

"A damned fool," I said with conviction.

"Well, you certainly don't look like an explorer. Those pants would disgrace an Indian! What about that piece of rope you've got tied around your middle for a belt? And those shoes!"

"What's wrong with them?" I looked them over, and couldn't see anything the matter, except for the need of a shine.

"Well, you've got the toes cut off for one thing. And your shirt is so full of holes. Your clothes won't last a week."

"Miss Pokorny—please. If you don't like my clothes, you can look elsewhere. They'll last. They always have. And another thing: I'm a bachelor, and I don't want you to forget it. You can henpeck the Iquitos Chamber of Commerce—but if you don't lay off me, I'll feed you to the fish so help me God." I stalked into my room.

"Put in your shirt tail!" she yelled. She had cheered up anyway.

On my bunk, where there was a little peace and quiet, I lit my pipe and got to thinking. Don Garcia had said even he had never forced a way through the tangle for more than a mile in back of the house; it was all *bravo;* unexplored. I thought for a long while about the Achuares hunting down Cocamas right here on the river, and of the Andoas, and the Muratos—homicidals inhabiting the lagoons of the Largo Anahco on the Rio Huasago, and in the Zaucude Yacu, and the Copal. Don Garcia knew almost nothing about these Indians, though he had lived many years here on the edge of the true unknown. As he did not attempt to enslave the Jívaros and other wild tribesmen, he had not been burned out. He was extremely anxious (I could see) to get us out of here, for fear the Indians might have their eyes on us.

Inez was a fine girl and I did not want to see her hurt, or tied to a Jívaro hut by one foot. But it was something else that laid a cold hand over my heart. All at once I realized what it was. All countries and regions over the world create for us certain impressions which abide with us: peace, confusion, gaiety, happiness, despair.... But here in the jungle the reaction psychologically was a chilling sense of incomprehensible mysteries and lurking types of malignant dangers.

But enough of worry. Inez wasn't afraid, and we would learn the numbing details soon enough; for at sunrise we were leaving.

ꙮ XIX. ꙮ

Headhunters in the Headwaters

*I*T was cool and just breaking dawn when Inez and I stood on the muddy bank in the shadowed well of towering green jungle, its upper blossoms all incandescent under a pink sky, and thanked old Don Garcia for his hospitality. He pointed out that the low-lying fog over the surface of the Marañón, was already burning off, and our vision would be clear very soon now for making our way upstream. The Achuare drums had stopped an hour earlier, which meant the Jívaros would be scattered in the jungle, maybe hunting for the pot, and maybe hunting for something else, and we must be careful.

"From now on, señor, in all these rivers, you will find headhunters—put out your fires at night; anchor in deep water when you sleep."

I carried our two bags and sack of food down to the dugout which the *patróne* had furnished according to our contract. It lay alongside the bank; being thirty feet in length and having a five-foot beam. Over this craft was bent a *tolda*, or *techa* (a half-round roof) of fresh-smelling green palm fans. In spite of its sturdiness, I was afraid of this dugout, for it was carved from a log of *espintana*, a very hard wood that sinks like lead; but upon remonstrating with Garcia, he said wearily it was all that was available—and if I didn't like it, I could lump it. I took my old money belt out of my bag and put it on under my shirt. It contained all the same essentials as formerly on the back rivers, and should the boat swamp, and all be lost, we might still get out. In this waterproof belt were also my oilskin packet of papers, Rubio's letter, police clearance (which allowed me to move with freedom) and my passport with Lima visa as well as the Iquitos visa.

Facing west upstream, the three coppery paddlers—their broad faces painted yellow and red—crouched naked in the bows amid a couple of tiny banana leaf packets containing all their provisions, mainly a handful of plantains and rock salt. They also had their muskets, but very little powder and shot. Inez and I carefully took our positions amidships just behind them, sitting side by side on the springy cane floor which was carpeted with an old rubber poncho (acquired from Bishop Arellano in Atalaya) that had already served so well on the Ucayali. Our bags I stacked behind us in the stern, in order to trim the tippy, round-bottomed craft properly. Even so, the gunwale was weighted to within three or four inches of the water.

Inez waved to Don Garcia as he pushed us off into the stream. He seemed greatly relieved at this last gesture which put an end to his responsibilities of the *contrato*.

"The *contrato* is fulfilled!" he barked, brushing his hands together.

"*Si*, señor, and if you ever swear on your grandfather's head again, I hope he comes out of his grave and bites your leg off."

"Shhhh ..." from Inez.

I gave the old buzzard a salute with thumb to nose, and he replied with a rock straight through the roof.

"You're impossible!" Inez cried. "That wonderful man found us this wonderful boat...why, I never!"

"I'll thank you not to rock the boat so much," I said, "and if we sink in the first rapids we come to, you'll think that old rattlesnake is a wonderful man all right."

In paddling, the Cocamas—with bulging muscles hard as flint—hit the water in split-second unison. It was a peculiarly quick, short, wrist-chop movement, with the inner edge of their platter-shaped, thin bladed, gaudy painted paddles. The result was a rhythmic chopping sound but definitely not the "drumlike sound" so often described. And with each quick chop, the dugout jerked forward a few inches against the swift current.

Globs of yellowish white foam, large as canoes, swirled over the Marañón's surface. Behind the south bank on our left ranged a seldom seen subtribe of Shuara—the over-all tribal name used by varions Jívaros. Soon the drums began rattling again, on our north. The paddlers said they were Murato and Cocama. The Muratos are Jívaros, and therefore headhunters and head-shrinkers. They are one of the easternmost Jívaros. The inland Cocamas are as wild, but are outside the head-cult. In spite of this psychological handicap, for the Jívaro head-cult strikes terror into other Indians' hearts, the Cocamas are fierce fighters and slave raiders, and are a cagey tribe numbering thousands. Consequently, there was little choice between the two banks.

The Indians decided to try the middle. But the current here proved too swift and we could make no headway against it. By this time we had dropped downstream from Valencia, and so finally had to skirt the more favorable left south shore, where the water's slower rate of flow allowed us to inch forward. Shoals of fish, some a hundred yards across, moved around us. The marvelously long plumed *picaflores* birds trilled and stood on fallen trees. Islands of bulbous flowers, tangled clots of roots and trees floated by with the usual crocodiles and hovering clouds of mosquitoes.

While fighting the current the Indians often came in very close to the shore. From the edge of our palm roofing, we peered out into a strange world of aquatic roots of every conceivable form and color, varying from delicate silky red stringers to lumpy muscular licorice-black cables. Using a pencil stub, Inez busied herself sketching them. Once in a while across the face of the high jungle hung a streamer of red or cream-colored flowers some ten feet long, not unlike a kite's tail. Later she drew the portrait of an *urubu rey* regally gliding in low circles overhead: it was the great, white king vulture.

Ever seeking slower water, the Indians took terrible chances, sometimes coming so close to the shore that tree stumps, reeds, caña, hyacinth, water grass, and snaggy limbs often touched our gunwales or raked the *techa*. In still water we would have been knifing along at about ten to twelve miles an hour, but in the swifter places here, we barely crept ahead—inch by inch. At such times ants climbed aboard. After the river made a long curve left, its course lay smoother, but still continued wriggling in broad loops so that shortcuts were usually made by crossing over and closing the half-mile width to the opposite shore. Thus we changed sides frequently; the grunting paddlers digging into the current, the paddles' *chop! chop! chop!* coming back fast and furious from the bow, spray flying wildly, and our tipsy craft lurching violently.

By noon, I calculated our position at 4° 15" south of the Equator, 75° 20" west longitude. This intrigued Inez: "I just don't see how you do it."

"I have my own system," I explained carefully, "First I rub my right ear, then add my ten toes (the shoes were indeed cut off, for comfort), subtract the hairs on my head—and so arrive at our position on the map."

"I thought you said the maps and the earth didn't match up."

"That's right," I agreed, "We could be a hundred miles from where the maps say we are. That's only one of our smallest worries though. But as long as I have my toes, my hair, and at least one ear, I'll make out all right."

The first Indian in the boat had dropped his paddle with a clatter, and was hurling his spear ahead of the bow into a curved fin cutting the yellow waters. As the spear struck, it floated back on the fast current; he grabbed its shaft and carelessly jerked aboard a two-foot *shirapira*, a white, scaleless fish with black bands. The Indian's dinner was intact but a toe was missing from the Number two paddler just behind; snapped clean off in the fish's mouth. As the blood was spurting, the others paddled shoreward. One of the Indians went a little way into the wall of trees, but soon returned with milk from the *sangre de leche* (blood-milk) tree. Big and rough-barked, its leaf is not unlike that of the balsa. This "milk" was drunk by the injured Indian. Within twenty minutes the spurting flow of blood had stopped, and the stump was bound in a fiber and leaf bandage. In generations to come this might well be a blessing to womankind, for the Cocama *brujos* use *sangre de leche* on hemorrhages suffered in childbirth.

Once more on our way, Inez read aloud from her pocket-sized library of the Amazon's immortals: La Condamine in the Ecuadorian highlands, Von Humboldt on the Orinoco, Spruce on the lower Amazon, and Darwin in the Galápagos Islands. These men were giants who generations ago had but scratched the possibilities of the heartland of this inner continental sea of vegetation. So much of it still lies unexplored! Even in the most active field, that of natural history, much remains to be done: less than fifty monkeys are known to science; the Indians say there are over a hundred. The plant life is at least 50 percent unknown—absolutely unrecorded. As to exploration, accurate mapping has not covered 1 percent of the jungle regions. As for the medicines alone, I believe that within a hundred years, many of them will have proven effective and will be made available. And as a final example of the virgin opportunities here for the young field scientist of future generations: that very day on the Marañón, our Number three paddler wore a basket headpiece decorated with eight small, brightly colored birds—beautifully skinned and stuffed with kapok. Five of these birds are unknown to science (I still have them).

Comida (lunch) was prepared on a muddy *playa*, and the speared fish together with a few plantains were boiled in our pot. Inez walked into the edge of the jungle which was composed of *gram alote*, fern umbrella trees and many kinds of palms, these last mostly spiky varieties. She explained on returning that even in the deep shade it was dripping hot, and the place crawling with incredible varieties of insects, especially spiders, ants, and mosquitoes. Every single leaf, great and small, held insects of some kind.

Lunch over, and the sand flies very bad, we hurriedly got under our palm palánquin once more. It is only while on the river, and moving, that the insects are endurable; here on the edge of the jungle they were awful—and I was rather annoyed when the Indians delayed. Before getting in the boat, the Indians took time out to burn copal, saying in Spanish mixed with their own dialect, that an *iguanchi* spirit was here—a Jívaro ghost-spirit.

All afternoon they kept at the work of paddling, and by nightfall we camped on a wrecked balsa raft, which may have slipped its moorings upstream at Borja still hundreds of miles by river in the west. But we first had to get rid of a stinking cargo of yellowish-black crocodile skins that lay on the raft, festering with maggots. Amazon crocodiles—amazingly enough—are slit full length down the spine, and not up the belly. A large rectangle is slashed out of the belly, since the hide is like armor plate and cannot be tanned. This leaves only about half of the original skin.

We got under our mosquito netting, and though it was hot, finally got to sleep. About two o'clock in the morning I awoke suddenly, and knew something was wrong. Moving my hand very slowly, I found my flashlight which was always inside my net. I snapped on the switch, and saw not a foot from my face an immense snake, coiled and ready to strike. The net I knew would not protect me. The body must have been four inches thick, a black color blotched with yellow, the neck very thin, the head flat and as large as a saucer. I dared not even blink my eyes. Not knowing what to do, for the slightest movement would cause it to strike, I lay there in an awful sweat.

Finally I had to do something or break under the strain. Knowing the snake was blinded by the light, I very slowly moved my right foot under my net and touched Inez through her net, which was about two feet away. She must have been awake, for I heard her say very quietly: "What is it?" She must have sensed something wrong, for her voice was strained, if quiet.

"What is it?" she repeated.

I could not answer. I knew my life lay in her hands, and whatever she did to save me she must do alone, and without the slightest mistake. She did not have a flashlight, for it had been lost overboard one night, and she was unarmed. Besides that, she was a rotten shot. I will not deny that I was thinking intently and I am not ashamed to say that I was thinking of God, in a completely detached way, and I was wondering if on death you saw Him, or if it was a light you saw—or if death was like dreaming in sleep, or utter unconsciousness, or absolute blackness. I felt with certainty that this was the end of the individual ego of one Leonard Clark, that he was nothing but a mass of chemicals to be used over and over again, and that from that moment on, he was in the hands of whatever force was moving the atoms and the worlds.

With the other half of my brain I heard Inez move; I knew she was raising her net. Any moment she would see the snake through my netting in the beam of my flashlight—would she scream....

The sweat was trickling down my face, and I was holding my eyes as still as I could, staring into the black eyes only a few inches away.

Next I felt something move under my head and knew it was her hand, feeling for my gun. The hand slowly withdrew. At least a full minute must have passed—the big automatic roared alongside my head, and the snake struck.

The open mouth flashed white against the netting; the long, white fangs hinged out from their pit-seats where they normally lie, and on coming in contact with the net's mesh, were instantly depressed—and venom spurted into my eyes. The fangs buried themselves in my neck, and in one cold and terrible movement I seized the snake behind the head and pulled it off, throwing it across the raft. The light showed blood on my hands, and I realized that Inez's shot must gone right through the pile of coils.

She let out a frightful scream. Everything was suddenly in complete darkness, for I had dropped the light. The pain was like the shock of twenty typhus hypodermic injections in one. Presently Inez had my netting pulled away, and after fumbling with her hands, found the flashlight and switched it on. The snake was lying some five feet away, crawling a little, turning over and over, coiling and uncoiling—badly hurt.

The three Indians were on their feet, dead-quiet, saying nothing. One of them crossed over to the snake, and holding it down with the stock of his musket, bent close and looked at it very carefully. He let out an exclamation, and one of the other Indians leaped off the raft and into the water; I could hear him splashing shoreward.

For a moment I thought of bleeding the wounds, slitting the fang holes with my sheath knife, but I had no sooner drawn the blade and pressed the point against my throat, than I stopped; the wounds were right alongside the jugular vein. Furthermore, there was no chance of applying a tourniquet. I couldn't help but laugh.

"For God's sake. Control yourself!" cried Inez.

"Oh, shut up! I'm all right. That snake was a *nacanaca*. That means I've got four to five minutes at the outside. Now listen to what I say. At daylight you will bury me, and then you will turn back to Garcia's. You will mail all my Marañón notes and maps to my brother Laurence—you will find his address somewhere. Do you understand?"

"Yes," she said, "I will. I know those notes mean a great deal to you. But—you won't die. There is something we can do."

I grabbed her by the arm, and held her, for she was extremely agitated. "Take it easy." I told her, "There is nothing on earth you can do. This is it. And don't start blubbering all over the place. Put my gun under your shirt, and keep it there out of sight—you may need it before you are out of here."

She started crying, and I lay on my back, trying to compose myself for what I knew would be a long, long sleep. Every man and woman who was ever born, I thought, has gone through this same experience. I was a little shocked, though I don't know why. I could feel the venom spreading, for the pain was creeping outward in a circle, and after about three minutes had lapsed, my jaws were paralyzed. My brain would go next. I realized the Indians were moving close, and presently all three of them were bending over me—the light blinding my eyes, which were beginning to feel as if they were on fire. One of the Cocama braves was sticking me all over the face, throat and chest with what felt like a long needle. And that was the last thing of which I was aware.

The next period of consciousness was a peculiar one. Though my eyes were open, for I raised my hands and felt of them, I was in total darkness. At first I thought I must have wakened in the middle of the night. The next instant I knew an Indian was standing very close, for I could detect the faintest odor of man. Normally you can't smell a river Indian, for he bathes as much as three or four times in a day. I felt something cold being laid over my face and eyes. By this time I was fully awake, realizing it was broad daylight, for a shadow had fallen across my eyes.

I must have started, some muscular reflex perhaps, for I heard Inez's voice:

"It's all right," she said, "Do you remember what happened?"

"Yes, I remember all about the snake. But I'm totally blind."

"The Indians are helping you," she answered, "They said you would be blind. Can't you see anything at all?"

"I only know that daylight has come."

"We have been here four days and nights."

"Have you eaten anything?"

"The Indians have been spearing fish." After a minute, during which she fed me with boiled fish, she continued: "On the afternoon of the second day I thought you were going to die. The Indians have been boiling something in a pot. About every hour they stick you all over the body with a long thorn which they keep dipping into the pot."

"What do they call the stuff?" I asked.

"Probably an Indian name. They call it *sanango*."

"That's Spanish," I told her.

"The blindness is from the venom which they say must somehow have gotten into your eyes. They are not *brujos*, but they are trying several things—that's what is on your eyes now. It's something they pour on a cloth."

I dozed off and it was not until hours later at midnight before I wakened. I sat up but was aware only that my netting was around me. The next thing I knew a light was shining in front of my eyes.

"I can see!" I shouted. Inez was laughing, switching the flashlight off and on. She pulled the net up and held the light very close, lifting the lid of my right eye with her fingers: "Your eyes are covered with a white film, and the edges are as red as blood."

With the first flush of dawn Inez and I ate fish, and she had the Indians load the dugout. Presently we were afloat in the fast current. By holding the upper lid of either eye, I could make out trees and the Indians and the canoe. Inez's face swam into view. She looked brown, thin and dog-tired.

It was not long before I realized we were not drifting with the current; the Indians were paddling, for the dugout was moving ahead in little jerks. That could only mean one thing.

"We're headed upstream?"

"Yes," she answered, "for Borja."

The only thing I could think of was—"What a girl!"

All day the Indians paddled against the current, stopping finally on a *playa.* Inez said it was 10:30 by my watch (which she had not forgotten to wind during all those other days). It seemed incredible that the Indians had kept at that back-breaking work for seventeen hours without a break, and in a boiling heat. All that same day, *huayranga* wasps, poisonous devils, had stung us, even through our clothing, and we could not sleep that night for the itching. Except for a splitting headache I felt well enough. The Indians continued their care of my eyes. This was part of their jungle code of helping any companion on a journey, and they in no way became more friendly than before, but remained cold and aloof. They speared fish by the light of a torch, and after boiling the catch, we ate. Inez watched while the Indians and I slept.

Next day, in desperation, Inez erected my big mosquito net in the canoe. Even so, the strong mesh was cut to ribbons by the *huayrangas.* More miles fell behind us, and at midnight we stopped and drank the last delicious drop of the corn coffee Bishop Arellano had so kindly given me on departing from Atalaya. My eyes seemed to be getting better, but I could not hold them open. I borrowed Inez's mirror and saw that they were opaque in the center, and fiery red all around the white areas. The headache was gone.

Near dawn, a twenty-foot flood crest rushed down from the Cordilleras of the unseen Andes, pouring over the *playas,* and all but swamping us. We were saved only by leaping overboard after the dugout had been dashed into the wall of jungle trees. Here we steadied her in the backwash.

With daylight we continued on; a white sun soon blazing in the sky over the Equator and withering our roof to a dingy yellow. At noon a gray, sandy *playa* furnished us with hot baths, as a sun-heated pool lay on the far side next to the jungle. I managed to put up a poncho screen for Inez, ramming two sticks into the sand and mud. The Cocama braves were becoming very curious of late to see the differences between their *nuas* (women) and the stranger. I feared they might be tempted, and as the last few days of hard paddling had soured them, they might suddenly decide against helping us, and even stage a bit of raiding on their own. I was standing with my back to the pool, where she was bathing, when two of them approached. When I ordered them off, they became angry, but returned to their fire where the third one was cooking a fish.

A butterfly hatch was resting on this *playa,* and for hundreds of yards there was nothing to be seen but countless wings flashing in the sun—a medley of black, yellow, and blue: millions of wings, opening and closing, opening and closing.

Later while paddling we came to a low shelving *playa,* littered with hundreds of crocodile skulls and carcasses, the awful, stenching leavings of a Cocama skin-hunting party. We skirted it wide for a horde of blue bottleflies rose up in a swarm and descended on us. Beyond, in the wide mouth of a whitish-yellow river called the Uritu-yacu, three Muratos were seen hunting nutria. These bark-loinclouted *bravos,* armed with muzzleloaders, ran into a patch of bamboo when they spotted our dugout. Yellow feathers were entwined in their long, black hair, and their enormous brown bodies were spotted in large yellow dots. Their arms and legs were painted a livid red. Seeing them, I knew I wasn't half as blind as I thought. Many Amazon tribes are of small types of men, or even thin and spindly. It came as a distinct shock to realize that these Jívaros were built the way blacksmiths are supposed to be but seldom are. Their shoulders were like nothing I had ever seen on a human body; their legs and arms were of a tremendous girth. All of them were over six feet tall. I had a distinct reaction that here was not only power, but a terrible cunning. Afraid, the Cocama paddlers crossed over to the south bank, and then really dug in their paddles, moving us forward faster than ever before.

Several times the dugout thumped against sunken logs. Obviously we were getting into shallower waters, and the current had increased to an average of eight knots: slotted channels, places where the river was pinched narrow, were running as high as fifteen knots—swishing and roaring with white water. So far, we had made our way along the edges in the quieter waters, and were still able to do so. It dawned on me that in order to make good a hundred miles against the current, the Indians were actually paddling somewhere between eight hundred and a thousand miles in slack water!—a third of the way across the United States…and all the while we had to proceed with great care, for our *espintana* log would certainly sink if overturned in the torrent.

By midafternoon we were hugging the north bank very close to the wall of trees, and once had to drag the dugout across a partly submerged tree. The top blocked our way by extending out from shore and into a very fast current. The crossing was done in fast water by laying strips of wet inner-bark down across the log, for skids, and then going overboard and hauling it by hand. We were in water up to our heads but it was the only possible method for getting the dugout past, for the log was twelve feet in diameter and we could never have cut through it.

Before our very eyes a whole forest, for a distance of four hundred yards, suddenly caved in and slipped with a roaring earthquake sound into the deep, swift waters. Had we been within two hundred feet of the bank, we would have been utterly destroyed, and instantly vanished under the surface of the river, pinned to the bottom under the limbs. These higher banks, I realized with elation, were sure signs of hills existing not over 150 bird-miles in the west. Waves rocked the dugout dangerously, but the Indians managed to steady it with their paddles, while Inez and I bailed frantically.

Night was not far off when the bow paddler called out that a Cocama camp lay on the right *playa* just ahead. Inez said smokes were rising from campfires, and that there were several lean-tos. Our three men were elated, for they had little stomach for this Murato country. That night we bivouacked in the middle of the camp. There were some fifty braves here. The *curaca*, who understood Quechua as do most Oriente tribes, explained mainly through our Spanish-speaking men that the "white" crocodiles have no value. And the mottled species, which he called *kaniotsa* (a Jívaro word), must be ten feet or longer, to bring forty soles-de-oro from the Pucate *patróne.*

The current here was considered too swift to greatly favor crocodiles, and most of their hunting was done inland on the hundreds of unknown *cochas* and seas. These, they said, were filled with the reptiles. Unfortunately they had been driven out by the Muratos, losing twenty-three braves.

One of the hunters, wearing a necklace of *tuick* wings (a Jívaro name for a certain green beetle), took a shine to Inez. Nor did the .45 thrust into the top of my pants discourage his admiration. He approached her and handed over a bamboo section containing some fireflies. Every night thereafter she used to take it out, put in a bit of sugarcane, and play with them. The fireflies became quite tame, for they refused to fly away, but would crawl around on her arms, winking signals. Another admirer in that camp gave her a rare orange-crested bird, the Jívaros' *sunga,* a sacred bird known to ornithology as the cock-o'-the-rock.

Strangely, there was no *paludismo* (malaria) in this belt of the jungle; the reason being, I finally concluded, that malarial germs had not yet been carried in by humans to the *Anopheles,* the mosquito native to the region. Undoubtedly infected humans must first be present before the mosquito carrier becomes dangerous. "Virgin" or "savage" rivers, upon which a *patróne* has not operated, are never "malarial rivers"! Some main rivers probably always (since the arrival of the Spaniards) have been malarial rivers, for the Jívaros use quinine, and this cure must have taken many years to find.

We were off that *playa* early and by midmorning I had killed a deer, though with my bad eyesight it was luck rather than accurate aiming. The deer had been swimming across the river, and was just emerging on a *playa,* when I saw it some hundred yards away on our right side. The busy Indians had not noticed it. After shooting, we landed, and before the Indians had the skin off, five shield-carrying Shimaco braves walked out of the jungle toward us. I made a dive for the canoe and got my gun, which I had foolishly left lying on the poncho. Apparently they came in peace, for they rammed the butts of their spears into the sand and looked on at the skinning, keeping up a running chatter of Quechua with the Cocamas.

Not ten minutes later came other Indians—a pair of Simarones, crowned in tall parrot feathers, and painted black with thick zigzags of yellow. And after these, five Cocamas—in shiny red paint, black hands and feet, and dressed in purple *kamakas* (bark loincloths). These last were armed with exceptionally long blowguns, perhaps twelve feet in length. I would never have guessed that an Indian, let alone twelve Indians, were close by in that thick, vermin-ridden jungle. The shot, of course, had drawn them.

One of the black-painted ones with the yellow zigzags, noticed my eyes, and began speaking Quechua to the paddlers. It turned out that this man was a Simarone *brujo* and well known to the other Indians. He walked into the jungle, but was back on the playa in an hour. In his hands were several leaves and sticks undoubtedly snapped off a bush. He built a small fire striking it with flint and steel, and soon had water boiling in a very small pot some two inches in diameter. Next he stuffed in broken sticks and leaves. One of the paddlers called the brew *makoa.*

After the stuff had been brought to a boil, and was cooling, he had me lie down in the dugout. Inez could see he was going to put a compress over my eyes, and so handed him a clean cloth. This he folded over my eyes and poured on the liquid. After that I told Inez to give the *brujo* the forequarters of the deer, and the guts and head to the others, and get us started on the river again.

The small pot, which the *brujo* had originally taken out of a monkey-skin bag (worn by all Indians), he left with us. About a year later, on analyzing a dehydrated sample of this brew, I learned that *makoa* is a powerful narcotic, in fact the modern drug belladonna, and an "old secret" among the *brujos* of the Oriente tribes. Within three days my eyesight was practically normal, though the eyes themselves were an ugly blood-red and remained so for many weeks.

That afternoon we worked our dugout inch by inch, in violent little jerks, along the high right bank. The river's surface was lashed with contrary currents and swirling foam, colored like the hide of an ocelot. We could make no headway against the current, and no matter how hard the paddles flew, we remained perfectly still in relation to the bank. We finally had to cross over, losing half a mile in so doing. Although the water was shallow on the south side, we gained about six miles. Then we crossed over again, desperately fighting the torrent of the swift-gliding Marañón, which from then on we were constantly recrossing. At times the river narrowed to only a few hundred yards across.

This treadmill obstacle was worse than anything we had encoun-tered. I was paddling now and the shallow waters and swifter currents flushing against our bow made navigation a dangerous puzzle. Once it became necessary to go ashore and track the dugout on vines cut from the trees. A sharp lookout was kept for Professor Rosell's giant electric rays; even freshwater sharks, and *paña, zúngaros*, water snakes, leeches. Once a herd of some thirty *delfíns* blew alongside, creating high waves that all but swamped the canoe.

But for my diary we would have lost all track of the days—and still no sign of Tres Unidos. Our Cocamas now confessed they had never been there. A hundred times Inez and I repeated Don Garcia's exact words, reproducing even his slightest inflections. I calculated we had come over a hundred miles, but due to the long, south slant and the river, we had probably advanced only up to 75° 35" west longitude—5° 18" south latitude.

Food in the sack was almost at the vanishing point—our biscuits and cans were long since gone. And other than a few parrots the jungle produced little for our pot. Spearing fish each evening became a neces-sity, and even the fish were becoming scarce. One night, using the beam of my flashlight, I shot an inquisitive *wambache*, one of the howler monkeys. It was roasted Indian hunter style, with the hair on, and so was strong-tasting.

We were both thin, and Inez was even gaunt. Our faces, arms and hands were burned a dark brown. For all our short rations, we were strong and determined, but how long we would stay so was the big question.

One night we moored alongside a twenty-foot bank, and because of bugs and the impossible tangle ashore, camped in the dugout. We were not yet asleep when a sudden cave-in began rumbling on the river's sur-face, the canoe heaved upwards with a lurch. Trees began falling out-ward into the river all around us, sending out terrifying waves, slamming hard against the water. A tremendous limb hit the stern, and instantly shipwrecked us, and we found ourselves struggling in the muddy water. The Indians were terrified, and immediately tried to find the dugout which (with the exception of the money belt's contents) had sunk with all our stuff. Even though it was black night I began diving under the tree. The limbs were all around me, and twice I was snagged, nearly drowning. I finally located the dugout on the bottom, pinned under a large limb. The Indians came over and together we went down and finally worked the boat loose, raising the bow, and actually walking it ashore for a distance of eighty feet.

Though I dived again and again, much of our gear was lost, carried downstream in the current; we still had our mosquito nets, which had become entangled in the thatched covering, but our paddles were gone. I found my machete and several other things at daybreak, and the Indians kept at the salvaging until they located their muskets and skin bags.

I made a list of what we still had:

1. The clothes on our backs.
2. Money belt (all its usual contents including diary, and one pencil).
3. .45 Colt (but only a clipful of shells).
4. Sheath knife.
5. Poncho.
6. Two nets.
7. Can (of Indian herbs, labeled).
8. Machete.
9. Wristwatch.

Everything else was gone—extra clothes, pipe and tobacco, pot, extra batteries, pencils (except one), sounding line, extra ammunition, medicines and mosquito dope, trade tobacco and salt. We were now without food of any kind, and this was very serious, for we both had lost too much weight already. The Indians took my machete and cut new paddles from the jungle. Never again were we to risk tying up to a high bank on the current side, but thereafter always found a *playa* on the flat, shallow side of the river.

Our first clean white-sand *playa* was glimpsed one noon on a bend in the left bank. It was actually crawling with hundreds of *jacaré*. And then at long last, around the bend, the Cocamas turned to us and pointed ahead with their chins. We must be coming to Tres Unidos!— the Oriente's central "city"—located at the junction of the three great rivers: the Huallaga; the Lower and Middle stretches of the Marañón.

The paddlers' violent *chop-chop-chop-chop* inched us around a palm point. We stared. There was no Tres Unidos…only waters and a wall of jungle.

The Cocamas began jabbering—as if frightened. The word *tunchi* could be heard. *Tunchis* were the souls of lost Jívaros hovering close to the ground in the shape of lights, who whistle a thin "*fi-fi-fi*," and make all Indians feel clammy cold on their approach.

The city was not there on the bank; it had vanished into the hot day fogs curling off the river. And in its place stretched only more of this eternal dismal swamp of trees. In the distance we could hear the beat of the Jívaros' giant *tundui*, signal drum. As we approached the high, right bank where Garcia eleven days before had said Tres Unidos lay. I saw a pole standing upright. It had been trimmed with a machete. Then I knew what had happened. The whole city had slipped into the river when the bank had been undercut by the current! The Indians caught hold of a root holding the canoe against the current. They kept pointing at the pole in awe.

Undoubtedly the houses and the entire population had been swept away into the river. I instinctively knew our circumstances had become desperate. Through a break in the trees and vines I saw hundreds of miles to the northwest, across the very heartland jungle of the Jívaro tribes. A sulfur-yellow coil was rising. This must be from the crater of an Andean volcano, perhaps unseen Sangay. Beyond that volcano, and in the high valleys of the Cordillera Orientale, lay the nearest civilization. There lay Ecuador, and its capital, Quito—our ultimate target beyond the jungle.

What should I do? El Dorado never seemed further from realization, though now it could not lie (according to my map) more than a couple of hundred miles as a parrot flies. Almost within the grasp of my hand lay that golden prize.

But like the kingdom lost for the want of a horseshoe nail, it was painfully obvious that a canoe and paddlers could not be had at Tres Unidos. The Cocamas jabbered excitedly when I questioned them about going farther. They would not go. Jívaro *bravos* were all around now on both sides of the river. There must have been several unrecorded tribes in here for the Indians kept shouting—"Zaparos! Zaparos! Zaparos!" They cocked their heads alertly as the drumbeats varied with the breeze, near one minute and far away the next. All the while the Cocamas made fierce faces and slapped their muskets to keep time. One of them also began yelling "Chapra! Chapra!" which according to the riverine Cocamas is a tribe of Jívaro.[1] The Jívaro country is believed to lie only north of the Marañón; we were to find that much more also lies *south*!

We were still holding our own against the current by hanging on to the root, when suddenly Inez pointed toward the shore, and I saw a man…a man in rags…stepping slowly out of the jungle just behind the pole. And he had his rifle aimed right at us. Wolf-lean, he stared hard, and finally lowered his rusty gun. I could see he was uncocking it. From this man's scrawny neck dangled a crucifix.

"*Patróne!*" called out the Cocamas, uncocking their own pieces.

The man still stared as if struck by lightning. Then he ran forward, sliding down the bank, falling, but getting up and coming on again—crying aloud all the while. He plunged into the river and I realized tears were streaming down his hungry face. I leaped out of the dugout and we shook hands, both of us standing waist-deep in the swirling yellow water.

"I am the *patróne*—Miguel Rojas," he shouted, wiping his face, which was wet from tears and sweat, on a ragged sleeve. Finally he got hold of himself, and told us that he and his family had been away when the disaster befell the "city" a month before, and by the grace of God had escaped death. We must be his "amigos."

He clawed aboard and gave directions to pick up his own canoe in tow and cross over to the south side of the river beyond the mouth of the Huallaga. Rojas was amazed to see a white woman here. The paddlers dug in, and we crossed over and soon entered a *cocha* among the trees. Then his clearing appeared just beyond on the edge of the swamp. The Indians beached, and when we had gotten out, they turned the dugout around and immediately started back for the Marañón.

Rojas said they were afraid of the spirit called Yucuruna (Man of the Waters), and his wife Yucumama. As I watched the Indians paddling away I thought that there vanished the last link we had back to Iquitos. Like Rojas, we were stranded. It was now September 25th, and the rains could begin any time. And if they did we would be stranded for six months until the waters subsided. It looked as if my plan had been shipwrecked.

---

1. Not yet reported outside the river.

We three waded through a flock of grounded vultures, barely ambling out of our way.

"*Mis amigos,*" laughed Rojas, "they feed here on the refuse disgorged by the Alto and Middle Marañón and the Huallaga."

A thatched shack now appeared, leaning over the swamp on crazy stilts. We climbed a ladder and came to a bamboo porch. In a dark comer squatted an Indian woman and a covey of half-breed children. Inez gratefully slung her hammock and mosquito net. I was given the table for a bed.

The señora soon proved to be a mission woman and therefore respectable. She was shocked to the depths of her black soul that Inez was not "Señora Clarka," of the same lofty status as herself, for it was impossible to attach innocence to such an impossible alliance.

That evening, Rojas, busy digging *niguas* out of his toes, said the Jívaros living just behind believed that a shot fired into a *lupuna* tree would cause rain. "She's a Jívaro—" he added, waving negligently toward the woman, "that's why they don't bother me. She tells me about the rain 'medicine.' The Indians' *cutipados* (*brujos*) are rain-makers, and that's one of the ways to bring rain when the inland rivers and *cochas* are too shallow for traveling by canoe."

"We need a little rain so we can paddle upriver on a raft," I said, "how about trying it?"

He laughed a bit nervously. "A raft's no good. Anyway, the rain-makers are crazy."

One of those 180-foot umbrella-topped giant trees was towering nearby. Out of curiosity I aimed the .45 at its white trunk and banged away. Five minutes later clouds were smashing together very low down just overhead, lightning crashed and rain sluiced earthward—all but sweeping the house away! Rojas wasn't very happy about it either.

With darkness, Inez and I played gin rummy under my net, Rojas' last candle lighting the table top. It was so hot that every few minutes the candle had to be straightened. The *patróne* squeezed in with us, for the bugs were active, and was soon filing away at the barbed head of his harpoon. Finally we got to sleep. Next morning a pair of pet parakeets landed on my net, wakening me. Rojas was studying the mouth of the Huallaga with his spy-glass, spotting caymans. Hunting them for skins was part of his livelihood. He greeted me, saying there was no food to be had here, only a few scraps of dried fish and two small yuca roots...one meal.

Both Inez and I were showing very serious vitamin deficiency. That day we could barely move about. No fresh meat or vegetables had been available for a long time. After leaving Don Garcia's, Inez had been dividing the food portions, until one day I realized with a shock that she was giving me nearly everything and keeping almost nothing for herself. After that, I was chief divider, but even so, both of us were always hungry.

I was in no shape to hunt that day. In the afternoon we mended our worn clothing (which was beginning to rot), sewed up the holes in our nets, and did our laundry. After that I experimented in Rojas' hammock, trying to rest up sufficiently for a hunting trip alone back in the jungle—for Rojas would not leave his clearing or the open river. There are many positions for lying in one of these contraptions. The most common position in the Amazon country is to sleep crosswise and never lengthwise—thus eliminating much of the sag. Curiously, the various positions are named by the Indians, and Rojas knew them all. There are hammocks in which four people can sleep, the Señor, the Señora, and two of the brats. There is also the double hammock, and of course the single. In addition there are hammocks for children. Hammockry has become a specialty, nay!—a cult. Columbus introduced them into Europe from the islands of the West Indies.

Back in the jungle I found some breadfruit; green, furry pods about an inch in length, containing forty to fifty nuts bedded in a mat of soft white pith. These Inez roasted, and they tasted like chestnuts. Others boiled by the Indian woman tasted very much like mealy lotus seeds. After this meager dinner Inez put our two plates into the river, and the *paña* cleaned them up.

Rojas importantly wound his alarm clock promptly at dawn, and every hour of the day thereafter. He could not go hunting with me because he had the "important business of the clock." And for no apparent reason that I could see, the alarm went off every hour. For days we heard it, hour by hour, and we used to play a game of counting the remaining seconds. Finally, I became so jittery I jumped every time it went off.

By day and by night the Jívaros' *tundui* drums were still broadcasting news of our arrival. Sometimes the Indian woman's eyes opened wide as she sat in her corner, listening. While hunting alone in the thick hedge of the jungle, miles inland from the river, I often had the feeling I was being watched. Once I even back-tracked at a run along my machete track, but try as I might, I could never find an Indian. If they were there, they certainly could have cut me off and killed me at their leisure.

The search for food over the next few days became a minor panic. If Inez and I had been alone, there would have been enough, for twice I brought in an armadillo of the type called *tatuejo*, weighing about ten pounds; or an iguana lizard; and once a pig; and then two small monkeys; but there was always Rojas' hungry family too. One of the children alone could eat twice as much as Inez and I together. Once a manatee snorted in the river behind the hut and I ran toward it, but could not hit the great beast in a fatal spot and I only wounded it with my old automatic. I was doubly sorry for it swam to the center of the Marañón and there was attacked by crocodiles, who tore it to pieces. The way crocodiles do this is to seize a leg (for example) in their teeth, and then spin their whole reptilian body around and around at an incredibly fast rate of speed. One day I managed to get a clutch of twenty small eggs laid by a *taricaya*. It was an accident, for turtles use only certain *playa*s year after year, and this stretch of the river was taboo.

Three Simarones came at dawn on the sixth day with a bundle of *sajino* skins. The *patróne's* store had a single shelf, a thinly stocked board with a few safety pins, a bolt of cotton cloth, some powder and shot, and a bean can half-filled with assorted buttons. For Indians who did not have contact with the curare makers, he had a commercial poison for their blowgun darts, and this had been made in Iquitos. All this stuff he happened to have in his canoe when Tres Unidos disappeared, for he and his family had been absent on a trading junket. The Simarones settled for a handful of the powder and shot. Their explanation for the bad hunting here was the presence of the spirit called the Chullachaqui (Horror of the Jungles), a Jívaro devil.

They turned their insolent eyes on me, and added if I did not stay in the house, the Chullachaqui would get me one day. They did not smile when I answered through Rojas that if I did stay in the house, the buzzards would get us all, anyway.

I started to hollow out a log, hoping to make a dugout canoe. It took me three days to fell a tree with my machete, and I knew it would take at least a month to finish the work. That folly was checked when a storm caused the swamp's waters to rise eight feet overnight, and my log was swept away into the Marañón. Sick at heart, we half planned to construct a raft and start back to Iquitos about four hundred miles away by river, two hundred airline.

One evening Inez wanted to try her hand at hunting. Herds of crocodiles lay in yellow and black bands on a long *playa* between the hut and the southwest corner of the Huallaga's mouth. Rojas took us in his own dugout and paddled us to the *playa*. Seated amidships,

Inez drew a bead on the largest, a big fellow some twenty feet long. At the .45's bark, the dusty-looking reptile wriggled toward us and hit the water like a torpedo. Rojas steadied with his paddle, yelling, "Señora! (He always insisted on that.) Hit the neck! Then the harpoon—throw the harpoon! Men die when they miss!"

Inez, I could see, had had about enough, and I slammed home the harpoon. Worms or no worms, we boiled the last foot of the crocodile's tail and ate it. Something had to happen, and soon....

⸲ XX. ⸴

Troubles and Revelations

*T*HAT night, owing to the drums and the burning heat, I did not sleep. Early next morning, just as the few clouds in the pale blue sky were turning pink—and it was high time to get up—I found myself dropping off. I had no sooner turned over on my side, than a strange sound crept out of the swamp from the direction of the Huallaga junction...*chugg-chugg-chugg-chugg.* That's a new one, I thought, probably a frog.

But I was fully awake now and swung my legs off the table, ducked under the netting, and respectably clad in my pants, walked yawning to the edge of the porch. I might as well go down to the *cocha* and have a bath. I was standing on the shore, dipping water over myself with a gourd, and looking lazily at the floating islands of water flowers when suddenly, some two hundred yards away, surging out of the fog, came a small power launch with a barge alongside.

"Inez! Rojas!" I called out, dropping the gourd in my surprise.

They rolled out of their hammocks and came bouncing across the springy floor overhead, their shirt-tails flying. The little boat chugged steadily toward us through the mists. Presently, though still a hundred feet away, we got a whiff of the cargo...*xarque*—dried beef.

"Thank God!" breathed Inez, "We eat."

Rojas was shouting: "Come in, *mi Capitán*. Slowly there, *mi Capitán*. Watch that sunken log, *mi Capitán*."

At last the dirty little trader bumped against our ladder and tied up.

"*Mi Capitán!*" I exclaimed, intentionally polishing Rojas' apple, "Your hand, amigo! Watch now! Careful!" I reached up and gave him a shove porchward. I followed at his bare heels.

"*Buenas dias,*" he growled when he reached the porch. That *capitán* was a river wolf in human form; he was only of medium height and very lean, but gave the impression of power and vitality. His face was pocked and scarred from disease and knife-fighting. He wore an old pair of white pants rolled to his knees. A dirty old t-shirt full of holes covered his large shoulders, but was rolled up revealing a very hairy torso. A curved knife in a snakeskin sheath was thrust into the back of his hide belt, hilt downward. That meant he was a knife-fighter, and an under-hand knife thrower at that—the most dangerous men in the world.

"Inez! A little liquor for *El Capitán*. Step lively, my pretty."

She fiercely grabbed my arm, and whispered, "There isn't any. You haven't got any. You gave Walter's two bottles of wine to Don Garcia!"

"Ah! *Mi Capitán*. Señora says '*pisco*' (white rum). Right away." And in English to the frantic Inez, "Empty Rojas' kerosene lamp—and hurry." I beamed, and pumped *El Capitán*'s steel-hard hand until a faint squeak of a smile crept up out of the dark depths and played faintly over that hard visage.

"Gringos?"

"*Si, compadre*. Gringos. A good joke—gringos—your very brother and sister."

He made a wry face: "*Hay dineros, pesos, soles, sucres?*"

"*Si, Capitán—muchas!* Ah, Señora Inez. *Pisco.*"

And so with Rojas' solitary tin cup in hand, I poured each a stiff drink, El Capitán Guillermo G. Mavila R., and then Rojas. I watched the trader anxiously as he rolled it on his tongue and swallowed hard....

The scarred face beamed with delight.

"Now where do you suppose she ever got that *pisco*?"—I thought. I tried an eye-opener myself, a big one—and it was out of the lamp—half kerosene and half fish oil.

We made a deal with the trader quickly. For twenty-six soles-de-oro we would be conveyed in style to Barranca, a soldiers' post halfway to Borja. A few days' journey—if we didn't mind sleeping on *xarque*.

"Everything is sanitary, señor," growled the trader, "I have the gringo gun of the 'fleet'—I swoosh-swoosh my cargo every day, absolutely."

"Dainty! Dainty!" I cried in American admiration of anything sanitary, though I could see maggots crawling over the cargo from where I was standing.

"*Si*, señor!" bellowed the *capitán* pounding his chest, "I am a Teniente Sanitario Reservo. An important cog in the World Sanitation Organization."

You don't look it, I thought, but complimented him: "Splendid! Splendid! Soon all these rivers will be paradise. Teniente, everything smells fine on the boat."

That night the trader slept aboard his barge, for his Indian crew was made up of some half a dozen mixed tribes and he didn't trust them, At dawn he replenished Rojas' trade stock and left him a sack of yuca and another of *xarque*, this in exchange for a thin bale of animal and crocodile hides and other truck, mainly tortoiseshell. It was 5 A.M., and as I stood on the porch waiting to leave, I realized the date was October 6th, and that thirty-three days had gone by since leaving Iquitos. And still no rainy season! After a couple of squirts from the *capitán*'s "fleet gun," we boarded the sanitary trading boat, a broad craft and some thirty feet in length, named the *Vaca Marina*.

"How come *Sea Cow*?" I asked the *capitán*.

"Because she gives plenty of milk, señor. I make all these *patrónes* into rich men."

I'll bet you do, I thought. We said goodbye to Rojas and his wife, cast off and left the *cocha*. We ran back out of the swamp and into the Marañón, turning left and heading upstream. The river was split into many confusing channels, apparently miles apart. Those we traversed were overhung with towering, multicolored jungles. The majority of the banks were of grayish sand and only a few feet high. Apparently we were leaving behind the low mud flats and high mud bars. A long, red grass grew in the region, and everywhere among the densely packed trees were thickets of fan *caña*, groves of spiky palms, giant pink-leafed trees, twenty-foot ferns and the white trunks of the *puna*—these last being the most common trees in the western Amazon.

Huge *camunguis*, jungle birds almost as large as condors roosted like horses in the dead trees where only shocks of ferns and orchid plants interfered with their fifteen-foot wingspread in alighting and taking off. Whole sections of this jungle were so covered by vines that nets—miles wide—appeared to have been flung from the sky.

At noon we had boiled chicken and yuca, cooked by one of the Indians in the crew.[1] It was our first real meal in a week. The maps were useless. Islands were everywhere; one was some fifteen miles long. The year before, the *capitán* told me, it had not existed, but there it was, and covered with a dense jungle. We struck bottom several times in shallow places, and proceeded cautiously in the deeper ones, sounding with a pole. We anchored off the south bank, the crew taking turns at guard watch.

The *capitán* spoke of headhunters, and kept a sharp lookout for them. Quite often he lost men to arrows or blowgun darts when he got too close to the jungle. On the second day at 3:45 P.M., we came upon the notorious Pastaza flowing from the north bank. The crew said it was a Jívaro stronghold and inhabited from its mouth northward, to its mid-regions, by Muratos, then by Ashiras, followed by a belt of Andoas, and still farther north, around the headwaters, by Zaparos.... All these tribes were headhunters, but none of them necessarily kept to their own districts, but were always moving around—hunting for game or heads or slaves (especially women).

We hugged the Marañón's south bank, keeping to the cover of palm leaves, and thus hidden, we worked slowly against the current. Safely past the Pastaza's mouth the *capitán* showed us his trading treasures, contained mainly in an old brass-studded rawhide trunk with an antique Spanish lock. In it among other items were tobacco twists, bamboos of blowgun poison, a bolt of red cotton cloth, two beer bottles filled with gold dust and nuggets, and nine shrunken heads.

A few miles farther on, we stopped at a "tame" Murato's house where the *capitán* traded two pieces of lumber for a wild Muscovy drake and an ancient phonograph. I asked how the Indian had ever come into possession of the phonograph and its several warped records. A crew hand said the Murato had killed a *patróne* near Barranca and burned him out, taking the "*mecánica*" as booty.

---

1. A chicken coop is part of the equipment of every Marañón trading boat.

"Did you say that Indian was 'tame,' señor?" asked Inez with interest, pointing at the giant, 200-pound, blue tattooed long-haired brave.

"*Si, si,* señora. Tame. *No es bravo!*" answered the *capitán* consolingly, "*Aguaruna es bravo*—very fierce. And Zaparos…Huambizas… Tutapishcos…Auhishiris…Payaguas…Cauranas…*y* Jacundas. *Si!* *Muchas tribos muy bravo. Muerte.*"

The *capitán's* maps showed the Rio Tuncay coming in on the south bank far east of the Pastaza's wide mouth. Actually, we saw it entered a mile to the west. Being infested with the *chichari,* flying beetles, whose bite causes blindness, the Murato said it was uninhabited. The sand bars at the Pastaza's mouth have altered since the old government mappers have been there, and islands now exist where none were shown on any of our modern maps.

As these days crawled by, we fell naturally into the routine of the crew. The *Vaca Marina* was about thirty feet long and had eight foot of beam. She had a canvas roof, and under this we slept in hammocks. Our meals were cooked by the crew over a box of sand on which they built their fire, and the meals were (except for the one of chicken) either fish or *xarque.* Inez got along so well with the *capitán* and crew that they constructed a shelter of palm leaves on the back of the barge towed alongside the launch, and here she did her bathing in privacy. The long hours were passed mostly in watching the jungle or talking with the *capitán,* who, for all his rugged exterior, became a sympathetic and loyal friend. With me alone he would have proved a tough nut, but he was just so much putty in the hands of Inez. I shall never forget the look of amazement when he saw a brassiere hanging on the clothesline, and came rushing over to ask me what the hell that was.

And so we felt our way up the river, noting that most of the Marañón's tributaries came in from the south, and not from the Oriente lying north, as shown on the maps. None of these great rivers has ever been explored. *Patrónes* who attempt to go up them, simply vanish. The *capitán* said many *patrónes* believe them to flow through flat jungle all the way southwest to the ramparts of the outlying Andean Cordilleras in the Moyobama area. The few Indians who have succeeded in getting in and also getting out report that all this region is inhabited by Jívaros. If this is true, then the Jívaro range is approximately twice as large as believed.

Von Wolfenegg's letter to the Reverendo Padre Cayetano, stationed at the Mission of San Lorenzo (or Barranca), was taken out of my money belt and its wrinkles somewhat eliminated under a board. It was 5:45 when we hailed Barranca. Here on red banks some twenty feet high on the north side of the river was the first "high ground" of the Amazon. I measured it as 620 feet above sea level. The little Capuchin Mission consisted of an adobe church some hundred feet long with a roof of corrugated iron. Also on the bank, clustered around the mission, were half a dozen bush huts. At the *casa* of the chief *patróne*, we drank warm beer. A page from my notebook best describes my impression of the four *patrónes* gathered there:

"*Barranca* patrónes—*indeterminate ages, gold teeth, dirty feet, pajamas, stubble chin whiskers and usually a mustache, lean and with a very wolflike and yellowish face. No other terrain on earth has bred so strong a face or so assured a bearing. Fiercely virile and devastatingly handsome— says Inez. Sometimes a* patróne *will elegantly wear boots, helmet, khaki or colored pants and a shirt to match having French rolled cuffs and jewel links. These men are usually aloof, conscious of being lords over thousands of wild Indians (if they can catch them), invariably holding a concession on an entire river hundreds of miles in length. Their houses are on piles, with palm floors and sides, having high-peaked pole and palm-thatched roofs; these are cool and comfortable. The Señora is invariably Indian. Death feuds between the* patrónes *are not infrequent. His guns, gasoline pressure-lamp and wife's sewing machine are usually in need of repair. Strangely, some* patrónes *are very rich men, even millionaires; while others are very poor.*"

Swatting mosquitos, we listened to the Padre's didactic lecture on there being no headhunters: "Absolutely not! Never since Peru has taken over the Oriente. The river Indians are now '*patróne Indios*,' and any *bravo* tribes without a *patróne*, are listed as 'dangerous and bad,' subject to *liquidación*."

On the whole, however, we were given a very cordial reception by the *patrónes*, who seemed amused at the priest trying to impress us, and even winked at us behind his back. This black-frocked, white-crossed missionary then began a very cold-blooded rant against us, saying we had no business here, and hinting broadly that it would be to our advantage to go back to Iquitos. It was different with Teniente Eduardo Rios Angulo, the Commandante in charge of the thirty-five troops.

This officer courteously invited us to dinner and said he would notify Capitán Gonzalez at Borja, by radio, of our approach.[2] Gonzalez was Commander-in-Chief of all forces in the Oriente west of Iquitos. The trading Capitán Mavila now offered to extend his trip to Borja, after the army officer supplied him with a fifty-gallon drum of gasoline.

From Barranca I could see the outlying spurs of the Andean Cordillera—perhaps eighty miles west. We were warned that it might be impossible to get beyond Borja, as the Jívaros were at the moment very restless.

On the following day we advanced to the Rio Morona, some thirty miles west. A soldier from Barranca escorted us as the week before Jívaros had killed nine *caucheros*.

A *patróne* whom we had picked up in Barranca offered to sell three human heads. He explained he had traded two *escopetas* (muskets) for each of them, and his price was 1,800 soles-de-oro for all three. So already the Padre's information was proved false, and headhunting still flourished, as everyone else had told us. These heads were not cut up the back as are many. The best Jívaro heads are cut in a deep, long cape into the back, chest and shoulders. There had been a great deal of speculation on all this in Iquitos, for no two "authorities" agree. Inez and I were soon to learn the truth of the matter.

Before reaching the Morona and about fifteen miles beyond Barranca, we saw our first real hill. This was a long, fifty-foot-high ridge on the right, which formed the Marañón's permanent bank a hundred yards north of the shore at low-water line in the dry season. This was in the vicinity of the Islas de Rapagua. Fifteen miles beyond that we turned right, and the *Sea Cow* chugged into the 100-yard-wide mouth of the Rio Morona. A few miles north on the right bank lay "Carabanchel," a very large bush-house on stilts. And beyond this about five miles we came to another house. Its *patróne*, a tall, lean man wearing a Van Dyke, was master of the river; that is, as far up into headhunting territory as he dared go—which was about twenty miles. Hundreds of rolled skins were in his house: anaconda, deer, pig, mon-

---

2. Peruvian army units stationed at dangerous outposts in wild Indian territory are usually equipped with a small receiver-transmitter radio set, which is operated with a hand crank generator.

key, otter, tapir, crocodile, jaguar, ocelot and "human." Human skin is used by certain bookbinders in the Orient and Europe; it is said to be the toughest skin known. Also there was *barbasco*, Indian baskets and pottery, balls of *caucho*, *tamshi* (one of the liana ropes), copal, various kinds of incense, some six hundred giant turtles, precious bird plumes such as egret, medicinals, rare woods, salted *paiche*...all the assorted jungle produce to be collected on this wild river.

The "Master" showed us a very fine *tsantsa*, the Jívaro name for their shrunken-head trophies. This one did not have a slit at the back. It was a perfect replica of a human head, every feature delicately preserved, and reduced to a diameter of only 2 1/4 inches across the temples. This was a rare *tsantsa* of the Zaparos, a Jívaro connection of our old Cocama paddlers' *chapras*. The long, black hair was tightly wrapped as a three-foot queue, in a twist of fibrous bark, to keep the malign spirits protected.

Other Jívaro tribes on the Morona are the Muratos and Huambizas; they too, of course, are headhunters. The *patróne* remarked that this head had come from a Huambiza.

"How do you know?" I asked. There was no intention of questioning his veracity, but only one of curiosity.

He flared back: "Because I recognize him. He used to work for me as a hunter."

The *patróne* and his hunters and *caucheros*, a dozen men altogether, warned that we could not go much farther west. Certainly we should not go among the Aguaruna Jívaros in the region of the Pongo de Menseriche. "Above the Pongo, all the rivers run with blood!" shouted the *patróne*.

Later, when the *patróne* cooled off a bit, he told us that anacondas "often" attacked his hunters. He said these constrictor snakes usually strike when a man is in the river, perhaps crossing at a ford or bathing. The snake usually (not always) approaches under water, seizes its victim in its jaws which are lined with powerful teeth. The snake then swims out to deep water, and there drowns the man. If the attack is made on land, the human victim is usually struck on the head by a "hammer blow" as the front of the snake's head is very hard and bony. Its victim unconscious, the great snake then coils around him and constricts, crushing the bones for convenient swallowing. The snake's large flat jaws are unhinged and the man taken headfirst. "The victim's head," explained the *patróne*, flicking his cigarette ash carelessly, "must be well laved and made very slippery. And a great deal of saliva and other reptilian kinds of slime are drooled over it."

No one spoke for quite awhile, and then an Indian hunter broke the silence by saying his brother had been struck and crushed so fast that it was impossible to run the two hundred feet separating them, before the brother was dead, blood running from ears, eyes and nose.

"What did you do to the snake?" I asked.

After a moment's hesitation, the man said, "I cut it into chunks, put it in my basket,[3] and brought it home. My family ate the snake; it was very good."

After feeding, the snake becomes comatose. It may not feed again for months. If an ant army finds it, all that remains is the skeleton of the reptile, for it is helpless if caught too far away from water. Anacondas not only could swallow a hundred-pound deer (a point often disputed by "experts" in Lima), but could actually swallow a domestic pig. When I voiced doubt, the *patróne* glanced at his men, then offered to wager $1,000 (U.S.), payable in Lima, and he would furnish both pig and snake.

After gazing at the 320 monstrous skins in their warehouse, I had to reconsider; these skins were from three to four feet wide, so that the snake was easily a foot in diameter! They said the skins were mostly of the mottled black peculiar to the middle Morona, though some were a beautiful brownish gold. Eighteen anaconda skins exceeding 20 feet were shown us, one which I measured at 26 feet, 8 ½ inches. In a fresh state they would have been longer, for these were dried and shrunken.

In addition to danger from snakes of this type, there were other pitfalls awaiting the professional hunter. There was no denying it was a hard life. Crocodiles had killed three hunters already that year; and five others had been lost to poisonous snakes. Nine from diseases. Another had drowned. Five pig hunters had been stalked and killed by Jívaros....

Beginning at dawn Capitán Mavila began trading with the *patróne*. By midmorning the *patróne* broke off and walked over to me where I was swinging in a hammock. He said he had a little "affair" arranged for

---

3. Jívaro baskets are large, being carried on the back of the hunter by a tumpline across his forehead.

los expedición arios. I decided one representative was enough, so leaving Inez behind, I followed him around the bush-house, and he told me Indians had been dispatched out on the river, and they had a snake. The pig pen was just yonder.

We strode up to the low bamboo fence and I saw a very large boar that must have weighed all of five hundred pounds. Now an Amazon boar can be a very dangerous animal, and this one had tusks. The *patróne* reached down and slashed its face with his machete, giving it a nasty wound. A double line of twenty Indians came running up, and I saw they held—straight out behind them so it could not constrict—a snake at least twenty feet in length. It was coal black, with a yellowish belly.

The snake was heaved over the fence and it landed on the boar. Instantly the boar attacked with its tusks, ripping into the monstrous coils, thicker than a man's thigh, slashing them so that the snake's flesh showed cotton-white, a bleeding and gory mess. All the time the pig was furiously grunting, but quite coolly going about the work of its butchery. The snake slowly raised its massive, flat head toward the boar, and apparently smelling the pig's blood, instantly struck. It had the boar by the long, upper snout where the tusks curled out, and it hung on, quickly thrashing the long, thick coil around the boar, until three coils were side by side, and then with a sudden and awful convulsion—squeezing.

The boar stood upright on its feet for quite a long time, absorbing what must have been a terrible punishment as its ribs were cracking. Then suddenly it grunted, and crumpled. You could see the coils grasp now, creeping, feeling for a closer vice-like hold, and then—squeeze. Blood flowed from the pig's mouth, then its ears.

After that the snake slowly uncoiled and started crawling away. The *patróne* had been fascinated, but now he was furious. He yelled at the Indians, and they leaped over the fence and laid hold of the snake, dragging it back to the pig, at the same time holding tight and stretching it out full length. This took all twenty of them, for the snake was bunching up and writhing, and the three men at the end of the tail were being knocked around. They finally succeeded in laying it full length on the ground, and a big Indian placed his feet inside the lower jaw and with his hands stretched the upper jaw, exerting the great power of his brawny legs, shoulders and arms, opening the mouth and throat wide. The other two Indians were dragging the boar over, and now rammed its head inside, getting behind and pushing, actually stuffing that 500 pounds of pig into the snake by sheer force....

Presently the snake took a mild interest, and the men loosened their hold. The snake began pushing its length forward, so that the pig gradually crept down into the neck. When the pig's hind feet had disappeared and the whole pig was well on its way to the snake's midriff, for it had now brought a coil up forward to assist in the leverage, the *patróne* turned to me, "Well, señor, here is the address of my agent in Lima. You may send me your $1,000 when you reach the coast."

I hadn't accepted the wager the night before, but there didn't seem much I could do about it. If I found El Dorado, I'd be glad to mail him a thousand dollars, but if I did not find El Dorado, he could go to hell. I put the card in my pocket.[4]

A good cargo was now aboard the *Vaca Marina*, a mixed skin cargo exchanged for powder and shot, and we headed back for the Marañón. We soon passed a large island on the left bank called Isla Límon, and behind it, flowing from the southwest was the unexplored Rio Apaga, inhabited by headhunters of an unknown tribe.

The forests were becoming ever denser if possible, practically bursting with the giant trees and palms. The Marañón's channels seemed to be more rigidly set and less impermanent. At one place we were very fortunate in seeing how islands are actually formed in the upper Amazon—that is, islands created in the river, and not those cut by new channels from the main jungle itself. When a single floating tree is snagged on the shallow bottom, and held, silt begins dropping behind it, precipitating and settling in the still waters of its lee. You could almost see these islands build up before your eyes. In a few months a single derelict tree, stopped in midstream, can form an island a mile or more in length, completely clothed in trees and other vegetation.

Torrents of rain came, and with them our first cool breeze. This rain struck fear into my heart. But there was no hurrying. Through gaps in the trees, a long north and south range, heavily vegetated, appeared from time to time. It lay fifty miles due west. This was the Cerros Campanquiz, the first true range of the Andean Cordillera, and (according to the governments of Ecuador and Peru) it had never been crossed

---

4. Later, in Quito, I mailed his agent a draft for soles-de-oro amounting to $1,000.

at any point in its approximately two hundred miles. Beyond this lay the *tierra incógnita* drained by the unknown Golden Serpent, and in the north by the Santiago. These were both headhunters' rivers with Aguarunas on the Golden Serpent, Huambizas on the Santiago. The Amazon River is actually divided into legs. From its mouth at the Atlantic to the Rio Negro, it is called the Amazonas; westward to the Napo—the Solimões; to the Huallaga—it is called the Lower Marañón; while beyond to the Cerros Campanquiz—the Middle Marañón. From that point just west of the Pongo de Menseriche, to its source high in the Andes (and far to the southwest) the river is named Alto Marañón, or more often, locally, the Golden Serpent.

By afternoon a dignified Huambiza *winchiyu* (*brujo*) joined us on the right bank. He had just finished cooking up a batch of blowgun poison. Jívaro curare, which he called *ampi*, (the *moca* of the Chamas) has many varieties. Certain secret leaves (often from twenty to thirty) including *Strychnos* (alkaloids) and various peppers of the *Capsicum* species, are gathered and boiled in sacred pots to which he had added the vine juices of *bucuna ucho, curupa-caspi, ampihuasca*, and *nacu sari*, to make it stronger. We saw the concoction was thick and syrupy, the color of dark chocolate. The *brujo* works alone, pounding and scraping the lianas, with no woman near, and the job often takes five days. The poison causes the blood to coagulate, and brings on paralysis to the muscles; to be effective the *ampi* must be fresh. The pathological qualities are significant; for today it is our greatest aid to surgery, heart diseases, infantile paralysis, chorea, rabies, epilepsy.

From this loin-clouted *winchiyu* pharmacologist, Inez—who had been industriously studying Jívaro—learned that *sangre pidipidi* (Spanish and Jívaro) is used for infection. This is a medium-sized plant whose bulbs (like small potatoes) are put into boiling water and when the resultant liquid becomes blood-red, it is taken off the fire and poured directly on the infection.

The witchman's secret for "bone healing" was a plant called *ucho sanango*, while extracts from the *renaquillo*, a small tree, are also used in the compound. Sitting at the deck's sandbox fireplace, the Indian placed the leaves of both plants in boiling water. The liquid is drunk by patients with broken bones, and the Indians say it will completely heal the bones within eight to fifteen days. I had heard the Muratos had one for bones, which will soften adult human bones like putty, and that the *brujos* know how to harden the bones after moulding broken bones that have been badly set, clubfeet and the like. During the time the patient cannot eat salt, grease, sweets, any high seasoning, or take *giamanchi*—the Jívaros' *chicha.*

From this Huambiza Inez also learned other *brujería.* If the tall tree *sangre de drago,* is cut in the manner of a rubber tree it expels a pure liquid. If this is taken orally, it is very good for "cuts" and *iguanchis* (bad spirits). Other *materia medica* was a Jívaro purgative, the latex of the *ojea* tree; an effective febrifuge, also. Such medicine men inject counter-irritants into the rectum. Quinine they use as we do, for malaria, calling it by its Quechua name of *quinaquina,* which they put in *giamanchi.* In upland Ecuador it is called *cascarilla.* Due to the Spaniards obtaining quinine from the Jívaros, the white man's conquest of the world's tropics was made possible. Today it saves millions of lives annually. The main supply comes from the Malay States and the East Indies, the South American cinchona trees (as in the case of rubber) having been transplanted to the Orient by the British and Dutch.

Inez learned for my benefit that *cetico,* a white-barked tree having a "fig-leaf," could be used medically for eye infection. For some days now my right eye had become very painful, and I was no longer able to sleep. Desperate, I showed the *brujo* my eyes. His method of treatment was based on a *mágico*-propitiatory conception, for he believed he was transferring the cause of the injury from me to the medicine itself. He also was convinced that his mind controlled matter, and so there was an intense mysticism present, especially when he began sweeping away ghosts with his fan and calling out in a great voice his *icaros* (holy oration) to the spirits. He placed the bark of *cetico* into boiling water and scraped out the inside residue. This poultice he placed over my eyes, which had been inflamed for three days, and were swollen and a solid red. In fact, I could no longer see with the right one, even when lifting the lid with my fingers. Two days later, the infection stopped and the eye cleared: normal vision returned.

As we continued to fight our way up the narrowing river, the first rocks appeared—small granite boulders, heralding our approach to the outlying Cerros. The current was becoming very fast and dangerous. The width of the river at most was a mere two to three hundred yards across. Whirlpools were skirted widely, as they were deep and fast. When caught in one, the pilot would instantly cut his engine switch, and let us spin. When we had revolved around once, and reached the lower edge of the whirlpool, he would throw on the switch, race the engine, and slam down his rudder hard—thus breaking away and heading downcurrent. He would put about and once more churn upstream, this time giving the whirler a wide berth.

In the north, on the right bank, and at the base of the east slope of the Cerros Campanquiz, we finally raised Borja over our bows. It still lay nearly a half-mile away, and only the thatch roofs were visible. The captain's spyglass showed this clearing was of several acres, with some dozen bush-huts. Like Barranca, it had been the scene of many Indian raids and massacres. According to legend, in the palmy days of the conquistadores a force of 3,000 Imperial troops had been stationed here. The people of Borja believed there had been a great cathedral with a tremendous bell of bronze and gold alloy. This bell was so heavy that three hundred men were required to lift it. The bell could be heard—so the story goes—in Iquitos, 600 river miles east (over 300 miles as the toucan goes)! Today in Loreto, this bell is believed to have been hidden by ancient *bravos* of a tribe no longer living, known as the Borjas. The Borjas had massacred the garrison and burned this, the greatest Spanish city in the Amazon Valley. The city was the conquistadores' only permanent foothold east of the Andes, and in the jungle itself. Historians have made no record of this story, for it is generally believed that Pizarro's followers took root only on the Pacific side of the Andes; and of course, the legend can never be proved—*or can it*!

As we approached closer to Borja, a shower fell on us, and afterwards when the sun broke out, the narrow sand and gravel *playas* steamed in the heat. Still some distance from Borja, we went ashore to visit one of the four *patrónes* based here, Don Vicanor A. Moray R. His *puesto* (a small plantation) was called "Eureka." The tiny citrus grove and gardens looked like an exotic Hollywood setting, the little bamboo house perched on posts.

The Don greeted us, saying food was difficult to find here in Borja. He was a tall and handsome man of about thirty, with waxed mustache, dressed in perfectly tailored khaki British bush jacket and shorts. We were given a cup of coffee during the *capitán's* transactions with the *patróne*, and then proceeded by the *Vaca Marina* up to Borja itself.

Von Wolfenegg had a house on the outskirts of the settlement. The trader stopped to discharge us. The house stood on high log stilts, and was capped with a red tin roof. It was the finest building in the entire Oriente, and was as substantial as a German baron could make it—with shower, two bedrooms, dining room, kitchen, storeroom. Von Wolfenegg had flown from Iquitos to Borja in the past. This was to be our headquarters.

The first important thing we learned from Señor Lopez, the caretaker, was that the only cow in our friend's half-wild herd of Hindu *cebu* cattle that could be milked had dried up. This was a great disappointment, as we had hoped for the milk. In hand, actually, were two eggs, some banana chips, two ounces of coffee, an inch of molasses in a small can. I knew we couldn't live very long on that, and must somehow get over the first Andean range of the Cerros Campanquiz without delay, for in this direction lay El Dorado. A fish spear might solve our problem there, if the water were not so swift as here at Borja. An explorer's life is one long series of "ifs," but *if* he didn't take on the IFs, he certainly wouldn't get very far up the Golden Serpent. That evening we ate one egg—the other "egg in hand" seemed to have slipped between the caretaker Lopez's fingers; but on the following day there was not a scrap of food to be had.

I scouted around Borja, a town of three *patrónes* and their families, some score of Jívaros (who owned the rest of the houses), and a garrison of fifty troops. The Señores Caballero and Gomez were the "big store owners" to whom Lewis Gallardy's father-in-law had given me a letter of introduction. I called on these traders, but the Señores—while very polite—assured me there was no food to be had in Borja, the store was empty, and, further, I could not possibly ascend the Pongo de Menseriche, that mighty gorge down which the Amazon (Alto Marañón) flows through the Cerros Campanquiz. Its thunder from where I stood, was certainly evidence of their assertions. Also the Huambiza and Aguaruna Jívaros were just beyond, on the west side of it—not six miles away!

"They are hunting heads," said one of the traders, "perhaps you had better go back to Iquitos."

I presented myself at the garrison, which lay at the base of the Cerro and against the Pongo's mouth, and there found Capitán Gonzalez in his hammock. I was kept waiting until he had finished his siesta, and then he spent two hours investigating my papers (passport and police clearance), saying they were out of order and I would have to return to Iquitos to have them validated.

Afterwards we inspected the garrison troops, mostly Quechuas from the Andes. The thick, stumpy Peruvian soldier, with his wrap leggings and bare feet, his long rifle with the bayonet usually fixed, heavy cartridge belt on suspenders, rather resembled a burly Japanese soldier. Unquestionably they were good soldiers, for being without imagination they jumped when spoken to and were tough as nails. In jungle fighting against Jívaros, however, their record is weak—for they are no match for the headhunters. Their mission is to make the Oriente rivers safe for occupation by *patrónes*. Since the Jívaros object to being dispossessed of their lands and also to becoming slaves, bad blood exists between them and the military. In many regions, without its being publicized or "official," the soldiers are engaged in a campaign of extermination. Lest this surprise many Americans, it will be remembered that not many years ago our government also used army, Indian mercenaries, and professional scalp hunters for the same purpose. The Peruvian soldiers' success lies in surprising villages or camps, machine-gunning everything and everybody in it, then burning.

In studying the Pongo's mouth, a great stony maw of cliffs, I learned that when a certain flat rock was not covered with water, the Pongo might possibly be negotiated by canoe; but if the rock was covered, there was absolutely no chance. I judged that fifteen feet of water were pouring over that rock. A peculiar wind blew from 6 A.M. till far into the night. It was known as the "Pongo wind."

Days passed. I watched the rock. Instead of going down, the flood was rising! When twenty-five feet of water flooded over it, I gave up watching. In the meanwhile I killed a few fish in the muddy river.

The soldiers began using the derogatory term of "gringo" to us. They followed the lead of their Commandante, Capitán Gonzalez who became curt before the Indians and even insulting. Under no circumstances were we to proceed beyond Borja. "I order you back to Iquitos!" he said, and handed us a written order. Inez and I ignored him from then on. His half a dozen officers were very cordial whenever we were alone with them.

The days continued very hot and sticky, for the air near the Pongo was humid, but the October nights were delightfully cool. The families of the *patrónes* called on us at all hours and showed off their children, for whom we usually found some small gifts. Indians also began coming, just squatting on the porch upstairs, staring at us. Inez at first was nervous, especially when they fondled her hair which was fine and light in color. When she realized they would do her no harm, she became at home with them, and even made a few friends among the women.

After we had been half starving for several days (I had lost twenty-five pounds since leaving Lima), I decided it would only be fair to tell Inez the reason why I was so determined to hang on and not turn back. One night sitting on the porch, the lamp between us on the table, I spread out my map of El Dorado, after unbuckling the money belt in which it had reposed in its waterproof wrapping for so long. I explained that this document, together with the writing on the back, showed Borja to have been founded in 1549.

I told her the information was not verifiable, for there is only a very brief account by one Juan Salinas, a Jesuit friar, who descended the Santiago and shot the Pongo in 1557. He reported finding gold, but did not mention a city, either Indian or Spanish. Two cities, however, were then actually in existence. They were San Francisco de Borja, founded in 1549 on the present site of Borja (or near it); and Santiago de las Montañas, at the mouth of the Santiago River just west of the Pongo where that river enters the Golden Serpent. Ancient Santiago de las Montañas had been founded by Juan Salinas de Loyola, and it was destroyed many times by savages. This central area west of the Pongo and back to the main Andes—was known to the old Jesuits as El Dorado, a very secret code name. Gold in tremendous weights, even for that day, taken from seven rich *lavaderos* (placers), was sent by secret caravan trails across the Cordilleras into Lima, seat of the Viceroy, and thence by the treasure road to Panama, and by galleon to Spain.

As for the quantities of gold involved, they were so stupendous that Spain took every measure to hide its operations. However, my informant in Lima and my own documented information showed that from one placer alone, in the years 1558 to 1652, the Spanish Crown was paid *in Spain* 500 to 800 kilos (modern weight) of twenty-three-karat gold. Another record shows that in each of four consecutive years (1570 to 1574) the Crown recovered an average of 9,700 kilos, about 25,000 pounds. The Crown's legal share was only one-fourth. As the mines were operated secretly there is no way of checking the total recovery, but there is reason to believe it was very much greater than the reported annual net clean-up of 100,000 pounds in dust and nuggets, worth today on the Tangier market (at $50 per gold ounce) over $50,000,000. A truer figure, though many times too conservative, would be four times that amount—which is the way costs, discounts and losses ran on other New World operations—or $200,000,000 annually.

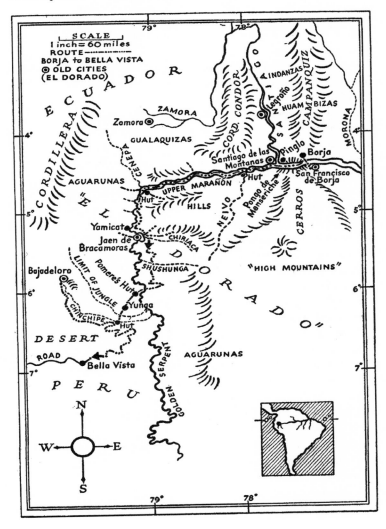

Therefore I believed that the old legend of El Dorado was founded not on whimsy but on a very real mining enterprise, and the Seven Cities of Cíbola, Manoa and Quivera searched for by Coronado, Vaca de Cabeza and Sir Walter Raleigh in North and South America were in fact seven actual cities of the Amazon headwaters.[5] After the seven cities of El Dorado had been established, diversionary propaganda was started by church secret agents (agents used by military forces today to establish "Diversionary Operatious aimed at misleading an 'Enemy Evaluation Section'"), which explains the fruitless searches made for El Dorado by the uninformed freelance conquistadores (on the outside of the operation itself). And these cities were not ancient Indian at all, but *Spanish cities!*—and located secretly on the sites of the ancient Inca placers themselves. So successful was the deception, that the only Englishman who ever tried to find El Dorado was Raleigh, and he went up the Orinoco instead of the Amazon. Only the old Spaniards could have done it, so cruelly sacrificing their own commanders to futile searches. However, it is unquestionably one of the greatest pieces of counter-intelligence ever accomplished in international intrigue.

The ancestors of the Huambiza and Aguaruna Jívaros probably were the "Borjas" of modern legend, who in actual fact did totally destroy these two Pongo cities, *and five others besides....*

These unknown Seven Cities of Cíbola, actually Seven Cities of El Dorado, were known only to Crown and Church agents as: Santiago de las Montañas, San Francisco de Borja, Legroño, San Reys, Jaen de Bracamoras, Bajadeloro, and Zamora. Here the Jesuits secretly mined gold.

Now, as to the exact locations of the seven cities—recently a Peruvian soldier under Gonzalez had found half a bronze bell near the mouth of the Santiago on its northwest corner. On its cast base was the number "15.."—the following numbers of the date missing. I knew also that when the old Indians attacked the seven cities of El Dorado, the Jesuits of Santiago de las Montañas hid their gold in two vaults under the floor of the church.

The seven ancient cities, then, were grouped around the hub of the mouth of the Rio Santiago. Eventually all their satellite placer camps

---

5. See my "Historical Note" at the beginning of the book.

were destroyed…and from El Dorado but a single survivor among the Spaniards ever reached Lima. Therefore the Jesuits abandoned gold mining in the headwaters of the Amazon Valley, and so it was that El Dorado was lost. And it proved utterly impossible (as in the case of lost Tayopa in Mexico) ever to find El Dorado, so perfect had been the system of security in bringing out the gold trains into Lima.

The lone survivor, an illiterate soldier, never dared to speak of El Dorado fearing the Inquisition's rack and the tortures of the officials. As an old man he made a crude map of the region, and on its back he had a scribe write some of the particulars still remembered by him. It was a copy of this document which I had taken from my tobacco pouch and spread on the table.

A clear statement of the situation was that I had purchased my map from a Señor Maldonado in Lima, who had inherited it through his family. And, as there was no indication that the mines had been exhausted before the destruction of the seven cities, great wealth must still lie there in the jungle at the seven placers.

I glanced across at Inez. "There it is. The cities' locations were only approximately indicated on the parchment—*each city marked with drawing of the Inca's golden eye.* They lie beyond the Pongo de Menseriche. These cities and their gold placers are what I am after. What do you think?—too rich for your blood? I go alone?" For I certainly expected her to ridicule the idea that El Dorado ever existed, much less that the golden land lay just beyond the Cerros Campanquiz, in the very heart of the Jívaro headhunting country.

Inez got up from the table and slowly walked to the railing of the porch, looking out over the Marañón and into the black night, the howling Pongo wind blowing her hair around her face. She turned and stared at me.

During the next hour I was told some astonishing things, not least among them why Inez had been so insistent on continuing west at Valencia when von Wolfenegg turned back to Iquitos. The plain facts were that she, *though a woman,* was also searching for El Dorado. She represented a syndicate, long formed, called The National Gold Bearing Society of El Dorado, with headquarters in London and Lima. They were capitalized for $175,000 and had a 700,000-hectare concession of land in which to search for the lost gold mines. If El Dorado were located, the Peruvian government would move troops into the disputed

Oriente territory east of Ecuador, and take one fourth of the gold production. In addition to this, I learned that the Borja *patrónes*—Caballero, Gomez and Moray—were not ordinary traders at all, but members of this same organization. So much for the essentials, now for the particulars.

The London Syndicate had chosen a woman because being the world's best undercover operators (in both military and commercial enterprises), the British had calculated the probability that a woman, especially an American woman, would be the last person to be suspected of ferreting out El Dorado, for secrecy was necessary as the Lima group had failed to locate El Dorado and yet refused cooperation to a representative of the main London establishment. Inez was felt to be qualified as she had traveled not only in nearly every country of the world, but also extensively throughout South America. I had no longer any least doubt about her capacities, abilities, experience and courage when I heard she had once been a "dancer" in Shanghai, in Budapest and in Constantinople. This lack of surprise on my part was due to my having had under my command in World War II some 700 women of all nations in one organization alone, operating as secret agents undercover throughout Asia, and I knew that there are many secret deals (including important commercial ones) going on about the world and that women play a very important part in them. I did not enquire into the nature of her activities in Shanghai and other places, as it was none of my business. I assumed however that they were connected with commercial enterprises.

Inez had taken ten persistent months (always a puzzling thing to me) to reach Iquitos from Pará, because she was learning the local dialects used along the river, acclimatizing herself to conditions as they existed in the Amazon country, and especially picking up information of all kinds as pertained to El Dorado and her getting there. Since, due to Indian troubles and the flareup of the border dispute with Ecuador, she could not form a regular expedition in Iquitos, she had seized upon the opportunity of joining me.

She had learned I was free to move west due to my medical report to the government, and that (to her best knowledge) I was not under serious local suspicion of being anything but what I professed to be—namely, an explorer. Von Wolfenegg knew nothing of her plans. She absolutely did not suspect I was after El Dorado. As a matter of fact (she now informed me to my discomfort), she had in Iquitos thought me to be a bit of a stuffed shirt of an ex-Colonel who was none too bright. She knew if she joined me she would be less conspicuous while traveling on the river. She felt I might get as far as Borja, and if stopped there, she would cut loose from me and continue up the main stem of the Amazon with Indians alone. She did not intend to reveal her plan to me, or anybody else at any time.

The Borja *patrónes* must not know of her intentions for going west of the Pongo de Menseriche. When one is playing a dangerous game for stakes as high as El Dorado, one does not take people into confidence (even people like von Wolfenegg) or in any way take chances other than those absolutely necessary. Inez was revealing this information to me now, because she comprehended for the first time the very great practical obstacles lying in the region west, and because I knew the approximate locations of the seven placers which she and the London and Lima organizations did not know.

At the end of that enlightening hour I sat back and lit my pipe, a corncob one and some tobacco which had been obtained at the Borja trading post. My reaction for the moment was very plain, if not altogether cryptic:

Well, I'll be darned! I thought.

∾ XXI. ↶

Stranded Among the Aguarunas

EXT morning I was summoned to the garrison. Instead of receiving help to get through the Pongo, which I had eagerly anticipated, I was handed a radiogram ordering us back to Iquitos on the first trader's boat that should reach Borja. In the meanwhile no more food would be sold to us from the commissary; in the past there had been little enough, a few pieces of yuca—nothing more. That was that! We were to get out, or starve.

Inez and I held out a few more days on a handful of rice and five plantains. In the meantime while hunting across the river, 500 yards beyond the south bank and at the foot of the Cerros Campanquiz, I found some very old man-cut sandstones which undoubtedly marked the site of ancient San Francisco de Borja. The stones had been up-turned by the action of tree roots displacing them, though obviously they had once formed the foundations and walls of buildings. I should never have guessed their significance but for the symbol identically placed on the treasure map. Obviously the *patrónes* knew of the site because Indians were panning gold by primitive methods They proved friendly. The miners were each recovering seven grams of dust per day, for which they were paid fifty soles-de-oro (on credit at the store), about $7.50. This is big money on the Amazon, but as the Indians had to work all day in deep water, and sickened and died as a result, they never stayed long on the job.

The score of Indians who lived in the Borja clearing believed that the cracks in the bottom of the Pongo de Menseriche contained the bulk of the Andean heavy gold. There was no way to divert the Marañón and get at it, and what they were recovering was merely the overflow of the flour-gold that was too light to settle.

I asked them if they thought the source of this gold lay in the mountains.

"The Golden Serpent and the Santiago drain two thousand miles of the Cordilleras," one of them told me. "There must be many sources— but who knows! No one can go there because of the headhunters."

There was no penetrating the thick jungles matting the steep Cerros Campanquiz range just behind, and not only did the water in the Pongo remain high (for the rains had already started higher in the Cordilleras), but the soldiers were now watching us.

Next morning we saw Señor Caballero weighing gold dust in his store—a bush shack half-way between the garrison and our house. When he saw us standing in the doorway, he stopped immediately. As the gold spilled out over the counter, for the scales were overflowing, he seemed very angry. But as we entered, he continued weighing the gold as if nothing had disturbed him.

A band of painted Huambizas in loincloths were squatting about on the floor. I realized they must be the owners of the two big dugouts I had seen drawn up on the bank outside. They could only have come through the Pongo, and brought this gold with them. Sacks made of wild pigskin were stacked on the ground.

"Where do these Indians find this gold?" I asked. Surely it was a natural question.

For a moment Caballero hesitated, then said with a smile: "They have found an ancient Spanish site midway up the Santiago with nine great stone troughs. I have never been there of course, but I call it 'Legroño de los Caballeros.'"

"Why Legroño?" I asked, managing to appear casual.

"Because, señor—Legroño was one of seven ancient cities up there somewhere, and we think all that country west of the Pongo is El Dorado...."

He then said that Moray, Gomez and himself were all trying to penetrate the Santiago and the Golden Serpent—because Moray had an "ancient parchment" in his family showing that El Dorado lay in this region. He even produced a large map (which with the help of the Indians he had worked out) of Legroño de los Caballeros. He had no objection when I copied the map on a sheet of paper which he supplied. The family came into possession of the original Moray parchment, on the death of an old soldier who had dictated what he knew to a scribe.

When I left the store, my mouth clamped shut, you can imagine the state of my mind. Inez thought the reason Caballero had said this, was that very few people ever believe the truth. If I had heard rumors, they now would be completely dispelled—for what *patróne* would reveal the source of great quantities of gold to a stranger? So Legroño actually existed, as did the ruins of old San Francisco de Borja. The location of

The Map:

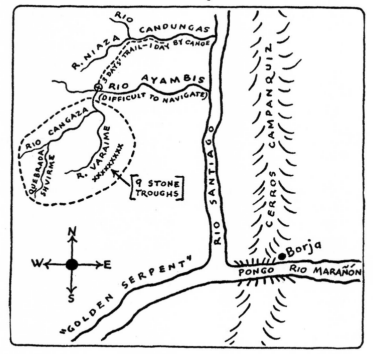

three of the cities was now known to me: San Francisco de Borja, Legroño, Santiago de las Montañas.

I walked back into the store—for above all, I must not let Caballero think I suspected anything of the real truth.

"Is that why Capitán Gonzalez won't let me go farther west?"

Caballero smiled. "*Si*, señor. The simple soldier is one of us."

Starving was easier after that....

On the 20th of October a cloudburst flooded through the canyon of the Pongo de Menseriche. The water rose to forty feet above the Aguaruna's rock marker.

That day we learned that electric eel is edible. But the first one I touched with my machete, after finding it on a mud bank, sent out a shock that all but paralyzed me.

Due to the lack of food, I had lost strength, and my eyes had now become so bad I could scarcely see. The old infection had returned, and was worse than ever. The doctor dared not risk court martial by treating me openly. Under cover of night he began treatments of belladonna, but after two days my eyes showed very little improvement. At last he gave up. Inez spoke to an Aguaruna *apamamacuna* (a class of *brujo*), and after playing a nose-flute to charm the spirit Anacondas, he suggested an injection of cow's milk. Inez "borrowed" the army hypodermic (while the doctor gallantly turned his back); and I roped one of the tamest of the *zebus* and milked her. This crazy treatment actually lessened the pain and my eyes cleared considerably. The *apamamacuna* now treated my eyes twice daily for a few days and finally cleared them of 80 percent of their film.

But in the meanwhile, storms lashed furiously against the tin roof of the house. All one day the storm continued: lightning sizzled in the tree tops and thunder boomed so loudly that we had to clasp our hands over our ears as the clouds were only a few hundred feet off the ground. Water began streaming over the ground, and pouring into the river. And the Marañón continued to rise. The Aguaruna *brujos*, one Indian said, were purposely "making rain" to keep us from going up the Pongo. Their medicine was potent stuff, for the river burst like some gigantic firehose, straight out of the narrow mouth of the Pongo. I was now balked at every turn: I was starving, my health was breaking down, I had practically no money left. The War Department in Lima, Gonzalez and the *patrónes* threatened me. And now, worse than all these, the river...the *Pongo*!

There are times when a man simply reaches the end of his rope. In desperation I finally said to Inez: "If we wait for permission to come from the War Department in Lima or for some chance canoe with paddlers, we are certainly done for.[1] I am going to try to get over the range alone. It is now less than a thousand miles to Quito in Ecuador, and I'll meet you there. You had better try and hire Indians to paddle you back to Iquitos."

"You mean you think you can escape from Gonzalez?"

"I once operated for nineteen months behind the Japanese Army lines, disguised as a Chinese," I returned. "And you have probably heard that there is a fourth *patróne* here in Borja. I still have enough money ($108) together with yours, to hire Guzman, who is not in the syndicate. I'll get his forty-foot dugout up through the slot somehow...."

I had only seen Guzman three or four times; he lived back in the jungle a mile or so. Guzman was a six-foot man, very lean and tough, perhaps fifty. He was said to be a terrific Indian fighter. This *patróne* owned the only heavy-duty outboard motor this side of Iquitos. He was also a very brave man who made his living by trading with the Huambizas and Aguarunas. It was said these Indians trusted him and let him go through the Pongo to a *playa* just beyond the mouth of the river. Here he bartered for their skins, gold, and other merchandise.

That night in the storm I left Inez. The soldiers were all under cover and I made my way safely through the trees to Guzman's house. We put our heads together. I did not tell him of El Dorado, but I made such a generous offer, that since he too wanted to explore on the Golden Serpent, he could not refuse. He agreed to try the Pongo at the next low water—it was absolutely impossible now. In the meantime we must hold out, wait.

Inez refused to return to Iquitos, and so she too secretly prepared to leave. The result of this desperate attempt on the Pongo was re- corded in my diary:

"*October 28—9 P.M.: Due to rain and wind this morning, before dawn, the soldiers were inside the Garrison. Under cover of darkness, with Indians at the paddles, Guzman steered his long dugout into the Pongo. Inez and I sat amidships. He kept to the right bank, under a cliff, where the current*

---

1. Later I learned that Capitán Gonzalez never sent my message.

was not so swift. The canyon he said was six miles long. Through this narrow slot of perpendicular stone wall some 2,000 feet high, flows the Marañón, a mad yellow torrent of roaring waters and foam. Government geologists earlier in 1945 reported that the Andean gold (as the Indians believe) may indeed be lying on its bottom. They had sounded it at low water, and no bottom could be found at 350 feet. The currents were so swift they could not get a line down deeper. Whirlpools, eddies, rapids and currents threw us about. Guzman now cranked up his motor, and tackled the canyon, the big motor roaring with the throttle wide open, and the Indians paddling desperately. The boat lurched wildly, taking in a great deal of water, and Inez and I started bailing. I have never been more frightened, scared all but stiff, in my whole life. He stayed near the rocks at the side, but we barely crawled forward. The din of the crashing waters, the echoing of the motor off the walls—was deafening. Once I glanced at Guzman who was crouching in the stern and swinging the rudder—his lean face was deeply lined and grim. He shook his head at me. The current in the center probably exceeded fifty miles an hour. Even at the edge, the torrent through which we crept was calculated at twenty miles per hour. The waves were terrific. Guzman yelled that at a certain place, just ahead—in fact we were then on its lower lip—was a tremendous whirlpool with a hundred-yard diameter. Four of Gonzalez's soldiers had been sucked down only the week before. I had already heard that no bodies are ever recovered from the Pongo. It is believed that the great zúngaros eat them. We crossed the river just below the whirlpool to the south side. All forward motion ceased altogether. We were on the left rim of the great pool. The current raced along our sides. The dugout was now a fifth full of water, though we were bailing madly. The whirlpool suddenly widened, and though we were only twenty feet from the rocks of the wall, almost grasped us; Guzman—his face an ashy white—slammed down the rudder, and with the big motor full open, swung out of his course and headed downstream. The current and the motor together gave us a speed that must have been nearly seventy miles an hour; we tore loose from the steep wall of the pool, and once in the current below, he cut the engine. The Indians kept our bow forward, and we shot out of the canyon's mouth. We were soaking wet, all but sunk, and the suspense was so overpowering that once we found ourselves in the open, and opposite Borja, Inez laughed. I don't think Guzman or the Indians ever will get over it."

So much for our first try. As we were approaching Puerto Patria, the red roof streaming with rain, a small hydroplane roared over and landed on the river, and out onto a pontoon stepped Walter von Wolfenegg!

We drifted alongside and caught hold. When I explained our desperate situation here, he shouted: "I have a plan!"

And without another word he got back into his plane, and immediately took off for Iquitos.

That night the storm continued, and the river was in full flood. Guzman splashed over from his house. "It's no use, señor," he said, "the rainy season has begun in earnest." Gonzalez, he had warned, was furious.

On the 30th the water was still rising, now sixty feet over the rock. More days passed, and the river rose over the banks and swirled under our house; fortunately the piles held. A mad tumult crashed deafeningly through the Pongo. I then realized I had lost the race started on the Perené and we could not get through for six months, until the end of the wet season. We packed, and I purchased a small balsa raft. As soon as I had strengthened it with vines we would drift back to Iquitos.

And then a miracle.

On the 3rd of November, Walter flew in again—this time in a big hydroplane. Before Capitán Gonzalez knew what he was about, our friend bundled us through the rainstorm, shouted orders to the pilot— Capitán Isaac Zapater V.—and immediately took off and flew over the Pongo. The Peruvian Air Force pilot landed beautifully on the log-jammed Marañón, then taxied over to the north bank, all the while fighting swirling currents and whirlpools, beached on a *playa* at the eastern lip of the Santiago. We had actually escaped to the unknown after being trapped for twenty-one days.

Here, to our great surprise—though known to Walter and the pilot—was a little army outpost called Pinglo, roosting on stilts high on the bank above the *playa*. The Teniente greeted us by saying we must return to Borja. Pinglo was under siege; Huambizas had just killed nineteen troops and taken their heads.

After one look at our disappointed faces, Walter turned to his pilot and winked. Capitán Zapater looked coldly at the post commander, and slowly strode up to him. "Señor!" he said, "If there is one thing lower than a snake's belly, it must be a foot soldier. If you don't know by this time that Americans are our friends, then it's high time you were informed. You are hereby ordered to shelter these people!" He turned on his heel and strode back to his airplane. We knew that in this storm, Gonzalez could never pursue us, and all we needed was two or three days. Inez moved in on the angry Teniente, and did her work of charming him so well, that he finally grudgingly consented to "three days."

After shaking hands, Walter and his pilot then flew back to Borja. Thinking a celebration was being held in our honor we put forth with all our best efforts in order to make ourselves congenial, for evidently the personnel of the post were preparing a party of some sort. That night Inez and I danced the whole night out under a sickle moon, just showing through breaking storm clouds. As it turned out, the event wasn't such a chore after all. The orchestra, oddly enough, was incredibly good; two spoons, a pair of gourd rattles, a guitar, drum, a bank of tom-toms and two reed flutes. The thirty private soldiers stationed here nonchalantly danced the rumba, the samba, and several other shuffles ending in "ba." Perfect manners were exhibited by each and every one, and some really beautiful dancing. The six Indian women, and the Peruvian spouse of the Commandante were all happily pregnant. We finally learned that this celebration was not one of welcome, but honoring the Teniente's birthday.

At dawn we saw that the Santiago was causing the main flood in the Pongo. The deeper Marañón was not flooded. This meant that a canoe could make way against the Marañón from this point, west. That day the waters in the Pongo fell forty feet. Guzman, already paid a substantial advance, had promised at the last moment that he would try to slip out of Borja, and pick us up at the Santiago's mouth. As I say, Guzman was an Indian fighter, and escaping from soldiers was an easy matter for him. Above all, this *patróne* wanted to learn the source of the gold traded to him by the Aguarunas and was willing to risk anything to ascend the Marañón. I knew in my bones that he would get through the Pongo.

I brought out my Marañón map, but saw from now on only a vague white blank with a dotted line running through the middle of it. The Teniente did not know about the Marañón above, nor was he very well informed on the tribes. His Indian scouts usually disappeared whenever they were sent out. I told him of Up de Graff's ascent of the Pongo sixty years ago, and of his encountering the Antipas tribe at the Santiago's mouth, where now stood Pinglo. The Peruvian did not know of any such tribe, and suggested that they might have been massacred by the Huambizas, or by the Aguarunas, or perhaps they had fled inland.

Many riverine tribes were leaving the rivers these days and taking to the interior jungles. The Aguarunas, the largest, bloodiest, and least known of all the Jívaros, were undoubtedly on the Alto Marañón, while the Huambizas hunted over the Santiago basin. Other headhunters were everywhere off these rivers and occupying the inland regions. We were shown a most curious and gruesome shrunken head; the teeth and jaws were of normal size, but the rest of the head had been reduced to the size of a baseball. We had to agree that the Huambiza had a nerve to sell it, as his victim had been one of the Teniente's own sergeants.

The 6th (November) rolled around, but no Guzman. The Teniente thought the water in the Pongo was low enough now to risk a large canoe for going downstream, and that on the morrow we would be taken to Borja.

That night I negotiated a deal with a reluctant old Aguaruna buck. Shortly after, Inez and I left Pinglo in his dugout. He was silent as a shadow, keeping to the right bank, after crossing the mouth of the Santiago, heading up the Marañón. We lay in the bottom of the dugout, thus escaping detection by the armed guard who challenged him. I shall never forget the thrill I had when we passed near the spot where the old bell of Santiago de las Montañas had been found by the soldier. I would have given much to have searched in the jungle here for that old stone floor of the ancient church of Juan Salinas de Loyola. Did the two vaults filled with bars of gold lie under it? the accumulated treasures of eight years of mining in all the cities of El Dorado?

All next day we continued up the jungle river. I took the stern paddle in order to help the old Aguaruna. By the evening of the 7th, he beached at the mouth of a river he called the Neivo (not marked on the maps). It came in on the south bank of the Marañón, through very dense, high jungles, and looked to be a new river. The mouth of the Neivo was some hundred yards wide, the channel very swift and deep— I should judge twenty feet.

There was a hut on the southwest bank of the river. This was backed by a high and very tangled jungle, and the ground all around had recently been flooded and was very muddy; altogether a desolate place. Here the old brave left us and paddled off across the Marañón, not daring now to return to Pinglo. He had scarcely hurried away when I saw a movement back in the jungle. I watched very closely. Presently I realized it was an Aguaruna brave. He was about 5 1/2 feet tall, and very thick, very brown, and painted with wavy lines of green and red. His loins were tightly wrapped in a red-and-black cloth, and his hair was bobbed in front just above the eyes, but streaming long in back over his shoulders. He was holding a blowgun. And above all, he was watching us as a snake watches its meal.

I grinned across the hundred feet at him. After a long while he slowly came out of cover. Like most Jívaros, this one could speak a few words of Quechua: it was very dangerous here, he let us know, and we must go back down the Marañón before dark. After I got a fire going inside the hut, I let him know we had no intention of swimming down the Marañón, to please him or anybody else. He seemed to accept what I said. He picked up a limb off the fire, and using it as a torch for luring fish to the riverside, soon speared a large *chambiri*. It was three feet long and very active; finally he killed it by biting on the spine just in back of the head. His teeth were sharp as needles and had no trouble piercing the thick skin and scales.

In Borja I had acquired an Indian hammock, and so, after eating, I swung our beds from the corner posts in the hut. We were soon in our nets and resting. I guarded while Inez slept. About midnight she took the watch. When dawn came I left with the Indian, for he had not gone far away in the jungle for the night, to try for another fish. We were hungry. Crouched on the *playa* we watched the surface of the Neivo.

Suddenly the Jívaro pointed up into the sky, and I saw that a hawk was dropping something on the shore rocks nearby. This proved to be a small turtle, whose shell the hawk was deliberately trying to break. We drove off the screaming bird, and pirated the turtle—our breakfast.

All day we sat in a drizzle, for the old roof of the deserted Indian shack was full of holes, and drums began talking. In about twenty minutes they were all around, far and near. Rain fell in the night, and by morning the Marañón was again in flood. The date was November 9th. The rains were on in earnest. Noon came. All at once I heard a spitting sound playing over the Marañón, and ran down to the *playa*. Half an hour later Guzman's big dugout poked its bow around a bend about a mile away.

Fearing he would not see us in the tangle of jungle, I signaled with the old .45 (the Borja doctor had given me twenty rounds); at first he swung away to the far side of the river, thinking an Indian was shooting at him. But later he crossed over to exchange a shot himself, and seeing my shirt waving, sharply turned his bow in shoreward. With Guzman's long thatched dugout alongside, we happily wrung his hand and chucked in our gear, and started off up the Marañón, the strange Indian jumping in too. Guzman didn't like the look of either the Neivo or the Golden Serpent (the last 350 miles of the unexplored Amazon), and he liked even less the looks of our Aguaruna. With Guzman was a crew of four tame Aguarunas.

The Marañón appeared to be freshly cut through a network of wandering channels separated by low islands of palms and trees. Hills were beginning to appear on both sides, Wild spices of cinnamon and vanilla almost overwhelmed us with their sweet perfume. We saw no Indians. The river lay under a pall of heat, reflecting two high walls of green jungle. Insects droned everywhere, and we itched incessantly.

Every few hours the canoe had to be tracked by hand around boulders and through rapids; at such times, Guzman, his crew of four Indians, Inez and I, would get out and tug the dugout along *playas* or wade in the edges of the river. The big Aguaruna would walk along, watching us, but made no offer to help or to hinder. At this time we picked up pieces of float ore which indicated the mountains contained copper and silver. Once an Aguaruna Indian paddled alongside our roaring motor, stopping long enough to point out fresh tapir tracks in the sand; the hind feet had four toes, the front, three.

Due to war with the Huambizas, the Aguarunas had apparently moved back from the river and vanished into the inner jungles. The river water was warm, and such a soupy creamy yellow, that it actually tasted good. With night we camped on a long *playa* only a few yards wide, and before dawn continued our weaving and winding in and out against the ever stiffening currents. By keeping to the less wild places along the flanks and close to the trees, poling and paddling hard, pulling on bushes and bamboos—all with the motor wide open—we inched forward, slowly gaining ground by the hour.

Camp was now pitched at an abandoned hut at the foot of a narrow and very swift *pongo*. Giant *tundui* signal drums pounded all night, and the Neivo Aguaruna disappeared—but no attack came at dawn, the favorite hour. We had just left shortly after daylight when I luckily shot a *danta*—a 600-pound, chocolate-colored tapir. The big .45 slug had hit the pachyderm's head as the beast swam across our bow. It climbed out on the high, right bank, and was walking into the trees; the range was

150 yards. My second shot fell short; but the third struck the *danta* in the shoulder, and it tumbled back into the river. Guzman put around, and we soon had the great animal by its ears and safely beached.

With plenty of meat on hand we felt better, and less apprehensive. The butchering was finished at 8 A.M., and we continued against the current, feeling our way cautiously through a narrow gorge, only a hundred yards wide, filled with wild eddies and whipping currents, fearful whirlpools and rocks partly awash. Above this *pongo*, crocodiles were sunning on small white beaches. In some stretches we made excellent time, putting the miles behind us. Ridges and small peaks began rising on both sides. Magnificent Equatorial jungles, very dark and gloomy, and filled with blue and brown morpho butterflies, now crowded the stony banks. At times cool winds rushed down from the north off the unexplored Cordillera Condor—the first great range of the Andean system. This range lies between the Santiago and the Zamora rivers, in a north-south direction, and is covered with jungle. Our Indians warned that the Condor was the stamping ground of Jívaros of the Indanzas, Huambizas and Gualaquiza (or Pantecunas) tribes. Due west of the great range lay the Zamora River, base for these latter headhunters—the Gualaquizas. All these people, they said, built forts of logs, with high towers.

My air maps showed wide, flat plains on each bank of the Golden Serpent; actually 2,000-foot hills existed on the right and perhaps even higher on the left, rising in places abruptly from the water's edge. One *pongo*, which trapped us for two hours, was barely a hundred and fifty feet across! The mighty Amazon was actually pinching down into a mountain torrent, rushing under an immense canopy of interlocking jungle.

That morning at eleven o'clock, we stopped at a little clearing on the left bank. Indians fled on our approach. There was a small rickety bamboo hut on stilts. Baskets, spears and blowguns were suspended from the rafters. Animal and reptile skins dried on frames of bamboo. After we had examined the hut, a pack of five giant Aguarunas crept out of the jungle, shouting "Apachis!" They yelled at our own tame Aguarunas that there was no food here for us. The Supay Chacara (Demon of the Garden) had sent a blight.

These warriors were the biggest and most fearsome Jívaros yet seen. They were very heavy-set and muscular—all bone and muscle, yet some must have weighed from 200 to 250 pounds; mostly 5 1/2 feet tall but a few over 6 feet. Their eyes were a dark brown, and their feet enormous. Their broad faces were scarred, their teeth filed and painted a shiny black with *nushumbi*—a preservative contained in the juice of a nut, and said by them to prevent decay. These *bravos'* faces were of a very broad Mongolian or Eskimo type, but incredibly heavy-jawed. Earlobes were stretched around thick plugs of wood, or calligraphically carved, four-inch bones and boars' ivory. Two men were heavily tattooed in blue. On their heads were coronas of basketry decorated with red and yellow toucan feathers. The chief's son was painted with large red spots all over his very brown face; while the others were painted red with *achiote* or black with *sua*, and slashed horizontally with an ocher-yellow. Their straight black hair was separated into three pigtails, tightly braided, and bound with colored beads strung on leather thongs ending in rosettes of feathers. Hair skirts, called *akuchus*, cut from the shrunken human heads, were woven into grim war trophy belts.

From these Aguaruna savages we quickly accepted halved gourds dipped into yard-high red *giamanchi* or *masata* (*chicha*) urns; to refuse, warned Guzman, would be an insult. Clots of saliva and other unpleasant matter of a very sour taste, were soon drunk up, followed by our smiles, as we rather foolishly cried in imitation of them—"*Winahu!*" ("I come!"). The Aguarunas' conversations start and stop with alarming abruptness, it was plaintive and petulant, bombastic, violent—something like radio static, accompanied by fierce facial expressions and startling gesticulations of their limbs and hands —every muscle straining. These Indians were anything but stoics, as they spat politely—with many a miss—between the two middle fingers held up in a Vee. Their talk continued incredibly loud, fierce, full of grunts, singsonging, clacks, hisses, whistles, and frightening shouts.

Guzman pointed out that no details are ever omitted in either manners or conversation, as the slightest offense may well cost a man his head. These savage Jívaros were certainly fierce, mentally alert, tigerish in their movements. I was afraid inside, and yet strangely fascinated.

Leaving a few *plátanos* and a piece of the tapir meat behind with Inez and me, and swearing on the Holy Mother he would be back on the morrow, Guzman (hoping no doubt to find gold) launched his dugout. He disappeared up a river called the Cenepa, which opened just across the way on the west bank of the Marañón. A powerful Gualaquiza Jívaro *brujo* from the Zamora just north lived in its headwaters. This witchman had once been in Borja peddling heads, where Guzman and he became friends. From this *winchiyu* (Brother of Life and Death), our *patróne* would not only trade for gold but discover whether the Aguarunas would let us ascend farther up the Golden Serpent. Guzman had assured me the Aguarunas had promised to take good care of us. Several times he had said there was no danger as long as I did not start trouble myself.

Several hungry and apprehensive days passed for Inez and me, and still no Guzman.

Even after the second day, we faced a crisis: due to starvation rations, an apathy had crept over us like a paralysis. Inez was thin and her face was drawn, but due to her natural courage and high spirits she escaped that haggard look which I momentarily expected. The Aguarunas came and stared sullenly, sometimes pointing out to each other our peculiarities—such as the color of our eyes, our hair, our clothes—and then filtered away, new ones always arriving, day after day; giants buttered with grease and paint, but absolutely empty-handed of food, though Jívaros grow yuca, corn, yams, *plátanos*, peanuts, and scores of other fruits and vegetables, many unknown to the outside world. Coconuts, of course, are not grown, as these palms flourish only near salt sea water.

Day and night sheets of rain trickled through our leaky roof. Since there was no mending the old thatch, we made raincoats out of banana leaves, wearing them inside the house. At night we slept on the Jívaro beds—short (five-foot) racks, or shelves, of split bamboos.

One morning during this long wait, my machete brought down a vampire bat which spurted blood all over the place. Alarmed, Inez spotted a small, eighth of an inch wound on a vein of my forehead. This bat's wingspread was only ten inches, yet from the amount of blood soaked up in my net, and its copious excretions puddled on the floor under my shelf, it must have extracted about three cups of blood. Actually, these small bats are capable of assimilating two pints of blood during a single feeding. They have no stomach, and the food passes directly through the intestines. They invariably tap a vein on the forehead, big toes, elbows, top of the head or neck, even the ears. The bottom jaw, we saw, had two pointed eyeteeth. Split open, the bat emitted a vile odor.

As Guzman had said, the Indians were friendly. I could see that just so long as we evaded an outright quarrel with them they would not attack. By withholding food from us they figured we must return downriver on a raft. It required all my patience in order not to argue with them on this matter of food.

We managed to examine some of the women, incredibly beautiful females: onyx-eyed, dusty red and orange in color, aquiline-nosed. Sticking straight out from the lower lip was a one-inch *tukunus* ornament, a small, hollow bird or monkey bone. Their dress is called the *tarachis*, a red dyed cloth gown somewhat like a Bengali sari. One breast is left exposed, and the arms are encircled with beautiful monkey-teeth bracelets. Their necks are banded with wide beaded necklace collars; while across the shoulder in bandolier fashion are wide belts of black seeds—*shankas*.

While the men weave the cloth, the women dye it—for cotton has a male soul, and the dye seeds a female one. These beautiful women are named after female plants. This is very complicated as yuca, for example, alone has fifty different names here. The women can tell you (in Jívaro) every single plant, blade of glass, and tree, that exists in the jungle. Polygamous, some men have as many as five wives (they are familiar with several aphrodisiacs), but are badly henpecked.

We found that the Jívaros live very complicated lives. They supply each and every family with food, weapons, canoes, and the thousand things necessary for life. Living in a world of the supernatural, and being animists, the Jívaros believe that all matter, organized and unorganized, has a soul, a *wakani*.

All objects offered to the devils and the gods are broken so as to kill the spirits, and thus release the soul to the sun. They believe that life here is only a dream state, unreality, and that spirits can enjoy the "soul-essence" of food offerings. Weapons and shields have male souls, therefore the men manufacture the weapons. The men weave the cloth on looms, using striped patterns of magnificent blues, reds, and browns. The ancient Incas raiding under Inca Roca in 1252 obtained these dyes from the jungle tribes, but today they are lost to the Quechuas and other highland peoples, and only Jívaros know the secret. Though vegetable, these gorgeous colors remind one of the ancient Egyptian mineral dyes.

At this time a raid was made on the Huambizas, and three of the Aguarunas came back triumphantly bearing heads. All headhunting has a religious significance. The practice has many ramifications—but this raid was part of a planting ritual.

The raid was very carefully prepared, and an enemy selected. Usually these raids are carried out between the various Jívaro subtribes, and sometimes even between clans within a subtribe. The sole object is to bring back heads, for they are not cannibals and do not kill to eat human flesh. The strategy is surprise, the tactics cunning. Jívaros are usually night "cat killers," but they are not cowards as has been claimed by Peruvians who have suffered defeat at their hands.

A witchman binds the warriors to the spirit world of the Dancing Anacondas; to do this the *brujo* goes under the influence of a narcotic, usually *natema* (Soul Vine), and plays a sacred flute calling the spirits of the Anacondas to join in dance with him, and so make his war-medicine strong. He enters the bodies of a tapir, anaconda, deer and tiger, and pleads with the River Gods, the Rain Gods, the Earth Goddess, the Jungle Gods, and makes attacks on the Supay (Devil), who brings about all man's misfortunes. The Great One of the Waters—the Rain God— who might bring storm and floods and so stop the raiders, is appealed to. He is the Odd-Footed One—having one human foot, and an animal one. During this time the witchman is not wakened, for to do so would cause his death, the soul being away from the body.

The headhunters in our camp underwent secret initiations of purification, including certain taboos—such as having a woman. The *enenima*, a head dance, was conducted to the accompaniment of drumming and piping and the clashing of shell bells. The *meseta*, headhunting war drum, which is different from the signal drum, was beaten when the headhunters left on their raid.

If the black-painted warriors proceeded by dugout (as these did), they approach the enemy under cover of night. Heavy stones are put in the canoes and they are sunk out of sight in the river. The surprise, the Jívaros claim, is invariably a success, and both male and female enemies are shot or cut down and their heads hacked off. Such women and children as can be rounded up are placed under guard. But all male warriors, including the wounded, are slain. The killers then flee homeward, fearing reprisals against the home *hea* (fortress house). The prize heads are then prepared according to complicated magic formulae, and so become the *tsantsa*—the shrunken heads of the Amazon.

At the *hea* the heads were first skinned, though due to the fear of spoiling this job is sometimes done at the scene of the massacre. Curiously, the eyes remain in the skull. This skinning is accomplished by sometimes splitting the skin up the back in order more easily to extract the skull. Huambizas however often extract the skull through the neck (after crushing the bones), no slitting being done at all.

With the skull out, the skin is sutured; the head is then boiled in water, being held by its long hair. The lips are fastened together with three upright *chonta* spikes (three or four inches in length) and bound with palm fibers. This holds the shape of the head and also prevents the malign spirit within from speaking evil against the head-takers.

Hot sand is now tossed around inside the shell; often a long and tedious task of weeks or even months (for the job need not be hurried). During the shrinking, the heads are kept in pickle jars, and taken out whenever another application of the hot sand treatment is desired. The skin is next pared down on the inside, ironed with a hot rock on the outside, and moulded with the fingers. The grease is thus removed; slowly, slowly, the *tsantsa* becomes dry, rigid, thin-shelled and mummified; and though the ears are a bit large and even "cauliflowered," the features are remarkably uniform and human. The head is now blackened with *sua*. The lip plugs are removed and three strands of palm fibers are woven into the three sets of holes, and these hang from the lips. At this time the head is usually decorated with feathers or a band of monkey skin around the forehead.

The Indian who captures the head, *muka hendinyui* (Taker of the Head) is painted red with either blood or *achiote* (a symbolic substitute as with the Campas). He diets according to custom, taking only certain foods. He has no sex relations with his wives. He dances the *hanlsamata* (Soul Killing Dance) so that the *tsantsa* will not cause death or accident to him or his clan.

The headhunter believes that the center of the universe is in the Jívaro tribes, and he drinks *natema* during the head-rites to dream of the Old Ones, the Old White Ancestors. These people believe they are descended from white men. The Old Ones tell him there is no time as we know it, life is a dream state, so he dreams and enters "reality," to see into the past and to forecast his own future. He beseeches the Old Ones to transmigrate the dead victim's soul into an animal, a plant, or a stone, or another human body, and so give it a home where it will not be free to plague him.

Then followed the *einsupani* (Victory Dance), during which tom-toms were tapped. Eight heads had been taken in this raid, but only one head was finished during our stay. The warrior who had completed his rites now stomped and chanted on the ground before the *hea,* the other Indians joining in chorus from time to time. After that last ceremony I was amazed that the *tsantsa* no longer had any value in the eyes of the Jívaros. It was stuffed away in an old earthen pot, and placed in the thatched ceiling of the house. Robbed of its soul, the savagely beautiful trophy no longer had any spiritual value!

The heads we saw later among the Aguarunas, some thirty of them, all had shaved scalps. These heads have been clipped and the long hair woven into girdles. I have heard people in Lima and in the States say that the long-haired heads are those of women and the short-haired ones of men. This is not so: both sexes wear their hair long in back, bobbed in front. When the hair appears uncut in front, the chances are the victim was not a Jívaro.

Far from exterminating themselves in these fratricidal raids, the Jívaros seem numerous. They live in scattered family groups and seldom concentrate in villages. Women are nearly always captured in the raids, and some women have lived in as many as ten or fifteen Jívaro subtribes. Polygamy is necessary as all women must have a husband and protector. In this respect they are kinder than we ourselves. If the headhunting rites were stopped, the tribes would lose interest in life, and eventually die out.

The reason Jívaro women follow at their *bravos'* heels, and usually carry the burdens, is not because the man is lazy, or that he is brutal and unkind, but so that his hands are free for handling weapons. His back is covered from attack either by spearmen or *iguanchis* (spirits). His big basket is carried on his back supported by a headband, so that his hands are free.

The bitter root soup comprising the *caapi* of the lower Amazon rivers in Brazil, called here *natema,* is also imbibed to make the sick strong again. In addition to headhunting rites, they use this same *haya huasca* (like the Campas) for provoking mystical visions, and often drink far into the night. Such visions last as long as two days and nights. *Natema* is taken during the ceremony at the "Dream House," presided over by the Arutumas, or Old Ones. Here the "Boa Brother:" spirit friend of the *brujo* and the tribesman comes and speaks wisdom.

Sick and dying Aguarunas are usually quarantined in a "sick house" out in the jungle. Amazingly, the Aguarunas are dead set against adultery, which must be penalized by pinioning the woman to the ground by four spears driven through her legs and arms. This is strange, for while infidelity is thus punished, it is considered proper that the bride spend her first marriage night with her own father and her father-in-law. Couvade is not practiced.

As the days progressed, more Aguarunas came with red and yellow feathers dangling in small dusters from their ears, squatting tensely in our bamboo house: immense, inert men they were, built like miniature rhinoceroses. Some wore foot-long earrings of thousands of a red and green beetle, which gave a rippling sound whenever they moved; these are known as *wawo*. Other warriors wore necklaces of feathers from the oilbird, a rare cave-dweller which is much prized.

The women with them wore spirit belts, *kungus*, snail shells that clanked whenever they moved. While the women were finely built, these men were the strongest human beings I had ever seen in my entire life.

All of the Jívaro tribes[2] have different dialects, distinguished by slight variations in the pronunciation of some of the words. Other words and especially names are identical. The Chulla Chagin or Sacha Runa spirit of the Huambiza, is the same for the Aguaruna. It is the "One-Footed Forest Devil," having one large clubfoot, and a smaller one which is hidden under leaves when walking. Supay is a universal Jívaro water devil whose floods, when it becomes angry, cause destruction in the *chacaras*. Again, the Sacha Mama is the big mythical serpent whose body sprouts ferns, trees and mosses, and which will not move unless stuck with a knife or spear.

Living among these Aguarunas was fascinating, but we were slowly starving. Every time I left the clearing to hunt, I was surrounded by spearmen and escorted back. Why they just didn't kill us and be done with it, I'll never know. Something had apparently happened to Guzman and the crew—perhaps they too were prisoners. One day a savage speared a jaguar which was swimming across the river, and I wanted to get its meat. The skin was stripped off, but the Indians would not let us have the meat, saying the tiger was an evil *brujo* whom the hunter had deliberately killed. They burned the tiger's body, thereby destroying forever that particular witch. The *brujo* himself had been killed a few

---

2. The Jívaros may number not six (as generally thought), but perhaps some twenty-five subgroups.

days before. The *brujos* of the Jívaros never live long—being nearly always murdered for one reason or another.

Inez happily discovered two dried-up ears of corn stuffed into the roof among some animal skulls; these food offerings we secretly boiled and ate. That same evening I shot an *agouti*, one of the large rodents. And so with the corn and this fifteen-pound rat, we really ate our fill for the first time in many a long day. This *agouti* tasted like goose; it had a thick rubbery skin which was too tough to masticate, but being fat, was strengthening.

An Indian woman brought Inez some ant larvae, which we ate with relish. Inez was wearing khaki boy's pants, heavy walking shoes and a cotton blue plaid shirt. She had lost fifteen pounds, I about thirty. One day a hunter came in with two monkeys which he had killed with his blowgun darts; their tails were tied together, and the carcasses conveniently slung about his shoulders. I joined the *bravo* in roasting the stomachs; the contents, partly predigested, were a Jívaro delicacy.

It was becoming difficult to sleep in the *hea*, as about twenty Aguarunas were now camping there with us. Magic spells were always being cast; all night long the Indians would wake up, grunt loudly, scout around outside, listen at the cracks of the wall intently, jabber at each other, while scouts came and went constantly. Curiously, a gaggle of wild geese with their wings clipped, acted as guards outside—for upon the approach of anyone they could always be counted upon to sound a warning, especially at night. For every guerrilla trick I knew, they knew ten. Day and night the Aguarunas were always restless, fearing attack by other headhunters.

An old *brujo* made endless spirit attacks against any such chance raiders who might be approaching. Jívaros long dead were buried in the dirt floor of our house, and others were entombed in canoes at a nearby "burial house." Quite often their spirits were questioned all night long.

Across the river were three *heas*, fortress houses about sixty feet long and twenty-five broad, built in an oval shape, thatched with green palm leaf. These were cleverly constructed of upright posts and canes so that it was possible to observe an enemy outside the fort, yet impossible for him to see inside. Purposely narrow wooden doors were strongly hinged by the use of "male and female joints" such as are used in China.

I befriended the *brujo* and learned that geographically the Jívaro nation is scattered over an immense jungle area of approximately 200,000 square miles. This is centered in the western half of the Oriente and in east Ecuador and north Peru. The region contains all the sub-tribes—some of which are small, while others are very large. The Jívaros do not have a head chief, nor do the subtribes. The Indians are individualists. Being ever jealous of their freedoms, only the elders of the house families are given a semblance of authority. And indirectly the *brujos*, of course, through religious prestige and their knowledge of medicines.

We saw that Jívaro canoes, usually of red cedar, are made by hollowing out whole logs. The means are fire and stone axes. The fine surface polishing is accomplished by wet sand and using stones as files. These canoes are beautiful, having elegant lines, curved bows and sterns with thin-shelled skins of a half to one inch in thickness. No woodworker in Iquitos has ever been able to match the Jívaro work for either water-worthiness or beauty.

One day I foolishly quarreled with an Indian over not getting food for us, or allowing me to hunt in the jungle. Guzman while pow-wowing with this fellow had said the man would feed us, should he be delayed. The Jívaro became furious, shaking his spear in my face and shouting like a crazy person. Alarmed, I went into the hut and got my .45. All that night Inez and I stood watches. The Aguaruna openly loaded his musket and tested the hammer several times. He posted other Indians around the house to keep watch on us. That night we climbed into the bamboo-floored upper story, which was open on the front, but had three rooms all around it. The watching Indians signaled by bird calls. Unfortunately for the plan, they used the calls of day birds, which warned us in time.

The warrior climbed into the upper story and took one of the three rooms, and we were separated from him only by a flimsy cane wall. Inez took my bed of bamboos, while I quietly switched over to her hammock. In this way the Indians did not know we had changed positions, and they watched the bamboo shelf where she lay huddled as if asleep.

Three times that night the Aguaruna approached silently, stood like a shadow in the doorway only fifteen feet away from us, but each time he silently withdrew. It was like a shadow show. His gun was always in his hands. Had he raised it toward Inez, I would have been compelled to shoot him dead before he could pull the trigger. This would have been practical since my .45 was aimed right through the back of the hammock in which I lay. Each time he put in an appearance, and my finger closed over the trigger, he was apparently, somehow incredibly, warned by the scouts outside that one of us had stirred and was possibly awake. Our situation could not go on forever; sooner or later, one of these nights, I would fall asleep.

ꜩ XXII. ꜩ

The Cities and the Gold
of El Dorado

*A*FTER an absence of eight days, Guzman arrived wild-eyed at noon. He was starving and all but done in. His dugout had capsized, dumping all the gear and food into the Cenepa. One of the crew was drowned. The others finally managed to salvage the gasoline drum and the dugout, and they continued up the Cenepa, and eventually reached Guzman's *brujo* friend. This Jívaro insisted on making medicine so that we could combat the bad spirits of the Tacu Runa (Keepers of the Waters). He also made ghost spears and cast them against the spirits of all our possible enemies among the Aguarunas. Above all, drum messages were pounded out that Guzman and I, together with Inez and the tame Aguarunas, were headed up the river under his own spirit protection. It was a normal practice for all travelers to move under the guidance of a *brujo* who was responsible to the other Indians.

Guzman didn't like the looks of the Aguarunas here, and so we boarded immediately and started upstream once more (November 20th). Ten minutes later giant *tundui* drums began throbbing out of the tangle on both banks. These are very large hollowed logs having a three-foot diameter, and square holes cut into them like rows of pigeon cotes. Guzman brought out nine grizzly little heads which his friend had traded to him, museum pieces which he knew would bring a good price. He also had a large calabash of gold dust and nuggets—weighing some three pounds. The Gualaquiza, he said, became angry when questioned about the source. That direction, the northwest, fit in very nicely with Zamora, one of the cities of El Dorado. Later I would try to reach it myself....

We moved forward steadily with the current. In spite of our weakness, Guzman and I paddled with the Indians, while Inez steered the big motor.

The Golden Serpent now bent from west to south, and was less than a hundred yards in width, narrowing down in the *pongos* to only a hundred and fifty feet. The current was faster than before, and the surface crawling with whirlpools. Whenever a whirler snatched out at us, Guzman would dive for the helm, cut the powerful motor, and drift backwards with the current, and then try the opposite side. This *patróne* was absolutely fearless, and skillful beyond words. At nightfall we pitched camp on a sandy *playa*. Our first job was to patch our rotten old canoe which was becoming badly honeycombed by borers. At the foot of a cliff close by, I found good samples of iron ore. The webbed tracks of *ronsoco* were everywhere, but the three Indians and I had no luck hunting them, though we tried for hours to whistle them close. That night the Indians were so hungry they took to sucking on pebbles placed under their tongues.

As soon as we could see next morning we were off. Between the *pongos*, and on the edges of the jungle, were white sand *playas*—broken here and there by tributaries flowing off the Andes and into the right bank of the Marañón. A piece of hard coal was found, and deposits of lime and salt. We passed a clear river coming in on the west bank, a deep, quiet river two hundred feet across its mouth; we camped on a *playa* just opposite. Hardly had we settled down to a meal of boiled boa—the kind known as *aboma*—when a dugout filled with fourteen Aguarunas, holding their long *pucunas* upright like a rowing crew, drifted slowly out of this stream. After looking us over, absolutely silent and motionless, they continued without the flicker of an eyelash, to drift down the main river. When they disappeared around a bend, Guzman spoke:

"I think we dare go a little farther." His eyes glistened, for all this while he was prospecting with his pan, wading deep into the river to scoop up gravel from the bottom of the roaring, wildly swirling waters. Everywhere he found colors, but nothing rich enough to warrant panning for profit, for if we did so, Indians would gather in the night—and that would be that.

Next day at a portage, Inez and I went ahead hoping to find game and walked knee-deep through two great petroleum seepages. All about lay banks of gravel and sand; out of them flowed oil. We kept to the river on a south bearing. For hundreds of yards, *cochas*, rock beds and puddles along the banks were golden yellow with the petroleum; the place stank. Our clothes up to our hips dripped with oil. All this region was disputed territory, claimed by Peru in the south, Ecuador in the north. Therefore though the seepage indicated the presence of an oil basin, no concession could be obtained from either Ecuador or Peru for exploitation, until these countries decided who owned it. A few miles south of the oil seepages we came upon nine big oblong Indian *heas* on an open flat beyond the right bank. The place was called Yamicat. The Indians all fled. We camped on a *playa*. Suddenly a single warrior strode out of the jungle, walked straight up to Inez and handed her three shrunken parrots about four inches long. Shrinking parrots was an art which he said was known to only one old Aguaruna. Later he went away and in the night returned with an entire human body, shrunk to a mere eighteen inches in length. In order to get this priceless object for science, she would have to come as his woman. It was a sad day for science, for this she refused to do.

Finally the Aguarunas returned, all painted and befeathered, and this time they held their ground. Due to our protection under Guzman's *brujo* on the Cenepa, whose drum messages were being relayed ahead of us, we were safe from these Indians as long as we didn't start trouble over food or something else. We found that in one of the *heas* were two warriors who had recently been mauled by a jaguar. Still clinging to them was the cat's smell, a strong glandular excretion given off when it is excited. By making a great fuss over them, we gained the friendship of the whole village.

Beyond Yamicat, the loyal Guzman would not go—fearing that the Cenepa *brujo's* prestige could not extend much further. Since Inez and I refused to return downriver with him, I paid him off. In addition to the agreed price, I also gave him a well-earned bonus. We shook hands and departed friends. At dawn he and the three tame Indians cast off, and started the long drift back to Borja, some 150 miles in the northeast. Later in Quito I learned from a letter mailed in Iquitos that before reaching the Cenepa, they were attacked and the three Indians killed. Guzman, however, veteran Indian fighter and bushman that he was, escaped through the jungle—making his way overland and eventually crossing the Cerros Campanquiz and arriving at Borja.

Inez and I stayed at Yamicat a few days, while I explored in the hot jungle, which was alive with birds, for the ruins of ancient Jaen de Bracamoras. A small Jívaro boy spent his days creeping about the *hea* into which we had moved, with a blowgun, shooting bats. Apparently he had appointed himself Inez's guardian and servant. During my periods of absence she mended holes in our hammock nets, patched clothing and did whatever she could to keep our small amount of gear in order. She was also drawing a map of the river above Borja. She had picked up about 400 words of the cryptic Jívaro, which were listed on several sheets of paper. My reluctance at Valencia and von Wolfenegg's fears were apparently not justified. By taking a real interest in their wives and children, Inez gained their confidence. They realized we would do them no injury. It was due to Inez's tact that the small boy was feeding us from the family *chacara*. I finally decided I could not find the ruin; I spread my map on the floor and studied it. It certainly showed them to be nearby, somewhere. I laid my compass on the map and worked out various azimuths.

One day a dugout overturned in the river, and an Aguaruna was killed by *zúngaros*. This brave's friends, in red body paint with white bars, immediately set out to hunt down a Jívaro whose medicine they believed responsible, for he had once made off with the dead man's sister and bad blood existed between them.

On this same day five *loro* snakes were killed in the clearing. They were six feet long, pale green and deadly poisonous. A toad was found in the belly of the first snake that was killed, and this the Indians declared was a bad omen. Gathering together their women and children, the Indians left the *heas* and departed upstream in their dugouts. We were now alone and at least a hundred miles from the nearest Peruvian outpost. Although there was now a great sense of loneliness, we had all the *chacara*s available for food.

On the fifth day, the 27th of November, a hunting party armed with blowguns floated down the big yellow river, paddles flashing, red paint and feathers glistening under the hot sun. In two canoes there were twelve Aguaruna warriors. Inez talked to them, with me chipping in occasionally, and seeing us without rifles they became friendly and came ashore. Guzman had been wrong—these savages had heard the drums and were willing to accept us. We engaged the two dugouts with all twelve paddlers; and that same afternoon reached the narrow mouth of a river called the Chiriaca. This surprisingly came in on the left bank, and must be the last important western tributary of the Amazon. Here in a hut I left Inez. I took one of the canoes and my machete and recrossed the Amazon. A mile from the mouth of the Chiriaca, on the opposite west side of the Amazon, among a group of low hills, I found only a few hundred yards beyond the river bank, and back in the jungle, several stone walls, marking the old site of the Conquistadores' Jaen de Bracamoras!—the fourth city in all probability so far located in lost El Dorado. I had now seen three of the city sites with my own eyes—and had a detailed map to Legroño west of the Santiago. The place was in a very high jungle, many of the massive trees having enormous blossoms. With considerable machete work I uncovered several sites having square or rectangular stone foundations. These were all that remained of the old Spanish houses of the city. Apparently the walls and roofs had been constructed of logs and thatch, which over the centuries had rotted away. Due to the large numbers of Spanish troops quartered in El Dorado, it apparently had not been considered necessary to erect stone fortifications against Indian attack. Symmetrical ditches following the contour of a hillside indicated that water had been brought into the city, probably not only for drinking and cooking, but for washing the concentrates for gold after these had been brought in from the widely scattered diggings.

Obviously the Aguarunas sometimes mined here. I began prospecting and found that nearby and in very deep and extensive gravel beds, reaching from the river bank about a mile west of it, gold lay in ripples on top of the sand trapped in the gravel deposits. I had no sooner seen this, when eight of my own Aguarunas came up. They themselves got busy with the large monkey-skin pans we had been seeing in the *heas*. They showed how they mined these vast deposits for the gold exchanged to traders for firearms. In several places they stripped off an overburden of gravel to get down to bedrock, and here they scooped up the heavy concentrates and washed them in the pans. The advantage of large skin pans over small metal ones is that more dirt is handled and that all of the fine gold adheres to the chamois-like skin instead of most of it washing out over the lip of the pan. According to what they said, seventy-eight Indians worked this mine, and yet they had hardly scratched the possibilities.

Although trees were growing thickly all over the deposit, which undoubtedly had been laid down by the Marañón at floodtimes, I saw long ridges of debris stacked in parallel lines, showing probably where the ancients had piled the tailings in order to get down to the gold-bearing levels. This location must have been one of the major sources of the Inca gold.

With the Indians I returned through the thick jungle to cross the yellow flood of the two-hundred-foot-wide Marañón. Inez as usual was surrounded by an admiring circle of Indian women and children. I saw that a basket of yuca had been brought for our use. The hut was only a temporary hunting shack having bamboo walls and a pole and thatch roof. A pile of ashes in the center of the floor showed how the food was to be cooked. It all seemed incredibly domestic. There was Inez in her pants and checkered shirt entertaining a crowd of painted Indians. Our hammocks were slung, and all that was lacking was a rug and a cat. And to think that seventy-eight of the largest, bloodiest and least known of all the Jívaros were our neighbors, all of then in loin-clouts and wearing paint and feathers. I could see that the real conquest of El Dorado had not been due to me at all, but to the efforts of one thin girl with a winning smile and a knack for the Jívaro dialect. Nevertheless I was damned pleased with myself; in the pockets of my khaki pants were two pounds of gold dust and nuggets.

Next day the mining continued, and working at Jaen de Bracamoras were seventy-eight Aguarunas.

On the second night, I traded every spare piece of equipment we could afford (razor, bullets, clothing) and all my trade tobacco, for this gold and other gold which had been mined but not yet sent out to a trader. There were five bamboo sections loaded with it! These bamboos were a foot long and three inches in diameter. The woody partition natural to them formed the bottom, and a long wooden plug furnished the means for sealing them. Each bamboo weighed some ten pounds, and all five of them totaled fifty pounds. Although a few nuggets were in the bamboos, most of the gold was of a dusty fineness. If the other six sites prove to be located on deposits as vast and rich as this of Jaen de Bracamoras, then indeed the secret sources of the major part of the old Spanish gold will have been revealed.

Now to get the boodle out of the jungle and across the high Andes to civilization where it could be disposed of and we could go home.

A plan gradually unfolded. It was obvious, after questioning the savages, that due to swift water we could travel by dugout no farther up the Golden Serpent. I wanted to go in this direction as my map showed that Bajadeloro must be there. We decided therefore to go overland along the river ways and attempt walking out of the basin. Thus we could eventually cross the Andes somewhere over into north Peru or south Ecuador. Some of the peaks lying above the jungle in the west were over 20,000 feet high, their summits covered with sheets of snow and cliffs of ice.

New Aguarunas from the upper Chiriaca, which drains out of great highlands in the east (out in the Amazon jungle proper) and up which their *brujos* were not permitted to go, flitted silently into our clearing to stare at us in disbelief. A pigtailed witchman in a blue loincloth striped brown and white told us that all this country east of the Marañón is forbidden Aguaruna country, which means that this inland Jívaro range must be approximately double that assigned to them in the Oriente *north* of the Marañón. The Aguarunas said that Jívaros exist all the way east to the west bank of the Huallaga itself—hundreds of miles of unexplored highlands and flat jungles. No explorer of course has ever penetrated it, let alone crossed that region. The Peruvian Air Force, whose planes have flown over some of the region, say that the Cordilleras are jungle-covered though they must go up to 3,000 feet. In this new Jívaro country you could place all the New England states and still have room left over. What lies out there no man can say.

One purple-painted, parrot-befeathered *bravo* strode in, parked his four-foot wood and stone war axe, and surprisingly handed Inez two baby ocelots. These beautifully spotted meat-eaters were the last thing I wanted, even if they only weighed a few pounds each, but not so Inez: she gave the warrior a silk scarf which he tied around his head. He then grabbed her by the arm and started off for the jungle. Giant Jívaros in green paint were standing all around the clearing and I dared not shoot. Instead I began beating my chest Aguaruna fashion and laid hold of her other arm, and between us we hauled back and forth. Finally the *bravo* conceived the idea that she was my property, and left in disgust. She kept the ocelots and there wasn't much I could do about it.

Inez had befriended a few Jívaros and they brought us to their *hea* about a mile upriver on the Chiriaca. It was necessary for them to get supplies, some dried skins for trading, and their weapons. Apparently the Indians needed only this mild excuse to send them in the direction of the nearest trader so that they could negotiate trade advantageous to themselves. Sometimes the traders cause trouble by refusing a fair price for Indian products and they felt that in our company a better deal could be made. Here we were confined, due to storms, for two days. Perhaps five hundred red-painted savages (with black pointed teeth) visited us during that time, and not one of them said a word—just squatted and stared. The officials in Iquitos, Barranca and Borja had said the Aguaruna tribe west of the Pongo de Menseriche could not number more than three hundred individuals. I do not think that five thousand is too high an estimate. These people, as we had seen, are not bloody savages at all if treated decently.

We left on December 2nd with four wild, young carriers on a secret Jívaro trade and raiding trail, heading south. Apparently they knew of a trader called Don Pomere. We squeezed our way through very thick vegetation, stumbling over roots and sliding along in the mud, for twenty miles or more—from 5:30 A.M. to 6:45 P.M. The ocelots rode like kings on one of the Indian's packs. The narrow thread took us over and down steep ridges packed tight with high palm-filled and vine-cinched jungle—for thirteen hours, and not a single rest period. Though they were heavily loaded with their own trade stuff, our remaining gear, food and the gold, we could hardly keep up with these young braves, none of them over eighteen.

Muddy, torn, and insect-gnawed, and utterly dog-tired, we finally camped on the stony bank of a small stream far east of the Alto Marañón. Inez was muddy, but she was wiry and made out surprisingly well.

Several Jívaros came slinking in, having left the Marañón's banks where they said only one hundred and fifty families now remained between Borja and Bella Vista. The reason they were leaving the river was that soldiers were going up the Santiago, and others were trying to get up the Marañón from Pinglo. Signal drums had told them of recent battles on both rivers.

Two women gave us a papaya from a nearby *chacara*, but their men seemed struck dumb that we should be here. I finally decided that the main reason we had not been killed was that we were not *patrónes*, missionaries, soldiers or traders. The drums had informed the tribe that we did not molest women, and that we killed no Indians or took slaves, and that we always bartered for food and did not pillage the *chacaras*. Two immense and greasy yellow-painted devils stomped over to our fire and without any preliminaries whatsoever, began to feel Inez all over, yelling at each other as they made various interesting discoveries. Instead of reaching for my gun—which would certainly have meant the end of everything—for some strange reason I could only sit on the ground and howl with joy.

"I never interfere with native customs," I finally managed to answer her look of astonishment.

All at once the inevitable happened. I heard a howl out of one of the bucks, and a businesslike "Stop that!" from Inez. With a large stick she was waylaying the two giant *bravos*, who, in astonishment, finally backed off and began nursing their heads.

Next day we waded across a deep meandering stream, eighteen different times. Once in thick jungle a pair of *cucupaccha* birds were flushed—the Jívaros' Spirit-Fountain birds. At a *hea*, several *bravos* and women fled at our approach, but soon they filtered back, and no trouble came out of their fright as the carriers said we were their friends. Apparently these Indians were our passport just as Guzman's Cenepa *brujo* had been before. Next day, still on the raiding trail known to them, we came to a wide river called by one carrier the Shushunga, and followed its jungly bank into a deep canyon. Forests of fern trees (all covered with red ants) alternated now with groves of hardwoods. Pig tracks were plentiful. Monkeys swung through the trees and parrots were uncommonly numerous.

At the upper end of this canyon we got a very bad start, when only a few feet away we suddenly came upon a band of Indians crouched in some bushes. They were extraordinarily stocky and heavy, armed with muskets and .44 Winchesters. Except for purple loincloths and red paint and feathers, they were naked. These Indians were not laying an ambush, they were hunting. They spoke not a word, nor did they move a muscle. Had I not noticed a gleam of bright red paint amongst the green leaves, we would have passed them that close and not known it.

Thank God the drums were still talking—and that we had made no enemy behind us.

We left the canyon and walked across white limestone sands that must once have been an ancient ocean floor. Each night after that, we camped in the thickest jungle we could find. The four Jívaros stood guard in alternate shifts. The reason for this was that we were now far south of their own stamping grounds, and were unknown among the Indians. We were still in Aguaruna country, and they knew the trail all the way out to their trader Pomere's, but that was no sure guarantee that all of us would not lose our heads.

At a very large, oval-shaped Aguaruna *hea,* a young *winchiyu* (*brujo*) arrived just in the dusk of the evening as we were making camp. He was dressed in a red-dyed grass skirt and wore a grass headdress. He explained he had been making *jambi* which is similar to *ampi* (curare). As he talked we realized there was little difference in his rites from those practiced by the *winchiyu brujo* we had picked up one afternoon on the Marañón's right bank forty miles below Borja. The "soul plants" he had used were the same, except that he mentioned a new one (*yura-caspi*). That night the *brujo* dipped the blowgun darts of our men into his pot of *jambi*, ringing our fire with them so they would dry. The ten-inch darts turned a bright red.

To kill, all that now remained was for the hunters to twist a bit of cotton around the butt of one of those darts, only some eighth of an inch in diameter, and fit it into the bone mouthpiece at the breech, and then hold the *pucuna* with the hands close up to the mouth, and finally give a big puff. The blowguns of our party were about nine feet in length, and weighed from eight to ten pounds. Each was made from two pieces of split *chonta* into which the bore groove had been scooped before placing together. The two strips had then been fitted tightly together, bound, shaped, tapered, gummed, and finally waxed for waterproofing—all of which made the gun a dark brownish black. The bore is ingeniously polished by a wet cord made rough with quartz sand. The finished bore is very fine. The Aguaruna killing range, as they had demonstrated on birds and monkeys, is up to two hundred feet. When using these blowguns, the Jívaro hunters could kill several pigs out of a herd, and always get them with the *jambi* poison. Although the animals run away, they are tracked down. With a musket or rifle the Indian may get only a single animal before the herd takes alarm and runs away to safety. Of the thousands of pig skins filtering through the traders into Iquitos, 90 percent are killed with blowguns.

On the day following, we again made several river crossings, and also waded through bearded tree-filled swamps which hummed with clouds of strikers; snakes were everywhere, but few crocodiles. That last meant we were steadily climbing up the edge of the Amazon basin. At nightfall we found a leaf shack, and bundled gratefully in out of a cold rain. Inez was muddy and wet, and looked as bedraggled as the pair of ocelots. On the following day the downpour didn't stop until 1 P.M., at which time we left our shelter, and began climbing a steep, muddy mountain trail. A swarm of little black blood gnats descended, nearly driving us crazy. We were cold; and the wind rattled in the palms overhead. We were so hungry that we finally cut down one of the palms, and ate some of the bitter-tasting heart, a whitish green bundle of leaves. We clambered painfully through the mud up to a ridge, and here the Indians finally camped on a high rim. The jungle looked like a wind-wrecked junkshop and was as thick as ever. Even the birds were quiet. Again rain fell, and this time, due to lack of dry wood, we had no fire over which to huddle and keep warm. Before nightfall the carriers had pointed out human tracks, which they believed to be those of Gualaquiza headhunters from the Zamora basin. Fearing trouble, we dared not light a fire of wet wood which would smoke. We stood watch all night.

With daylight breaking we decamped and sloshed through tremendously high dripping jungles to the east bank of the Golden Serpent, the first time we had seen it since leaving the *hea* on the Chiriaca. The water was high and yellow with mud, and the Indians wouldn't chance swimming it. Rain fell all that day as we cut our way along the east bank. The four young braves trudged along heads down, tiring under their packs. At midafternoon death was very close, but I did not know it. I just missed stepping squarely on a tremendous snake, a *macanchi*, one of the local varieties of bushmaster called by the Aguarunas *nocompo*.

I stopped dead in my tracks as its head sprang back. It was a beastly thing (as we saw later), nine feet long, four inches in diameter, brown and mottled with black, with a thin neck and a broad flat diamond-shaped head.

The toe of my right shoe already touched one of the thick, moving folds in the great coil which reached a third of the way up to my knee.

There was no leaping over the snake, or running away. The shock of my inevitable fate was so great and so instantaneous that I felt no fear, only an odd detachment from my body standing there—waiting.

Presently I was aware that someone was chopping at a tree. I raised my eyes and saw that one of the Jívaros had my machete—he had been using it to clear a trail—and was furiously hacking away at a sapling some four inches in diameter and a dozen feet high. When it fell, he picked it up by the thin end and approached me to within a distance of fifteen feet. The next thing I knew he had slammed the small tree down on the great snake; and at the same instant somebody behind placed his hands on my back and gave me a shove. I picked myself up and saw that it was Inez. The snake was slowly uncoiling, for its back was broken, and the Indian brought down his tree again, again, again....

Once more we started out on a line about five hundred yards away from the Marañón and parallel to it. An hour later we stumbled on an Aguaruna's *hea*. In relating the narrow escape we had had from the *nocompo* snake, the big red-painted Indian here became friendly. He fed us with a monkey stew, and then told us we must cross over the Marañón to the west bank, as a shortcut existed to the trader's. This Indian carried his dugout down to the bank and ferried us across one at a time. I gave him six .45 cartridges, one in payment for each of us. The four carriers soon located the new trail according to directions given them by the Aguaruna. In a drizzling rain we struck into a narrow Indian trail lasting four sweating hours, and going uphill. The flowers on the ground became more plentiful, which meant the mass of trees, palms and fern trees must be thinning out, and ground orchids were everywhere. (Many wild jungle orchids, incidentally, have a wonderful odor.) We moved back several miles inland from the river, keeping to a fairly consistent southwest compass azimuth of 225°. And though we could not see it below us, we could hear a great roaring of waters, and by nightfall at last came to Don Pomere's, which was a bamboo bush-hut on the side of a steep jungle-smothered hill. Pomere proved to be an old gray-headed Negro trader, with an Aguaruna wife. We had at last reached the edge of civilization. After shaking hands with us, hugely grinning, Don Pomere greeted the four young Jívaros whom he knew from trading once before. For their bundles of deer hides he offered canvas pouches of lead shot and powder. Apparently they had left their guns behind on the Chiriaca as they were without the means for firing them. After much customary haggling they finally accepted. The pig hides, which were not so heavy, they would carry beyond to a place called Yunga where a better price could be obtained. The trading over, to everybody's huge satisfaction, I did a little trading on my own.

I bought a brace of guinea-pigs. The trader had several—for, multiplying rapidly and easy to feed, they are kept as food all through the Andes—and along with meat we ate the kind old man's mashed *plátanos*. Pomere told us that once a month pack mules from Yunga, in the high Andean Cordillera above, are driven down to him where they are loaded with hides and *caucho* which he and his sons trade from the Aguarunas. There were no mules at the moment and we would have to walk. From Yunga a *camellóne* (trail) led west across the Andes to north Peru and the Pacific Ocean!

Dawn of December 9th saw us leaving Pomere's. He would not take money for sheltering us so we gave him a gift of Peruvian cigarettes, after buying four packs from his wife. To say he was surprised would be putting it mildly. And then we and the four Indians climbed on a wet trail, through dripping jungles for three sweltering hours.

And then suddenly we walked out of the jungle.... Inez and I stood in the open, muddy and sweating in our khaki pants and tattered shirts. With all that direct sunlight on us, we looked like hell. But our joy was tremendous; we stood at the western edge of the Amazon rain-forest. The first Andean granite jutted close above. Just before us a few fly-bitten, long-horned Spanish cattle blinked dully. From Inez I expected some profound verbal expression of gratitude and wonder at reaching this jungle-free country. She opened her mouth and yelled— "Beefsteak!"

Three hours more on the trail, through a weird, twisted, pygmy-sized bush of a jungle brought us to the approaches of Yunga. It was a Quechua colony of a score of thatched bush houses inhabited by "cattlemen," who wore leather pants, red serapes, enormous straw sombreros with silver buckles, and carried sheathed machetes. They went barefooted even when they rode ponies.

Our carriers, naked but for their loincloths, feathers and paint (which they put on just outside of town), blinked in astonishment at these Quechuas; and the "savages" were in turn gazed upon in awe by the men of civilization. Our Jívaros spoke only two Spanish words: "*Adios! Cabeza!*" which somehow amused me—"Goodbye! Head!"

On the outskirts of the little settlement Inez stepped over a pink-and-white-banded coral snake, some five feet long. She wouldn't believe it was dangerous until I smashed its head with my snake stick, and two little streams of a golden fluid spurted from the fangs.

Straddling two worlds, the jungle and the open Cordillera, we slept, dead-tired. We were guests in the high stilted house of one Señor Flores. Below was an oxen-driven *trapiche* (sugar mill). The loft was the sleeping quarters for eight of Flores' offspring and ourselves. The ocelots slept in a basket with a wooden lid which banged up and down all night. A boy had fed them with a crow and apparently they were not only eating but mauling the crow as well.

All the scrub jungle in this region was fascinating, wild, and oddly enough unexplored, lying between the massive Amazon jungle proper and the high, open, windswept Andean grasslands, or *páramos*. It was not unlike that dry, brittle, pestiferous region of the Brazilian *sertão*. Flores warned that beyond the low jungle lay a wide belt of desert, and only beyond that, and much higher in the mountains, did the grass start.

My search was not yet over. According to my El Dorado map, Bajadeloro, one of the ancient seven cities, lay at the headwaters of a river west of us. There was no indication that the river flowed through a desert. I could not have been more surprised, for I had thought all of El Dorado lay entirely within the Amazon forest region itself. When Flores was not around, I spread the map on the floor of the loft and took my compass bearings. There could be no mistake! That river and Bajadeloro must certainly lie in the desert spoken of by our host. That was the plan, then, to go in search of that lost city—the fifth.

After a couple of days at Flores', we hired two derelict saddle horses, a pack mule, and a Quechua guide. The four Jívaros said goodbye and left for their Aguaruna jungles; with them went not only powder and shot but four new sheath knives (which I obtained from the trader)— just what their hearts desired. It was December 12th, we decided to make Quito, in Ecuador, by Christmas. We still had six hundred miles to go. The plan was to leave Yunga for Bella Vista, a town lying high in the Cordillera and having road connection across the mountains with the coast. Before reaching Bella Vista, and while still in the desert belt, we would turn right (north) up the river marked on my map and try to find Bajadeloro. After that we would retrace our way back down the river and continue west to Bella Vista. We left Flores' at 4 A.M., first riding five hours through the scrub. The ocelots rode on top of the packs on the mule, their sharp claws digging into the cloth covers. Condors perched in the low trees. The tracks of tapir, a white and a red deer, bear, fox, four kinds of monkeys, *huangana* and *sajino*, puma, jaguar, and ocelot—lay everywhere on the sandy ground. Flocks of green parrots burst out of the thickets.

We broke out of the jungle and into the open. Before us stretched a brown sandy desert with giant cactus rising fifty feet toward the blazing sun. The temperature was 123 degrees, our skins burned and wind-blown dust clogged our throats. We had no sooner started into the desert than we struck the edge of a locust plague, billions of three-inch red hoppers, and not a blade of the poorest desert grass was left. As they whirred from under the hoofs of the three animals, it was all we could do to keep our saddles—for the two old nags started to buck. We finally calmed them down, and started through once more. For two hours we rode through locusts.

I steered west by compass until we hit the low gravel bank of a shallow desert river which our guide called the Chinchipe. This could only be the river marked on the treasure map. From our high vantage point we could see off to the left that this river poured into the Marañón about fifteen miles southeast, on a compass bearing of 120°. A desolation of desert edged the Marañón now (though the jungle's margin could be seen far to the east), and it lay broadly yellow and shallow in a deep and wide stone-rimmed valley. Just in front of us, an old Indian on a balsa raft put out from the opposite bank to fetch us, and after our animals had swum across the 200-yard wide Chinchipe, and we had crossed by raft, our Quechua guide was dismissed and sent back to Yunga. He would make it all right, for he was riding a good mule. Inez fed her cats with fish obtained from the old Indian. This Indian lived in a bamboo-thatched hut, which I marked well in my mind, as we must return to it.

Alone now, and according to the Yunga plan, Inez and I left the ferryman, turned right along the west bank, and, heading north, followed the Chinchipe across the desert upstream toward its headwaters. For the next few days we plodded along, sometimes leading the horses and mule, sparing them when we could. At night we would camp, building a fire out of dead cactus limbs. We had obtained a supply of *camotes*, a kind of sweet potato in Yunga, and, baked, these were our staff of life. Even so we nearly starved. I had bought two half-sacks of corn in Yunga, but this was used to keep the animals going. Inez wore a straw hat obtained in Yunga, as the sun was blazing hot. Our pants and shirts stuck to us. At night we would wash at the river bank. Except for blood gnats there were few real insect pests. Scorpions and desert spiders were in plenty, but were welcome after what we had been through in the lower country. Although Inez was very thin, she seemed strong, and I noticed the bug bites on her arms and face had disappeared. She was deeply tanned. While she fed the cats (who rode on the mule pack) with a dead fish found on the bank, I shot a bird.

Near the source high in the hills, we found the site of ancient Bajadeloro—the fifth city of El Dorado. From the desert near the river bank we saw heaps of bare stones lying on hills a great distance off. The map had been correct! It was no great accomplishment to detect this mining operation. However, the Arymaya about were unaware that the ridges of gravel and rock were the tailings left over from the old Spanish miners. All that remained to show the former occupation were tumbled walls of irregular stones, the adobe mortar long melted. Apparently the roofs here had been constructed of poles and thatched with bundles of *páramos* grass, a custom prevailing unchanged today. Only to the practiced eye, however, could a mining operation in the past have been detected, for unless you were looking for an old mine, the place might be mistaken for a natural erosion.

Somewhere, about 15° to right of north, deep in the Amazon jungle again, must lie ancient Zamora on the headhunters' Rio Zamora. Indians told us that a Jívaro town called Zamora existed west of the Condor range.

We had now located six of the seven cities of El Dorado—only San Reys remained unknown. In my notebook I listed them:

Santiago de las Montaños (Mouth of Santiago, west bank).

San Francisco de Borja (South bank of Marañón at Borja).

Legroño (Midwest side Rio Santiago, foot of Condors, nine stone troughs).

San Reys (Location not found).

Jaen de Bracamoras (Near Yamicat, walls and old diggings).

Bajadeloro (Headwaters Chinchipe).

Zamora (In Gualaquiza Jívaro country, Rio Zamora, west of Condor Range).

That no gold was found at Bajadeloro was no disappointment. My main objective had been gained: El Dorado was found! And no small amount of the lost gold of El Dorado was already packed on our horses and the mule. Now we must get out if we could.

In retracing our steps back to the ford we had of course to cross over the same desert again along the Chinchipe's west bank. The two horses died on the first day. Old gall sores on the mule's back had to be treated with salt and water before we could continue. Desert ticks clung to the poor animal, ticks fat with its blood, which we picked off like grapes. The mule stumbled so often, that I took the approximately fifty pounds of gold on my own back, but two days later I could no longer walk, and buried two of the ten-pound bamboos in the top of a knoll under a very large candle-cactus. That night I killed a small rock boa which I boiled and we ate.

Next day, eight days from the time we had left and departed with the Yunga guide, we made the hut of the old Indian at the ford, and knew we had a good chance of reaching Bella Vista. The Indian fed us fish and we slept in safety and without fear of a jaguar killing the mule. Out in the desert they had prowled close nearly every night. That night, however, the mule died.

I was suddenly desperate, for the plan was in jeopardy. I offered the Indian two handfuls of gold for his donkey, and he laughed at me. Gold, of course, is a regular medium of exchange in the Andes. When I increased it to four, he led the donkey up. I loaded on the bamboos. Due to there having originally been five rather large and heavy bamboos (on the Chiriaca), and two of these now buried in the desert, the three remaining ones could not be properly packed on the donkey. As a result I took a few of the smaller bamboos comprising the walls of the hut, and repacked all the remaining gold—about thirty pounds now—into six lengths of bamboo plugged at the bottom by the natural partition. In that way the bamboos could be loaded evenly on the pack animal— three to a side, each side weighing fifteen pounds. The bamboos and our remaining gear were so heavy together that the old, insect-chewed beast could hardly keep its feet. Again we started into the desert—this time due west of the Chinchipe.

There was nothing but sand—oceans of fine brown sand—and strange cactus thickets, cactus that sprouted from a long thick stem and seemed like snakes twisting in long branches some twenty feet in length, and all covered with white spines. By early afternoon we became tangled in one of these thickets, which rose up over us to a height of from twenty to thirty feet, and in backtracking we lost half a day. I kept high on the ridges, out of the gullies, after that, moving always west by the compass. On the second morning I changed course to the left on a bearing of 220°. We found no water, and the Indian's old calabash jug was empty. In a sack I was again carrying two of the bamboos (totaling ten pounds), the donkey four (totaling twenty pounds). Once in a damp gulch we saw the tracks of lion. Here I dug down for water, but hit hardpan at four feet—dry as a bone.

All this time Inez had been marching along like a trooper, her shirt sticking to her back, her shoes all run down at the heels. She was getting skinnier and had more bones showing than an old maid schoolmarm. Instead of me taking care of her, she was taking care of me, hanging Our hammocks from the cactus and building the fires. It was my job to collect bits of grass and brush for the mule as fodder. But whenever I looked at Inez, one thought took hold of my mind: that woman has plenty of guts, but brother-does she look beat up!

We stayed in the gulch that night, and in the moonlight while watching for the lion (for the donkey was braying and going crazy), I saw a movement among the cactus and quickly fired. Cautiously I approached, holding the .45 in readiness, and saw to my astonishment that I had killed one of the big white deer peculiar to the desert. We soon had a fire going of old cactus branches, and the meat broiling.

It was a bitter decision next day, but we abandoned an eight-inch tube of the gold in favor of a venison hindquarter. I have heard it said that one should never eat under such conditions, unless water is available. This is a lot of rot; we ate the liver raw, getting considerable moisture out of the meat. These white deer, incidentally, can exist without water holes. They are a desert animal and get their moisture out of their browsing, That morning we passed ant castles some ten feet high.

It was midmorning when a large ant-bear ambled by, and oddly enough it was not in a cactus thicket, but right out in the open. I judged the bear to be about sixty pounds in weight. It was covered with long, shaggy, yellow hair. At the moment Inez was walking behind the donkey, grimly prodding it along with a branch of cactus, and she was carrying the gun to relieve me of the weight.

There was no time to drop my load and get the gun too; I just dumped the bamboos and started hard after that bear. It ambled into a thicket and I thought it was lost, but a few minutes later while I was prowling around, I saw a movement high up and there it was climbing a thorny cactus tree. In a few minutes I had cleared a way and climbed after it. The bear moved back out on the end of a limb, and since I dared not cut the limb and drop it to the ground for fear it would get a way in the thicket, I crawled out after it, and slashed at its head with my machete. The blood gushed over me, and the bear screamed in pain, but a few moments later its grip loosened and it fell to the ground—dead.

I recovered the carcass and returned to Inez and the donkey. I tossed the bear up on the donkey's load. We continued on our way. An hour later, Inez pointed out the Marañón's headwaters, gleaming in a swampy valley of reeds and cactus, fed by a stringer heading, I knew, yet hundreds of miles due south in a high Andean *barranca*. Exposed to view was the drainage system of the entire eastern slopes of the Cordillera on the Peruvian segment. Hundreds of small tributaries would be carrying flakes of gold down into the river, which in turn brought the gold into the El Dorado region. Here it was deposited in gravel and sand, and here one day—after the disputed territory had been settled between Ecuador and Peru—mining operations on a large scale would once more be carried out.

Not long after, the poor donkey dropped in his tracks. The pack animal could not get up, and there it died, its head in the brown sand, moaning pitiably. We abandoned what was left of the deer haunch, and also the bear. I had no idea how wide this desert was, but decided to risk everything on one throw of the dice. I put all of the remaining five little bamboos of gold in my sack and we started out, the sweat pouring off my face, the shirt sticking to my back under the twenty-five-pound sack.

"You're crazy," cried Inez, "leave the gold and take the meat." She still had the cats, leading them now on a string leash.

I would have tried to get through the desert eastwards and reach the Marañón's swamp, but it lay all of forty miles away, with terrible dry gulches all the way as we could see. Inez handled the compass and we stayed on 220°, very close to southwest. All that day we walked (and the ocelots with us), and when night came the air felt so cool that we kept right on for twelve hours without stopping except to rest a few minutes. The ocelots gave out and I carried them, for Inez was near tears. An hour after dawn we stumbled out of a high thicket, and spread out before us was the town of Bella Vista—the La Merced of the northern slopes of the Cordillera....

After resting a while we started out again, and went in among the thirty-odd adobe houses strung around a bare plaza. I had a long-forgotten letter of introduction to a *patróne* here. A Peruvian missionary by the name of Rubio had given me the letter in Iquitos. We found Rubio's friend sick in an adobe house. He and his wife could not take us in, but the Señora's father owned a trading post on the plaza and here we were brought. In spite of the poor quarters and our exhaustion, we ate *chunta* (mutton stew and potatoes) on the plaza, and were elated. It was December 24th. We could not make Quito by Christmas but we would celebrate Christmas there anyway. We found that the empty storeroom faced the dusty square, fortunately unoccupied by anything but a pair of indifferent donkeys. I got the five eight-inch bamboos under ground, and we lay with the cats beside us on the stone floor and fell asleep.

About nine o'clock we wakened when a dog barked at the doorway, and we went out on the plaza. Several Peruvians and any number of Quechuas were about and they stared hard at us. Bella Vista, we soon learned, was indeed connected by a dirt road to the west coast. The village trader had no sooner gotten this out of his mouth, when the bimonthly *camión* (bus) rattled around the dusty plaza and pulled up in front of his store. I bought two small empty baskets with lids and soon had the five bamboos in their bottom, and covered over with corn which Inez bought in the market.

Surely the gods were kind.

At the American Consulate in Quito it was learned that the Peruvian and Ecuadorian Ministries of War had informed the State Department, through their Foreign Chancelleries, that we had been "lost to Jívaros, somewhere on the unexplored Alto Marañón...."

There was a packet of letters at the Consulate. MacCrae and Wright (it was in their station wagon that Jorge and I crossed the Andes to Tarma, just above La Merced) invited me down to Oroya for a two weeks' jaguar hunt. Jorge was now head of his family and *patróne* of "vast estates."... Reading on, I saw that he longed for Cumaria, and that he might possibly get away now to try for El Dorado, though he frankly doubted whether it really existed since taking it up with the historians and his attorneys. Julio and Guido wanted some new music and a box of the 180-grain rifle shells I had spoken of. Father Antony hinted for a photograph of his beloved mission. Johnny Rokes opened his mouth with: "Haw! yourself! You old dog!" El Capitán, of the sanitary *Sea Cow*, sent a signed book written by a missionary friend of his, trying to convert me to the true religion, and a very decent letter in English to—"Mi dare freens and fallo exploradores…" Walter's crested letter informed me that an old shirt had been left at Puerto Patria, and was it mine, and if so—what in hell was he to do with it? Stone's note wanted to know about conditions lower down on the Perené…and "how about my oil?" Van de Putte's postcard mentioned he was having a whale of a time in Iquitos, wished we were there, and that I could have his Pastaza shrunken head should I fail to get one of my own. (I had fifteen: one for each of my South American friends. Of course, they are forbidden farther north.)

Christmas in Quito!

At the airport, for funds had arrived by cable, Inez was grappling with several suitcases she had had forwarded here months before, flowers (financed by an ex-Governor of the Galápagos Islands), and those wild cats, embarking for Panama and London. That chic creature with lipstick on and dressed in a neat suit was a far cry from the old Inez. Keeping away from the claws of those confounded cats, I slipped the shrunken parrots into her pocket (she had given them to me as a Christmas gift).

The Pan-American skyliner's engines started with a bang, and the door slammed. There went the best friend any explorer ever had. And the first woman to ascend the Amazon River.

That day through a gold broker (no bank would buy gold from "disputed Oriente territory") I disposed of the five bamboos for—$16,000. We had agreed on a higher price, but the broker skipped out over the Colombian frontier before the balance was paid. I mailed a draft to Inez (all in legal brass sucres), another (in soles totaling $1,000) to that snake-betting *patróne* on the Morona. Inez had insisted that the concession legally belonged to her company, and that I need pay back only half the expenses incurred from Borja on (which she had advanced). But I was not yet finished with El Dorado. Until international boundaries were established, it was no-man's-land, and anybody's gold. I got off a wire to Jorge:

"The Inca really did have golden eyes. I look for the seventh in Shuara country. Can you meet me Guayaquil in a week?"

On the following evening I received his answer *extra-urgente*. It was brief:
"Leaving mañana!—Jorge."

APPENDIX

The following material, gathered in the course of the author's journey of exploration in the western Amazon region, is intended to provide some concrete scientific background for those whose interest in this region is more than superficial. The facts given are from the author's notebooks, supplemented by such research as was possible, and by the aid of many friends. It is understood that the scientific identifications of the numerous plants and animals listed are those which were obtainable from the authorities consulted: no final validity can be claimed for all of them, and for those lacking such identification it is hoped that the descriptions will provide clues for further investigation and research. This is especially true of List No.6, Jungle-Indian Pharmaceuticals.

The Lists are in seven parts, as follows :

1. Dangerous Snakes.

2. Edible Fish and Turtles.

3. Valuable Trees.

4. Useful Flora.

5. Fruits and Food Plants.

6. Jungle-Indian Pharmaceuticals.

7. Campa Indian Vocabulary.

1. DANGEROUS SNAKES

Of the thirty-two varieties of dangerous snakes observed by the author, the fourteen most feared by natives of the western Amazon region are listed, with descriptions. The names are necessarily local (a combination of common Indian and Spanish). Five of these snakes have been positively identified. Much of the region has not been covered by herpetologists and the list may contain new varieties, particularly of *Lachesis*.

Aguaje-machacuy. A quick-moving, slender snake measuring up to nine feet. Coloration from orange to reddish chocolate. Long-fanged. After striking goes into coils and waits for victim to die. Probably *Lachesis*.

Alfaninga. Many localized varieties, usually gray to black; one and a half to three feet in length. Deadly poisonous. Aggressive.

Carachupa-machacuy. A large thick snake with head resembling a rat's. Teeth marks can produce a two-inch bite.

Cascabel (*Crotalus terrificus*). Two-color, thick-bodied rattler up to seven feet long. Semiaquatic. Slow-moving except when coiled, and striking about half its length. Has a ground color of either yellow or olive-green. Pair of dark bands encircle neck. On each variety is a chain of large brown yellow-edged patches extending along spine to tail. Small heads with top covered by tiny scales. Venom white, extremely plentiful, breaks down red blood corpuscles. Much swelling at point of strike (entire leg may swell greatly and flesh turn dark as blood is attacked). The cascabel does not usually sound warning on the approach of man but coils and lies ready to strike.

Coralito (*Micrurus corallinus*). This colubrine snake is related to the African mamba and the Indian cobra. It has a red coral color placed as rings on a crown to black body. Up to four feet in length. Is a cannibal. Has small blunt head. Scales opalescent. Due to short fangs the coralito has developed a peculiar side-swinging strike and hangs on after piercing the flesh. Immediately this snake begins a quick chewing motion, puncturing the flesh in a series of bites. Death is cased by shock to nervous system. Victim apparently dies from lack of breath, and in extreme pain when blood becomes watery and breaks out through the eyes.

Fer-de-lance (*Bothrops atrx*). This is one of the most terrible snakes of the Amazon. All of them are very large and aggressive. The fer-de-lance is one of the bushmaster's relatives as well as being related to the poisonous tree vipers. It is thick-bodied, flat-headed and has cat-like eyes—that is, with a pupil. It is slower than the colubrines but strikes faster from a coil. Long poison fangs eject a great amount of venom, which attacks the blood system, causing internal hemorrhage. A deep pit between eye and nostril is thought to be the organ of some unknown special sense. Behind the lance-head the rough-scaled seven-foot body is gray crossed by dark bands margined with yellow or green. This snake is viviparous, having thirty to thirty-six young in a litter. Nocturnal. When swallowing prey, dislocates each side of jawbones. Will attack man without provocation.

Jergon (*Bothrops picta*). This is a palm viper whose bite is 70 percent fatal. There are many varieties, including climbers, ground, and water. Coloration ranges from earthy, usually plum to red most common. Length up to six feet. The top of the flat head is protected by small scales. This is one of the crotalines.

Loro-machacuy. Different kinds, blue, white and black, green. Up to eight feet in length. Thin, and move with great swiftness. Some are tree climbers. Very abundant.

Mantona-venenosos. An orange snake, sometimes yellow, white; length up to nine feet. Indians claim it will follow man and strike without provocation.

Motelo-machacuy. Head resembles a turtle's. The body is mottled yellow and white, also many other colors. Length up to seven feet. This snake is usually fatal to white men, though the Indians have a cure and are rarely victims to its venom.

Naca Naca. Several varieties, yellow, white, black and red, black and white, up to six feet. Deadly.

Pucuna-machacuy. Various mottled types, very large. Is swift and will strike if approached. It has been named after the Jívaro blowgun which shoots poisoned darts. The effects of its strike are said to resemble those of curare, which could make it one of the colubrines.

Shushupe (*Lachesis muta*). Three varieties of the pit viper bushmaster. Usually (if it has not been fed recently) fatal to man in five minutes. Up to twelve feet in length and slender. This terrible snake lives in holes in the ground. The fangs, which unhinge from the top of the mouth, are 1 1/2 inches long. The body scales are almost as rough as pineapple. The coloration is reddish to yellow, sometimes pink, with black bands. It is the only crotaline which lays eggs. Very alert and aggressive, probably exceeding the cobra in this respect. It will follow a man and kill either by day or by night. The Indians say this snake will not strike just once, back off and wait, but will continually strike until the victim is dead.

Yguana-machacuy. Head resembles an iguana's. Body up to six feet, marked like a boa's—brown and black. Not very aggressive but deadly if victim cannot find aid from an Indian *brujo*.

2. EDIBLE FISH AND TURTLES

This list comprises forty fish and six turtles, descriptions prepared from the author's notebook, identity established by capture of specimens. Scientific names have been ascertained for ten of the fish and three of the turtles. All others listed by common local names having a Spanish derivation. New varieties are undoubtedly reported here. Body length given in most cases.

Anguilla (*Gymnotus electricus*). This electric ray is six to seven feet in length. Coloration ranges from white to sandy yellow. Indians claim it is capable of paralyzing a man or even an ox at thirty feet through water. Greatly feared.

Bagre. A beautiful six-inch fish, silvery. It provides an excellent yellow meat which is without bones.

Boquichico. Fifteen inches long. This is a scaled fish, silvery with gray back. The meat is white and delicious but difficult to eat because of the spiny bones.

Bujurqui. A six-inch fish with dark silver scales, good meat. These fish run in schools and are plentiful.

Carachama. A foot in length, this fish is very dark in color, running from gray to blotched black. Head large, body tapering. A very good food fish.

Carachama mama. Thirty inches long. Because of its black, shell-like bony covering, this fish is usually taken by spear. The meat is excellent.

Carahuash. The scales are yellow on the lower sides, black on top of the spine. This variety is twelve inches long and is usually taken by bow and arrow. The Indians smoke this fish and use it on long journeys.

Chambira (*Myletes paco*). Usually this fish runs to eighteen-inch length. Scales small and silvery. It is a largemouth type, a bottom feeder. The meat is palatable but bony. When Indians spear this fish they turn the canoe bow upstream, so that when casting the spear it will rebound back on the current. After boating the fish they bite it on the back of the head, where the small scales offer little protection.

Corbina (*Corbina nigra*). A favorite river fish, seventeen inches in length, with silvery scales. The meat is fine-textured and good eating, being somewhat like whiting.

Denton. A small five-inch fish with tiny silvery scales. A school fish, this one is usually taken in a round casting net. Good meat, but bony.

Dorado. This beautiful river fish is a foot and a half in length, the scales golden. The meat makes it one of the favorite fishes of the western Amazon system of rivers. Usually speared.

Gamitama (*Serrasalmus rumbus*). A great food fish, twenty-eight inches in length. The scales are a dark yellow. This type is plentiful in the rivers and when split and dried is excellent for long trips. Because of the oil in the meat it is very nourishing. One of the favorite food fishes. Usually speared, though first barbasco root is pounded and tossed on the water, which seems to impair breathing in the fish. The flesh is not affected by the poison. If not speared, the fish recovers.

Lenguada. A small five-inch fish with tiny dark scales. A delicious fish but hard to get at as the schools are not heavy.

Lisa (*Cobites taenia*). White with black bands, fifteen inches long. Good meat but very bony. Common.

Macana. A beautiful twenty-inch fish without scales, dark reddish. A fine food fish.

Mañana Me Voy. A tiny school fish of only two to three inches, silvery scales. Inhabits island lagoons as well as rivers. Plentiful but must be obtained with barbasco and nets.

Maparate. Gray-backed, this is a silvery fish about a foot in length. Good flesh, plentiful.

Majaras. A sardine-like fish common in all waters. It is three inches long, with silvery, red-tipped scales. Sometimes captured in fish traps.

Mota. No scales, lead-colored, length thirteen inches. A fine fish whose flash is much esteemed.

Paco (*Arochilodus sp.*).One of the fine fishes, some twenty-two inches long, with silvery scales and gray stripes. Good even when laid across greenwood twigs and sowly broiled over hardwood coals. Usually speared.

Paiche (*Arapaima gigas*). The great food fish of the upper Amazon rivers. These fish run up to nine feet in length and are very thick, sometimes reaching a weight of 400 pounds. The flesh is palatable either salted or fresh. Oily and nutritious. Silvery color. Taken by harpoon. Has been greatly exploited because of high commercial value and some rivers are virtually depleted of them.

Palometa (*Pyocentrus piraya*). An oblong-shaped fish, flat and scaly. The sides are silver with orange spots. Length nine inches. This is a bottom feeder and the flesh is very fine in texture and tasty.

Pana (*Serrasalmo*). A well-fleshed, common six-inch variety. Two classes—red and white. Meat delicious.

Peje Torre. A thirty-inch fish taken by spear. The skin is without scales and the color is red with yellow spots. A good quality food fish. Much sought and not very common.

Piro. Dark skin edging off at sides and bottom to yellow. Length seventeen inches. Good flesh.

Pununderos. A very plentiful fish some five inches in length. The habitat is mostly inland on *cochas* (lagoons and lakes) off the river banks. Caught with barbasco.

Punuysiqui. A very plentiful food fish, thirteen inches in length. Dark gray scales.

Raya (*Raya nasuta*). Forty-inch stingray with flat nose. Ashen gray skin, very rough, like sandpaper. Has a long bony tail with poisonous barb midway along the shaft. Uses this as a striker. Common in shallow waters where it lies in sand and mud. Sometimes causes death through gangrene resulting from sting.

Sabalo. A great favorite. Twelve inches long, silver-sided, dark back. Very common along sides of rivers.

Salton. Good eating fish with firm flesh. Twenty-four inches long with lead-colored skin. No scales. Usually taken by spear.

Sapochunchi. Small fish, five inches long, no scales. Skin a dark gray. A wonderful broiling fish.

Sardina. Running in schools these fish, while plentiful, are of rather poor quality. The scales are silvery. Length seven inches.

Shirapira. Twelve inches in length, no scales, white with some black on sides and spine. One of the common food fishes.

Shirui. The meat is white and delicious though the fish is only three to four inches long. A very fine dark-yellow skin.

Shuyo. The Indians spear this fish from canoes along the shallow river banks. The average run is eleven inches, the scales dark reddish.

Tucunare. Excellent eating, seven-inch fish, with reddish black scales. Abundant.

Turushuque. No scales, dangerous side-spurs which are poisonous. A twenty-one-inch fish having excellent meat. Gray to silver.

Yahuarachi. An inland school fish some six inches long. Dark silvery scales. Caught with barbasco and netted.

Yulilla. A river and *cocha* fish which is very plentiful. Five inches in length, with small silvery scales.

Zungaro (*Trichomycteros*). A six and a half-foot tiger fish, considered very dangerous. Skin smooth and scaleless, color a spotted gray. It is said by officers of the Peruvian army at Borja that this fish will attack a man whose canoe has overturned in the Pongo de Mencheriche. They say no bodies are ever recovered in this gorge because of the zungaro. It is, however, an excellent food fish. Must be taken by harpoon.

Asna charapa (*Chelus fimbriata*). This turtle is sixteen inches in length, long-snouted, with eyes well forward. The shell is a dark gray and very knotty. Some of the armor plates are movable and are said by Indians to be used as flashers to decoy fish. Very alert and difficult to approach. Meat good.

Charapa (*Podocnemis expansa*). A large turtle some forty inches long. The shell is flat and wide, colored olive gray. Head very flat. Lays about 300 small eggs in one night, using the same *playas* (riverine beaches). Much sought for its eggs and delicious flesh.

Cupiso. Twelve inches long, shell-gray. The meat. is good but this turtle is so alert that it is hard to approach. Indians sometimes catch them in fish traps.

Motelo. A very common turtle measuring sixteen inches in length. The shell is rough, colored gray and yellow. Good red meat.

Taricaya (*Peltocephalus tracaxa*). Large turtle about eighteen inches long, with dark gray rough shell. Lays about 80 eggs in a night. Much sought for eggs and meat.

Teparo. Very much resembles the cupiso. Is a foot long and covered by mud-gray shell very difficult to see. Exceedingly shy. Meat is red and palatable.

3. VALUABLE TREES

List comprises fifty-eight trees, of which thirty-seven are scientifically identified. In all cases the local Spanish-Indian name is given, with brief descriptions to aid in further identification.

Acapu (*Andira ambletti*). A durable and brittle wood which comes in black; white, yellow, and blotched varieties. Water-resistant, it is used in building construction.

Aguano or Caoba (*Swietenia mahogani*). One of the best of the many fine soft-wood mahoganies. Trunk is very long and straight, often sixty feet, by four feet in diameter. It is floated down the Loreto and Oriente rivers to the mills in Iquitos and shipped in the form of logs and lumber to Europe and the United States.

Alfaro or Lagarto caspi. An excellent softwood for making canoes and any marine constructions. Strongly water-resistant. There are millions of these giants in the Amazon jungle.

Bacury (*Platonia insignis*). This tree grows to a height of seventy-five feet. It is one of the favored woods for constructions because of its resistance to water and humidity. It is a gray wood and the tree is one of the rubber producers.

Balata. Two types: white and red. Used at present only for extracting latex.

Cabiuna (*Dalbergia nigra*). A beautiful red wood, rarely cut.

Canela muena (*Laurus cinnamomum*). This very fine "cinnamon laurel" can be floated. Twelve varieties are known in the jungle; a few are used in local carpentry .

Capinuri (known also as lagarto caspi, cuchara caspi, charapa caspi, cocacuma, ana caspi, machim mango, chuchuhuasi caspi, charapilla, urco cumaceva, taracuca, tarrafa caspi, chontaquiro, maipuco, palo violeta, tortuga caspi, yutobanco, ango caspi, etc., etc.). All of these are notable for their wonderful colors, magnificent grains, and varied hardness. They are abundant but usually pass unrecognized in the jungle. Nearly all are heavier than water, making transportation difficult. A few can be floated out to be made available for domestic and export uses.

Capirona (*Capirona aparinaceas*). Occurs in several varieties which reach tremendous dimensions. Mainly confined to the low alluvial lands where, as soon as the *playas* (beaches) of the periodically flooded rivers are formed, it is the first tree to appear. Soft and fine-grained, it would be excellent for carpentry and cabinet work, being of a light yellow color. Prized as best for burning in river launches, which is the only use it has been put to.

Catahua (*Rura crepitans*). A magnificent redwood, used now only for dugouts and boat plankings.

Caucho (*Castilla elastica*). Rubber.

Cedro. This giant tree floats. The wood is straight-grained, easily worked, durable, and constitutes the second of all woods in Amazonic regions in commercial importance. The stands along the Ucayali River banks are being depleted by *patrónes*, and tributaries of this system will not all be worked out for some time because of labor shortage and depredations of bravo Indians. Chiefly used in furniture making and house construction.

Cedro (*Cedrela odorata*). One of the fine cedars, floatable. Varieties are white, brown, yellow, red. Tree is one hundred feet tall and from six to eight feet in diameter. Mainly furniture and construction.

Cetico (*Cecropia peltata*). A very light wood used for constructing rafts. Contains a high percentage of cellulose. Will be an important source of wealth for the region if a paper mill is installed. Very abundant, especially on the great rivers, where are found islands covered solely with these trees. Incidentally, the Indians believe that certain bats eat of its fruit and the seeds, undigested and retaining their germinative powers, are thus dropped in all parts of the jungle.

Chicle (*Achras sapota*). Base for chewing gum.

Cocobolo or Guayacan (*Guayacum arboreum*). Very heavy, stone-like. Color, texture, grain, and patina make it precious. But tooling is difficult and uses most probably restricted to the arts.

Culebra caspi. Very fine-grained wood, mottled with markings similar to those of snakes. Little used but would be precious for carvings.

Cumaceva (*Cesalpina echinata*). This wood is notable for its toughness and hardness. Exceptionally heavy and difficult to work. Coloration red to chocolate. Locally it is used for harpoons on very large fish. Because of its fine straight grain it will one day rank with other precious woods, especially in artwork.

Cumala. This tree is very abundant, two varieties being recognized locally. From its beautiful woods are fashioned white boxes, sometimes carved; and red window casings, doors, and furniture. Like most of these fine woods, it is not being exported.

Espintana. Very hard wood when dry; very abundant. Used mainly for building by local *patrónes*.

Eipo (*Machoerium leucapterium*). A fine hardwood tree.

Estoraque (*Myrus erythroxylon*). Of balsamic bark. The heart of this wood possesses an aromatic fragrance. The wood is fiery red, hard, and very weather-resistant. The grain is not suitable for wide uses commercially, because of its unworkability. At present used for fine carvings, frames, and house trimmings.

Genipapo (*Genipa brasiliensis*). A hardwood used for walking sticks, spears, etc.

Huacamayo caspi or Puca caspi. This splendid rose-redwood is very fine-grained. Little used even in Amazon regions.

Huacapu (*Vonacapona americana*). This wood is practically indestructible. The main supporting braces of the houses of the region are invariably of this wood. Poles buried in wet, hot, tropical earth rot off quickly, and for this reason the huacapu is highly valued. Resistant to borers.

Huacapurana. This grand tree produces wood which is of extraordinary hardness and weight. The color is very beautiful, being red-veined with a golden yellow.

Huito or Jagua (*Genipa americana*). In addition to the medical uses of its fruit, this tree supplies a very soft fine-grained pale wood of white and yellow designs. The logs float. At present a few carvings are made from it; also used in making cots.

Incira. Two varieties: one canary yellow, the other a darker hue. It is a soft wood and practical for working though the grain is much twisted. Locally goes into house frames, window casings, doors. Abundant.

Ishpingo. This tree is abundant, a softwood suitable for construction in large, buildings.

Itahuba (*Ocotea magaphilla*). Laurel-like, of various kinds and many colors. Very resistant wood, preferably used in naval and other marine structures.

Jacaranda (*Swartzia flemingi*). A forty-foot-high banana tree.

Jebe or Shiringa (*Hevea brasiliensis; Shiphonia elastica*). Rubber.

Kapok (*Ceiba pentandra*). Silk cotton tree.

Leche caspi. Balata.

Louro. Construction wood, very hard. Grows in swamps.

Lupuna (*Ceiba pentandra*). King of the forest. Individuals have been measured up to sixty meters high by three in diameter at the base and forty meters in diameter around branches. Resembles an umbrella or flattened cupola. Navigation is often laid from tree to tree during flood time. Too large for economic handling, and the wood itself is soft. Due to the shallow humus of the Amazon basin's floor and the hardpan close to the surface, this tree is shallow-rooted. Although thousand-year-old trees exist, usually these giants are uprooted by winds and floods, since the roots seldom reach a depth exceeding a few feet.

Marfil vegetal (*Hiarina tagua*). Palm, produces ivory nuts.

Mashonaste (*Olmedia erytrixilea*). A gigantic tree having wood of many colors, with a twisted grain. The texture is heavy and extremely hard. Little used at present except for the resin excretions.

Mazaranduva (*Mimusops balata*). One of the fine rubber producers.

Moena. This tree supplies wood as good as cedar and yet more resistant to weather and insects. Abundant, but little used. Graded into five qualities.

Nervio amarillo. A yellow-ribbed wood, similar to Palo marfil. This is perhaps the most dense and finest-grained of all Amazonic commercial woods. Almost unknown, even locally. Commands big prices when found.

Nispero. Produces fruits and a smokeless firewood. Used in the river launches.

Nogal. A raft wood used in furniture construction.

Oje (*Ficus anthelmentica*). The tree is abundant, wood very soft. Best for boxes, packing cases, etc.

Palillo. Used as wood in metal boilers.

Palo cruz (*Brommea grandicipes*). Probably the finest wood of the region, and the most pleasing to sight and touch. Its color is yellow sepia veined and striped with marble black. The tree is not large and, to prevent splitting when it is worked, the wood must be allowed to dry in a damp place at least for a year. At present it is only used locally for canes, rulers, parquetry, and various small objects.

Palo marfil. This "ivory wood" is very hard, practically indestructible, and of a beautiful texture comparable to elephant ivory. It is believed to be scarce and little known.

Palo mullato (*Pentaclethra filamentosa*). A fine heavy wood which burns even when green.

Palo sangre (*Genipa oblongifolia*). Occurs in three grades. This "blood wood" is a very fine-grained, straight-grained wood of bright red hues, and splendid, for any fine work of carpentry, carvings, and cabinet work. Though not difficult to fashion, it is extraordinarily hard and non-porous. It takes varnish without losing its bright color. The tree grows to gigantic proportions, and though abundant in numerous stands it will not float and its transportation is extremely difficult. The wood is considered locally to be more water-resistant than any other.

Pau ferro (*Swastria tormentosa*). This "iron wood" is practically indestructible. The tree grows to about sixty feet.

Quillo bordon (*Caryocar toxiferum*). A floatable wood of a rich creamy color. The texture is very fine-grained, the patina like velvet. It is used in local cabinet work and highly prized. Plentiful.

Quinilla. This wood is found in various colors, the grain very irregular and even tortuous. The tree is abundant and has many of the characteristics of the Palo sangre. Its commercial development is arrested in favor of more precious or better-known woods and so is relegated at present to the woodpile.

Remo caspi (*Styrax acuminatum*). The wood is soft and of a yellow rich and consistent, and maybe worked into very thin slices (veneers). It is resistant, pliable, and light in weight. Locally it is merely used to make the wide-bladed oars of the region. The logs float. Would be good for construction and furniture.

Sucupira (*Bowdichia virgilioides*). A fine construction wood, color white and yellow.

Tahuari. There are two grades, both very hard. Clear-grained and multi-colored; used for furniture and in construction.

Topa or Palo de balsa (*Ochroma sp.*). Used locally for rafts (*boatas*). Considerable exportation. It is very porous, light in weight, white in color. The down covering the seeds of the flower is used for pillows, etc.

Zapallo (*Cucurbita moschata*). A large tree having many local uses among the wood-wise Indians. Durable.

Zapote (*Matisia cordata*). Large tree; produces a delicious dark-brown fruit. The bark is girdled for chicle, the base of chewing gum.

4. USEFUL FLORA

Thirty-one miscellaneous plant varieties useful to the Indians are briefly described under their local names; of these, eighteen are scientifically identified. The local names are used among all tribes and by the Peruvians and are Spanish, derived usually from the Indian.

Atadijo. Tree used in the making of water canisters.

Bijao. Plant used as a substitute for paper such as wrapping tamales, fashioning canisters, etc.

Bombonaje (*Carludovica palmata*). A very large palm from whose leaves are fashioned hats, baskets, canoe tops, fish traps, etc.

Cabuya. A resistant tree fiber used for ropes. Very resistant to water and humidity. Probably stronger than good hemp.

Calla brava (*Guadua latifolia*). A palm cane used as ceilings in houses, lasts fifteen years; the *chicosa* species is even more durable. Thickets of this cane are sometimes miles wide. Produces best fish spears due to toughness of wood and the large air pockets inside. Could be used for furniture. Light.

Calla dulce (*Saccharum officinarum*). This sugarcane grows wild in some regions. It is about fifteen feet tall.

Chambiri (*Astrocaryum tucuma*). A textile palm, fiber much in demand by the Indians.

Chaquira. A plant whose small fruits are used as ornaments.

Chonta (*Euterpe oleracea*). Black, straight-grained palm heart. Probably the hardest wood known which is workable; arrow heads, bows, and spears. Spikes are made of it to pinion the logs of balsas (river rafts).

Copal (*Hymenaea courbaril*). A gum used to burn before the gods and spirits. Aromatic. Has high commercial value.

Gamalote. Nature's best preservative from Amazon soil erosion. Artificial flowers made from pith of this plant.

Huacra pona (*Iriartea ventricosa*). Palm wood, very durable as timbers in house construction. Workable yet very hard.

Huimba (*Xilum ceiba*). A fine-grade tree fiber may be obtained from the fruit. Filler for pillows, very cool.

Inayuga. A palm supplying wood from which many tribes make their *pucunas* (blowguns). Grain very straight, lightweight but tough.

Lacre. This tree produces a sticky resin used in boat and other construction.

Machingo. Hardwood best for kitchen utensils. Tough, red in color.

Marona (*Bambusa guadua*). A palm cane type of bamboo used for house walls. Tough, light, and very resistant to rot.

Mirity (*Mauritia flexuosa*). From this palm is obtained fine textile fibers.

Mishquipanga. Plant supplying large leaves for Indian paper.

Pichana (*Attalea funifera*). Indians use this tree bark as scrub brushes.

Pijuayo. Tree fruits cooked with *chicha*. Also source of cooking oil.

Pona (*Iriartea exorhiza*). Palm used in house construction, also for bows and arrows, spears, etc.

Punga. Cording, very tough.

Shapaja (*Attalea speciosamarti*). A palm whose oily nuts are excellent fuel for smoking rubber. The wood is excellent for house construction.

Tagua (*Phytelephas macrocarpa*). Buttons and ornaments are cut from this ivory palm nut. Has important commercial value.

Tamshi (*Carludovica trigona*). Lianas used in making water-resistant ropes. Also used for canisters and house construction.

Tobaco (*Nicotiana tabacum*). Plant producing tobacco.

Tutumo (Crescentia cujete). The fruit rinds of this tree are used as cups, dippers, etc.

Vainilla (*Vainilla aromatica*). The aromatic vanilla which is used by Indians as a fine perfume.

Yanacaspi. From the heart of this tree the Indians weave a fine quality of rope.

Yarina. Same as tagua; used as beams in house construction.

5. FRUITS AND FOOD PLANTS

Forty-five kinds are listed by common or local names, with short descriptions. Of these, thirty-five are scientifically identified; the others may be simple varieties or locally cultivated types.

Achira. A plant whose fruit resembles ginger to the taste. Probably a local variety.

Almendro (*Terminalia catalpa*). A giant tree producing vast amounts of fruit. A favorite in jungle regions.

Anona (*Rollinea ortopetala*). A very abundant tree on the Ucayali River. produces an excellent and delicious fruit of the pulpy, softshelled type.

Anonilla (*Rollinea selvatica*). Wonderfully flavored fruit resembling the chirimoya.

Arbol del pan (*Artocarpus incisa*). Produces breadfruit in the form of nuts which are contained in a large hard-shelled pod and protected by pith. When boiled these nuts taste like lotus seeds. One of the standard foods of the western Amazon regions.

Avocado (*Persea sp.*). Small soft fruit which is exceedingly oily. Very nutritious. Colored green with rough skin and has large black pit. Meat soft and a whitish green.

Camote (*Convolvulus batata*). A delicious white variety is grown along the banks of the Ucayali. A soft fruit.

Chiclayo (*Phaseolus mungo*). A variety of small bean. A *playa* (river beach) crop which is grown easily without care.

Chiclayo verdura. A localized bean used fresh in salads, Mostly a *playa* crop. Quick-growing. ,

Chirimoya (*Anona sp.*). One of the custard apples.

Cocona. The fruits of this bush are dried and used as a cereal. One variety used as a sweetening in *chicha*.

Cumaru (*Coumarouna sp.*). This giant tree supplies an excellent fruit black in color and very nutritious.,

Frejol (*Phaseolus vulgaris*). This *playa* crop bean is widely used on the rivers because of its rapid growth. Labor required in cultivation is almost nil. At beginning of dry season the seeds are broadcast in the wet sand and mud, with no care or weeding required.

Goma huayo (*Hymenonea chapadensis*). A rare localized fruit but highly appreciated. Soft and pulpy.

Granadilla (*Passiflora macrocarpa*). Dainty fruit of the passion flower. Sometimes preserved.

Guava (*Inga spectabilis*). This fruit is a deep pink in color and very sweet and pulpy. Makes good preserves.

Guayaba (*Psidium guajava*). Apple-like fruit from which preserves are made. Very much appreciated because of its rich texture and ability to keep after cooking.

Huasai (*Euterpe oleracea*). Palm producing a fine and abundant fruit.

Huitina. A vegetable tuber flourishing in the shallow soil of the Amazon valley.

Huito or Jagua (*Genipa americana*). A tree fruit very agreeable to taste. Soft-skinned. Great favorite. Very abundant.

Limon corriente (*Citrus aurantifolia*). A large lime, sweet.

Lucumo. Very large and easily grown fruit. Hard-shelled. Delicious to the taste.

Maiz (*Zea mays*). Jungle variety grown on *playas* and in clearings. Small ears, pulpy.

Mandarina (*Citrus nobilis*). Small and very sweet orange with loose skin, highly prized. Keeps well.

Mango (*Mangifera indica*). Very succulent fruit, somewhat like a cross between pear and apple in size and outline. Juicy but small and fibrous. Usually eaten in semi-rotten state with a spoon. Common.

Melon (*Cucumis melo*). A melon grown usually in the *playas* or sometimes in a chácara (clearing). Not very tasty though desirable on boat trips where weight is not a factor. Keeps well.

Naranja (*Citrus vulgaris*). Sweet but small orange; pulpy. Much esteemed.

Palta or Aguacate. Same as avocado.

Papaya (*Carica papaya*). This fruit grown on a thin-stemmed tree with fig-like leaves. Fruit up to a foot in length, yellow, and green, with segments on shell. After seeds and pulp are removed, the whitish yellow meat is sliced with a knife. Delicious. Very common.

Parinari (*Parinarium sp.*). Large and very abundant, tree fruit. Delicious and easy to pack.

Pepino (*Cucumis sativa*). A melon rarely grown, though excellent to taste.

Pifayo (*Bastris sp.*). The fruit of this palm is often used as fodder for cattle and pigs. Oily.

Platano (*Musa paradisiaca*). Cooking-type banana; usually boiled or baked. Large and hard fibrous type. Cannot be eaten raw.

Pupunha. Palm with yellow fruit used in fermented drinks.

Sacha mango (*Gustativia augusta*). Fine pear-shaped fruit. Packs very well.

Sacha papa. A local wild fruit known sometimes as father of the mountains. Soft and delicious..

Sandia (*Citrullus vulgaris*). The juice of this fruit is used in water as a cooling hot-weather drink. Grown on *playas*. Abundant.

Shimbillo. A wild tree-fruit small and soft-skinned. Juicy and delicious.

Tumbo (*Passiflora quandrangularis*). Small fruit crushed and served as a refreshing drink in water. Jigger of gin and sugar makes this one an excellent and cooling drink.

Ungurachui (*Aenocarpus bacaba*). This palm supplies a tremendous quantity of rich fruit. Can be dried.

Uvilla (*Chondodendron convolvulaceum*). This is a small fruit resembling a bunch of grapes. Soft. Grown on a very large tree.

Yuca (*Jatropha dulcis*). Tuber. One of the main foods of the upper Amazon basin. These roots grow on a small tree only 8 or 10 feet high.

Yuca (*Manihot utilissima*). A potato-like tuber root. Source of tapioca.

Zapallo (*Cucurbita moschata*). A very large fruit of greenish color. Used on long boat journeys because of its hard protective shell.

Zapote or Sapote (*Matisia cordata*). Plum size, brown, soft delicious fruit. Wild. Though it cannot be picked and shipped, it has been called the finest tasting fruit produced anywhere in the world.

6. JUNGLE-INDIAN PHARMACEUTICALS

Of these seventy-one drug plants only a few have been previously reported in technical literature (curare by Gill, 1940; oje by Woodroffe, 1914, and Gill, 1940). Local Indian-Spanish names are given, and positive scientific identifications are provided for twenty-one. Few Europeans and Americans realize that the Indian *brujos* (witch doctors) have long used "our" belladonna, cocaine, quinine, etc. Most of the native compounds are secret formulas, made up of unidentified plants. Descriptions of properties and Indian claims of cures are given. Curare is a compound made up usually of some twenty plant types, only a few of which are identifiable by local names (also, included).

Abatua (*Coeculus platyphylla*). Liana root of yellow color, bitter to the taste. Has diuretic properties; is a febrifuge. Indians use it for dropsy.

Achiote (*Bixa orellana*). Related to paprika. India body- and face-paint; now used in cosmetics such as lipstick. Common tree whose seeds furnish an orange-red food and cloth dye; also used for clearing skin blemishes; Indians say it is an insect repellent.

Aguaje (*Mauritia flexuosa*). A palm whose fruit is a source of excellent alcohol used in mixing herbs.

Ajosacha (*Ajo silvestre*). Used to cure headaches, being applied as a plaster.

Albahaca. The sap of this plant is used as a general tonic, especially after long illness.

Almendro. A tree producing excellent medicinal oil.

Amashisa. A resin used on inflammations.

Anguilla (*Gymnotus electricus*). On either side of upper portion of the spine of this stingray is found a yellow strip of flesh running parallel to the spine. This is eaten as an aphrodisiac by old or impotent men.

Assacu. A poison used on leprosy patients in the form of plasters. Said to be far more effective than standard chaulmoogra oil injections.

Ayahuasca or Soga de muerto; A vine yielding a powerful narcotic similar to opium in results. One of the "souhines" which produce visions lasting up to 24 hours. Taken by mouth. This is a Jívaro name; the Chamas call it Oni; Brazilian tribes call it Caaupi.

Ayamullaca. An herb used to make very good soap for bathing wounds and infected areas.

Barbasco or Cube (*Lonchocarpus* and *Tephrosia spp.*). A tree-root narcotic. It is pounded into pulp and poured into lagoons and creeks to poison fish. This is the *timbo* of Brazil. Foundation of the insecticide rotenone. It is poisonous only to cold-blooded creatures. Also used in certain medical formulas by Indian witch doctors.

Belladonna (*Atropa belladonna*). The deadly herb nightshade. Indian uses are in the main identical to those of medical science.

Buranham. A tree-bark juice used as a blood purifier.

Cacahuillo (*Theobroma sp.*). Used to relieve stomach troubles, also at time of arrow or spear thrust through abdomen. *Brujos* (witchmen) say this one has medical properties effective in certain ailments of the throat.

Cacao (*Theobroma cacao*). Used for lumbago.

Caferana (*Tachia guianensis*). A white bush root used as a febrifuge. Bitter.

Canela. A tree bark used in preparing a powder for mixing drinks said to give strength; also used in preparing sweets.

Carana. An excellent tree resin used externally for many ailments.

Cascarilla. This tree exists in great numbers and is a source of quinine, used by *brujos* for curing malignant malaria. The early Spaniards are thought to have obtained the quinine cure for malaria in Ecuador. *Brujos* usually brew the bark in *chicha*. Very bitter.

Catahua (*Hura crepitans*). Indians say rag soaked in juices of this tree and tied around a limb (leg or arm) at the limit of infection causes poison to recede to original point. Often used after battles in which snake venom has been detected on arrows or spears. It supplies the narcotic resin used to cure leprosy. Leprosy is a new disease in the

Amazon, brought in by *patrónes*, and probably a higher percentage of lepers exist there than in any area in the world. Only recently have *brujos* been claiming cures. Baron Walter von Wolfenegg, of Iquitos, has documented two such cures by Rio Blanco Indians..

Cetico. A white bark, fig-leaved tree, sometimes used for rafts as a substitute for balsas. After bark is placed in boiling water, take it out and scrape out the inside residue. When placed in an infected eye it offers relief from pain, and clears away infection after several days of treatment. (Author's eyes probably saved by this, after Peruvian Army doctors had given up.)

Chuchuhuasha (*Erythroxylon catauba*). The tree bark is pulverized and mixed in alcohol. Taken orally it is said by *brujos* to cure cancer.

Coca (*Erythroxylon coca*). A shrub leaf resembling the laurel which is used as an anesthetic. From this we obtain the Indian's cocaine.

Cocobola. The resin of this tree is used for curing pulmonary infections through smoke inhalations.

Copaiba (*Copaifera sp.*). A tree whose sap is excellent for curing open wounds and diseased areas. Used in many formulas.

Curare (also Ampi, Moca, Jarnbi). Primarily a blowgun poison secretly brewed from various palms, leaves, vines, lianas. Also taken to relieve heart and muscle contractions, blood pressure, troubles resulting from animal and snakebite. It is an anesthetic. "Soul plants" used include approximately twent—unreported new ones are Ampi-huasca, Curupa-caspi, Bucuna-ucho. Science has not yet found a cure for curare poisoning. The Indians use rock salt which they swallow in water, also they slash the area around the dart wound and rub in more salt. For this reason blowguns are used in war only on white men, while guns, spears, and war-axes are used in Indian fighting Indian.

Curarina. Bush extract for infections.

Gapuy. Shrub root boiled and prepared for use in ophthalmia.

Guayaba. For conjunctivitis.

Huacapu. A tree extract used in the cure of conjunctivitis and other inflammations of the eye.

Huacrapona (*Iriartea ventricosa*). Palm whose fruit is used in preparing base for any type of jelly fed to patients.

Huaman samana. The leaf is crushed and rubbed (together with alcohol) on skin to kill insects and egg sacs developing under the surface.

Huayra caspi. A tree having a red bark whose milk is rubbed on boils and certain insect bites. A common cure for minor skin ailments.

Huayusa. A shrub used as a tonic to promote appetite. Found mainly on Rio Tambo.

Huito. Ornamental black paint for face and body. Frequently used as war paint but also to cut down sun glare on rivers. Medical properties cleanse skin of blemishes. Also cures internal canero fish poisoning.

Ishpanga. A cure for amebic dysentery.

Lacre. Produces a medicinal tree resin used in preparation of skin medicaments.

Lancetilla. An inhalant for bronchitis.

Leche de oje (*Ficus anthelmentica*). Same medicine reported by Woodroffe in 1914 and Gill in 1940. On Rio Santiago this tree latex (after preparation) is used for internal parasites such as worms (papaya seeds also taken for same purpose). It is a violent purgative, and a febrifuge.

Malva. This bush furnishes leaves which when boiled are a very effective heart stimulant. Sometimes it is applied to a warrior dying of wounds.

Marona or Huama. A giant grass resembling bamboo. The lower section contains water which is used by the Jívaros to cure liver ailments.

Morapirama. A bush root infused after boiling for local paralysis.

Murure. A tree-bark juice used as a blood purifier.

Nacu sari. Ingredients used in ampi (one of the curares), Ucayali River. These are secrets of the witchcraft *brujos* of the Brotherhood of the Dancing Anacondas. For that reason separate names were unobtainable.

Nucfio pichana. A brew is made from this herb which cures certain fevers, brings down temperature. The *brujos* have many such febrifuges.

Nushumbi. Used to paint Jívaros' teeth black; a black nut. Said to prevent decay. The Peruvians are working on a bleaching agent as this has been used on troops and found effective.

Paico. Stomach medicine used for curing fish poisoning.

Paujil huasca or Paushi. A vine which when cut into lengths of three or four feet and held vertically so that its juice may be drunk in quantity is said to be a cure for tuberculosis.

Pijuayo. Fruits are cooked with *chicha* (fermented saliva and vegetable or fruit juice beverage) for their concentrated food value; also a source of medicinal oil.

Piri piri. The tuberous roots are boiled to obtain an oral antidote for curing certain types of snakebite. Perfume is also obtained which is said by the Indians to have aphrodisiacal properties.

Posan-ka. A Chama tribe aphrodisiac. Rio Perené.

Puchury (*Nectandra puchury*). From the bark is made a powder used in acute dyspepsia cases.

Quinaquina. One of the malaria-control drugs.

Quinoa (*Chenopodium quinoa*). A plant burned to provide an ash which is used in the preparation of the coca quid (chewed for its coca content).

Retama. A tree having many medical uses among the *brujos*.

Sacha curarine. A bush or small tree similar to palm. From the seeds, bark. and leaves are extracted juices used to cure snake poisoning (for shock, applied through the rectum).

Sangre de drago. A tree which when bled in the manner of a rubber tree expels a pure liquid. Taken by mouth this liquid is apparently a conditioner after fever, "very good for cuts," and often used in this manner to cure internal infections from arrow and spear wounds.

Sangre de leche. A thick tree of rough bark, leaf similar to that of balsa. Upon bleeding, a brilliant red liquid may be recovered, and taken orally as a cure for internal hemorrhage in childbirth, spear wounds, etc. Also used on patient bleeding internally as result of strike by any crotaline snake, especially the fer-de-lance.,

Sangre pidipidi. The bulb-like "potatoes" are placed in boiling water; when liquid becomes red it is taken off the fire and applied to infected area. Often used in amputation of limbs.

Sinai or Cinami. A palm used in making a special *chichi* for the sick. Its oils are used as abase for certain fine perfumes.

Shiric sanango (*Brunfelsia sp,*). Used externally with alcohol to bring down temperature. Something like an ice pack.

Sucuba (*Pulmeira phagedencia*). A tree sap used as a vermifuge. Also as relief from acute rheumatism.

Tohe (*Datura insignis*). A sleeping draught.

Topa (*Ochroma sp.*). Used extensively as an antiseptic. It also closes cut or gunshot wound.

Ubos. A tree whose fruit furnishes the base for several medical formulas.

Ucho sanango. A tree whose leaves are boiled together with those of the Renaquillo tree, and taken by mouth. It is found that broken bones will heal completely in eight to fifteen days. This is a secret of the Morona Jívaro tribe called the Murato (lower Pastaza), and when they use it the patient eats no salt, grease, sweets, seasoning, or alcohol (*giamanchi* or *chicha*). They say adult bones are softened to the consistency of putty by external compresses. In shaping badly set bones, clubfeet, etc., the *brujos* have a means of hardening the bones afterwards. Resin also used for snakebite.

Verbena. An herb used as a base in medical formulas.

Yotoconti. A plant extraction used to preserve teeth. This weekly treatment leaves the teeth black. Old savages of the Campa and Oriente tribes invariably have good teeth. At the moment Peruvian scientists are experimenting on troops, say all dentists in Loreto units have been transferred elsewhere.

Yuquilla. A tree extract used in the cure of conjunctivitis and other inflammations of the eye.

Zarzaparilla (*Smilax sp.*). A *brujo* blood conditioner.

7. CAMPA INDIAN VOCABULARY

The following list comprises some 400 words used by the Campa Indians. It is not intended as a scholarly linguistic contribution, but as a practical aid to any traveler on the Perené or Upper Ucayali rivers in Peru, enabling him to enter into a closer relationship with the isolated and sometimes very savage Indians of these regions. The best English equivalents are given in the first column (arranged alphabetically), followed by the Campa word. The list includes words deriving from the great Arawakan linguistic family but will be of little use to anyone but the explorer, since no classification has been attempted, nor have any dialect variations been offered. Translation was made from the purely practical point of view; pronunciation of the Campa equivalents should be according to the usual English phonetic values, which is close enough to give useful results. Had I possessed such an "unscientific" list before descending the Perené, my journey would have been immeasurably simplified.

ache	*catsihararense*	brother	*iye*
adventure	*andakangare*	brother-in-law	*atni*
adversary	*ishiniatandingare*	butterfly	*shaveta*
afternoon	*shaitene*	canal	*uiauarense*
air	*tampea*	cancer treatment	*chuchuhuasha*
airfield	*shiakomendotse*	canoe	*pitodse*
airplane	*aracomendoxe*	carbine	*cuberi*
alligator pear	*acapa*	cat	*michi*
alone	*apinti*	cattle	*iramentopirotse*
arm (limb)	*noshoqueta*	cave	*muruna*
arrow	*peu*	cedar	*santare*
ashes	*samanpo*	chief	*pingatsare*
ask	*asemiter*	chin	*eshpatone*
baby	*enseaniqui*	chocolate	*heneito*
back	*notapi*	chonta	*palmkiri*
bamboo	*tantsdse*	Christ	*Pawa*
banana	*parente*	clever	*trongamesate*
band (head)	*etsanoriki*	clothes	*sarentse*
barking	*otsheti*	cloud	*mencori*
basket	*canteri*	cock (bird)	*chiranpare*
bat	*pigeiri*	coffin	*cajonarnise*
beads	*mamendotse*	cold	*katsingare*
beans	*mashake*	colony	*ashtakaurarose*
bear	*milne*	comb	*shiri*
bed	*mamento*	come	*hate*
bird	*sinicri*	cook	*gotsuarente*
birth	*timause*	copper	*muytonte*
black	*kisare*	corn	*shinqui*
body	*guatra*	cotton	*ampe*
bones	*tonqui*	cow	*vacau*
born	*timy*	coward	*saronte*
bow (weapon)	*shakopse*	crop	*avateri*
box	*caja*	curious	*ameningare*
boy	*entse*	dagger	*satamendotse*
bracelet	*mengetski*	dance	*shingirotse*
branch (twig)	*ocheo*	danger	*cuengare*
brave (warrior)	*tiopenachori*	daughter	*chagui*
broom	*pishimendotse*	day	*quitaiteri*

dead	*kamingari*	favor	*pingatakaina*
deer	*maniro*	feather	*chivanque*
devil	*kamari*	feeble	*matsare*
deity	*guabane*	feed	*kataroshi*
dirty	*patsere*	feet	*noiti*
doctor (witch)	*abendandingare*	fellow	*espabinsale*
dog	*otsiti*	female	*eshnan*
door	*astacorouse*	fetid	*estibare*
dream (soul)	*koshoquirene*	fever	*katierena*
drink	*nire*	fierce	*katsimare*
drunk	*shingitenkare*	fight	*autabakanse*
eagle	*paquitsa*	fighter	*andandingare*
ear	*yianvita*	find	*nomensagare*
early	*kapstiekitartere*	finger	*noshetaqiu*
earth	*quipatse*	fire	*pumaare*
earthquake	*unila*	fish	*sbima*
east	*kirinka*	fishing	*ashimacba*
easy	*tuetmestiare*	fist	*nosoiye*
eat	*noya*	flea	*pa toke*
edge	*sobe*	floor	*salicki*
edible	*tinaetere*	flower	*chaquiagui*
egress	*iguanake*	food	*guarense*
enemy	*huariri*	fool	*masonte*
enter	*anke*	foreign	*pukmgare*
entrance	*kiamendotse*	free	*esparuankir-*
errand	*yanse*		*erakiri*
essence	*pinarotse*	fresh	*tambsegiaka*
eye	*notqui*	friend	*shanitka*
eyelash	*chinpishoke*	frog	*mashero*
fable	*chatona*	funeral	*bitstare*
face	*noboro*	girl	*eguangaro, ense*
false	*saigire*	glory	*guarenkarotse*
fang	*nopangana*	God	*Pawa*
far	*daina*	gold	*kishongare*
farm	*quantse*	good afternoon	*abaiteni*
farmer	*enaspaco*	good morning	*tailaribe*
fat	*guatsante*	goose	*bopsi*
father	*apa*	grandfather	*sharine*

grandmother	*isba*	jealous	*itakanse*
grass	*tokare*	journal	*andavarence*
great	*antaroite*	juice	*ashinisare*
green	*naturea*	jungle	*ashambisbe*
grow	*sbibucanse*	kill	*moyeri, otiche*
guard	*kisole*	kitchen	*onkosamendotse*
guilty	*cregotaranskaro*	knife	*cotsiru*
gun	*tungaventodse*	lamb	*uisba*
hair	*noisbi*	lamp	*suamendotse*
hammock	*kiebotse*	landscape	*daina*
hand	*naco*	late	*shaviteni*
handsome	*kanesare*	laugh	*shirondantse*
happy	*kimocheti*	laundry	*kiguaguambu-*
hard	*kisole*		*dotse*
hatchet	*shacha*	law	*kandakandedro*
hate	*maguisaneateri*	lay	*guatikere*
he	*riore*	lazy	*perante*
head	*noito*	leaf	*ashe*
heart	*nasangane*	leap	*amitage*
heavy	*tenari*	leather	*meshinanse*
hell	*kiaratse*	leave	*hokanakero*
here	*asa*	left	*aupiete*
hide	*amaya*	leg	*nobore*
high	*autare*	leper	*patsarangare*
house	*paugotse*	leprosy	*patsaranse*
how	*sucuandaca*	life	*ayantare*
how are you?	*aviro*	light	*shometse*
hungry	*ashenti*	lip	*shera*
hunter	*kovinsare*	little	*orifanke*
hunting	*kovingare*	live	*nosaique*
husband	*nohime*	liver	*danatare*
hut	*paukoshense*	log	*shakarake*
I	*naka*	loom	*ontesguamin-*
ice	*caisingare*		*dotse*
idea	*kingishandare*	louse	*netsi*
idler	*perante*	love	*nitasutane*
innocent	*carioratsine*	love potion	*posan-ka*
insane	*phingebitsare*	lover	*takotause*

low	*shavie*	new	*iraquerare*
loyal	*kiariore*	night	*steneidi*
lunch	*huarense*	north	*okakeroka*
lung	*novihuncare*	nose	*noirina*
machete	*saviri*	nor	*te*
mail	*sanginaretse*	notice	*yanse*
malaria	*karkametstase*	obey	*angensante*
male	*chiransare*	ocean	*mama cocha*
malediction	*kamaretanse*	offer	*tiangare*
man	*champari*	old man	*chiraukarakyas-*
mandioca	*kaniri*		*piri*
man-of-gold	*pahua*	order	*amenanse*
margin	*sapea*	origin	*timalanuetse*
matches	*shengirstse*	ornate	*potsotingare*
medicine	*akendaronse*	oven	*tashimento*
messenger god	*pachukuma*	owl	*paigonnae*
milk	*sunkare*	owner	*cistarore*
mirror	*amenarotse*	pack	*oisuaite*
money	*kirerki*	paddle	*cunarosi*
monkey	*shitone*	pallid	*kiteriri*
monster (myth)	*sucuruju*	palm	*siaro*
moon	*cachiri*	papaya	*mapocha*
morning	*scaitegiuere*	parrot	*kintaro*
mosquito	*sito*	patch	*noavitero*
moth	*chapitse*	peccary	*tavriqui*
mother	*ina*	pelt	*nomishima*
mountain	*antami*	pepper	*estskane*
mouse	*unkiro*	picture	*shiakanse*
mouth	*nowante*	pig	*shintore*
mud	*sunboatsa*	pillow (wood)	*mametetotse*
musician	*sonkare*	pineapple	*tibana*
native	*pashimetariatsiri*	pity	*tiyueider*
natural	*timaishtashare*	place	*kamciseiteri*
nature	*iraca*	plantation	*pankiwarense*
navigate	*amapate*	plate	*guamentose*
necessary	*kuashare*	play	*nepasash*
negative	*sanendance*	plenty	*usheiki*
neighbor	*chaningare*	poison	*kepiare*

poisonous snake	*maranki,*	snake	*marangui*
poor	*aishuotgaugare*	snow	*menkare*
potato	*mosagui*	son	*notomie*
potato (sweet)	*carete*	south	*antackeronta*
powerful	*slimsiki*	speak	*ayablta*
pray	*ahiane*	spear	*satamendotse*
punishment	*guashankidanse*	spirit	*itasolenga,*
puppy	*ostegamki*		*shiakanse*
pursue	*infamatase*	spring (season)	*roaguelainta-*
quarrel	*meyes*		*pagare*
quick	*espayene*	staple	*oshinsehare*
quiet	*marete*	star	*empoguiro*
raft	*shintipu*	start	*ansparer*
rain	*ingani*	stay	*nigateni*
revenge	*asarmatandin-*	stick (wood)	*shake*
	gare	stomach	*nonaohia*
rich	*sharitgangare*	stone	*mapi*
right	*tambatika*	storm	*estenikiri*
river	*niga*	stranger	*puningare*
road	*avotshanigin*	straw	*kasavesi*
robber	*cushente*	stray	*peingaere*
rock	*emperta*	stroke	*posanse*
sacrifice	*huinioshirenkar*	strong	*shiniare*
savage	*antamikire*	sugarcane	*canks*
sea	*engajols*	suicide	*tongashare*
see	*amene*	summer	*osarensi*
sell	*aplmante*	sun	*ureatsere*
shame	*pashueitingare*	sungaro (fish)	*iotse*
shelter	*nampirense*	sunrise	*stuapakeoriasi*
shot	*tongatse*	sure	*ariorika*
sick	*manseare*	suspend	*quashondvagero*
silence	*pimagerette*	swear	*seiningare*
silver	*kireki*	sweet	*pushari*
skin	*meshinatse*	swim	*namate*
sky	*inquite*	tail	*itinko*
slave	*manipirisi,*	tall	*antariti*
	nankiretse	taste	*kanutsa*
sleep	*amage*	teach	*yotante*

teeth	*nahi*
terror	*sarotse*
throat	*noyamento*
tigre (jaguar)	*manite*
tired	*hari kiri*
toga	*uma*
tongue	*nene*
toucan	*opempe*
tracks	*shetaki*
trap	*nofate*
trap (fish)	*keperotse*
trap (animal)	*samerense*
traveler	*hatingare*
tree	*chato*
tribe	*atshiri*
true	*kiaria*
uncle	*pabachare*
unhappy	*kutikastarne*
union	*patoirense*
valley	*tengana*
village	*nampitse,*
	seraganasere
volcano	*toungare*
walk	*anite*
wall	*tantodse*
war	*wairi*
warm	*maswirense*
warrior	*manatingare*
was	*saikavetingarski*
water	*nija*
waterfall	*otaki*
wave	*shingue*
weak	*matsare*
weapon	*tugamenkidotse*
wedge	*stironsti*
well (health)	*matya*
west	*katonko*
where	*hauca*

whip	*pasanaendotse*
whisper	*santikoimi*
whistle	*asuabuaeti*
white	*taimroki*
widow	*kamaimentingaro*
wife	*nohina*
wild	*ishingare*
wind	*tampea*
window	*onioro*
wing	*shibanke*
winter	*quiare*
wire	*ashirutsa*
witch	*matse*
witchdoctor	*abendaningare*
with	*espatariri*
wither	*shinpetake*
wolf	*parare*
woman	*caya*
wood	*enshato*
wool	*nlashero*
worm	*shapite*
wound	*patsaronse*
wrinkle	*ampitsare*
you	*aviro*
young	*equangare*

Inez Pokorny

Tsantsa, Jívaro shrunken head

Jorge Mendoza

ABOUT THE AUTHOR

Leonard Clark was perhaps one of the greatest of all twentieth-century explorers. He did not believe in big expeditions and elaborate paraphernalia—he was a man who carried his own belongings and charged ahead. This same trait enabled him to perform extraordinary feats of military intelligence and reconnaissance in difficult and dangerous areas during World War II. Clark attended the University of California, then joined the army, attaining the rank of colonel. During the war, he spent many months in China behind Japanese lines organizing guerrilla activity. His post-war expeditions began in Borneo, and over the years he made trips to Mexico, the Celebes, Sumatra, China, India, Japan, Central America, South America, and Burma. He was the author of two other books, *A Wanderer Till I Die* and *The Marching Wind*. He passed away in 1957 at the age of 49, while on a diamond-mining expedition in Venezuela.

Leonard Clark examining his dinner at Borja